Infant Development and Risk

An Introduction

Second Edition

by

Anne H. Widerstrom, Ph.D.
San Francisco State University
San Francisco, California

Barbara A. Mowder, Ph.D.
Pace University
New York

and

Susan R. Sandall, Ph.D.
University of Washington
Seattle

with invited contributions from

Robert E. Nickel, M.D.,
Helen Harrison, and Harriet Able-Boone, Ph.D.

PAUL H. BROOKES PUBLISHING CO.

Baltimore • London • Toronto • Sydney

Paul H. Brookes Publishing Co.
Post Office Box 10624
Baltimore, Maryland 21285-0624

Typeset by Signature Typesetting & Design, Baltimore, Maryland.
Manufactured in the United States of America by
Vail-Ballou Press, Binghamton, New York.

The photographs in this volume were taken by Susan R. Sandall or provided by Barbara A. Mowder and Kawana Reed.

Most of the case studies described in this book are completely fictional. Any similarity to actual individuals or circumstances is coincidental, and no implications should be inferred. Selected case studies are composites based on the authors' experiences; these case studies do not represent the lives or experiences of specific individuals, and no implications should be inferred. Case studies based on real people or circumstances are presented herein only with the individual's written consent.

Library of Congress Cataloging-in-Publication Data

Widerstrom, Anne H.
Infant development and risk : an introduction / Anne H. Widerstrom, Barbara A. Mowder, and Susan R. Sandall.
p. cm.
Includes bibliographical references and index.
ISBN 1-55766-269-X
1. Handicapped children—Services for—United States. 2. Infants—Services for—United States. 3. Handicapped children—United States—Development.
4. Infants—United States—Development.
I. Mowder, Barbara A. II. Sandall, Susan Rebecka. III. Title.
HV888.5.W53 1997
362.4′048′083—dc20

96-42168
CIP

British Library Cataloguing in Publication data are available from the British Library.

Contents

Infant Development and Risk

About the Authors

Anne H. Widerstrom, Ph.D., Professor of Special Education, Department of Special Education, 4 Tapia Drive, San Francisco State University, San Francisco, California 94132

Dr. Widerstrom is Professor of early childhood special education and Coordinator of the early childhood special education program at San Francisco State University. Her professional experience includes classroom teaching in both general and special education; service as an educational diagnostician; supervision and program coordination; and university teaching, research, and administration. Dr. Widerstrom has published several books and numerous journal articles on early intervention.

Barbara A. Mowder, Ph.D., Director of Graduate Psychology Programs, Associate Chair of the Psychology Department, and Professor of Psychology, Psychology Department, Pace University, 1 Pace Plaza, New York, New York 10038-1502

Dr. Mowder is Director of Graduate Psychology Programs, Associate Chair of the Psychology Department, and Professor of Psychology at Pace University in New York City. She is a Fellow of the American Psychological Association and is active in many organizations, such as the National Association of School Psychologists, New York Academy of Sciences, New York State Psychological Association, and the School Psychology Educators Council of New York State. She has written extensively in the areas of school psychological services and is conducting research on parenting issues, early child development, and special services.

Susan R. Sandall, Ph.D., Research Coordinator, Early Childhood Research Institute on Inclusion, University of Washington, Box 357925, Experimental Education Unit, Seattle, Washington 98195

Dr. Sandall completed her undergraduate work at the University of California at Berkeley, her master's degree in special education at the University of Oregon, and her doctor of philosophy in education (special education) at the University of Washington. Her initial work was as a teacher at the Center on Human Development Preschool at the University of Oregon. While in graduate school, she coordinated the program for infants with disabilities and their families at the Experimental Education Unit. As a faculty member at the University of Colorado in Denver and the University of Delaware, Dr. Sandall coordinated personnel preparation efforts in early intervention and early childhood special education. Dr. Sandall is the Research Coordinator for the Early Childhood Research Institute on Inclusion at the University of Washington.

Robert E. Nickel, M.D., Clinical Director, Regional Services Center, Child Development and Rehabilitation Center, and Associate Professor, Department of Pediatrics, Oregon Health Sciences University, 901 East 18th Avenue, Eugene, Oregon 97403-5254

Dr. Nickel is an associate professor of pediatrics at the Department of Pediatrics and the Child Development and Rehabilitation Center (CDRC), Oregon Health Sciences University, and he is the medical director of the Eugene office at CDRC. He has been instrumental in the production of materials related to developmental monitoring activities, including the *Ages & Stages Questionnaires: A Parent-Completed, Child-Monitoring System,* the *Infant Motor Screen* (screen test/manual and videotape) and *Developmental Screening for Infants 0–3 Years of Age,* part of a training program for primary health care professionals. As a developmental pediatrician, he attends a number of clinics for children with special health care needs in the Portland and Eugene CDRC offices and at outreach sites.

Helen Harrison, 1144 Sterling Avenue, Berkeley, California 94708

Mrs. Harrison is the mother of two children, Edward, born prematurely in 1975, and Amy, born at term in 1980. Edward survived his premature birth with multiple disabilities. In 1982, Mrs. Harrison was one of the founding members of Parent Care, the international support organization for parents of infants at high risk for delay or disability. She is the author of *The Premature Baby Book* (St. Martin's Press, 1983). In 1992, she and Dr. Jerold Lucey, the editor of *Pediatrics*, organized a parent–professional conference, "Intensive Concern: Parents and Physicians Discuss Neonatology" to consider ethical issues in the care of premature infants. As a result of this conference, "The Principles for Family-Centered Neonatal Care," drafted by Mrs. Harrison and a group of parents of prematurely born children, was published in *Pediatrics*. This document, the first article by parents ever to appear in *Pediatrics*, has proved influential in changing caregiving practices in neonatal units. Mrs. Harrison lectures and writes on bioethical issues, developmental care, pain control for neonates, and on the medical problems and outcomes of premature infants. She has served on the boards of several organizations devoted to providing services for children and adults with disabilities. She is at work on a second edition of *The Premature Baby Book.*

Harriet Able-Boone, Ph.D., Associate Professor, School of Education, University of North Carolina at Chapel Hill, 111 Bonaparte Drive, Hillsborough, North Carolina 27278

Dr. Able-Boone is an associate professor of early childhood in the School of Education at the University of North Carolina at Chapel Hill, where she conducts research regarding ethics and early intervention issues. She teaches undergraduate and graduate courses focusing on infants and families in early childhood service delivery. Dr. Able-Boone received her graduate degree from George Peabody College of Vanderbilt University in early childhood special education with an emphasis on ethics and public policy.

Foreword

In the United States as well as other parts of the world, professionals and the general public are becoming increasingly concerned about infants and toddlers who are at risk as a result of medical, biological, and environmental factors. This concern for babies who are at risk parallels already-established intervention efforts for infants and toddlers who have disabilities. Public awareness of, and professional involvement with, very young populations who have problems or a significant likelihood of developing problems have been stimulated in part by media attention to medical technology that increases survival in infants who have significant disabilities, to the growing impact of poverty on children in particular, and to the biological and environmental effects of substance-abusing parents. Growing interest is also attributable to the many professionals who are speaking out about the need for increased resources and services for infants who have or may develop problems. Finally, the passage in 1986 of the Education of the Handicapped Act Amendments (PL 99-457), which was subsequently incorporated into the Individuals with Disabilities Education Act, has provided an expanded base for addressing the needs of young populations at risk for disability and developmental delay. This law, and in particular Part H, offers incentives to U.S. states and territories for the development or expansion of an array of services for infants and toddlers with disabilities. In addition, Part H permits states and territories to develop eligibility guidelines for including in these services populations who are at risk.

Although public and professional awareness of young children who are at risk for or who have disabilities has increased, it appears that most U.S. states and territories will not choose to expand their eligibility definitions to include groups at risk. The failure to expand state eligibility requirements results primarily from financial constraints. Most administrators, perhaps all interventionists, and large segments of the public support conceptually and practically the need to provide programs for infants and toddlers who are at risk; however, adequate federal, state, or local funds to include infants and young children in early intervention programs are generally not available. Until adequate financial resources are developed, it is likely that most early intervention programs will have to limit services to infants and young children who have diagnosed disabilities and their families.

The inability of states to expand their eligibility guidelines is unfortunate, for it is clear that many babies who are at risk will develop mild to serious disabilities. Early identification and intervention can often do much to counter or attenuate the effects of a disability on a child. As public awareness continues to grow and as professionals assemble empirical evidence on the importance of early intervention, garnering financial resources to provide services to infants and toddlers who are at risk for or who have disabilities should grow. As the number of programs increases, the field faces several major challenges: the development of appropriate screening, assessment, and evaluation tools; expansion of curriculum efforts; meaningful family involvement; increased integration into community programs; and, most critical, preparation of quality personnel to deliver services.

As we approach the 21st century, the significant shortage of trained early intervention personnel, including occupational therapists, physical therapists, communication specialists, social workers, nurses, pediatricians, and special educators, has been amply documented (Widerstrom & Abelman, 1996). Equally troubling is the fact that many of the personnel providing early intervention services have had no formal training in early intervention. The quality of services offered to infants and young children and their families is often poor because personnel lack appropriate experience and training. Developing solutions for the shortage of personnel has been a topic of concern for professional organizations, government agencies, institutions of higher education, and local program administrators who find themselves unable to hire appropriate experienced and prepared personnel. Topics frequently addressed by these groups and individuals include whether to prepare infant and toddler specialists, how to prepare them, who should prepare them, what competencies should be identified, and what types of licenses or certification should be required. It is not likely that uniform solutions will be agreed on or that satisfactory solutions will be developed soon. Nevertheless, increasing numbers of institutions of higher education are recognizing the need to prepare personnel who can provide high-quality services to infants, toddlers, and their families. It is now generally recognized that personnel preparation employing a team approach is most effective and most closely reflects the actual delivery of infant and family services (Bricker & Widerstrom, 1996). To assist in this training effort, quality materials such as this book with its interdisciplinary focus are needed.

This book was originally written to address the need for current information about newborns and infants who are at risk for disabilities or developmental delays that would be useful to various professionals representing the multiple disciplines involved in early intervention. Like the first edition, this second edition is also based on the assumption that, though many professionals have been working with infants and toddlers for lengthy periods, their knowledge base is unidisciplinary, primarily restricted to their own particular field of training. A general book such as this one is needed for students and professionals from diverse fields to become conversant with the literature, research, and intervention premises associated with relevant disciplines.

In a growing market of textbooks focused on young children who are at risk, this volume has much to recommend it for use in introductory classes, by individuals new to the field, and by those whose formal training has been minimal. First, this volume provides comprehensive coverage of early intervention populations and services. Second, readers will find the chapters straightforward and pragmatic. Most chapters begin with a list of objectives and conclude with a list of follow-up activities as well as resources for students wishing more information. Third, this textbook juxtaposes typical and atypical development, which will assist the reader in understanding normal developmental phenomena and how they can be derailed. Finally, this volume addresses the major issues and trends confronting those who are or will be working with infants and toddlers and their families.

The original purpose of this edition is the same as that of the first edition: to present information useful to students and professionals from various disciplines. In addition to updating the original chapters, however, the authors have expanded the book to include new chapters on ethical issues in neonatal care, on medical factors placing infants at risk, and on several new aspects of early intervention service delivery. The second edition profits from the contributions of three additional authors, two experts in the ethics of treating infants and toddlers at risk for or with disabilities and an expert on the medical aspects of infant disability. In short, this volume has assembled and synthesized information that will be of great use to the practitioner working with young children.

Although there is much we do not know, the authors of this volume have assembled, in large measure, what we do know and have presented it in a clear, readable fashion. The reader of this volume will be better equipped to understand and intervene with infants and toddlers who are at risk or who have disabilities and their families.

Diane Bricker, Ph.D.
Professor of Special Education
Associate Dean for Academic Programs
College of Education
University of Oregon, Eugene

REFERENCES

Bricker, D., & Widerstrom, A. (Eds.). (1996). *Preparing personnel to work with infants and young children and their families: A team approach.* Baltimore: Paul H. Brookes Publishing Co.

Widerstrom, A., & Abelman, D. (1996). Team training issues. In D. Bricker & A. Widerstrom (Eds.), *Preparing personnel to work with infants and young children and their families: A team approach* (pp. 23–41). Baltimore: Paul H. Brookes Publishing Co.

Preface

Writing a book with several other authors is a task that is both challenging and satisfying. It is challenging because many viewpoints and opinions must be reconciled in order to present a unified discussion, and it is satisfying because the book is enriched by the specialized expertise and varied experiences that authors from varied disciplines contribute. The first edition of this book, *At-Risk and Handicapped Newborns and Infants: Development, Assessment, and Intervention,* was written by one psychologist and two early interventionists, each of whom had an interest in infants who were considered at risk for developmental disabilities or delay. Since that edition was published in 1991, the early intervention field has seen many changes—in technology, law, and practices related to service delivery. In order to present in this new edition a more complete and timely discussion of infants at risk, an expanded pool of authors and viewpoints was necessary. In this second edition, we are fortunate to have a rich collaboration of authors, including the parent of a child with disabilities and professionals from the fields of medicine, psychology, and early intervention.

The content of the second edition has been considerably expanded. To reflect the broader base of this edition, we have changed the book's title to *Infant Development and Risk: An Introduction*. We have updated the background chapters on typical and atypical infant development and on preterm and low birth weight infants that appeared in the first edition and have added chapters to discuss early intervention services, including assessment, intervention techniques, programs, and service coordination, for infants who are at risk for or who have disabilities. Also addressed in new chapters are the difficult ethical and legal issues confronting early interventionists, especially in the area of neonatal intensive care.

The formatting of the chapters has been modified as well. Objectives have been added at the beginning of most chapters to guide readers on what to expect from each chapter. At the end of most chapters is a list of activities suggested to assist readers in understanding and applying the concepts and issues discussed in each chapter and to lead them toward opportunities to expand their knowledge of the topics. These additions will be particularly useful for students using the book as a text in courses related to atypically developing infants.

This edition, like the first, is also intended to be used to introduce professionals working in human services to atypical infant development and risk. As the early intervention field has expanded to include a greater variety of services to families, professionals from an increasing number of disciplines have become involved in service delivery. Many professionals from fields such as social work, child care, psychology, and health care are becoming involved in early intervention services for the first time even though they have been practicing their professions for many years. We hope that they, too, will find the book useful as a means of updating and expanding their knowledge of infants who are at risk for or who have disabilities. The book also should be of interest to parents of atypically developing infants. In particular, we hope that Chapter 7 by Helen Harrison and Chapter 8 by Harriet Able-Boone on the ethics of neonatal care will be useful to parents and other caregivers. We appreciate the important contributions of Helen Harrison and Harriet Able-Boone as well as the valuable work of Robert E. Nickel on Chapters 3 and 4, which address medical issues related to infant development.

The handsome photographs of babies and their families, which make the book so pleasant to read, were taken by Susan R. Sandall or provided by Barbara A. Mowder and Kawana Reed. We are grateful for their talent and generosity.

Anne H. Widerstrom, Ph.D.

Infant Development and Risk

SECTION I

INTRODUCTION

CHAPTER 1

Newborns and Infants at Risk for or with Disabilities

Anne H. Widerstrom

Objectives

- To understand and appreciate the historical context in which the field of early intervention developed
- To gain an understanding of current legislation governing the delivery of services to infants at risk for or with disabilities
- To become aware of advances in technology affecting neonatal care and the ethical issues associated with such advances
- To become aware of recommended practices in early intervention

Since the mid-1980s, there has been a growing interest in intervention programs for infants considered at risk for developmental delays. This interest was fueled in 1986 by the emphasis placed on the infant/toddler age group in the Education of the Handicapped Act Amendments (PL 99-457). In a larger sense, it also reflects a commitment to early intervention based on years of efficacy research.

A substantial body of research from education, psychology, medicine, and related fields supports the importance of providing interdisciplinary, family-focused services to young children who are at risk for or who have disabilities. The research includes an array of both longitudinal and cross-sectional studies of children from birth to age 6 with a variety of disabilities, documenting the educational and economic benefits of early intervention for infants and young children at risk (Lazar, Darlington, Murray, Royce, & Snipper, 1982; McWilliam & Strain, 1993; Meisels, 1984; Shonkoff, Hauser-Cram, Krauss, & Upshur, 1988; Smith & Strain, 1988). The House Report accompanying PL 99-457 summarized the benefits of early intervention as follows:

1. Intelligence is enhanced in some children.
2. Substantial gains are made in all areas of development, including physical, cognitive, language and speech, psychosocial, and self-care development.
3. Secondary disabling conditions are inhibited or prevented.
4. Family stress is reduced.
5. Dependency and institutionalization are reduced.
6. The need for special educational services at school age is reduced.
7. The nation and society are spared substantial health care and education costs. (Smith, 1989)

Other indicators of the current interest in infant development and intervention are the growing number of early intervention programs for infants at risk for or with disabilities and the number of journals devoted to infants and toddlers available to professionals in psychology, medicine, education, and related fields. A list of some of the major journals in each field that address this important area appears in the appendix to this chapter.

HISTORICAL PERSPECTIVE

Early intervention for infants and toddlers first gained importance in federal policy in the 1960s with the passage of PL 88-156 in 1963 and the Elementary and Secondary Education Act (PL 89-10) in 1965. The former expanded maternal and child health services for expectant mothers from low-income families to prevent mental retardation. The latter provided federal funds to state-operated schools for children with disabilities. States continue to make use of this funding source (Smith, 1989).

Project Head Start

The funding of Project Head Start in 1965 represents a major milestone for early intervention. Project Head Start's goal is to help preschool children from low-income families to overcome the effects of poverty on their development and school achievement. From the beginning, an important characteristic of Head Start was its comprehensive and multidisciplinary scope, offering educational, health, nutritional, and parental support services to eligible families. Only 4-year-olds were eligible for enrollment until 1972, with the establishment of the first parent–child centers for infants and their parents. Today, a large network of parent–child centers serves low-income infants and toddlers in every state.

Handicapped Children's Early Education Program

The establishment by Congress in 1968 of the Handicapped Children's Early Education Program (HCEEP) (PL 90-538) represents another landmark in early intervention. Research on the effects of early intervention has been funded since the 1970s by

HCEEP, subsequently renamed the Early Education Programs for Children with Disabilities (EEPCD). Comprehensive funding under EEPCD has supported model programs, the development and dissemination of assessment and curriculum materials, and technical assistance on a national basis (Smith, 1989). The result of this comprehensive funding has been a vastly increased knowledge base related to the effectiveness of early intervention, more than 500 model demonstration projects for serving infants, toddlers, and preschool children, and a large number of innovative assessment and curriculum materials. This knowledge base proved to be particularly important in establishing a rationale for the passage of PL 99-457 in 1986.

Political Factors

Four states mandate early intervention beginning at birth, and all 50 states have some type of services for infants and toddlers with delays or disabilities. The United States is within reach of the goal of universal access to services beginning at birth for all children at risk for or with disabilities and their families. It has been necessary to justify the provision of services to young children at risk for or with disabilities, whereas the efficacy or cost effectiveness of programs for primary and secondary school children has not been subjected to the same kind of scrutiny by legislators. Parents of school-age children have not had to fight as long or difficult a battle for publicly funded special education programs as have parents of infants, toddlers, and preschoolers. It is encouraging to view the progress that has been made since the 1960s in this regard, as well as the present high level of interest and activity related to the well-being of infants. However, there are serious threats from Congress to reduce or eliminate funding of infant/toddler programs during times of economic downsizing. Achieving the goal of universal access to services will require continued partnership between parents and professionals in the political arena.

TRENDS IN INFANT INTERVENTION

The developmental well-being of newborns and infants and their families has been of concern to professionals from various disciplines for many years. Since the 1980s, new models of service delivery, new legislation, and advances in technology have changed the delivery of early intervention services and have at the same time raised new ethical issues in newborn and infant care.

Service Delivery Models

The first infant intervention programs in the 1960s were called infant stimulation programs and usually were located in hospitals. These programs emphasized providing additional sensory stimulation to the infant to compensate for impairments resulting from birth trauma or defects. Intervention focused on medical and physical impairments, and health specialists provided short-term physical therapy, which parents were encouraged to follow up at home.

Early intervention programs have evolved significantly from these early stimulation programs. First, most programs are staffed by an interdisciplinary team working together as a closely knit unit in carrying out assessments and program implementation. Second, the infant/toddler curriculum has grown from a narrow focus on the child's motor, physical, or health problems to a concern for the infant's overall optimal development, including cognitive and communication skills, emotional well-being, and parent and peer interactions. Third, programs today are family focused rather than child focused. Whether the infant/toddler programs are based in communities or hospitals, early interventionists agree that greater benefits result from intervention that considers factors affecting the child but originating in the family. Having the full participation and support of the child's family increases the effectiveness of the intervention. A final difference found in contemporary infant/toddler programs is their location. While the need for short-term, hospital-based follow-up care continues, especially for infants with complex health care needs and severe disabilities, the trend is to provide intervention services during the first 3 years of life in community-based settings that include the services of professionals from many disciplines in addition to health-related services.

Legislation Affecting Service Delivery

The Education of the Handicapped Act Amendments (PL 99-457), governing services to newborns and infants with risk or disability, was passed in 1986 as an amendment to the Education for All Handicapped Children Act of 1975 (PL 94-142). In 1991, these amendments were incorporated into the reauthorization (Individuals with Disabilities Education Act Amendments; PL 102-119) of the Individuals with Disabilities Education Act (IDEA; PL 101-476). PL 99-457 has two parts governing services to children below age 5: Part H for infants and toddlers to age 3, and Part B for preschool children ages 3–5. The law requires each state to serve preschool children with identified disabilities (Part B), but states may elect to serve infants and toddlers at risk for or with disabilities (Part H). As of 1997, all states had elected to serve infants and toddlers. Each participating state is required to establish a comprehensive system for the identification, assessment, and treatment of children birth to age 3 with disabilities and their families. An interagency coordinating council (ICC) in each state must develop the state's system, with members appointed by the governor, representing the array of participants in the early intervention process: administrators, service providers, and families receiving services.

The ICC must develop a state's comprehensive system to include the following 16 components:

1. A definition of the term *developmental delay*
2. A central directory of public and private early intervention resources and services available in the state, research and demonstration projects being conducted in the state, and professionals and other groups that provide assistance to eligible children and their families
3. A timetable for serving eligible children
4. A comprehensive Child Find system that includes primary referral sources such as hospitals, physicians, parents, and child care providers and that is coordinated with other state agencies that serve young children
5. A public awareness program that informs the public about the state's early intervention program, the Child Find system, and the central directory
6. Performance of a timely, comprehensive, multidisciplinary evaluation of each child, birth through age 2, referred for evaluation, including assessment activities related to the child and the child's family; nondiscriminatory assessment and evaluation procedures must be adopted

7. An individualized family service plan (IFSP) for all eligible children and their families that includes service coordination
8. A comprehensive system of personnel development, including preservice and in-service training for providers that includes understanding the basic components of the state's early intervention system, meeting the interrelated social, emotional, health, developmental, and educational needs of eligible children, and assisting families in enhancing the development of their children
9. Personnel standards that define entry-level requirements for state-approved certification or licensing for work in early intervention
10. Procedural safeguards for the parents' rights of due process including the right of appeal and confidentiality, the right to examine records, and the right to communication in parents' native language
11. Supervision and monitoring procedures, including the provision of technical assistance
12. Procedures for resolving complaints that a public agency is in violation of the requirements of Part H
13. Policies and procedures related to financial matters, including how early intervention services will be funded, which services will be provided at no cost to parents of eligible children, and which will be subject to a system of payments including a sliding scale; in addition, the policy must stipulate that the inability of parents to pay for services will not result in the denial of services to the child or the child's family
14. Development of interagency agreements with other agencies within the state that serve eligible children and their families to delineate each agency's financial responsibility, describe procedures for resolving disputes, and ensure the cooperation and collaboration among all agencies involved in the state's early intervention program
15. Policy for contracting or arranging for early intervention services with public and private providers including the requirement that all services must meet state standards
16. Data collection procedures that the state will use to compile data on the statewide system, including sampling and reporting methods
(Individuals with Disabilities Education Act Amendments of 1991)

At the time of this writing, all states and territories have agreed to participate in Part H through their state legislatures with the passage of enabling legislation. This commitment process took the better part of 10 years. It is a remarkable achievement that all states formally acknowledge the importance of early intervention services for infants and toddlers, despite lack of funding. Although the law provides for federal funding to implement both Parts B and H, to date neither section of the law has received full funding.

Whereas Part B for preschool-age children must be administered by the department of education or instruction in each state, Part H may be administered by a department of education, health, or developmental disabilities or by another human services agency. Therefore, there is great variability from state to state in the content, eligibility for, or administration of infant/toddler services. For that reason, it has been difficult in many states to put into practice a seamless system of service delivery from birth to age 5 for children with disabilities. Only those states whose infant/toddler programs are administered by the state education agency along with preschool services offer consistent program services from birth to age 5.

Eligibility Criteria

Because children ages 3–21 must have a specific disability in order to receive special education services, it was acknowledged that later disabilities might be prevented if infants who were at developmental risk could receive services. Under Part H, therefore, eligibility for services is defined loosely.

Definitions of Developmental Risk and Delay Services may be provided to infants and toddlers who have developmental risk or delay as defined in the following:

1. Delays in one of the developmental domains (i.e., cognition, communication, physical development, psychosocial development, or self-care)
2. A physical or mental condition that has a high probability of resulting in developmental delay (e.g., Down syndrome, cerebral palsy)
3. Medical or environmental risk for substantial developmental delay if early intervention is not provided

Each state is responsible for developing more specific definitions of developmental risk and delay, as well as criteria for determining eligibility for services for the infants, toddlers, and their families residing in that state. States must also establish the appropriate diagnostic instruments that are used in determining eligibility, a difficult and time-consuming task. How narrow or broad a definition is influences the numbers and types of children receiving services, the types of services provided, and ultimately the cost of an early intervention system. Several states have conducted extensive impact and cost studies before finalizing their definitions (Shakelsford, 1992).

Definitions of Risk Three categories of risk for adverse developmental outcomes are 1) established risk, 2) biological/medical risk, and 3) environmental risk. Children with established risk associated with a diagnosed physical or medical condition are, by Part H law, eligible for services. If a state decides to include in its eligibility definition children in other risk categories, it must identify the risk factors that will make a child eligible for services.

Children determined to be at *established risk* have "a diagnosed physical or mental condition which has a high probability of resulting in developmental delay" (IDEA Amendments, 1991, 34 C.F.R. Sec. 303.16 [a][2]). These conditions may include Down syndrome and other chromosomal abnormalities; sensory impairments; metabolic disorders; microcephaly; severe attachment disorders, including failure to thrive; seizure disorders; and fetal alcohol syndrome. Children in this category are eligible for Part H services by virtue of their diagnosis, regardless of whether a measurable delay is present.

Children considered at *biological/medical risk* have a condition that makes them more likely to develop a delay than children without the condition. Examples of biological and medical risk conditions that states have identified include low birth weight, intraventricular hemorrhage, chronic lung disease, and failure to thrive. Certain conditions may be labeled established risk by one state and biological or medical risk by another. Examples of this ambiguity are failure to thrive, prenatal substance exposure, and HIV-positive test at birth.

Environmental risk is even less clearly defined than established or biological/medical risk. It includes factors related to the child's caregiving environment and family situation. Examples of environmental risk factors that states list among their

eligibility criteria include parental substance abuse, poverty, parental developmental disability, parental age and educational attainment, and child abuse or neglect.

At the time of this writing, 10 states and 2 territories (Guam and the Virgin Islands) have elected to serve at-risk infants. Of these 12, three are serving only those infants with medical or biological risk conditions (Arkansas, Louisiana, and Mississippi), and one serves only infants who are at risk because they have parents with developmental delays (Colorado). Kansas and Texas leave it up to local communities to decide, based on the availability of funds, whether to serve infants at risk. In addition, six states have elected to track and monitor infants at risk. Several states are studying the feasibility of serving infants at risk exhibiting neither a delay nor an established risk condition.

Definitions of Delay Individual states have defined developmental delay variously as exhibiting a certain percentage of delay in one or more developmental areas, lower functioning than expected for chronological age, informed clinical judgment, atypical development, or a combination of some or all of these definitions. Those criteria measured by standardized assessment instruments are expressed in standard deviations from the mean; percent delay; number of months delay; or a developmental quotient (DQ), similar to an IQ score. Criteria that are less quantifiable include atypical development as judged by a trained clinical professional or a multidisciplinary team (Shakelsford, 1992).

Some states employ more than one criterion for defining developmental delay. In Table 1.1, 15 states are listed with their definitions of developmental delay. The table illustrates the wide variation among states in the criteria they use to determine who is eligible for early intervention services.

Definitions of risk and delay can range from inclusive, leading to the serving of larger numbers of infants and toddlers, to exclusive, resulting in the exclusion from services of children who may be at risk for disabilities. The decision is usually based on the availability of funds to perform the assessments that determine eligibility

Table 1.1. Some examples of states' definitions of developmental delay

State	Definition of developmental delay
Alaska	1. *From state application:* Mild/moderate delay—Birth to 12 months: delay in months of less than ½ chronological age in two or more areas; older than age 12 months: less than 6 months' delay in two or more areas Severe/profound delay—Birth to 12 months: delay in months of more than ½ chronological age in two or more areas; older than12 months: greater than 6 months' delay in two or more areas 2. *From legislation* 15% below chronological or corrected age or 1.5 *SD* below age in one or more areas
Arkansas	2 *SD* in one area or 35% delay in months for birth to 18 months; 2 *SD* in one area, 1.5 *SD* in two areas, or 25% delay in months for ages 18–36 months
California	Significant difference between expected level of development and current level of functioning determined by qualified multidisciplinary team (MDT), including parents; atypical development determined by informed clinical opinion
District of Columbia	Abnormal physiological characteristics (prematurity, low birth weight, cognitive, and motor delays) for birth to 12 months; 25% delay or 2 *SD* in one area for ages 13–36 months
Florida	Age less than 2 months: atypical development, clinical opinion Age 2–12 months: 2 months' delay in one area Age 13–24 months: 3 months' delay in one area Age 24–36 months: 4 months' delay in one area
Illinois	2 *SD* or 25% delay in one area; 1.5 *SD* or 20% delay in two or more areas or in one area with addition of other environmental risk factors; clinical judgment
Maine	Younger than 24 months of age: MDT professional judgment Older than 24 months of age: 1. Delay of 2 *SD* or 25% or more below chronological age in one area 2. Delay of 1.5 *SD* or 15% below chronological age in two areas 3. In one area with additional risk factors: delay of 1 *SD* or 10% below chronological age in one area of development with a high probability for further delay because of additional established conditions or biological factors
Maryland	25% delay in one area; atypical development/behavior; professional judgment
Michigan	Informed clinical judgment of MDT and parents; multiple sources of information including developmental history, observational assessment, recent health status appraisal, and an appropriate formal assessment measure
Minnesota	Substantial delay in one or more of the following developmental areas with the following criteria: Cognitive: total score of 1.5 *SD* below the mean Communication: 2.0 *SD* below the mean Physical development: Motor: 2.0 *SD* below mean for children birth–18 months Physically impaired: 1.0 *SD* below mean Hearing: medical documentation and informed clinical opinion Vision: medical documentation and informed clinical opinion Social or emotional: informed clinical opinion Adaptive development: informed clinical opinion Noncategorical criteria: delay in overall development demonstrated by a composite score of 1.5 *SD* below the mean

(continued)

Table 1.1. *(continued)*

State	Definition of developmental delay
New Hampshire	Informed clinical opinion to determine developmental delay or atypical development in one or more areas; MDT decision and consensus
Ohio	Child has not reached developmental milestones for chronological age—a "measurable delay"
Oregon	Child's developmental age: 56%–75% of chronological age in three or more areas 40%–55% of chronological age in two areas less than 40% of chronological age in one area
Texas	Age less than 2 months: atypical behaviors or medical diagnosis Ages 2–12 months: 2 months' delay in one area Ages 13–24 months: 3 months' delay or more in one or more areas Ages 25–36 months: 4 months' delay or greater in one area Atypical behavior
Washington	1.5 SD or 25% delay in one area; informed clinical opinion

SD: Standard deviation from the mean.

and to provide the recommended services. Evidently, states have, for economic reasons, turned away from serving infants at risk under Part H. Yet infants at risk who lack identified disabilities stand to benefit the most from early intervention. Effective preventive programs most likely would result in fewer children referred for special education and other remedial services at older ages. In that sense, early intervention dollars would be well spent in early prevention programs.

Two unique aspects of Part H of IDEA require special comment. First, an IFSP is required for each infant found to be eligible for services. This resembles the individualized education program (IEP) first mandated in 1975 for school-age children by the Education for All Handicapped Children Act of 1975 (PL 94-142). The IFSP contains the following sections:

- A statement of the child's present levels of functioning in cognitive, communicative, motor, emotional, social, and self-care development
- A statement of the resources, priorities, and concerns of the child's family
- A statement of goals and objectives for the family and for the child
- Detailed plans for achieving each goal and objective, including resources to be provided, who is responsible, and a time line for completion

The IFSP is more fully discussed in Chapter 10.

A second unique requirement of Part H of IDEA is for a service coordinator to be assigned to each family to oversee the implementation of the IFSP. The service coordinator may belong to any of several disciplines involved in the family's intervention program but must be a professional with whom the family is familiar and comfortable. The service coordinator's primary responsibility is to perform advocacy for the family in interactions with service delivery agencies. See Chapter 6 for a more detailed discussion of service coordination.

Because Parts B and H have different requirements for serving preschool children and infants/toddlers, the law has essentially resulted in the division of the early intervention service delivery system into two distinct parts. Differences in licensing and certification requirements, personnel training, and service delivery are the result (Widerstrom & Abelman, 1996). Licensing or certification in most states and in most early intervention disciplines is awarded across the entire birth-to-5 age range (Bricker & Widerstrom, 1996). Qualified professionals are thus eligible to work in either infant or preschool programs.

By contrast, training of service providers must cover two quite distinct service delivery systems with specific requirements for infants and toddlers with disabilities and for preschool children with disabilities. Professionals must understand the difference between an IFSP and an IEP, for example, and the underlying assessment techniques required for each. Training for work as a member of an interdisciplinary team necessarily differs according to the service delivery system, whether infant or preschool. For example, familiarity with home visiting procedures may be more important for infant service delivery, while knowledge of techniques to promote inclusion may be more useful for preschool service delivery. While some of these differences appear to be inherent between the two age groups, deriving from their particular characteristics, the differences are exaggerated by law. It is interesting to note that some of the requirements of Part H, notably the IFSP, the family-centered services, and service to children developmentally at risk, are seen by early interventionists as entirely appropriate for preschool-age children.

Advances in Technology

The continual improvement in technology available to assist newborns born at risk for or with disabilities presents a notable incentive to develop new programs for infants. Many infants survive traumatic birth conditions to spend considerable time in intensive care units and follow-up hospital programs. The need has increased proportionally for long-term community-based programs to continue the care of these infants once they leave the hospital. Such programs tend to be scarce and expensive (Frederick, 1996; Lewit, Baker, Corman, & Shiono, 1995; Pomerance, Pomerance, & Gottleib, 1993; Robertson, 1993).

Infants born at risk for developmental delay are often preterm or small for gestational age (SGA). In the United States, low birth weight (defined as less than 2,500 grams) is a major public health problem, a major contributor both to infant mortality and to childhood disability. The principal determinant of low birth weight in the United States is preterm delivery, a phenomenon of largely unknown etiology. Preterm delivery (defined as birth prior to 37 completed weeks of gestation) is more common in the United States than in many other industrialized countries. It is the factor most responsible for the relatively high infant mortality rate in this country (Paneth, 1995).

Although all racial and ethnic groups experience some degree of low birth weight, the highest rates in the United States are found in the African American community. Poverty is strongly and consistently associated with low birth weight, but the precise social and environmental conditions that lead to preterm delivery and low birth weight remain unidentified (Paneth, 1995). It was previously thought that a lack of prenatal care increased the risk of low birth weight, but there is not a strong correlation between increased access to prenatal care and lowered rates of preterm delivery (Alexander & Korenbrot, 1995). In fact, both the low birth weight and the preterm delivery rate have remained unchanged in the United States since the 1970s, despite a great improvement in the delivery of prenatal care to pregnant women (Paneth, 1995).

Since the 1970s, neonatologists have developed many new and effective technologies for all newborns, including full-term, preterm, and low birth weight infants. One result has been a substantial increase in the number of infants at risk who survive the neonatal period. According to several studies, the number of infants with birth weight less than 1,500 grams who survived the newborn period approximately doubled between 1960 and 1980 (Bennett, 1987; Hack, Klein, & Taylor, 1995). Of those who survived in 1980, 75% had normal outcomes, whereas in 1960, 75% of the survivors had developmental disabilities. The statistics for infants with birth weights less than 1,000 grams are even more striking: About 50% survived in 1980, compared with 10% in 1960. Of the survivors, 25% in 1980 had disabilities, compared with 75% in 1960 (Bennett, 1987). A review of several studies of long-term developmental outcomes of extremely low birth weight infants (less than 1,000 grams) revealed that more than half of the survivors had no developmental disabilities, while about one quarter demonstrated some degree of below-average functioning (Hack et al., 1995).

Numerous long-term follow-up studies indicate that, although severe disabilities in infants at risk are prevented through improved care in neonatal intensive care units (NICU), there is an increase in the number of infants with minor neurodevelopmental and neurobehavioral delays in cognition, attention, and neuromotor functioning (Bennett, 1987; Hack et al., 1995; Klein, 1988). The delays continue to be observable at school age and during adolescence in a variety of academic and behavioral manifestations. They include mild mental retardation, mild communication and attention disorders, minor neuromotor problems, and emotional immaturity. As with severe disabilities, the incidence of these minor disabilities increases as birth weight and gestational age decrease. At greatest risk are the very low birth weight infants (less than 1,500 grams) and extremely low birth weight infants (less than 1,000 grams) (Hack et al., 1995). Statistical data show that male survivors are more likely to develop mild delays than are females (Saigal, Rosenbaum, Stoskopf, & Milner, 1982).

For premature and low birth weight infants, different complications tend to lead to different prognoses and outcomes. Complications associated with good developmental outcomes include respiratory distress syndrome, hyperbilirubinemia, hypogloxemia, and hypocalcemia. Those associated with a poor prognosis or developmental outcome include intraventricular hemorrhage, bronchopulmonary dysplasia, sepsis, and periodic apnea. As might be expected, the chance for a good prognosis decreases for infants who are both low birth weight and preterm or for those from low income families (Guralnick & Bennett, 1987; Hack et al., 1995; Parmalee, 1989).

A related issue involves the cost of caring for low birth weight infants. The cost of sustaining babies in intensive care for extensive periods of time is very high (Lewit et al., 1995; Pomerance et al., 1993). Parents and professionals have raised questions about whether our society should be allocating so many resources to the survival of marginally viable infants (Harrison, 1994; Paneth, 1995; Robertson, 1993). Topics related to low birth weight and preterm infants, including long-term developmental outcomes and the costs of neonatal intensive care, are more closely examined in Chapters 3 and 7.

Ethical Issues in Newborn Care

As federal legislation and technology coincide to promote neonatal developmental intervention, there are two parallel debates influencing the rationale and the direction of policy development. The first debate involves the way in which a neonate should be perceived. On the one hand, is a newborn an extrauterine fetus in need of interventions that simulate the womb? If so, the NICU should seek to re-create the warm, quiet, peaceful atmosphere of the intrauterine environment. Or, on the other hand, does a premature infant differ significantly from a fetus of similar gestational age because the infant has undergone the birth process that automatically triggers independent functioning of major organ systems? If so, perhaps the NICU should simulate the extrauterine environment experienced by full-term infants. The type of intervention carried out in the NICU is determined by which view of the preterm newborn prevails.

The second debate concerns the nature of the NICU as an extrauterine environment. Early interventionists have questioned whether the intensive care unit is either a source of sensory deprivation requiring additional sensory stimulation of the neonate or a source of overstimulation requiring less handling and more uninterrupted sleep for the neonate. A third supposition is that the problem is not of too much or too little stimulation, but rather of an *inappropriate pattern of interaction* (Bennett, 1987; Heriza & Sweeney, 1990). The stimulation may be adequate but of poor quality and administered by the wrong person (namely, a professional instead of the infant's parents). Infants in NICUs often are deprived of social interactions, for example, particularly those interactions with their mothers that are necessary to later optimal development (Gottwald & Thurman, 1990).

Several ethical issues in infant care concern the role of families. These issues all have to do with the idea that parents should be offered *informed choices* concerning their infant's care. Issues of importance to parents of premature or low birth weight infants with complex health care needs include the following:

- Parental access to complete and objective information about their child's medical condition
- The parents' role in medical decision making concerning treatment and its termination
- The overtreatment of marginally viable or severely compromised infants
- The undertreatment of neonatal pain
- The effects of the NICU environment on the newborn
- The availability of follow-up care and support after NICU treatment, throughout childhood and into adulthood if necessary (Harrison, 1994)

These topics are more fully explored in Chapter 7.

THE INTERDISCIPLINARY EARLY INTERVENTION TEAM

Interdisciplinary infant/toddler service delivery reflects the interest from a range of professions in infant development discussed at the beginning of this chapter. IDEA requires that infants and toddlers at risk for or with disabilities and their families receive services by professionals from several disciplines working cooperatively for the benefit of the child and family.

The number of professional disciplines represented in early intervention programs varies somewhat according to the needs of the children, the approach taken, and the financial constraints under which the program operates. IDEA mandates that services must include special education, speech-language therapy, audiology, occupational and physical therapy, social work, family counseling, health/medicine,

and nutrition. A brief description of professional roles in each of these disciplines is found in Chapter 11.

In all stages of planning, implementing, and evaluating the early intervention plan, the child's parents are considered by law to be members of the team. In fact, the original intent of PL 99-457 was to bring a family focus to early intervention services, reflecting what was considered to be best practice in the field at that time. This view of the child as a member of the family system replaced the more traditional view that the child with disabilities, not the family, should be the primary focus of the intervention. Current law requires that an IFSP be developed by the interdisciplinary team including parents and professionals and that it contain goals and objectives for the child and for the family based on multidisciplinary assessment.

The roles of team members in programs for infants and toddlers may differ markedly from those of service providers in preschool programs that lack a family focus. In infant programs there is typically more contact with parents on a daily basis, and professionals are accustomed to giving informal support to parents as needed. Infant specialists are often the professionals that parents come to know best and to trust. They conduct the family assessment, help the family develop goals related to their child's disability, and often serve as the family's service coordinator and advocate.

RECOMMENDED PRACTICES IN EARLY INTERVENTION

Parents sometimes question whether early intervention is necessary or even helpful for their infant or toddler. They point to the lack of hard data from early intervention programs documenting gains for their children and for themselves as families. While definitive results have been difficult to come by in this field, given the difficulties involved in studying very small samples with many confounding variables, some consensus has developed over the years about what constitutes effective early intervention. Several studies have shown that early intervention works in general, but information about what works best for which child is ambiguous (Bronfenbrenner, 1986; Lazar et al., 1982; McWilliam & Strain, 1993; Meisels, 1984; Ramey & Suarez, 1984; Shonkoff et al., 1988). Most early interventionists would agree that there is a need for more specific information about the effects of early intervention on specific disabilities. Research to provide such information is ongoing, funded in the form of research institutes by the U.S. Department of Education.

In examining the content for effective early intervention, four factors describe recommended practices in the United States:

1. Services that are based in the community rather than in hospitals or clinics work best for families.
2. Services that are made available in the child's natural environment or in settings with typically developing children are less restrictive.
3. Services that are coordinated among the various agencies that offer them give parents the ability to do "one-stop shopping."
4. Services that offer various sources of support to the child and family promote optimal development.

Services that Are Based in the Community Rather than in Hospitals or Clinics Work Best for Families An important concept developed by the early intervention field in the United States is the emphasis on offering health-related services out in the community where families live and work. Many other countries confine early intervention services, whether educational or health related, to hospitals and clinics. This means that, to obtain services for their child, parents must often make numerous appointments, spend time waiting to see specialists, and leave their child for extended periods in unfamiliar and often intimidating settings. By contrast, community-based services are usually more user friendly. They are located close to where the family lives, often provide regular and reliable transportation, and offer services on a schedule that is compatible with the parents' busy life.

Services that Are Made Available in the Child's Natural Environment or in Settings with Typically Developing Children Are Less Restrictive The regulations governing early intervention require that, to the greatest extent possible, services be delivered in the least restrictive environment. For infants and toddlers, this means that children must be placed in programs with typically developing infants and toddlers (e.g., infant/child care programs), or, alternately, they must be provided services at home, in the infant's natural environment. Natural settings generally are more comfortable for both child and family than either segregated or clinical settings; and having typically developing children to play and interact with affords a richer language environment and a more creative play environment for many children with disabilities. When children are relaxed and feel at home in their environment, it is reasonable to expect that they can perform closer to their optimal levels.

Services that Are Coordinated Among the Various Agencies that Offer Them Give Parents the Ability to Do "One-Stop Shopping" Although interagency coordination or collaboration may be difficult to achieve, life is much simpler for parents of a child with a disability if they can receive the required services through a single point of contact.

Services that Offer Various Sources of Support to the Child and Family Promote Optimal Development Infants and toddlers at risk for or with disabilities and their families often require multiple services that may include education, allied health-related care, speech therapy, social work, counseling, or support from other disciplines. It is this aspect of early intervention that probably best distinguishes it from special education for older children. Comprehensive support is considered by some professionals to be the key to the effectiveness of early intervention (Bronfenbrenner, 1986; Ramey & Suarez, 1984).

SUMMARY

The field of early intervention is a relatively young field. It has been since the mid-1970s that intervention services for infants and toddlers and their families have been generally available and publicly funded. In the ensuing period, professional training programs have been developed and advances in technology have been made, resulting in more generally available services of higher quality. Another result is the emergence of difficult issues related to family roles, team training, service delivery, funding, ethical considerations, and others.

At present, the field is at a critical juncture at a time when all states have made a commitment to the idea of providing some level of services for infants and their families. Now that there is an opportunity to realize universal, high-quality early intervention, funds for achieving this goal are in jeopardy in an era of economic downsizing. Nevertheless, it seems possible that despite low funding resources, the dedication and energy that have moved the field so far in a relatively short time will prevail, and a comprehensive, interdisciplinary system of service delivery will emerge.

REFERENCES

Alexander, G.R., & Korenbrot, C.C. (1995). The role of prenatal care in preventing low birth weight. *The Future of Children, 5*(1), 103–120.

Bennett, F.C. (1987). Infants at biological risk. In M.J. Guralnick & F.C. Bennett (Eds.), *Effectiveness of early intervention for at-risk and handicapped children* (pp. 79–112). New York: Academic Press.

Bricker, D., & Widerstrom, A. (Eds.). (1996). *Preparing personnel to work with infants and young children with disabilities: A team approach.* Baltimore: Paul H. Brookes Publishing Co.

Bronfenbrenner, U. (1986). Ecology of the family as a context for human development: Research perspective. *Developmental Psychology, 22*, 723–742.

Education for All Handicapped Children Act of 1975, PL 94-142, 20 U.S.C. § 1400 *et seq.*

Education of the Handicapped Act Amendments of 1986, PL 99-457, 20 U.S.C. § 1400 *et seq.*

Elementary and Secondary Education Act (ESEA) of 1965, PL 89-10, 20 U.S.C. § 241 *et seq.*

Frederick, J. (1996). Implications of managed care on early intervention services for infants and toddlers. *Infants and Young Children, 8*(3), vi–viii.

Gottwald, S.R., & Thurman, S.K. (1990). Parent–infant interaction in neonatal intensive care units: Implications for research and service delivery. *Infants and Young Children, 2*(3), 1–10.

Guralnick, M.J., & Bennett, F.C. (1987). *The effectiveness of early intervention for at-risk and handicapped children.* New York: Academic Press.

Hack, M., Klein, N.K., & Taylor, H.G. (1995). Long-term developmental outcomes of low birth weight infants. *The Future of Children, 5*(1), 176–196.

Handicapped Children's Early Education Act of 1968, PL 90-538, 20 U.S.C. § 621 *et seq.*

Harrison, H. (1994, October). *Parents' perspectives on neonatal ethics: Setting compassionate limits to the use of technology.* Paper presented at Grand Rounds, Community Hospital, Santa Rosa, CA.

Heriza, C.B., & Sweeney, J.K. (1990). Effects of NICU intervention on preterm infants: Part 1: Implications for neonatal practice. *Infants and Young Children, 2*(3), 31–48.

Individuals with Disabilities Education Act (IDEA) of 1990, PL 101-476, 20 U.S.C. § 1400 *et seq.*

Individuals with Disabilities Education Act Amendments of 1991, PL 102-119, 20 U.S.C. § 1400 *et seq.*

Klein, N.K. (1988). Children who are very low birth weight: Cognitive abilities and classroom behavior at five years of age. *Journal of Special Education, 22*(1), 41–54.

Lazar, I., Darlington, R., Murray, H., Royce, J., & Snipper, A. (1982). Lasting effects of early intervention: A report from the Consortium for Longitudinal Studies. *Monographs of the Society for Research in Child Development, 47*(2–3, Serial No. 195).

Lewit, E.M., Baker, L.S., Corman, H., & Shiono, P.H. (1995). The direct cost of low birth weight. *The Future of Children, 5*(1), 35–56.

McWilliam, R.A., & Strain, P.S. (1993). Service delivery models. In DEC Task Force on Recommended Practices, *DEC recommended practices: Indicators of quality in programs for infants and young children with special needs and their families* (pp. 40–46). Reston, VA: Council for Exceptional Children.

Meisels, S.J. (1984). The efficacy of early intervention: Why are we still asking this question? *Topics in Early Childhood Special Education, 5*(2), 1–11.

Paneth, N.S. (1995). The problem of low birth weight. *The Future of Children, 5*(1), 19–34.

Parmalee, A.H. (1989). The child's physical health and the development of relationships. In A.J. Sameroff & R.N. Emde (Eds.), *Relationship disturbances in early childhood: A developmental approach* (pp. 145–162). New York: Basic Books.

Pomerance, J.J., Pomerance, L.J., & Gottleib, J.A. (1993). Cost of caring for infants weighing 500–749 grams at birth. *Pediatric Research, 4*, 231A.

Ramey, C.T., & Suarez, T.M. (1984). Early intervention and the early experience paradigm: Toward a better framework for social policy. *Journal of Children in Contemporary Society, 17*, 3–13.

Robertson, N.R. (1993). Should we look after babies less than 800 grams? *Archives of Disease in Childhood, 68*, 326–329.

Saigal, S., Rosenbaum, P., Stoskopf, B., & Milner, R. (1982). Follow-up of infants 501–1500 grams birth weight delivered to residents of a geographically defined region with perinatal intensive care facilities. *Journal of Pediatrics, 100*, 606–613.

Shearer, A. (1985). Everybody's ethics: What future for handicapped babies? *Early Child Development and Care, 18*(3–4), 189–216.

Shonkoff, J.P., Hauser-Cram, P., Krauss, M.W., & Upshur, C.C. (1988). Early intervention efficacy research: What have we learned and where do we go from here? *Topics in Early Childhood Special Education, 8*, 81–93.

Smith, B.J. (1989). Early intervention public policy: Past, present and future. In J.B. Jordan, J. Gallagher, P.L. Hutinger, & M.B. Karnes (Eds.), *Early childhood special education: Birth to three* (pp. 213–229). Reston, VA: Council for Exceptional Children.

Smith, B.J., & Strain, P.S. (1988). Early childhood special education in the next decade: Implementing and expanding PL 99-457. *Topics in Early Childhood Special Education, 8*, 37–47.

Widerstrom, A.H. (1991). At-risk and handicapped newborns and infants. In A.H. Widerstrom, B.A. Mowder, & S.R. Sandall, *At-risk and handicapped newborns and infants: Development, assessment, and intervention* (pp. 1–14). Englewood Cliffs, NJ: Prentice Hall.

Widerstrom, A., & Abelman, D. (1996). Team training issues. In D. Bricker & A. Widerstrom (Eds.), *Preparing personnel to work with infants and young children and their families: A team approach* (pp. 23–42). Baltimore: Paul H. Brookes Publishing Co.

Widerstrom, A.H., & Goodwin, L.G. (1987). Effects of an infant stimulation program on the child and family. *Journal of the Division for Early Childhood, 11*, 143–153.

1 ACTIVITIES

1. Visit a Head Start program for parents and infants younger than age 3. Find out as much as you can about services offered to infants with disabilities. Find out what the eligibility criteria are for participation in the program.

2. Ask your senator or congressperson for a copy of the most recent authorization of the Individuals with Disabilities Education Act (IDEA). Read carefully the sections of the law (Part H) dealing with infants between birth and 3 years of age.

3. Visit a hospital that serves infants at risk for or with disabilities in a Level III nursery (neonatal intensive care unit) and observe the procedures used. Find out how much access parents have to the nursery.

4. Visit an early intervention program in your community to observe an interdisciplinary team at work. If possible, interview the educator, occupational therapist, physical therapist, speech-language pathologist, and the social worker to find out what their special responsibilities are.

Appendix

Suggestions for Further Reading

The following journals publish articles related to infant behavior and development, infant assessment, and/or early intervention and programming. They can be found in most university libraries.

Typical and Atypical Child Development

Child Development
Infant Behavior and Development
Young Children

Psychology

Journal of Abnormal Psychology
Journal of Counseling and Consulting Psychology
Journal of Pediatric Psychology
Professional School Psychology
Psychology in the Schools

Health

Developmental Medicine and Child Neurology
Journal of Behavioral and Developmental Pediatrics
Journal of Behavioral Medicine
Journal of Pediatrics
Pediatrics

Special Education

American Journal on Mental Retardation
Journal of Early Intervention
Journal of Special Education
Journal of The Association for Persons with Severe Handicaps (TASH)
Topics in Early Childhood Special Education

Interdisciplinary

Child: Health, Care and Development
Infants and Young Children
Journal of Children in Contemporary Society

Note: Not included in this list are the many journals concerned with special fields, such as speech, occupational, or physical therapy or nursing.

SECTION II

TYPICAL AND ATYPICAL INFANT DEVELOPMENT

CHAPTER 2

Typical Infant Development

Barbara A. Mowder

Objectives

- To review methods of research in infant development
- To understand genetic and biological development
- To learn stages of language and cognitive development
- To understand social-emotional development

The field of infant development has a long and distinguished history, and much of what is known about how and why infants grow and develop is from systematic observation, theoretical developments in psychology, and the utilization of experimental techniques. Scientific interest in infant development can be traced to the 1800s when, in 1877, Charles Darwin made a scientific, systematic observation of a child's behavior (Kessen, 1965). This event is usually noted by child developmentalists as the beginning of the study of child growth and development (e.g., Bornstein & Lamb, 1988).

Chronologically, other milestones in the evolution of infant and child development include the early theoretical formulations of G. Stanley Hall (e.g., 1891, 1904), particularly his contributions on adolescent growth and development, followed by the extensive psychoanalytic writing of Sigmund Freud (e.g., 1917, 1923/1962, 1940) at the turn of the century and later. Arnold Gesell (e.g., 1925, 1940, 1945) and his theory of the importance of maturation, and John Watson's (e.g., 1924, 1928) theory of behaviorism in the late 1920s and 1930s also helped shape the field. The enormous contributions of Jean Piaget on cognitive development (e.g., 1929, 1951, 1952, 1954) and the work of Albert Bandura on social learning theory (e.g., 1969, 1977, 1986) are an integral part of current thinking and research about young children (Miller, 1993).

The concept of development is key to this chapter. *Development* means the pattern of change that starts with conception, continues throughout life, and ends with death. Development is a complex concept that involves an interaction of biological and physical development, cognitive development and learning, and social-emotional development. Further complicating the construct is the fact that development does not occur in a vacuum, but rather is an interactive process, occurring within a physical environment and social context, with other individuals who are developing at the same time.

RESEARCH METHODOLOGY IN INFANT DEVELOPMENT

Beyond the theoretical formulations regarding infant and child development such as those previously mentioned are the methods that have evolved for studying developmental phenomena. It is critical to understand research methodology because much of what we know, understand, and accept in the infant and toddler developmental literature derives from experimental research. Research and experimental techniques have allowed developmentalists to move beyond observation to sophisticated methods for examining infants and their growth and development, to make assertions about developmental progress, and to develop and test theories (Miller, 1987).

As a field, infant development considers growth in terms of norms and expected ranges of development as well as individual differences. When physical growth and development is studied, for example, researchers examine many infants to establish the average rate of growth; then, within the determined range, individual differences among infants are considered. The range also establishes the parameters by which differences between groups of infants (e.g., infants born to mothers who smoked during pregnancy and those born to mothers who did not) are examined. This is known as the concept of norms, and it is important in the examination of infant development.

Research Designs

Research designs for studying infants for the most part have focused on group data and ranges of normal development. There are many research designs (e.g., Hetherington & Parke, 1993; Maccoby & Martin, 1983; Martin, 1981; Seitz, 1988), and infant developmental research tends to correspond to one of five primary designs:

1. Longitudinal research
2. Cross-sectional research
3. Short-term longitudinal research
4. Cross-sectional/short-term longitudinal research
5. Single-subject research

No one research design is the ideal methodological model; each has advantages and disadvantages, strengths and weaknesses. Researchers may select a particular design depending on the developmental issue studied, along with various considerations such as the importance of discerning individual differences or focusing on group trends and practical concerns such as availability of groups of children over time, research time commitment, and cost issues.

Meredith

Meredith's parents were concerned when she was born 3 weeks before her due date and just more than 5 pounds. She seemed to sleep through her first 2 weeks of development. After that initial period of time, however, Meredith exhibited a combination of traits. She responded to her parents whenever her name was said by turning her head in response. In addition, she molded to her mother's arms by moving and snuggling into a comfortable position, and shortly she began to smile. Her distress cues were very clear to her parents and almost exclusively were for hunger, wetness, and the need to sleep. Her parents met her needs quickly, and the easy-going nature of her temperament extended through her first year of life. By the end of the first year, Meredith approached most people with a ready smile and was actively exploring her environment. She continued to enjoy the physical proximity and touch of her mother, and this remained a consistently effective way to soothe Meredith on the rare occasions when she was distressed.

The same combination of personality traits—easy social interaction, continual smile, and pleasant temperament—has continued right through to her preschool and elementary school years, where teachers consistently note a self-reliance and independence and an overall comfort with self. Meredith is sought out by other children for play, actively explores and seeks out novel situations, and continues to display a joyful outlook on her world.

Longitudinal Research Longitudinal research requires that a population be identified, that each subject within the population be studied, and that the study occur over at least a 5-year span of time. This type of research provides rich data by identifying individual differences within populations and noting how these differences develop over time. A disadvantage of this research design is that it requires a relatively stable population, because attrition (loss of subjects over time) can seriously affect assertions that may be made about the data collected (Loeber & Farrington, 1994; Simons, Ritchie, Mullett, & Mingarelle, 1989; Verhulst & Koot, 1991). Classic developmental longitudinal studies include the Terman Gifted Child Study started in 1921; the Berkeley Growth Study in 1928; and, in 1929, the Berkeley Guidance Study, the Fels Research Institute Project, and the Harvard Longitudinal Study (Mednick & Mednick, 1984). A recent example of longitudinal research is the study by Caspi and Silva (1995) in which temperamental qualities at age 3 were related to personality traits in young adulthood at age 18.

Cross-Sectional Research Cross-sectional research requires that several different groups of infants are studied, which are identified at specific developmental ages or stages, or chosen for other specific characteristics. For instance, Hubert (1989) studied parents of 6- and 24-month-old children to discern parental reactions to temperament behavior. She found high correlations between parent ratings of their own pleasure and infant temperament ratings, ratings that were not affected by other classification variables (e.g., age, birth order, gender). By utilizing cross-sectional research, developmentalists collect data within a relatively short period of time, which allows them to make statements about developmental issues without waiting for a certain group of babies to mature. Because the analysis focuses on group change, however, individual developmental differences are lost.

Short-Term Longitudinal Research Short-term longitudinal research is a design developed to capture individual differences in development without investing an enormous amount of time. In this method, one group of infants is identified and studied over a relatively brief period of time, typically 1–5 years. Berlin, Cassidy, and Belsky (1995), for example, examined loneliness in young children and infant–mother attachment. They found that the most loneliness was reported by young children who had been classified as insecure-ambivalent in infancy and the least loneliness by those classified as insecure-avoidant. An intermediate level of loneliness was reported by youngsters classified as secure in infancy. The advantage of this research design is that individual differences may be studied over time without the attrition of subjects that can occur in longitudinal research. One distinct disadvantage is that some developmental issues may not be amenable to a short time span of study.

Cross-Sectional/Short-Term Longitudinal Research The cross-sectional/short-term longitudinal research design is a combination approach, incorporating cross-sectional research with short-term longitudinal methods, which attempts to capture many of the advantages of both. In this design, groups of individuals at different ages or developmental stages are identified and studied over 1–5 years (e.g., Anderson, 1993). In this way, some assertions regarding individual differences may be made, as well as limited statements regarding developmental issues. Kline, Tschann, Johnston, and Wallerstein (1989), for example, considered children's adjustment in joint and sole custody families by considering children ages 3–14. They studied the group for 1 year after the parents filed for divorce, and then again 1 and 2 years later, and found no difference in child postdivorce adjustment with sole and joint custody. Several problems occur with this approach, however. The different groups must have an adequate measure of similarity in order to make assertions regarding long-term developmental issues. Furthermore, statements regarding individual differences are limited, and the logistics of studying several different groups of children simultaneously over a specified period of time is difficult.

Single-Subject Research A design recently adopted for use with infants is the single-subject research design, in which one baby or a very small number of infants are studied extensively over a specified period of time. This type of design has been particularly amenable to behavioral examinations of children in which a specific behavior is identified, an intervention or treatment program developed and implemented, and an evaluation reported. Lamm and Greer (1988), for instance, used behavioral methods to induce and maintain swallowing with three infants who did not swallow food or liquid. Problems with this approach exist, in that only two or three infants are usually studied. This makes it difficult to make generalized assertions regarding infant and child growth and development. However, single-subject research designs have been suggested as a solution to some of the methodological difficulties encountered in studying young infants (Pomerleau, Malcuit, Chamberland, & Laurendeau, 1992).

Research Techniques

Within the various research designs, specific techniques have been developed for the study of infants. The need for specific techniques, different from those used in studying older children, adolescents, and adults, is clear. Infants do not have the cognitive, language, motor, physical, or social-emotional maturity evidenced at other developmental levels and stages. Therefore, techniques that accommodate to their specific developmental functioning are necessary (Miller, 1987) (Table 2.1).

Early research techniques included the use of infant diaries, case studies, or journals. Darwin (Kessen, 1965), as well as others, wrote journals regarding specific infant development. This technique is still in use (Wallace, Franklin, & Keegan, 1994) and provides a rich source of data on day-to-day individual infant and toddler developmental progress. However, it does not necessarily yield information that may be generalized to other children. Another technique that has been used successfully over time is systematic observation. Indeed, this tool was the primary technique employed by both Freud and Piaget in developing their landmark theories. Although their theories focus on different developmental issues, both theoreticians systematically observed children, made careful, documented statements regarding development, and advanced comprehensive theories on how infants and children grow and develop.

More recently, techniques such as habituation-dishabituation, visual preference, strange situation, questionnaire and survey research, and standardized testing have been developed. *Habituation-dishabituation* refers to research that examines how infants respond to and ignore various repeated stimuli such as objects or sounds (e.g., Bornstein & Benasich, 1986; Bornstein, Pecheux, & Lecuyer, 1988). Tamis-LeMonda and Bornstein (1989) considered infant attention as a predictor of toddler language, play, and representational competence. They drew infants' attention to a stimulus panel and, once the babies were oriented, projected a visual stimulus. After the infant habituated and stopped looking at the stimulus, they presented a new visual stimulus. Researchers recorded continuous measurements of the infants' looking behaviors. Using this technique, they found that infants who habituate to visual stimuli in a mature manner have more flexible language comprehension, have more pretend play, and exhibit more advanced representational abilities as toddlers than infants who habituate in a less mature manner.

Visual preference and *visual search* are other techniques developed to study infant development. Fantz (1958) originated these techniques by developing a situ-

Table 2.1. Infant study research techniques

Research techniques	Description
1. Diaries, case studies, and journals	One of the earliest forms of infant research in which individual infant development is recorded on an ongoing basis
2. Systematic observation	Systematic, careful, well-documented observations of infants
3. Habituation-dishabituation	The cessation of an infant's response to repeated stimuli, response recovery to the same stimuli
4. Visual preference	The systematic study of what and how long an infant views stimulus material
5. Visual search	Techniques developed to monitor infants' eye movements and complex visual behaviors
6. Strange situation	A systematic set of situations designed to assess the infant's attachment to the parent
7. Questionnaires and survey techniques	Paper-and-pencil assessment materials designed to study an array of infant development issues
8. Standardized assessments	These materials are developed to have strong psychometric properties for studying infants in a standardized manner

ation in which a trained observer systematically studies what an infant is viewing and the amount of time the infant spends observing a specific stimulus. Other researchers have developed more sophisticated techniques to monitor infants' eye movements, scanning patterns, and complex visual behaviors (Snow, 1989). For example, Langlois, Ritter, Roggman, and Vaughn (1991) examined infant attractiveness preferences in four types of faces: white adult female and male, black adult female, and infant. Using a visual preference paradigm, infants viewed pairs of faces. Subjects showed significant preferences for attractive faces across all facial types; the results indicate infant preferences for attractive faces regardless of race, gender, or age.

The *strange situation technique* is a tool developed specifically to study the issue of attachment; because it has been used almost to the exclusion of any other research technique in the issue of infant attachment, it has become a technique in its own right. In this technique, an infant is placed in a room with its mother and measures are taken with the mother, without the mother, and with and without a stranger being present (Lamb, Thompson, Gardner, & Charnov, 1985). Hubbs-Tait, Wierzbicki, Gray, and Englehart (1994), for example, used a videotaped episode of the strange situation in part of their study to examine perceptions of adopted infant boys' behaviors and mental health issues. The effects of the adoption term were not significant; subjects perceived the resistant baby as least socially competent and most negative in affect and the secure infant as least independent.

Questionnaires and survey techniques have also been developed to study infant growth and development. These techniques typically rely on the administration of written questionnaire and survey materials to the infant's primary caregiver. Izard, Haynes, Chisholm, and Baak (1991), for example, asked mothers to fill out emotion and temperament questionnaires. They found that mothers' emotion experiences, expressive behaviors, and personality traits significantly predicted the level of security of the infant–mother attachment. Mothers' perceptions of their infants' expressive and temperamental characteristics were also significant predictors of infant–mother security.

More recently, *standardized assessment instruments* have been used to study infant growth and development. Instruments and measures, such as the Bayley Scales of Infant Development (Bayley, 1993), afford researchers a standardized method for studying infant development. Bondurant-Utz and Luciano (1994) have presented a guide to infant and preschool assessment in special education, and Meisels and Wasik (1990) have examined when and how often children at risk should be assessed, the validity issues surrounding screening and assessment instruments, and meaningful assessments with children at risk and their families. Other standardized assessment measures have been used to examine the infant's environment. For example, Spieker and Bensley (1994) used the Home Observation for Measurement of the Environment (HOME) to examine the relationship between social support from adolescents' mothers and adolescent mother–infant living arrangements. One of their findings was that adolescents living alone had better teaching interactions but lower HOME scores compared to those living with their mothers.

Other methods also have been developed to measure infant responses. Physiological measures include, for example, simple reflex behaviors, such as sucking and eye blinkings, as well as voluntary behaviors, such as grasping, head turning, and looking. Measuring heart rate is the most commonly employed physiological measure (Field, 1990). Research has also considered infant cries as a method for assessing infants at risk for disabilities (Meisels & Wasik, 1990).

The study of prenatal development has employed different and diverse techniques, from the early use of direct observation of surgically exteriorized animal fetuses or aborted human fetuses, to the more recent indirect manipulation of the fetus and the use of inference from subsequent developmental consequences (Smotherman & Robinson, 1987). The latter methodology is common in teratological research, but Smotherman and Robinson (1987) cautioned that reliance on the postnatal approach influences the conduct of research, shapes the questions being asked, and brings possible bias to the field of infant study. More sophisticated methodologies have been developed recently, such as external fetal monitoring (Patrick, Campbell, Carmichael, & Probert, 1982) and real-time ultrasonography (Birnholz & Benacerraf, 1983), yet there remain many methodological issues in human behavioral teratology research (Jacobson & Jacobson, 1990).

ISSUES IN INFANT DEVELOPMENT

Historically the issue most frequently debated in the developmental literature is that of nature versus nurture (Miller, 1993). That is, what is the relative role of biological processes as opposed to environmental influences on development? Because infants are both biological as well as social beings, the issue is what the relative influence of each is and whether one predominates over the other. Extreme positions have been taken on this issue over time. Arnold Gessell (1925, 1940, 1945) held the view that maturational factors supersede all other considerations, whereas B.F. Skinner (1957, 1966, 1976) took the opposite position.

Another issue that has emerged in infant development is whether development is a collection of changes that occur over time or if development is qualitatively different at different points in development. This issue of quantitative versus qualitative changes (Miller, 1993) is more clearly seen when one views a variety of theoretical positions on infant development. Piaget (1929, 1951, 1952, 1954), for example, posited that development is qualitatively different at different stages. The infant is developmentally and qualitatively different from the preschooler, and the preschooler is qualitatively different from the elementary school–age child. Skinner (1972, 1976), however, believed that behavioral development occurs as a collection of learnings. That is, learning for the infant is essentially no different from learning for an adolescent or an adult.

A further issue with developing infants is whether they are active or passive in the developmental process (Sroufe, Cooper, & Marshall, 1988). In other words, do infants' actions and activities have an impact on their development, or are infants passive recipients of events or factors over which they have no control? Watson (1930) maintained that an infant is passive in the developmental process, whereas Piaget (1952, 1954) maintained that the infant must be active in order to progress through the developmental stages.

The role of past experience in development has also been a major concern for infant developmentalists. What, for example, is the effect of an extremely deprived first 3 months of life? Does serious neglect early in an infant's life result in life-long developmental problems, and, if so, can these developmental issues be overcome with time? Freud (1940) maintained that the effects of early experience are fundamental and affect all aspects of later development. Learning theorists, such as Bandura (1977, 1986), however, took a different point of view by demonstrating significant changes in behavior that can occur based on presentations of different models with various reinforcement histories.

Finally, the goal of development is a major issue for developmentalists. What are the expectations for developing infants? Is it anticipated, for example, that they successfully complete the stage of sensorimotor development and demonstrate object permanence (Piaget, 1970)? Or is there no particular expectation in terms of development? Is each individual infant becoming a toddler, preschooler, child, adolescent, and then adult without any particular landmark in the developmental sequence?

GENETICS AND BIOLOGICAL DEVELOPMENT

The study of infant development begins with a consideration of genetics and biological development. Genetics plays a crucial role in development from conception and fertilization through birth and further development. There is a profound developmental complexity within the mother's womb prior to the infant's birth. That complexity includes genetic characteristics and environmental factors. These factors continuously interact and affect physical characteristics as well as the infant's behavior.

Genetic Makeup

An infant is a biological being whose development begins with conception, when a male gamete (sperm) unites with a female gamete (egg cell or ovum). After the ovum is fertilized, biochemical changes prevent other sperm from penetrating (Sutton, 1975). The single-celled zygote, which is formed at conception, contains the infant's entire complement of genes and chromosomes needed for development (Rosenblith & Sims-Knight, 1985).

Chromosomes are structures within human cells composed of DNA (deoxyribonucleic acid). Genes, in turn, are small bits of DNA (Nora & Fraser, 1989). Each of the 23 pairs of chromosomes found in every human body cell contains thousands of genes. Together, chromosomes and genes form the blueprint for development, specifying the structure of every individual human cell. (See Chapter 3 for a more complete discussion of the way genes and chromosomes affect development.) The actual combination of genetic material is referred to as the *genotype*; genotypes are never directly observed because they are the genetic material that resides within the human cell. *Phenotypes* differ from genotypes because they are observable, measurable characteristics. Phenotypes include characteristics such as height, skin pigmentation, and weight. *Polygenetic inheritance* refers to the interaction of many different genes, which, in turn, affect development. It is important to understand that not all developmental factors derive directly from specific individual genetic activity.

Biological Development

Prenatal Growth and Development From research, we know that after conception the zygote undergoes extremely rapid growth and thus begins the germinal stage of prenatal development. The germinal stage lasts approximately 2 weeks, and during this time the zygote moves through the fallopian tube to the uterus where it attaches itself to the uterine wall. By the end of this period, implantation has occurred and the cells have already begun to differentiate. The inner layer of cells, the *blastocyst,* will develop into the embryo, and the outer layer of cells, the *trophoblast,* will provide nutrition, protection, and support for the developing embryo.

The embryonic period begins approximately 2 weeks after conception and extends through the end of the eighth week. As this period starts, the embryo is firmly attached to the uterine lining and consists of two layers of cells, the endoderm and the ectoderm. The inner layer, the *endoderm,* will develop into the digestive tract, glandular system, liver, and respiratory system. The outer layer, the *ectoderm,* becomes the skin, hair, nails, sensory organs, and nervous system. Finally, approximately 3 weeks after conception, a third layer of cells develops between the endoderm and the ectoderm, called the *mesoderm.* The mesoderm will form the skeletal, muscular, circulatory, reproductive, and urinary systems.

During the embryonic period the supporting membranes, including the amnion, placenta, and umbilical cord, are also developing. The *amnion* is a protective wrapping of clear, salty liquid in which the embryo floats. The *placenta* is a vital link between the embryo and the mother, providing passage of antibodies, nutrients, waste products, oxygen, and hormones. The mother's and embryo's bloodstreams do not actually mix because they are separated by thin membrane walls; however, oxygen, nutrients, and waste products are easily exchanged through the placenta. From the placenta, a bluish red *umbilical cord* develops in which very small molecules, such as oxygen and food from the mother's blood, may pass between the infant and the mother.

Within a short period of time, by 4 weeks, the embryo and supporting membranes are approximately the size of a pea (Snow, 1989). A primitive heart is pumping blood, a rudimentary system for digesting and assimilating food is being formed, and parts of the brain are already in evidence. Limb buds are visible, eyes begin to appear, the spine has started to form, and the first of the kidney-like structures is present. The first bone cells appear at about 6½ weeks (Musick & Householder, 1986); the skeleton is one of the first recognizable tissues to develop during the embryonic period (Ross, Mimouni, & Tsang, 1988). An obstetrician may use a technique known as ultrasonography, or ultrasound, during this period of time to determine developmental age, evaluate growth, detect twins, and find anatomical abnormalities (Nora & Fraser, 1989). Ultrasound imaging uses sound waves, which are passed through the amniotic fluid to the fetus. The waves produce images received as two-dimensional pictures on a screening monitor.

The first fetal movements can be observed at 7½ weeks' gestation (DeVries, Visser, & Prechtl, 1982; Ianniruberto & Tajani, 1981), and the first sign of true responding appears about this time in the form of a head movement from the site of stimulation, from gentle brushing in the nose and lip regions (Bremner, 1994; Hooker, 1952). By 8 weeks, tremendous growth and differentiation have occurred. The head represents almost half of the body's length, facial features begin to form, and limbs become more evident. The brain has developed in size and complexity (Kolb & Fantie, 1989), all major body systems are present in some form of development, and the embryo is clearly recognizable as a developing human organism. By 8–9 weeks, quick startles and slow general movements are observed, followed quickly by hiccups and isolated arm and leg movements (Prechtl, 1987). Motion pictures show the mouth opening and closing beginning at 8½ weeks; swallowing, and lip and tongue movements between 10½ and 12½ weeks; squint-like and sneer-like expressions at 14 weeks; and strong gagging by 18½ weeks (Chamberlain, 1988). By the end of the embryonic period, the embryo is approximately 1 inch in length and weighs about one thirtieth of an ounce. Because growth is so rapid during the embryonic period, it is a time of extreme vulnerability. A new technique referred to as chorionic villus sampling, or CVS, allows cells to be suctioned from the placenta by a small tube passed through the vagina and cervix. This relatively safe procedure, by which the fetus's genetic makeup is examined, can be performed within 8–12 weeks' gestation (Chervenak, Isaacson, & Mahoney, 1986).

The fetal stage begins with the ninth week after conception and extends to birth. At the beginning of this period, the fetus continues dramatic growth and development. Prechtl (1987) found that from 10 weeks onward rhythmic breathing movements can be observed, the head can be rotated, and by 10½ weeks jaw opening and complex stretch movements are added to the fetal repertoire. Yawns, rhythmic sucking, and swallowing follow closely at 11 and 12 weeks. From the beginning of this period to approximately 14 weeks is a time of spurting brain growth, when billions of cells develop into neurons (Strom, Bernard, & Strom, 1987). Taste buds function by 15 weeks (Bradley & Stern, 1967), and the fetus will experience the taste of a range of acids, proteins, salts, and other chemicals in the amniotic fluid for some time before birth (Mistretta & Bradley, 1977). From 10 to 18 weeks of gestation, as well as the last 3 months of pregnancy through the first 18 months of postnatal life, brain tissue can be damaged by toxic substances, nutritional deprivation, disruption of oxygen and carbon dioxide exchange, and combinations of these and other factors (Hunt, 1983).

As the third month of development after conception progresses, the fetus can kick its legs, turn its limbs and head, open its mouth, swallow, and make a fist. By the end of the third month, or 12 weeks, the external sex organs are observable and the fetus exhibits substantial movement. At this time the fetus is almost 3 inches long and weighs approximately 1 ounce.

During the fourth month of development, the mother begins to show her pregnancy and feels the fetus moving for the first time. Growth continues to be extremely rapid, with limbs, hands and feet, heart, and reflexes undergoing striking development. When the fetus is 16–20 weeks of age, an obstetrician may perform an amniocentesis. With amniocentesis, a hollow needle is inserted into the amniotic sac and fluid is withdrawn (Finegan, Quarrington, Hughes, & Doran, 1987). The amniotic fluid is analyzed to discern chromosomal abnormalities and a range of possible defects and disorders. Neural tube defects, including absence of part of the brain or skull or failure of the spine to close, may be found through amniocentesis because alpha-fetoprotein is leaked from the fetus into the amniotic sac (Brock, 1983); both a high or low level of alpha-fetoprotein has diagnostic implications (Lippman & Evans, 1987).

By the fifth month, the skin of the fetus is covered by a cheese-like substance called *vernix caseosa* (Snow, 1989), which protects the skin during the long immersion in the amniotic fluid. Extensive brain growth occurs, as well as formation of sweat glands, growth of eyebrows and eyelashes, and development of a soft, fine hair called *lanugo* that covers the body. At the end of the fifth month the fetus is approximately 12 inches long and weighs about 1 pound.

During the sixth month, the fetus engages in many reflexive activities such as sucking, swallowing, and grasping. The eyes and eyelids are completely formed,

irregular breathing occurs, and the fetus moves and sleeps at regular periods of time. Fetal skin is still covered with vernix, and there are few fatty deposits under the skin for insulation and protection. If the fetus is expelled from the womb at this point, the chances of survival are mixed. The respiratory and digestive systems, in particular, are generally not mature enough to support the fetus as a neonate. Six months after conception the fetus is usually about 14 inches long and weighs almost 2 pounds.

By the end of the second or early in the third gestation trimester, the fetus is capable of auditory perception (Birnholz & Benacerraf, 1983); data suggest the fetus responds to sounds as early as 12 weeks (Hepper, 1992). At 7 months of gestation, or 28 weeks, the fetus may survive if expelled from the womb; even infants as young as 24–25 weeks may now survive with significant medical assistance. This period is called the "age of viability" and means that the respiratory system, brain functions, digestive and circulatory systems, and other developmental aspects of the fetus are mature enough to exist, with special care and attention, if birth occurs. However, Drogtrop, Ubels, and Nijhuis (1990) found that fetal heart rate patterns, body movements, and eye movements do not occur simultaneously in fetuses between 25 and 30 weeks' gestation, suggesting that behavioral states that imply a high level of linkage are not present in fetuses of this age. By the end of the seventh month, the fetus is usually 16 inches long and weighs about 2 pounds.

From 8 to 9 months after conception, the fetus gains weight, the functioning of biological systems is refined, and the fetus becomes increasingly sensitive to light, sound, and touch. In the final weeks before birth, the fetus displays changes in activity level that correspond closely to the neonate's states of sleep, quiet wakefulness, and active wakefulness (Nijhuis, 1992). The placenta facilitates the transfer of the mother's antibodies to the fetus, but begins to break down and becomes progressively less efficient in meeting the needs of the fetus. The fetus becomes ready for birth and at birth weighs approximately 7 pounds and is about 20 inches in length.

There are a number of scales developed for screening and predicting perinatal risk. Molfese (1989) discussed the University of Colorado Neonatal Morbidity Risk Scale, the High-Risk Pregnancy Screening System, the Obstetrical Complications Scale, and the Maternal–Child Health Care Index, as well as many other scales and systems. All of these scales include measurements of the mother's age, marital status, parity (number of previous births), income and education level of the mother and father, prenatal care, maternal physical factors, maternal nutrition, placental factors, and fetal factors. Molfese stressed the importance of perinatal risk scale development, as approximately 85% of perinatal mortality and morbidity cases can be identified as coming from the approximately 25% of pregnancies that have antepartum or intrapartum complications.

Birth and Effects of the Birth Process Birth moves the fetus from the protective environment of the womb, where the temperature is controlled and consistent, sounds muted, and nutritional needs continuously met, to a world where the newborn must breathe, eat, and cope with a large array of needs and stresses. *Childbirth* is the process that moves the fetus out of the uterus and into the complex world awaiting it. While nearly 95% of all infants are born within 2 weeks of their expected delivery date (40 weeks' gestation), scientists are not clear about what actually causes labor to begin (Snow, 1989).

The birth process includes three stages. During the first and longest stage, labor begins with the muscles of the uterus contracting. The contractions are involuntary, and they cause the cervix to stretch, open, and prepare to expel the fetus. As labor progresses, the contractions come closer together, from initially being 15–30 minutes apart to every 2–5 minutes; they also increase in intensity. At the end of this stage, the cervix has approximately a 4-inch opening that is large enough to allow the infant to move through the birth canal.

The second stage of labor is the birth of the child. The contractions, with the help of the mother's abdominal muscle pushing, continue to move the infant out of the womb. Typically, the baby is in the head-first position; after the head appears, the rest of the body is eased out of the birth canal. In the third stage of labor, the placenta is delivered. This stage is the shortest and involves the uterine muscles expelling the fetal membranes, placenta, and umbilical cord.

Difficulties can occur during the birth process, including a baby being in a problematic birth position, a prolonged and complicated delivery, detachment of the placenta during the birth process, and anoxia or lack of oxygen for the baby. These and other birth-related issues are covered in greater detail in Chapters 3, 4, and 5.

Development of the Neonate The newly born infant, or neonate, typically has grown in the womb for 37–40 weeks and weighs about 7 pounds. The average gestation is 38 weeks, with 70% of neonates delivered at 36–40 weeks, and roughly 98% between 34 and 42 weeks (Meredith, 1978). The average 38-week-old neonate weighs 7.3 pounds and is 19.9 inches in length.

After birth, neonates must adjust quickly to their new, complex circumstances. They breathe on their own, ingest and digest food for the first time, and eliminate waste. Their body temperature adjusts to their environment. There appears to be

Typical Labor and Birth

Ann and Joseph had prepared for their first child by attending Lamaze childbirth classes. In the classes, they learned to prepare for their child's birth by practicing exercises that would help the delivery and birth. They also discovered that an average labor for a first-born child was about 8 hours' duration, with the range being approximately 3–24 hours.

With this in mind, on the morning Ann's water broke (indicating that their baby would soon be born), the soon-to-be parents took their time getting to the hospital. Thinking that labor would be at least the typical 8 hours in length, Joseph had breakfast and Ann picked up a few things around the house. However, within a short period of time it was clear that the contractions were coming more frequently and that if they didn't get to the hospital soon, their baby would be born at home.

After rushing to the hospital, they went through the obligatory check-in procedures, including Ann being taken to the delivery area in a wheelchair. Once in the labor room (a dismal area painted dark green with a single light bulb housed in wire mesh), the nurses took over preparation for delivery. They encouraged the use of the Lamaze exercises and integrated Joseph into their preparations while explaining the fetal monitors and other equipment in the room. Shortly, however, the contractions were in close proximity to one another and Ann was brought into the delivery room. Within minutes, baby Melissa was born and was given her first Apgar score, a perfect 10.

much variability in the relative coordination of sucking, swallowing, and breathing at birth (Woolridge & Baum, 1988).

Newborns exhibit many reflexive behaviors. A *reflex* is an automatic reaction or a built-in response to a stimulus (Sroufe et al., 1988). Table 2.2 gives examples of infant reflexes. Some reflexes serve critical life survival functions, such as breathing, and others help the infant deal with threats to the developing body.

All senses are functional at birth, although they are immature and capable of significant refinement and development (Field, 1990). The infant can see at birth, but visual acuity for two dimensions is poor for several months after birth and only gradually increases during the first year (Banks & Salapatek, 1983). Very young infants will attend to something moving across their line of vision and will show little interest in static objects and scenes (Gibson, 1988). Infants' acuity improves with time, achieving nearly adult levels by 6 months to 1 year of age (Acredolo & Hake, 1982; Rose & Ruff, 1987). Studies of newborns' eye scanning movements suggest that they are preprogrammed to search with their eyes and that their eye actions are spontaneous rather than reflexive in nature (Haith, 1980).

Hearing is also present at birth, although it takes a few days for the neonate's auditory canals to be clear of amniotic fluid and for hearing to become fully functional. Infants selectively respond to human sounds, particularly the female human voice (Freedman, 1971) and especially the mother's voice (DeCasper & Fifer, 1980).

Table 2.2. Examples of infant reflexes

Reflex	Description	Developmental pattern
Blink	To a flash of light or a puff of air, an infant closes both eyes.	Permanent
Babinski	When the side of an infant's foot is stroked from the heel toward the toes, the toes fan out and the foot twists inward.	Disappears around 1 year
Babkin	When an infant is lying on his back, pressure applied to the palms of both hands causes the head to turn straight ahead, the mouth to open, and the eyes to close.	Disappears around 3 months
Grasping	Pressure on an infant's palms produced by an object like a parent's finger causes the fingers to curl with a strong enough grasp to support the infant's own weight.	Weakens after 3 months and disappears by 1 year
Moro	The reflex pattern, which involves extending the arms and then bringing them rapidly toward the midline while closing the fingers in a grasping action, can be triggered by several kinds of startling stimuli, such as a sudden loud noise or holding the infant horizontally face-up and then rapidly lowering the baby about six inches.	Disappears around 5 months
Rooting	When an infant's cheek is stroked lightly, he turns his head in the direction of the stroked cheek and opens his mouth to suck the object that stroked the cheek.	Disappears around 4 months
Stepping	When an infant is held above a surface and then lowered until the feet touch the surface, the infant will make stepping movements like walking.	Disappears around 3 months
Sucking	When an object such as a nipple or a finger is inserted into an infant's mouth, rhythmic sucking occurs.	Changes into voluntary sucking by 2 months
Tonic neck	An infant placed on his back tends to turn his head to one side and to extend the arm and leg on that side while flexing the limbs on the other side (like a fencing position).	Disappears around 4 months

From Sroufe, L.A., Cooper, R.G., & Marshall, M. (1988). *Child development: Its nature and course.* New York: Alfred A. Knopf; Copyright © 1988, reprinted by permission of The McGraw-Hill Companies.

In fact, research shows that newborns will increase their rate of nonnutritive sucking in order to gain access to tape recordings of their mother's voices. They appear to prefer their own mother's voice to that of unfamiliar females (DeCasper & Fifer, 1980). Furthermore, newborns show preference for the sound of the maternal heartbeat (DeCasper & Sigafoos, 1982), and they can discriminate between their father's voice and unfamiliar male voices (DeCasper & Prescott, 1984). Additional research also suggests that prenatal experiences with the mother's voice influence early postnatal auditory perceptions in terms of infant reaction and orientation (Spence & DeCasper, 1987).

Hearing and looking systems appear coordinated from birth and unite in the infant's attention to auditory/visual stimulus (Gibson, 1988). Babies also feel, smell, and taste at birth. Infants respond to touch by reflexive action. Newborns can discriminate between strong odors at birth (Rieser, Yonas, & Wilkner, 1976; Steiner, 1977) and breast-feeding infants are adept at responding preferentially to their mother's breast or axillary odors (Cernoch & Porter, 1985). Newborns exhibit a clear preference for sweet liquids as opposed to salty or tasteless ones (Lipsitt, 1977) and readily learn a discrimination task when offered a sweet reward as one of the stimulus choices (Reardon & Bushnell, 1988).

INFANT PHYSICAL GROWTH AND MOTOR DEVELOPMENT

Infants are born with little physical control over their bodies. Reflexive behaviors predominate at birth. Two patterns govern infant physical growth and development (Sroufe et al., 1988). The first is the *cephalocaudal pattern,* in which the greatest growth occurs at the top of the body and proceeds downward; thus, the head develops first, then the neck, trunk, and so on. The second pattern is that growth occurs in a proximodistal direction, in which the growth and control begin at the center of the body and move toward the extremities. This is clearly exhibited in the muscle control of the trunk and arms compared with the hands and feet.

As the infant develops muscle coordination, it is important to recognize that there are gross motor skills and fine motor skills that evolve. *Gross motor skills* include large muscle activities such as crawling, sitting up, and walking. *Fine motor skills* refer to the dexterity infants develop, for example, in learning to pick up objects with their hands. When infants are born, they have little coordination of the arms, chest, or legs; their gross motor and fine motor skills are extremely limited.

Growth is rapid within the first year of development, and in a short period of time, typically within 2–3 months after birth, the infant begins to smile in response to external stimuli, usually an adult's face. Within 3–4 months, the infant can lift shoulders and chest, arms extended, in a prone position. There is evidence that infants point as early as 3 months of age (Hannan, 1987) and can grasp at objects in their line of vision. By 6 months of age, an infant usually sits up with some aid and support (Cratty, 1986). There is a great deal of variation in maturation patterns; some infants develop very quickly, reaching expected motor milestones early, while others develop more slowly or unevenly, with some abilities developing early and others later than expected. Specific maturation rates or patterns are little related to later growth and development; therefore, children's early, late, or uneven maturation patterns are not particularly predictive of later growth, skills, or abilities.

The study of motor skills acquisition has been revived recently. Thelen (1995) found that multidisciplinary approaches are offering new insights into the processes by which infants learn to control their bodies. She thinks that the new research is less concerned with how children perform and more interested in how developmental components cooperate to produce changes in behavior. The new focus is on the contextual, fluid, multicausal, and self-organizing aspects of developmental change. Bertenthal, Campos, and Kermoian (1994), for example, examined how infants' locomotor experience is related to the development of various new behaviors.

INFANT LANGUAGE DEVELOPMENT

An infant's cry is the baby's first use of language. The cry begins as a reflex and emerges as a major means of communicating discomfort and distress. Cooing, a response to comfort, occurs at approximately 2 months of age, followed closely by babbling, between 3 and 6 months. *Cooing* consists primarily of vocal sounds, and *babbling* includes consonant sounds and consonant-vowel combinations (Grieser & Kuhl, 1989).

By around 9 months, infants display an understanding of some words spoken to them. From early in development, language comprehension consistently precedes language production (Lamb & Bornstein, 1987), and a baby's first words typically occur at about 1 year of age. From this point, language development is rapid and infants increasingly use words to communicate as well as understand more of what is said to them. By 18 months, they typically comprehend body parts and respond to simple questions. Their expressive vocabulary ranges from 3 to 50 words, and they use one-word sentences like "Up!" (Baby wants to get up), "More" (I want some more milk), and "All gone" (My dinner is all gone).

By 24 months, toddlers produce approximately 250–300 words and can speak intelligibly in two- and three-word phrases. They understand much of what adults communicate to them, as well.

Language development is rapid and not well explained by traditional learning theories. Sophisticated theories of language development have emerged to explain the rapid, universal development of this remarkable human skill (Chomsky, 1993; Garton, 1992; Lenneberg, 1993; Sokolov & Snow, 1994). Skinner (1957) was an early language theorist, with the view that language developed as any other learned behavior. He maintained that language could be explained as a conditioned set of responses; infants make sounds similar to words, adults respond enthusiastically, and sounds that approximate words are therefore selectively reinforced. In this way language develops as a response to parental reinforcement. He went further to propose that infants, toddlers, and young children learn language frames, such as "I want _______," then learn new words to place in the frame. This view of language has been criticized for generally not explaining the rapidity with which language occurs, the universality of language, and the production and comprehension of novel utterances.

Another early attempt to explain language development was made by Noam Chomsky (1993), who proposed that language was a biological phenomenon; humans were born with an innate disposition for language learning called the *language acquisition device* (LAD). Related to Chomsky's theory is that of Lenneberg (1967, 1993), who proposed a critical period for the development of language. He maintained that language learning is a universal human activity, illustrated by the fact that children the world over learn language in a similar manner, achieving language milestones in an unvarying order.

More recently, researchers have argued that children learn language in a social context and have stressed the communication aspect of language (Bruner, 1983; Garton, 1992; Pinker, 1984, 1989; Shatz, 1987). This viewpoint suggests that some innate language learning ability, combined with environmental stimulation in the form of adult–child interactions, is responsible for children's language development.

Language development is an area of intense research interest. Researchers in this area seem in general agreement that there are universals for language acquisition and that it includes the complex interaction of phonology, syntax, semantics, and pragmatics. Researchers are considering a variety of issues, including whether language is indeed species specific, the relationship between language and cognition, and the acquisition of language comprehension and production skills. For example, Bloom, Beckwith, and Capatides (1988) found a pattern of results that suggests an interactive, mutual influence between developments in language learning and affect expression. Morford and Goldin-Meadow (1992) found that infants use words in combination with gestures; their findings are consistent with Bates, Thal,

Whitesell, Fenson, and Oakes (1989), who found evidence for the common roots of gestural and language systems.

Pye, Ingram, and List (1987) proposed that children learn the phonology of a language in a uniform manner, but children acquiring different languages develop different phonological systems. They find that children quickly develop a highly predictable phonological organization within their own given language.

Pinker (1984) proposed a *continuity assumption,* by which children have innate cognitive and language acquisition mechanisms similar to adults. Nelson (1987) developed the theory of the *rare event,* which states that the crux of language growth lies in rarely occurring language instances. Challenging and useful adult input strings are seized by the child's system and put into storage and compared with previously stored similar forms. To support his assertions, Nelson noted that only about 10% of adult utterances to children are selected and used in their language learning. That 10% represents adult language that expands on children's previous utterances and that is at children's current level of language learning. Thus, adult utterances that are useful and challenging are incorporated into child language learning.

Snow, Perlman, and Nathan (1987) proposed the notion of *scaffolding,* in which children can imitate and incorporate adult model utterances or phrases into their own lexicon. Children imitate adult words that they do not fully understand, and this process provides a boost to the child in learning new words and phrases. Thus, scaffolded utterances are less demanding to produce than spontaneous utterances. Verbal scaffolding has been used to facilitate conversational participation and language acquisition in children with pervasive developmental disorders (Kirchner, 1991).

Bootstrapping is the idea that children construct their own knowledge of language by using what they already know to learn more advanced forms (Shatz, 1987). The early use of the bootstrapping concept applied to syntax to explain that a child's grasp of abstract forms of syntax or grammar was based on a more basic semantic or pragmatic level of learning. Later, Pinker (1989) and Shatz (1987) expanded the idea of bootstrapping to include the child's use of communication in general. Thus, children use whatever knowledge of language they have to gain an understanding of new forms, content, and uses. For example, they use gestures, smiles, and vocalizations to elicit language from those around them, which, in turn, facilitates language learning. They also use strategies for maintaining discourse and storing and analyzing language information in their own active role in language learning (Shatz, 1987).

There have been a number of attempts to explore the relationship between the mother and infant in the infant's language development (Ginsburg & Kilborne, 1988; Iverson, Capirci, & Caselli, 1994; Murray, Johnson, & Peters, 1990; Pine, 1992; Vibbert & Bornstein, 1989). For instance, Yoder and Kaiser (1989) proposed alternative explanations for the relationship between maternal interaction style and the infant's language development. They found that early attempts to explain the relationship between a mother's speech and a child's later language development assumed a direct maternal influence model; more recent attempts have considered pragmatic and discourse aspects of maternal speech (e.g., Hoff-Ginsberg, 1986). Indeed, Olsen-Fulero (1982) provided a model of maternal pragmatic and discourse features that may positively and negatively influence child language development.

Finally, there have been attempts to tie language learning to the research in infant cognition and learning. Gopnik and Meltzoff (1987) linked language development with Piaget's stages of cognitive development. For instance, they noted that, around 18 months of age, toddlers start to name many objects around them. The "naming explosion" seems to be linked to the development of categorization.

INFANT COGNITION AND LEARNING

The field of infant learning is dominated by a number of theoretical perspectives. One early learning theory is known as *classical conditioning.* The key concepts involve an unconditioned stimulus (US), which automatically elicits an unconditioned response (UR); an example of an US is a puff of air directed toward the eye, and the UR is an eye blink. Additional concepts include the conditioned stimulus (CS), a previously neutral stimulus that becomes conditioned after being paired with the US over time. The CS takes on the properties of the US and itself elicits a conditioned response (CR); for example, a light that is turned on prior to a puff of air hitting the eye will elicit, itself, over time, the eye blink response (Houston, 1986). In regard to infant learning, the mother, initially a neutral stimulus, becomes paired over time with meeting the infant's various needs for affection, food, and warmth. The mother soon becomes a signal to the infant that pleasant experiences, such as feeding, will occur (Miller, 1993; Sluckin & Herbert, 1986).

A view of learning related to classical conditioning is known as *operant conditioning.* Operant conditioning theorists maintain that individuals are active in the learning process, and their activity results in consequences. The consequences may be positive reinforcements, negative reinforcements, punishments, or no response. Reinforcements increase the likelihood that the behavior will occur again, and punishment causes a behavior to cease. No response to a behavior will eventually, but not immediately, cause the behavior to diminish (extinction). The use of infant operant learning research has been debated in the literature. Pomerleau et al. (1992), for example, presented methodological problems, and Schlinger (1993) challenged assertions that principles of reinforcement are not enough to explain infant learning and behavior.

The main proponent of operant conditioning is B.F. Skinner, who maintained that most behaviors are learned. This view of learning is called *behaviorism.* When it is used as a teaching method, it is called *applied behavior analysis.*

Another theory related to classical and operant conditioning is *social learning theory.* This behavioral theory extends the view of learning to include individual development and the social context in which learning occurs. Albert Bandura (1977, 1986) proposed a social learning theory in which he expanded operant conditioning to include learning without reinforcement. That is, individuals learn without receiving direct individual reinforcement simply by observing others. The concepts of vicarious reinforcement, vicarious punishment, and modeling explain much about how individuals learn by observing others. Infants, for example, early in their development, attempt to imitate those around them. The mimicking of an older child's behavior by the 9- or 10-month-old infant is an example of social learning theory. In later years, individuals learn new behaviors by observing others perform and by viewing the consequences of those behaviors. The vicarious consequences, in turn, influence the likelihood of the observer performing the same behaviors.

Since the 1980s, learning theorists have focused on cognitive development and how children process information. There are a variety of points of view on this matter, employing artificial intelligence paradigms, mathematical processing models, and cognitive architecture (e.g., Langley, 1983; Rabinowitz, Grant, & Dingley, 1987; Wilkenson & Haines, 1987). Some of the information-processing models view human learning as analogous to information being processed by a computer.

Jean Piaget studied learning as it occurs within the developing individual. He and the neo-Piagetians were among the first to consider learning in a developmental and social context. Two fundamental, invariant human characteristics describe Piaget's theory: organization and adaptation (Shulman, 1985). *Organization* refers to Piaget's belief that human cognitive development is a highly coordinated activity, rather than chaotic or without form. *Adaptation* refers to the continual adjustments that infants make to their environment.

Piaget maintained that infants are active in their cognitive development; in fact, this is a cornerstone of his work. Infants are born with reflexive actions; the reflexive actions are the infant's first activities. As the infant develops, the reflexes give way to voluntary actions. These sensorimotor activities form the basic components for the construction of knowledge. What the infant is trying to do, indeed what impels all cognitive development from Piaget's perspective, is to construct his or her own view of reality.

Piaget theorized that there are four primary developmental stages through which individuals pass. Two of these are pertinent to this discussion. The neonate begins in the sensorimotor stage of development, in which information is received through the infant's sensory apparatus and motor activities. This stage begins at birth and extends to approximately 18–24 months of age. Piaget declined to tie specific age expectations to his developmental stages, maintaining that development was to a great extent dependent on internal, individual characteristics such as maturation rate. However, much detailed observation of children during the first 2 years has led other researchers to attach age approximations to Piaget's stages.

During the sensorimotor stage, the typically developing infant moves from basic reflex activities to complex actions. The infant develops significant abilities to store, remember, organize, and utilize sensory and motor experiences and information. The sensorimotor stage is divided into six substages, beginning with the *reflexive* stage; it occurs from birth to approximately 1 month of age and involves primarily the reflex actions of sucking and looking. The next substage, *primary circular reactions,* begins at approximately 1 month of age and extends through 4 months. During this period the infant attempts to make the body do things, such as trying to get the thumb to the mouth and attempting to reach objects with his or her arms. The third substage is termed *secondary circular reactions,* beginning at approximately 4 months and lasting to 10 months of age. The infant begins to perform coordinated actions with objects to achieve a result, such as attempting to make a toy move by hitting it.

The fourth substage begins at 10 months and extends through 12 months of age and is known as the *coordination of secondary schemes.* In this substage, the infant increasingly combines activities to reach an end result. For example, he or she might crawl to an object, reach for it, move it to his or her mouth, and begin to suck. The fifth substage, *tertiary circular reactions,* begins at 1 year of age and extends to approximately 18 months. This substage is characterized by increased motor development and the ability to use improved motor abilities in new ways through trial and error. The final substage is termed *mental combinations* and starts at approximately 18 months. The toddler has some language and basic motor skills; mental representation is clear in his or her use of objects and words to stand for people and objects not present.

The typical toddler then moves to the second major developmental stage, *preoperational thought.* Characteristic of this stage is the child's egocentrism and basic unawareness of the thoughts and feelings of others. In this stage, the toddler tends to focus on one perceptible aspect of a situation or activity at a time; for example, he or she can attend to "short" or "fat," but not "short and fat" simultaneously.

Bremner (1994) found that recent research in infant perception causes some reevaluation of Piaget's theory. In particular, there appear to be perceptual factors that determine whether or not infant visual search occurs. The infant's perception of spatial relations, rather than level of cognitive development, may determine whether object permanence is displayed and the infants search their visual field. This analysis is based on research by Baillargeon and her colleagues (Baillargeon, 1987; Baillargeon, Spelke, & Wasserman, 1985) in which very young infants, even at 3½ months, seem to understand object permanence and the rules that govern movement of objects. Spelke, Breinlinger, Macomber, and Jacobson (1992) tested even younger infants and found evidence that, as young as 2½ months of age, infants understand that one thing cannot move through another object in its path.

Infant learning and cognitive development is a major interest area for developmentalists. The field has moved from a strict consideration of observable infant developmental characteristics to a fuller, richer view of how infants learn and organize their cognitive understanding of the world. Researchers are focused on such issues as eye contact and infant cognition (Phillips, Baron-Cohen, & Rutter, 1992), attention and verbal expression (Heinicke & Lampl, 1988), and stability of infant measures of intelligence (Cardon & Fulker, 1991; DiLalla, Thompson, Plomin, & Phillips, 1990; Ramey, Lee, & Burchinal, 1989; Rose, 1989). The relationship between infant growth and cognition (Rose, 1994), preverbal communication and cognitive development (Papousek & Papousek, 1992), the role of genetics in learning (Plomin, 1989), the development of new theories of intelligence (e.g., Feldman, 1982, 1986; Gardner, 1983, 1984; Sternberg, 1984, 1986), and enrichment programs and cognitive development (Honig, 1991).

INFANT SOCIAL-EMOTIONAL DEVELOPMENT

Infants become attached to their parents, and parents bond to their infants. This attachment-bonding activity forms the beginning of the infant's social-emotional development.

Attachment

Attachment is critical and is the basis for the infant's social-emotional well-being and the foundation for all other infant attachments and subsequent relationships. The issue of attachment has received significant interest by developmentalists. The early study by Skeels and Dye (1939), in which orphaned, institutionalized children were examined for the effects of a lack of human interaction, is frequently considered the beginning of this field of endeavor. The work of John Bowlby (1969, 1973, 1980) and that of Mary Ainsworth (1973, 1982) and her students (e.g., Main & Cassidy, 1988) dominate thinking on the issue of attachment.

Attachment is usually described as an emotional tie or bond of affection between the infant and parent. Attachment includes many behaviors such as calling out for contact, clinging, crying, seeking eye contact, smiling, and touching. It is not the particular behavior itself or the frequency of one or many of the behaviors that describes attachment, but rather the pattern of attachment behaviors that indicates the quality and strength of the attachment between infants and their parents.

Ainsworth (1982) and her associates (Ainsworth, Blehar, Waters, & Wall, 1978) identified stages of attachment. Phase 1 is the *initial preattachment* (baby shows orientation and signals without discrimination of figure) that occurs during the first 1–2 months of life. The infant behaves in a way that elicits the proximity of adults; behaviors include crying, cuddling, and smiling, all of which tend to promote parent–infant contact. In Phase 2, *attachment-in-the-making* (baby shows orientation and signals directed toward one or more discriminated figures), the infant begins to discriminate familiar from unfamiliar faces at approximately 2–7 months of age. In Phase 3, *clear-cut attachment* (baby maintains proximity to a discriminated figure by means of locomotion as well as signals), from approximately 7 to 24 months of age, infants tend to have one person to whom attachment behaviors are directed. Not only does the infant direct the attachment figure to approach, but the infant will also make crawling and creeping attempts toward the attachment figure. In Phase 4 (formation of a goal-directed partnership), from 24 months on, infants tend to develop *multiple attachments* (Lamb et al., 1985).

Research on attachment usually uses the *strange situation paradigm* (Ainsworth et al., 1978). This laboratory procedure studies the quality of the mother–infant attachment during separation and reunion (Table 2.3). The procedure (Ainsworth et al., 1978) involves eight, approximately 3-minute episodes of observing the mother and child. The episodes create increasing levels of stress for the 12- to 24-month-old infant so that researchers can determine how babies organize their behavior around attachment figures (Lamb et al., 1985). The parent and stranger are specifically instructed to avoid initiating behavior with the infant, but to respond appropriately to the baby.

The scoring of attachment behavior is based on the infant's proximity and contact-seeking behavior, contact-maintaining behavior, resistance, avoidance, and searching for the parent. Infants are classified as secure (Type B) if they greet the parent positively upon reunion, are soothed if distressed, and exhibit little or no avoidance or resistance toward the parent; insecure-avoidant (Type A) infants actively avoid and resist the parent upon reunion; and insecure-ambivalent infants (Type C) show high levels of distress throughout the strange situation and show weak to strong proximity seeking with a mild-to-obvious resistance and inability to be settled by the parent (Main & Solomon, 1986). The proposal of a Type D attachment classification (Main & Solomon, 1986) comes from researchers' difficulty in classifying a small portion of infant attachment relationships; in almost all of these cases, the infants were disorganized in the presence of only one parent. The Type D, or insecure-disorganized/disoriented infant, typically displays contradictory behaviors:

- Disordering of expected temporal sequences (e.g., the infant initially greets the parent with bids for contact and then turns away and looks blankly ahead)
- Simultaneous display of contradictory behavior patterns (e.g., approaching the parent, but from a sideways position or even backwards rather than face-to-face)

- Incomplete or undirected movements and expressions, including stereotypes (e.g., striking out at the parent's face, but with weak and nearly undirected movements)
- Direct indications of confusion and apprehension (e.g., upon the approach of the parent, the infant may express confusion and apprehension)
- Behavioral stilling: "dazed" behavior and indications of depressed affect (e.g., an unfocused, "dead" stare with mouth and chin limp)

Babies are assigned to attachment categories by means of interactive rating scales that measure contact-seeking, resisting, avoiding, and other behaviors (Table 2.4).

Ainsworth, Bell, and Stayton (1971) conducted classic, or foundational, research on mothers' responsiveness to their infants. They categorized mothers according to four aspects of the mothers' sensitivity and responsiveness toward their babies: 1) *sensitivity-insensitivity*, the extent to which mothers are aware of their infant's needs and respond to them; 2) *acceptance-rejection*, the mother's general acceptance of the problems, limitations, and responsibilities of having a baby; 3) *cooperation-interference*, the degree to which mothers allow their infants autonomy or impose control; and 4) *accessibility-ignoring*, a measure of mothers' attention to their babies' cues and signals.

Table 2.3. The strange situation procedure

Sequence	Participants	Situation
1.	Mother, baby, and observer	An introductory session during which the mother and infant become familiar with the room, which is usually a carpeted playroom laboratory with children's toys and available chairs.
2.	Mother and baby	The mother and baby are alone together in the research room.
3.	Stranger, mother, and baby	A female stranger enters the research room with the instruction to sit quietly for about 1 minute and then to converse with the parent for approximately 1 minute and finally to engage the infant in play so that the parent can leave the room; the parent leaves unobtrusively after 3 minutes.
4.	Stranger and baby	First separation episode. The stranger and the baby are alone; the parent is instructed to speak loudly before reentering the room so as to attract the infant's attention; as she returns to the research room she is asked to pause for the infant to respond to her presence. The parent is to make the baby comfortable and reinterest the child in toys; the stranger leaves.
5.	Mother and baby	First reunion episode. The mother and infant are alone together when the parent is instructed to leave the playroom.
6.	Baby alone	Second separation episode. The infant is left alone for approximately 3 minutes unless particularly distressed; the stranger returns to the playroom.
7.	Stranger and baby	The stranger and the baby are together in the playroom; when the mother returns to the playroom the stranger leaves.
8.	Mother and baby	Second reunion episode. The mother and child are alone together in the playroom.

From Ainsworth, M.D.S., Blehar, M.C., Waters, E., & Wall, S. (1978). *Patterns of attachment.* Hillsdale, NJ: Lawrence Erlbaum Associates; adapted by permission.

Table 2.4. The interactive rating scales

Scale	Abbreviated description of selected anchor points[a]
Proximity and contact seeking	7. Very active effort and initiative in achieving physical contact (e.g., fully approaches the adult and achieves contact through its own efforts)
	5. Some active effort to achieve physical contact (e.g., approaches but is picked up without any clear bid for contact)
	3. Weak effort to achieve physical contact or moderately strong effort to gain proximity (e.g., approaches, does not request pick up, and is not held)
	1. No effort to achieve physical contact or proximity
Contact maintaining	7. Very active and persistent effort to maintain physical contact (e.g., while held more than 2 minutes, infant at least twice actively resists release)
	5. Some active effort to maintain physical contact (e.g., while held for less than 1 minute, the infant actively resists release once)
	3. Some apparent desire to maintain physical contact but relatively little active effort to do so (e.g., infant initiates contact at least twice in an episode, but on each occasion the hold is brief, and its cessation is not protested)
	1. Either no physical contact or no effort to maintain it
Resistance	7. Very intense and persistent resistance (e.g., two or more instances of: repeatedly hitting the adult, strong squirming against hold, temper tantrum, repeated angry rejection of the adult or toys)
	5. Some resistance—either less intense or more isolated and less persistent (e.g., at least 3 instances of the above, without as great a degree of anger)
	3. Slight resistance (e.g., two rather modest instances of resistance)
	1. No resistance
Avoidance	7. Very marked and persistent avoidance (e.g., no attention to adult despite repeated attempts by her/him to attract attention)
	5. Clear-cut avoidance but less persistent (e.g., 30 seconds of ignoring in the absence of attempts by the adult to gain attention)
	3. Slight isolated avoidance behavior (e.g., brief delay in responding)
	1. No avoidance
Search[b]	7. Very active and persistent search behavior (e.g., approaches door promptly and actively bangs or attempts to open it)
	5. Some active search (e.g., approaches door after delay or fails to make active effort to open it or bang)
	3. Some apparent desire to regain the attachment figure, but the search behavior is weak (e.g., infant looks toward door for at least 30 seconds)
	1. No search
Distance interaction	7. Very active and persistent distance interaction (e.g., reciprocal interaction for more than 45 seconds)
	5. Active distance interaction (e.g., smiles and vocalizes to parent at least four times)
	3. Little distance interaction (e.g., looks frequently at adult, and orients for at least 15 seconds)
	1. No distance interaction (e.g., just occasional glances)

From Lamb, M.G., Thompson, R.A., Gardner, W., & Charnov, E.L. (1985). *Infant–mother attachment: The origins and developmental significance of individual differences in strange situation behavior.* Hillsdale, NJ: Lawrence Erlbaum Associates; reprinted by permission.

[a]Full details regarding the rating scales are provided by Ainsworth et al. (1978). *Patterns of attachment* (Appendix III). Hillsdale, NJ: Lawrence Erlbaum Associates.

[b]Rated only in separation episodes

Clarke-Stewart (1973) found that, when mothers are rated on responsiveness, expression of positive emotion, and social stimulation, high-scoring mothers have more securely attached infants than low-scoring mothers. Infant–mother attachment does not differ significantly between experienced and inexperienced mothers (Mercer & Ferketich, 1994). Additional research (e.g., Goldberg, MacKay-Soroka, & Rochester, 1994; Isabella, 1993) demonstrates that the number of interactions between the mother and infant early in the child's development affect each member of the pair; this confirms that attachment is a critical concept in understanding mother–infant interactions (Rosenblith & Sims-Knight, 1985). The relationship between attachment as measured in the laboratory setting and the sensitivity of care in the home (as documented by home observations in the first year of an infant's life) is well established (Bates, Maslin, & Frankel, 1985; Egeland & Farber, 1984; Grossman, Grossman, Spangler, Suess, & Unzer, 1985; Sroufe, 1985). Importantly, van den Boom (1994) developed an intervention program focused on promoting secure attachment by improving mothers' skills in perceiving, monitoring, and responding to their infants. She found that at 12 months of age, more intervention than control dyads were securely attached.

Research has been conducted on attachment behaviors and stranger sociability (Lutkenhaus, Grossman, & Grossman, 1985; Plunkett, Klein, & Meisels, 1988), attachment and temperament (Belsky, Rovine, & Taylor, 1984; Bradshaw, Goldsmith, & Campos, 1987), and attachment and social play (Connell & Thompson, 1986; Roggman, Langlois, & Hubbs-Tait, 1987). Attachment is further discussed as it relates to social-emotional disorders (Chapter 4) and as it relates to family dynamics (Chapter 6).

Theories of Infant Emotional Development

The earliest and one of the most well-developed theories of emotional development is that of Sigmund Freud (1923/1962). Freud based development on early experience. He proposed that the human mind is divided into three systems: the id, the ego, and the superego. The *id* strives for immediate gratification by any possible avenue and is the source of all motivation. For Freud, the id is present at birth, while the other two structures, ego and superego, develop over time. The *ego* continually tries to control the id by being responsive to social conventions and expectations; therefore, the ego is responsible for the appropriate expression of emotions, delay of gratification, and perception and thought. The *superego* is the guide of morals and ethics. Together the three structures mediate need-gratification with social and environmental constraints.

Freud's importance lies in the comprehensiveness of his theory and his landmark influence on psychology. Despite his historical importance in the field of social-emotional development, his theory has lost prominence with theorists who take into account the influences of social and environmental factors and, more recently, cognitive factors on emotional life.

Another prominent theory of social-emotional development is that of Erik Erikson (1950). Erikson is considered a neo-Freudian because he accepted many of Freud's essential tenets. Erikson departed from Freud, however, in his consideration of the social context in which development occurs. Freud stated that development occurs primarily as a result of factors within the individual, but Erikson believed that development is far more dependent on the social issues that the devel-

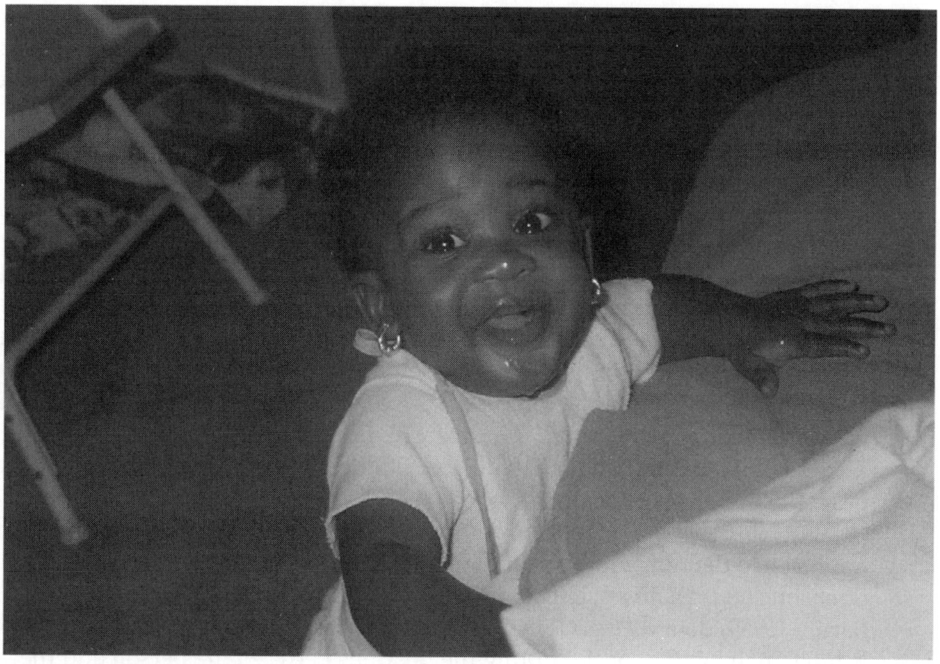

oping individual faces. His theory of social-emotional development focuses on primary developmental issues, or "crises," which the the individual encounters over the developmental life span. The social context and culture, indeed, play important roles in infant socialization. Zayas and Solari (1994) reviewed research on early childhood socialization and found that parent and child behaviors are the result of processes encompassing specific cultural values.

For the infant, Erikson believed that the primary issue is the development of basic trust or mistrust. By meeting the infant's needs in a reliable manner, the caregiver instills in the infant a basic sense of trust in the world. If needs are not met, or met in an unsatisfactory manner, the infant tends to develop a sense of mistrust. At about age 2, the toddler enters the stage of autonomy versus guilt. During this time, the toddler moves about in the environment and, if the exploratory behavior of the child is fostered, a sense of autonomy is developed. Erikson's other stages trace emotional development into adulthood and old age.

Temperament and Emotions

In considering infant social-emotional development, an important issue is infant temperament (Halverson, Kohnstamm, & Martin, 1994; Kagan, Arcus, & Snidman, 1993; Rothbart, 1991; Rothbart, Ahadi, & Hershey, 1994). Is social-emotional development more heavily dependent on social factors and environmental context or on the infant's temperament and personality traits? Two primary issues have dominated work in this area: the dimensions or characteristics of temperament and the stability of temperament over time and place (Lamb, 1988). Although personality factors are associated with temperament, the expression of these characteristics is dependent on the child's environment, including changing expectations and relationships. Culture is an important feature as well (Flanagan & Hardee, 1994).

Research in the 1990s in social-emotional development takes a more longitudinal approach (e g., Caspi & Silva, 1995), focusing on interpersonal exchanges and the links between temperament and social factors like parental sensitivity and environmental context.

Worebey and Lewis (1989) studied infant response to stress and found that individual differences do exist and may reflect important temperamental differences. The consistencies that they identified in infants over time suggest that the relationship among newborn temperament, early environment, and later growth and development should be explored. Worebey and Blajda (1989) found that temperament may be studied in infants as young as 2 weeks of age by obtaining ratings from the mothers (see Table 2.4). Levels of activity and emotionality are stable over the first 2 neonatal months. Distress-related responses that characterize early irritability may predict difficult temperament, other aspects of emotionality, and maternal behavior in caregiving. Importantly, however, Bohlin, Hagekull, Germer, Andersson, and Lindberg (1989) did not find that early temperamental characteristics influenced later attachment behaviors.

Another aspect of social-emotional development is emotions. A recent approach to defining emotions and their measurement and regulation is an interactional one (e.g., Denham, Renwick-DeBardi, & Hewes, 1994). Campos, Campos, and Barrett (1989) defined emotions as not mere feelings, but rather "processes of establishing, maintaining, or disrupting the relations between the person and the...environment" (p. 395). Their view stresses how emotions are formed, the function of emotions in adapting to the social world, and emotions as a basis for personality development. According to this viewpoint, person–environment interactions form the center for studying emotion regulation.

The common thread among conceptualizations of emotional development is the attempt to understand how children respond to aversive environmental stimuli (Dodge, 1989) such as child abuse (Rieder & Cicchetti, 1989), economic deprivation (Duncan, Brooks-Gunn, & Klebanov, 1994; Garrett, Ng'andu, & Ferron, 1994), and marital discord (Gottman & Katz, 1989). Kopp (1989) suggested that an interaction between reflex responses and cognitive development makes possible the control of negative emotions early in life. Gottman and Katz (1989) posited that children learn regulatory behaviors through interactions with parents and that, when the interactions are disrupted through marital discord, this learning is interrupted. Rieder and Cicchetti (1989) proposed that children exposed to abusive situations lose their ability to use cognitive controls over aversive stimuli.

Further research on social-emotional development has taken several different directions. For example, Stifter, Fox, and Porges (1989) found that an infant's facial expressions give her or him a method to communicate with caregivers. A more expressive infant may be more competent in eliciting caregiving behaviors than less expressive infants. Sroufe (1985) also suggested that sensitive caregivers adjust to the infant's characteristics.

In their studies of mother–infant interaction based on mutual gazing, Messer and Vietze (1988) found that previous analyses may have overestimated the influence of the partner in initiating gazing and may have underestimated the role of physiological responses. Fox (1989) also uncovered psychophysiological correlates of emotional reactivity in infancy. Stifter et al. (1989) demonstrated that the infant's level of emotional expressivity at 5 months is related to physiological responses such as heart rate. These studies appear to lead to the conclusion that emotions have a biological basis, but are mediated by environmental factors.

By contrast, Emde (1980, 1983, 1988), taking a more psychodynamic view, stressed the relationships in which the infant is developing and the effect that the relationships have on social-emotional development. It is thus evident that the subject of infant emotional development remains a rich area for continuing research.

SUMMARY

Infant growth and development is a large and comprehensive field that includes infant physical, cognitive, behavioral, and social-emotional development. In a brief period of time, typical infants move from a position of total dependence on their adult caregivers to functional children who, by age 2, can express themselves to some extent with language, regulate motor activity, communicate and express emotions, feed themselves, and interact successfully with their environment. The field of infant development is heavily research oriented, with the focus on exploring how infants grow and develop within their environment.

SUGGESTED READINGS

Bornstein, M., & Lamb, M. (1992). *Development in infancy.* New York: McGraw-Hill.
Bremner, J.G. (1994). *Infancy* (2nd ed.). Oxford, England: Blackwell Publishers.

REFERENCES

Acredolo, L.P., & Hake, J.L. (1982). Infant perception. In B.B. Wolman & G. Stricker (Eds.), *Handbook of developmental psychology* (pp. 244–283). Englewood Cliffs, NJ: Prentice Hall.

Ainsworth, M.D.S. (1973). The development of infant–mother attachment. In B.M. Caldwell & H.N. Ricciuti (Eds.), *Review of child development research* (Vol. 3). Chicago: University of Chicago Press.

Ainsworth, M.D.S. (1982). Attachment: Retrospect and prospect. In C.K. Parke & J. Stevenson-Hinde (Eds.), *The place of attachment in human behavior* (pp. 3–30). New York: Basic Books.

Ainsworth, M.D.S., Bell, S.M.V., & Stayton, D.J. (1971). Individual differences in strange-situation behavior of one-year-olds. In H.R. Schaffer (Ed.), *The origins of human social relations* (pp. 17–52). New York: Academic Press.

Ainsworth, M.D.S., Blehar, M.C., Waters, E., & Wall, S. (1978). *Patterns of attachment.* Hillsdale, NJ: Lawrence Erlbaum Associates.

Anderson, E.R. (1993). Analyzing change in short-term longitudinal research using cohort-sequential designs. *Journal of Consulting and Clinical Psychology, 61*(6), 929–940.

Bailey, D.B. (1987). Collaborative goal-setting with families: Resolving differences in values and priorities for services. *Topics in Early Childhood Special Education, 7*(2), 59–71.

Baillargeon, R. (1987). Object permanence in 3.5- and 4.5-month-old infants. *Developmental Psychology, 23,* 655–664.

Baillargeon, R., Spelke, E.S., & Wasserman, S. (1985). Object permanence in five-month-old infants. *Cognition, 20,* 191–208.

Bandura, A. (1969). Social-learning theory of identificatory processes. In D.A. Goslin (Ed.), *Handbook of socialization theory and research* (pp. 213–262). Chicago: Rand McNally.

Bandura, A. (1977). *Social learning theory.* Englewood Cliffs, NJ: Prentice Hall.

Bandura, A. (1986). *Social foundations of thought and action: A social cognitive theory.* Englewood Cliffs, NJ: Prentice Hall.

Banks, M.A., & Salapatek, P. (1983). Infant visual perception. In P.H. Mussen (Ed.), *Handbook of child psychology* (Vol. 2). New York: John Wiley & Sons.

Bates, E., Thal, D., Whitesell, K., Fenson, L., & Oakes, L. (1989). Integrating language and gesture in infancy. *Developmental Psychology, 25,* 1004–1019.
Bates, J.E., Maslin, C.A., & Frankel, K.A. (1985). Attachment security, mother–child interaction, and temperament as predictors of behavior-problem ratings at age three years. In I. Bretherton & E. Waters (Eds.), Growing points of attachment, theory and research. *Monographs of the Society for Research in Child Development, 50*(2, Serial No. 209).
Bayley, N. (1993). *Manual for the Bayley Scales of Infant Development—Second Edition Manual.* San Antonio, TX: Psychological Corporation.
Belsky, J., Rovine, M., & Taylor, D. (1984). The Pennsylvania Infant and Family Development Project: III. The origins of individual differences in infant–mother attachment: Maternal and infant contributions. *Child Development, 55,* 718–728.
Berlin, L.J., Cassidy, J., & Belsky, J. (1995). Loneliness in young children and infant–mother attachment: A longitudinal study. *Merrill-Palmer Quarterly, 41*(1), 91–103.
Bertenthal, B.I., Campos, J.J., & Kermoian, R. (1994). An epigenetic perspective on the development of self-produced locomotion and its consequences. *Current Directions in Psychological Science, 3*(5), 140–145.
Birnholz, J.C., & Benacerraf, B.R. (1983). The development of human fetal hearing. *Science, 222,* 516–518.
Bloom, L., Beckwith, R., & Capatides, J.B. (1988). Developments in the expression of affect. *Infant Behavior and Development, 11,* 169–186.
Bohlin, G., Hagekull, B., Germer, M., Andersson, K., & Lindberg, L. (1989). Avoidant and resistant reunion behaviors as predicted by maternal interactive behavior and infant temperament. *Infant Behavior and Development, 12,* 105–117.
Bondurant-Utz, J.A., & Luciano, L.B. (1994). *A practical guide to infant and preschool assessment in special education.* Needham, MA: Allyn and Bacon.
Bornstein, M.H., & Benasich, A.A. (1986). Infant habituation: Assessments of short-term reliability and individual differences at 5 months. *Child Development, 57,* 87–89.
Bornstein, M.H., & Lamb, M.E. (1988). *Developmental psychology: An advanced textbook* (2nd ed.) Hillsdale, NJ: Lawrence Erlbaum Associates.
Bornstein, M.H., Pecheux, M.G., & Lecuyer, R. (1988). Visual habituation in human infants: Development and rearing circumstances. *Psychological Research, 50,* 130–133.
Bowlby, J. (1969). *Attachment and loss: Vol. 1. Attachment.* New York: Basic Books.
Bowlby, J. (1973). *Attachment and loss: Vol. 2. Separation: Anxiety and anger.* New York: Basic Books.
Bowlby, J. (1980). *Attachment and loss: Vol. 3. Loss, sadness and depression.* New York: Basic Books.
Bradley, R.M., & Stern, L.B. (1967). The development of the human taste bud during the fetal period. *Journal of Anatomy, 101,* 743–752.
Bradshaw, D.L., Goldsmith, H.H., & Campos, J.J. (1987). Attachment, temperament, and social referencing: Interrelationships among three domains of infant affective behavior. *Infant Behavior and Development, 10,* 223–231.
Bremner, J.G. (1994). *Infancy.* Oxford, England: Blackwell Publishers.
Brock, D.J.H. (1983). Amniotic fluid tests for neural tube defects. *British Medical Bulletin, 39,* 373.
Bruner, J.S. (1983). *Child's talk: Learning to use language.* New York: Norton.
Campos, J.J., Campos, R.G., & Barrett, K.C. (1989). Emergent themes in the study of emotional development and emotion regulation. *Developmental Psychology, 25,* 394–402.
Cardon, L.R., & Fulker, D.W. (1991). Sources of continuity in infant predictors of later IQ. *Intelligence, 15,* 279–293.
Caspi, A., & Silva, P.A. (1995). Temperamental qualities at age three predict personality traits in young adulthood: Longitudinal evidence from a birth cohort. *Child Development, 66,* 486–498.
Cernoch, J.M., & Porter, R.H. (1985). Recognition of maternal axillary odors by infants. *Child Development, 56,* 1593–1598.
Chamberlain, D.B. (1988). The mind of the newborn: Increasing evidence of competence. In P. Fedor-Freybergh & M.L.V. Vogel (Eds.), *Prenatal and perinatal psychology and medicine: Encounter with the unborn.* Lancaster, England: Parthenon Publishing Group.
Chervenak, F.A., Isaacson, D., & Mahoney, M.J. (1986). Advances in the diagnosis of fetal defects. *New England Journal of Medicine, 315,* 305–307.

Chomsky, N. (1993). On the nature, use, and acquisition of language. In A.I. Goldman (Ed.), *Readings in philosophy and cognitive science* (pp. 511–534). Cambridge, MA: MIT Press.
Clarke-Stewart, K.A. (1973). Interactions between mothers and their young children: Characteristics and consequences. *Monographs of the Society for Research in Child Development, 36*(6, Serial No. 153).
Connell, J.P., & Thompson, R. (1986). Emotion and social interaction in the strange situation: Consistencies and asymmetric influences in the second year. *Child Development, 57,* 733–745.
Cratty, B.J. (1986). *Perceptual and motor development in infants and children.* Englewood Cliffs, NJ: Prentice Hall.
DeCasper, A., & Fifer, W. (1980). Of human bonding: Newborns prefer their mothers' voices. *Science, 208,* 1174–1176.
DeCasper, A., & Prescott, P.A. (1984). Human newborns' perception of male voices: Preference, discrimination, and reinforcing value. *Developmental Psychobiology, 17,* 481–491.
DeCasper, A., & Sigafoos, A.D. (1982). The intrauterine heartbeat: A potent reinforcer for newborns. *Infant Behavior and Development, 6,* 19–25.
DeVries, J.I.P., Visser, G.H.A., & Prechtl, H.F.R. (1982). The emergence of fetal behaviour: I. Qualitative aspects. *Early Human Development, 7,* 301–322.
Denham, S.A., Renwick-DeBardi, S., & Hewes, S. (1994). Emotional communication between mothers and preschoolers: Relations with emotional competence. *Merrill-Palmer Quarterly, 40,* 488–508.
DiLalla, L.F., Thompson, L.A., Plomin, R., & Phillips, K. (1990). Infant predictors of preschool and adult IQ: A study of infant twins and their parents. *Developmental Psychology, 26,* 759–769.
Dodge, K.A. (1989). Coordinating responses to adversive stimuli: Introduction to a special section on the development of emotion regulation. *Developmental Psychology, 25,* 339–432.
Drogtrop, A.P., Ubels, R., & Nijhuis, J.G. (1990). The association between fetal body movements, eye movements and heart rate patterns in pregnancies between 25 and 30 weeks of gestation. *Early Human Development, 23(1),* 67–73.
Duncan, G.J., Brooks-Gunn, J., & Klebanov, P.K. (1994). Economic deprivation and early childhood development. *Child Development, 65,* 296–318.
Egeland, B., & Farber, E. (1984). Infant–mother attachment: Factors related to its development and changes over time. *Child Development, 55*(3), 753–771.
Emde, R. (1980). Emotional availability: A reciprocal reward system for infant and parents with implications for prevention of psychosocial disorders. In P. Taylor (Ed.), *Parent–infant relationships.* Orlando, FL: Grune & Stratton.
Emde, R. (1983). The prerepresentation self and its affective core. *Psychoanalytic Study of the Child, 38,* 165–192.
Emde, R. (1988). Development terminable and interminable: I. Innate and motivational factors from infancy. *International Journal of Psychoanalysis, 69,* 23–42.
Erikson, E. (1950). *Childhood and society.* New York: Norton.
Fantz, R. (1958). Pattern vision in young infants. *Psychological Review, 8,* 43–49.
Feldman, D.H. (1982). Transcending IQ in the definition of giftedness. *Early Childhood Review, 23,* 15–18.
Feldman, D.H. (1986). Giftedness as a developmentalist sees it. In R.J. Sternberg & J.E. Davidson (Eds.), *Conceptions of giftedness.* Cambridge: Cambridge University Press.
Field, T. (1990). *Infancy.* Cambridge, MA: Harvard University Press.
Finegan, J.K., Quarrington, B.J., Hughes, H.E., & Doran, T.A. (1987). Infant development following midtrimester amniocentesis. *Infant Behavior and Development, 10,* 379–383.
Fisher, C.B., & Lerner, R.M. (1994). *Applied developmental psychology.* New York: McGraw-Hill.
Flanagan, D., & Hardee, S.D. (1994). Talk about preschoolers' interpersonal relationships: Patterns related to culture, SES, and gender of child. *Merrill-Palmer Quarterly, 40,* 523–537.
Fox, N.A. (1989). Psychophysiological correlates of emotional reactivity during the first year of life. *Developmental Psychology, 24,* 364–372.
Freedman, D.G. (1971). Behavioral assessment in infancy. In G.A.B. Stoelinga & J.J. Van Der Werff Ten Bosch (Eds.), *Normal and abnormal development of brain and behavior.* Leiden, The Netherlands: Leiden University Press.

Freud, S. (1917). *Psychopathology of everyday life.* New York: Macmillan.
Freud, S. (1923/1962). *The ego and the id.* New York: Norton.
Freud, S. (1940). *An outline of psychoanalysis.* New York: Norton.
Gardner, H. (1983). *Frames of mind: The theory of multiple intelligences.* New York: Basic Books.
Gardner, H. (1984). Assessing intelligence: A comment on 'testing intelligence without IQ tests.' *Phi Delta Kappan, 65,* 699–700.
Garrett, P., Ng'andu, N., & Ferron, J. (1994). Poverty experiences of young children and the quality of their home environments. *Child Development, 65,* 331–345.
Garton, A.F. (1992). *Social interaction and the development of language and cognition.* Hove, England: Lawrence Erlbaum Associates, Inc.
Gesell, A. (1925). *The mental growth of the preschool child.* New York: Macmillan.
Gesell, A. (1940). *The first five years of life: A guide to the study of the preschool child.* New York: Harper & Row.
Gesell, A. (1945). *The embryology of behavior.* New York: Harper & Row.
Gibson, E.J. (1988). Exploratory behavior in the development of perceiving, acting, and the acquiring of knowledge. *Annual Review of Psychology, 39,* 1–42.
Ginsburg, G.P., & Kilborne, B.K. (1988). The emergence of vocal alternation in mother-infant interchanges. *Journal of Child Language, 15,* 221–236.
Goldberg, S., MacKay-Soroka, S., & Rochester, M. (1994). Affect, attachment, and maternal responsiveness. *Infant Behavior and Development, 17,* 335–339.
Gopnik, A., & Meltzoff, A. (1987). The development of categorization in the second year and its relation to other cognitive and linguistic developments. *Child Development, 58,* 1523–1531.
Gottman, J.M., & Katz, L.F. (1989). Effects of marital discord on young children's peer interaction and health. *Developmental Psychology, 25,* 373–381.
Grieser, D., & Kuhl, P.K. (1989). Categorization of speech by infants: Support for speech-sound prototypes. *Developmental Psychology, 25,* 577–588.
Grossman, K., Grossman, K.E., Spangler, G., Suess, G., & Unzer, L. (1985). Maternal sensitivity and newborns' orientation responses as related to quality of attachment in Northern Germany. In I. Bretherton & E. Waters (Eds.), *Growing points of attachment theory and research* (pp. 223–257). Monographs of the Society for Research in Child Development, 50(1–2, Serial No. 209).
Haith, M.M. (1980). *Rules that babies look by.* Hillsdale, NJ: Lawrence Erlbaum Associates.
Hall, G. (1891). Notes on the study of infants. *The Pedagogical Seminary, 1,* 127–138.
Hall, G.S. (1904). *Adolescence (Vols. I and II).* Englewood Cliffs, NJ: Prentice Hall.
Halverson, C.F., Jr., Kohnstamm, G.A., & Martin, R.P. (Eds.). (1994). *The developing structure of temperament and personality from infancy to adulthood.* Hillsdale, NJ: Lawrence Erlbaum Associates.
Hannan, T.E. (1987). A cross-sequential assessment of the occurrences of pointing in 3- to 12-month-old human infants. *Infant Behavior and Development, 10,* 11–22.
Heinicke, C.M., & Lampl, E. (1988). Pre- and post-birth antecedents of 3- and 4-year-old attention, IQ, verbal expressiveness, task orientation, and capacity for relationships. *Infant Behavior and Development, 11,* 381–410.
Hepper, P.G. (1992). Fetal psychology: An embryonic science. In J.G. Nijhuis (Ed.), *Fetal behaviour: Developmental and perinatal aspects.* Oxford: Oxford University Press.
Hetherington, E.M., & Parke, R.D. (1993). *Child psychology: A contemporary viewpoint.* New York: McGraw-Hill.
Hoff-Ginsberg, E. (1986). Function and structure in maternal speech: Their relationship to the child's development of syntax. *Developmental Psychology, 22,* 155–163.
Honig, A.S. (1991). Piagetian and psychometric development of 12 month old disadvantaged infants in an enrichment program. Special Issue: Varieties of early child care research. *Early Child Development and Care, 68,* 71–87.
Hooker, D. (1952). *The prenatal origin of behavior.* Lawrence: University of Kansas Press.
Houston, J.P. (1986). *Learning and memory.* Orlando, FL: Harcourt Brace.
Hubbs-Tait, L., Wierzbicki, M., Gray, D., & Englehart, R. (1994). Perceptions of infant boys' behavior and mental health: Relation to infant attachment. *Infant Mental Health Journal, 15*(3), 307–315.
Hubert, N.C. (1989). Parental subjective reactions to perceived temperament behavior in their 6- and 24-month-old children. *Infant Behavior and Development, 12,* 185–198.

Hunt, J.V. (1983). Environmental risks in fetal and neonatal life as biological determinants of infant intelligence. In M. Lewis (Ed.), *Origins of intelligence: Infancy and early childhood.* New York: Plenum Press.
Ianniruberto, A., & Tajani, E. (1981). Ultrasonographic study of fetal movements. *Seminars in Perinatology, 5,* 175–181.
Isabella, R.A. (1993). Origins of attachment: Maternal interactive behavior across the first year. *Child Development, 64,* 605–621.
Iverson, J.M., Capirci, O., & Caselli, M.C. (1994). From communication to language in two modalities. *Cognitive Development, 9*(1), 23–43.
Izard, C.E., Haynes, O.M., Chisholm, G., & Baak, K. (1991). Emotional determinants of infant–mother attachment. *Child Development, 62*(5), 906–917.
Jacobson, J.L., & Jacobson, S.W. (1990). Methodological issues in human behavioral teratology. *Advances in Infancy Research, 6,* 111–148.
Kagan, J., Arcus, D., & Snidman, N. (1993). The idea of temperament: Where do we go from here? In R. Plomin & G.E. McClearn (Eds.), *Nature, nurture, & psychology* (pp. 197–210). Washington, DC: American Psychological Association.
Kessen, W. (1965). *The child.* New York: John Wiley & Sons.
Kirchner, D.M. (1991). Using verbal scaffolding to facilitate conversational participation and language acquisition in children with pervasive developmental disorders. *Journal of Childhood Communication Disorders, 14,* 81–98.
Kline, M., Tschann, J.M., Johnston, J.R., & Wallerstein, J.S. (1989). Children's adjustment in joint and sole physical custody families. *Developmental Psychology, 25,* 430–438.
Kolb, B., & Fantie, B. (1989). Development of the child's brain and behavior. In C.R. Reynolds & E. Fletcher-Janzen (Eds.), *Handbook of clinical child neuropsychology* (pp. 17–39). New York: Plenum Press.
Kopp, C.B. (1989). Regulation of distress and negative emotions: A developmental view. *Developmental Psychology, 25,* 343–354.
Lamb, M.E. (1988). Social and emotional development in infancy. In M.H. Bornstein & M.E. Lamb (Eds.), *Developmental psychology: An advanced textbook.* Hillsdale, NJ: Lawrence Erlbaum Associates.
Lamb, M.E., & Bornstein, M.H. (1987). *Development in infancy: An introduction.* New York: Random House.
Lamb, M.E., Thompson, R.A., Gardner, W., & Charnov, E.L. (1985). *Infant–mother attachment: The origins and developmental significance of individual differences in strange situation behavior.* Hillsdale, NJ: Lawrence Erlbaum Associates.
Lamm, N., & Greer, R.D. (1988). Induction and maintenance of swallowing responses in infants with dysphagia. *Journal of Applied Behavior Analysis, 21,* 143–156.
Langley, P. (1983). Exploring the space of cognitive architectures. *Behavior Research Methods and Instrumentation, 15,* 289–299.
Langlois, J., Ritter, J.M., Roggman, L.A., & Vaughn, L.S. (1991). Facial diversity and infant preferences for attractive faces. *Developmental Psychology, 27*(1), 79–84.
Lenneberg, E. (1967). *Biological foundations of language.* New York: John Wiley & Sons.
Lenneberg, E.H. (1993). Toward a biological theory of language development. In M.H. Johnson (Ed.), *Brain development and cognition: A reader* (pp. 39–46). Oxford, England: Blackwell Publishers.
Lippman, A., & Evans, J. (1987). Screening for maternal serum of fetoprotein: What about the low side. *Canadian Medical Association Journal, 136,* 801.
Lipsitt, L.P. (1977). The study of sensory and learning processes of the newborn. Symposium on Neonatal Neurology. *Clinics in Perinatology, 4,* 163–186.
Loeber, R., & Farrington, D.P. (1994). Problems and solutions in longitudinal and experimental treatment studies of child psychopathology and delinquency. Special section: Childhood psychopathology. *Journal of Consulting and Clinical Psychology, 62*(5), 887–900.
Lutkenhaus, P., Grossman, E.E., & Grossman, K. (1985). Infant–mother attachment at twelve months and style of interaction with a stranger at the age of three years. *Child Development, 56,* 1538–1542.
Maccoby, E.E., & Martin, J.A. (1983). Socialization in the context of the family: Parent–child interaction. In P.M. Mussen (Ed.), *Handbook of child psychology: Vol. IV. Socialization, personality, and social development.* New York: John Wiley & Sons.

Main, M., & Cassidy, J. (1988). Categories of response to reunion with the parent at age 6: Predictable from infant attachment classifications and stable over a 1-month period. *Developmental Psychology, 24,* 15–26.
Main, M., & Solomon, J. (1986). Discovery of an insecure-disorganized/disoriented attachment pattern. In T.B. Brazelton & M.W. Yogman (Eds.), *Affective development in infancy.* Norwood, NJ: Ablex.
Martin, J.A. (1981). A longitudinal study of the consequences of early mother–infant interaction: A microanalytic approach. *Monographs of the Society for Research in Child Development, 46*(3, Serial No. 190).
Mednick, S.A., & Mednick, B. (1984). A brief history of North American longitudinal research. In S.A. Mednick, M. Harway, & K.M. Finello (Eds.), *Handbook of longitudinal research.* New York: Praeger.
Meisels, S.J., & Wasik, B.A. (1990). Who should be served? Identifying children in need of early intervention. In S.J. Meisels & J.P. Shonkoff (Eds.), *Handbook of early childhood intervention* (pp. 605–632). Cambridge: Cambridge University Press.
Mercer, R.T., & Ferketich, S.L. (1994). Maternal–infant attachment of experienced and inexperienced mothers during infancy. *Nursing Research, 43,* 344–351.
Meredith, H.V. (1978). *Human body growth in the first ten years of life.* Columbia, SC: State Printing Company.
Messer, D.J., & Vietze, P.M. (1988). Does mutual influence occur during mother–infant social gaze? *Infant Behavior and Development, 11,* 97–110.
Miller, P.H. (1993). *Theories of developmental psychology* (3rd ed.). San Francisco: W.H. Freeman.
Miller, S.A. (1987). *Developmental research methods.* Englewood Cliffs, NJ: Prentice Hall.
Mistretta, C.M., & Bradley, R.M. (1977). Taste in utero: Theoretical considerations. In J.M. Weiffenbach (Ed.), *Taste and development: The genesis of sweet preference.* Washington, DC: U.S. Government Printing Office.
Molfese, M.J. (1989). *Perinatal risk and infant development: Assessment and prediction.* New York: Guilford Press.
Morford, M., & Goldin-Meadow, S. (1992). Comprehension and production of gesture in combination with speech in one-word speakers. *Journal of Child Language, 19,* 559–580.
Murray, A.D., Johnson, J., & Peters, J. (1990). Fine-tuning of utterance length to preverbal infants: Effects on later language development. *Journal of Child Language, 17,* 511–525.
Musick, J.S., & Householder, J. (1986). *Infant development: From theory to practice.* Belmont, CA: Wadsworth Publishing Company.
Nelson, K.E. (1987). Some observations from the perspective of the rare event cognitive comparison theory of language acquisition. In K.E. Nelson & A. Van Kleek (Eds.), *Children's language* (Vol. 6, pp. 289–331). Hillsdale, NJ: Lawrence Erlbaum Associates.
Nijhuis, J.G. (1992). The third trimester. In J.G. Nijhuis (Ed.), *Fetal behaviour: Developmental and perinatal aspects.* Oxford: Oxford University Press.
Nora, J.J., & Fraser, F.C. (1989). *Medical genetics: Principles and practice.* Philadelphia: Lea & Febiger.
Olsen-Fulero, L. (1982). Style and stability in mother conversational behaviour: A study of individual differences. *Journal of Child Language, 9,* 543–564.
Papousek, H., & Papousek, M. (1992). Beyond emotional bonding: The role of preverbal communication in mental growth and health. *Infant Mental Health Journal, 13,* 43–53.
Patrick, J., Campbell, K., Carmichael, L., & Probert, C. (1982). Patterns of gross fetal body movements over 24-hour observation intervals during the last 10 weeks of pregnancy. *American Journal of Obstetrics and Gynecology, 142,* 363.
Phillips, W., Baron-Cohen, S., & Rutter, M. (1992). The role of eye contact in goal detection: Evidence from normal infants and children with autism or mental handicap. *Development and Psychopathology, 4,* 375–383.
Piaget, J. (1929). *The child's conception of the world.* New York: Harcourt & Brace.
Piaget, J. (1951). *Play, dreams and imitation in childhood.* New York: Norton.
Piaget, J. (1952). *The origins of intelligence in children.* (M. Cook, Translator). New York: International Universities Press.
Piaget, J. (1954). *The construction of reality in the child.* New York: Basic Books.
Piaget, J. (1970). Piaget's theory. In P.H. Mussen (Ed.), *Carmichael's manual of child psychology* (3rd ed., pp. 703–732). New York: John Wiley & Sons.

Pine, J.M. (1992). Maternal style at the early one-word stage: Re-evaluating the stereotype of the directive mother. *First Language, 12,* 169–186.
Pinker, S. (1984). *Language development and language learnability.* Cambridge, MA: Harvard University Press.
Pinker, S. (1989). Language acquisition. In M.I. Posner (Ed.), *Foundations of cognitive science* (pp. 359–399). Cambridge, MA: MIT Press.
Plomin, R. (1989). Developmental behavior genetics: Stability and instability. In M.H. Bornstein & N.A. Krasnegor (Eds.), *Stability and continuity in mental development: Behavioral and biological perspectives* (pp. 273–291). Hillsdale, NJ: Lawrence Erlbaum Associates.
Plunkett, J.W., Klein, T., & Meisels, S.J. (1988). The relationship of preterm infant–mother attachment to stranger sociability at 3 years. *Infant Behavior and Development, 11,* 83–96.
Pomerleau, A., Malcuit, G., Chamberland, C., & Laurendeau, M. (1992). Methodological problems in operant learning research with human infants. *International Journal of Psychology, 27*(6), 417–432.
Prechtl, H.F. (1987). Prenatal development of postnatal behaviour. In H. Rauh & H.C. Steinhausen (Eds.), *Psychology and early development* (pp. 231–238). Amsterdam: North-Holland.
Pye, C., Ingram, D., & List, H. (1987). A comparison of initial consonant acquisition in English and Quiche. In K.E. Nelson & A. Van Kleek (Eds.), *Children's language* (Vol. 6, pp. 175–190). Hillsdale, NJ: Lawrence Erlbaum Associates.
Rabinowitz, F.M., Grant, M.J., & Dingley, H.L. (1987). Computer simulation, cognition, and development: An introduction. In J. Bisanz, C.J. Brainerd, & R. Kail (Eds.), *Formal methods in developmental psychology: Progress in cognitive development research.* New York: Springer-Verlag.
Ramey, C.T., Lee, M.W., & Burchinal, M.R. (1989). Development plasticity and predictability: Consequences of ecological change. In M.H. Bornstein & N.A. Krasnegor (Eds.), *Stability and continuity in mental development: Behavioral and biological perspectives* (pp. 217–233). Hillsdale, NJ: Lawrence Erlbaum Associates.
Reardon, P., & Bushnell, W.Q. (1988). Infants' sensitivity to arbitrary pairings of color and taste. *Infant Behavior and Development, 11,* 245–250.
Rieder, C., & Cicchetti, D. (1989). Organizational perspective on cognitive control functioning and cognitive-affective balance in maltreated children. *Developmental Psychology, 25,* 382–393.
Rieser, J., Yonas, A., & Wilkner, K. (1976). Radical localization of odors by human newborns. *Child Development, 47,* 856–859.
Roggman, L.A., Langlois, J.H., & Hubbs-Tait, L. (1987). Mothers, infants, and toys: Social play correlates of attachment. *Infant Behavior and Development, 10,* 233–237.
Rose, S.A. (1989). Measuring infant intelligence: New perspectives. In M.H. Bornstein & N.A. Krasnegor (Eds.), *Stability and continuity in mental development: Behavioral and biological perspectives.* Hillsdale, NJ: Lawrence Erlbaum Associates.
Rose, S.A. (1994). Relation between physical growth and information processing in infants born in India. *Child Development, 65,* 889–902.
Rose, S.A., & Ruff, H. (1987). Cross modal abilities in human infants. In J. Osofsky (Ed.), *Handbook of infant development* (2nd ed., pp. 318–362). New York: John Wiley & Sons.
Rosenblith, J.F., & Sims-Knight, J.E. (1985). *In the beginning: Development in the first two years.* Monterey, CA: Brooks/Cole.
Ross, R., Mimouni, F., & Tsang, R.C. (1988). Fetal and neonatal skeletal growth and mineralization. In B.S. Linblad (Ed.), *Perinatal nutrition.* New York: Academic Press.
Rothbart, M.K. (1991). Temperament: A developmental framework: In J. Strelou. & A. Angleitner (Eds.), *Explorations in temperament: International perspectives on theory and measurement. Perspectives on individual differences* (pp. 61–74). New York: Plenum Press.
Rothbart, M.K., Ahadi, S.A., & Hershey, K.L. (1994). Temperament and social behavior in childhood. *Merrill-Palmer Quarterly, 40,* 21–39.
Schlinger, H.D. (1993). Learned expectancies are not adequate explanations. *American Psychologist, 48,* 1155–1156.
Seitz, V. (1988). Methodology. In M.H. Bornstein & M.E. Lamb (Eds.), *Developmental psychology: An advanced textbook* (2nd ed., pp. 51–83). Hillsdale, NJ: Lawrence Erlbaum Associates.

Shatz, M. (1987). Bootstrapping operations in child language. In K.E. Nelson & A. Van Kleek (Eds.), *Children's language* (Vol. 6, pp. 1–22). Hillsdale, NJ: Lawrence Erlbaum Associates.
Shulman, V.L. (1985). *The future of Piagetian theory: The neo-Piagetians.* New York: Plenum Press.
Simons, C.J.R., Ritchie, S.K., Mullett, M.D., & Mingarelle, C.C. (1989). Subject loss and its implications for a high-risk population. *Infant Behavior and Development, 12,* 139–146.
Skeels, H.M., & Dye, H.B. (1939). A study of the effects of differential stimulation on mentally retarded children. *Proceedings and Addresses of the American Association on Mental Deficiency, 44,* 114–136.
Skinner, B.F. (1957). *Verbal behavior.* New York: Appleton-Century-Crofts.
Skinner, B.F. (1966). *The behavior of organisms: An experimental analysis.* New York: Appleton-Century-Crofts.
Skinner, B.F. (1972). *Cumulative record: A selection of papers* (3rd ed.). New York: Appleton-Century-Crofts.
Skinner, B.F. (1976). *About behaviorism.* New York: Vintage Books.
Sluckin, W., & Herbert, M. (1986). *Parental behaviour.* Oxford, England: Blackwell.
Smotherman, W.P., & Robinson, S.R. (1987). Psychobiology of fetal experience in the rat. In N.A. Krasnegor, E.M. Blass, M.A. Hofer, & W.P. Smotherman (Eds.), *Perinatal development: A psychobiological perspective* (pp. 39–60). San Diego: Harcourt Brace Jovanovich.
Snow, C.E., Perlman, R., & Nathan, D. (1987). Why routines are different: Toward a multiple-factors model of the relation between input and language acquisition. In K.E. Nelson & A. Van Kleek (Eds.), *Children's language* (Vol. 6, pp. 65–98). Hillsdale, NJ: Lawrence Erlbaum Associates.
Snow, C.W. (1989). *Infant development.* Englewood Cliffs, NJ: Prentice Hall.
Spelke, E.S., Breinlinger, K., Macomber, J., & Jacobson, K. (1992). Origins of knowledge. *Psychological Review, 99,* 605–632.
Spence, M.J., & DeCasper, A.J. (1987). Prenatal experience with low frequency maternal-voice sounds influence neonatal perception of maternal voice samples. *Infant Behavior and Development, 10,* 133–142.
Spieker, S.J., & Bensley, L. (1994). Roles of living arrangements and grandmother social support in adolescent mothering and infant attachment. *Developmental Psychology, 30*(1), 102–111.
Sokolov, J.L., & Snow, C.E. (1994). The changing role of negative evidence in theories of language development. In C. Gallaway & B.J. Richards (Eds.), *Input and interaction in language acquisition* (pp. 38–55). Cambridge: Cambridge University Press.
Sroufe, L.A. (1985). Attachment classification from the perspective of infant–caregiver relationship and infant temperament. *Child Development, 56,* 1–14.
Sroufe, L.A., Cooper, R.G., & Marshall, M.E. (1988). *Child development: Its nature and course.* New York: Alfred A. Knopf.
Steiner, J. (1977). Facial expressions of the neonate indicating the hedonics of food related chemical stimuli. In J. Wiffenbach (Ed.), *Taste and development: The genesis of sweet preference* (pp. 173–204). Bethesda, MD: National Institutes of Health (DHEW Pub. No. NIH 77–1068).
Sternberg, R.J. (1984). Testing intelligence without IQ tests. *Phi Delta Kappan, 65,* 694–698.
Sternberg, R.J. (1986). *Intelligence applied: Understanding and increasing your intellectual skills.* San Diego: Harcourt Brace Jovanovich.
Stifter, C.A., Fox, N.A., & Porges, S.W. (1989). Facial expressivity and vagal tone in 5- and 10-month-old infants. *Infant Behavior and Development, 12,* 127–137.
Strom, R.D., Bernard, H.W., & Strom, S.R. (1987). *Human development and learning.* New York: Human Sciences Press.
Sutton, E.H. (1975). *An introduction to human genetics.* New York: Holt, Rinehart & Winston.
Tamis-LeMonda, C.S., & Bornstein, M.H. (1989). Habituation and maternal encouragement of attention in infancy as predictors of toddler language, play, and representational competence. *Child Development, 60,* 738–751.
Thelen, E. (1995). Motor development: A new synthesis. *American Psychologist, 50*(2), 79–95.
van den Boom, D.C. (1994). The influence of temperament and mothering on attachment and exploration: An experimental manipulation of sensitive responsiveness among lower-class mothers with irritable infants. *Child Development, 65,* 1457–1477.

Verhulst, F.C., & Koot, H.M. (1991). Longitudinal research in child and adolescent psychiatry. Special section: Longitudinal research. *Journal of the American Academy of Child and Adolescent Psychiatry, 30*(3), 361–368.
Vibbert, M., & Bornstein, M.H. (1989). Specific associations between domains of mother–child interaction and toddler referential language and pretense play. *Infant Behavior and Development, 12,* 163–184.
Wallace, D.B., Franklin, M.B., & Keegan, R.T. (1994). The observing eye: A century of baby diaries. *Human Development, 37*(1), 1–29.
Watson, J.B. (1924). *Behaviorism.* New York: Norton.
Watson, J.B. (1928). *Psychological care of infant and child.* New York: Norton.
Watson, J.B. (1930). *Behaviorism.* Chicago: University of Chicago Press.
Wilkenson, A.C., & Haines, B.A. (1987). Learning a cognitive skill and its components. In J. Bisanz, C.J. Brainerd, & R. Kail (Eds.), *Formal methods in developmental psychology: Progress in cognitive developmental research.* New York: Springer-Verlag.
Woolridge, M.W., & Baum, J.D. (1988). The regulation of human milk flow. In B.S. Lindblad (Ed.), *Perinatal nutrition* (pp. 669–678). New York: Academic Press.
Worebey, J., & Blajda, V.M. (1989). Temperament ratings at 2 weeks, 2 months, and 1 year: Differential stability of activity and emotionality. *Developmental Psychology, 25,* 257–263.
Worebey, J., & Lewis, M. (1989). Individual differences in the reactivity of young infants. *Developmental Psychology, 25,* 663–667.
Yoder, P.J., & Kaiser, A.P. (1989). Alternative explanations for the relationship between maternal verbal interaction style and child development. *Journal of Child Language, 16,* 141–160.
Zayas, L.H., & Solari, F. (1994). Early childhood socialization in Hispanic families: Context, culture, and practice implications. *Professional Psychology Research and Practice, 25,* 200–206.

2

ACTIVITIES

1. Describe the advantages and disadvantages of each child development research design.
2. Explain why there is a need for specific research techniques.
3. Describe the function of phenotypes and genotypes.
4. What purpose does the trophoblast serve in an embryo's development?
5. How long does the fetal stage of development last?
6. How are abnormalities and defects detected in vitro?
7. What gross motor skills are developed within the first year of life?
8. Initial reflexive behaviors proceed in what direction?
9. Explain Piaget's theory of organization and adaptation in relation to cognition in infants.
10. Explain the function of Freud's three systems of emotion and development.
11. What effect does temperament have on an infant's emotional development?

CHAPTER 3

Determinants of Risk in Infancy

Anne H. Widerstrom and Robert E. Nickel

Objectives

- To understand the concept of risk for developmental delay as it applies to infants
- To understand the various biological risk factors that can occur in the prenatal and postnatal periods, including premature birth, low birth weight, prenatal alcohol or drug exposure, and perinatal asphyxia
- To understand the various environmental risk factors that can affect the newborn, including mothers of adolescent age, parental drug or alcohol abuse, or parents who have disabilities

The infant at risk has become a great concern to professionals in medicine, developmental psychology, special education, and related fields (Rossetti, 1986), and each field gives somewhat different meaning to the term. For this discussion, the following definition adapted from Rossetti (1986) is used:

> An infant who because of low birth weight (<2500 grams), prematurity (<37 weeks gestation), the presence of serious medical complication, or adverse environmental conditions has a greater than average chance of displaying developmental delay or later cognitive or motor deficits or a combination of these. (p. 3)

The definition of the risk must be broad because there is increasing evidence that the quality of familial, medical, therapeutic, and educational care provided to the child immediately following birth has great influence on the ultimate quality of that child's life

(Snyder-McLean, 1986). Inadequacies in any of these areas place the infant at risk for developmental delay.

This chapter examines the various biological and environmental risk factors that can occur in the prenatal, perinatal, and postnatal periods (Table 3.1). Biological factors include premature birth, prenatal alcohol or drug use, and perinatal asphyxia. Environmental factors include maternal age, parental alcohol or other drug use, and parents who have developmental disabilities. Children with a combination of biological and environmental factors are at a greater risk for developmental problems than children with either factor alone.

DETERMINING DEGREE OF RISK

The concept of multiple-variable risk is important in the field of early intervention. With the introduction of the terms *reproductive risk* and *caretaking causality* by Sameroff and Chandler (1975), professionals in psychology and education began looking at nonmedical factors that might place a child at risk for developmental delay. Sameroff and Chandler proposed a continuum of caretaking causality to illustrate the fact that the degree of biological risk in infancy cannot accurately predict later developmental outcomes, because socioeconomic and familial factors may outweigh biological factors. Since that time, greater attention has been given to the entire range of risk variables, including genetic factors, socioeconomic factors, health factors, and child abuse (e.g., Cicchetti & Toth, 1987; Sameroff, 1989).

Use of Risk Indices

One of the most important areas of study in the prevention of physical and cognitive disabilities in young children is the development of techniques that can accurately identify those who are at risk for later difficulties. Of particular interest are the high-incidence, low-severity problems such as learning disabilities, behavioral difficulties, and mild delays in intellectual functioning that are economically and psychologically costly but that may be ameliorated if remediation is provided early in development.

Several authors have attempted to develop risk indices for use with infants that accurately predict achievement in later childhood (Broman, Nichols, & Kennedy, 1975; Littman & Parmalee, 1978; Ramey, Stedman, Borders-Patterson, & Mengel, 1978). Siegel (1985) has developed such an index containing 13 variables in three categories (Table 3.2) that has been relatively successful in predicting cognitive and language delays at ages 2, 3, 5, and 6. The index appears to be a better predictor of later IQ scores than various infant IQ tests (Siegel, 1985). Siegel's index is based on the concept of *cumulative* or *multiple risk factors.* Like other authors (e.g., Bee et al., 1982; Keogh & Kopp, 1978), Siegel argued that risk is not due to a single factor but to a variety of biological and environmental factors.

Table 3.1. The periods surrounding birth

Term	Description
Prenatal	The period extending from conception to birth
Perinatal	The period from the twelfth week of gestation through the fourth week after birth
Neonatal	The first 20 days after birth
Postnatal	The period from 28 days following birth to 11 months

Table 3.2. Siegel newborn risk index variables

Reproductive variables
Gravidity (birth order)
Amount of maternal smoking during pregnancy
Number of previous spontaneous abortions
Perinatal variables
Birth weight
Apgar scores (1 minute and 5 minutes)
Gestational age (if preterm)
Severity of respiratory distress (if preterm)
Severity of birth asphyxia (if preterm)
Severity of apnea (if preterm)
Demographic variables
Socioeconomic status
Sex
Mother's educational level
Father's educational level

Adapted from Siegel (1985).

INCIDENCE OF INFANTS AT HIGH RISK

Estimates of the incidence of infants at high risk range from 5% to 15% of all newborns (Rossetti, 1986), depending on classification criteria. The most commonly used indicators of risk are birth weight and gestational age. Infants at high risk tend to come from non-Caucasian families with lower socioeconomic status. African American infant and neonatal mortality rates continue to be more than twice those of Caucasian rates (Table 3.3) (Guyer, Strobino, Ventura, & Singh, 1995). The reasons for this discrepancy are complex; however, these statistics reflect the lack of prenatal care available to low-income families in the United States, as well as the risk factors related to mother's age and behavior during pregnancy.

The infant mortality rate reached a low in 1994 of 7.9 deaths per 1,000 live births (Guyer et al., 1995). Concomitant with this improvement in the infant mortality rate is the improvement in the survival of very low birth weight (VLBW) infants. Although more VLBW infants survive, the overall incidence of serious neurodevelopmental deficits among these survivors has remained stable. Table 3.4 shows the types of sequelae and the numbers of infants affected in two birth weight groups from a study by Hack and colleagues (1994). These data emphasize that children with a birth weight of less than 750 grams are at high risk for neurodevelopmental problems. The limit of viability for VLBW infants is now 24–25 weeks of gestation (Allen, Donohue, & Dusman, 1993).

PRENATAL FACTORS

The infant's environment in utero is critical to its future well-being. That is why many prenatal risk factors have to do with the mother's health and behavior. The mother's age, her general state of health and nutrition, and the adequacy of prenatal care are important maternal risk factors. Certain maternal health problems increase the risk for birth defects (e.g., seizure disorders, diabetes) or increase the likelihood of premature birth (caused by sexually transmitted diseases [STDs]). It is also well-known that smoking and the use of alcohol and other recreational drugs may

Table 3.3. Infant mortality rates by age and race, selected years[a]

Year	1994[b]	1993[b]	1992[c]	1990[c]	1990[d]	1980[d]	1960[d]	1940[d]	Decline in %	
									1940–1992	1940–1994
Total[e]	7.9	8.3	8.5	9.2	9.2	12.6	26.0	47.0	81.9	83.2
White			6.9	7.6	7.7	11.0	22.9	43.2	84.0	
Black			16.8	18.0	17.0	21.4	44.3	72.9	77.0	
Black:white ratio			2.4	2.4	2.2	1.9	1.9	1.7		
Neonatal[e]	5.0	5.4	5.4	5.8	5.8	8.5	18.7	28.8	81.3	82.6
White			4.3	4.8	4.9	7.5	17.2	27.2	84.2	
Black			10.8	11.6	10.9	14.1	27.8	39.9	72.9	
Black:white ratio			2.5	2.4	2.2	1.9	1.6	1.5		
Postneonatal[e]	3.0	2.9	3.1	3.4	3.4	4.1	7.3	18.3	83.1	83.6
White			2.6	2.8	2.8	3.5	5.7	16.0	83.8	
Black			6.0	6.4	6.1	7.3	16.5	33.0	81.8	
Black:white ratio			2.3	2.3	2.2	2.1	2.9	2.1		

From Guyer, B., Strobino, D.M., Ventura, S.J., & Singh, G.K. (1995). Annual summary of vital statistics—1994. Reproduced by Permission of PEDIATRICS, Vol. 92, Page 1036, Copyright 1993.

[a]Data from National Center for Health Statistics.

[b]Provisional, estimated from a 10% sample of deaths; rates per 1,000 live births; 1940–1992 final, rates per 1,000 live births.

[c]Race according to race of mother (introduced in 1989).

[d]Race according to race of child.

[e]Includes races other than white and black.

Table 3.4. Neurosensory and growth outcomes

	Birth weight	
	Number (%)	
Condition	<750 g (*N*=68)	750–1499 g (*N*=65)
Cerebral palsy[a, b]	6 (9)	4 (6)
Visual disability[b, c]	12 (25)	3 (5)
Blindness[d]	4 (6)	1 (2)
Vision $\leq$ 20/200[c]	8 (17)	2 (3)
Hearing disability[e]	13 (24)	8 (13)
Deafness	1 (1.5)	1 (1.5)
Mild hearing loss[b, e, f]	12 (22)	7 (11)
Subnormal growth[a]		
Weight[b]	15 (22)	7 (11)
Height[b]	17 (25)	3 (5)
Head size[b]	24 (35)	9 (14)

Adapted from Hack, M., Taylor, H.G., Klein, N., Eiben, R., Schatschneider, C., & Merguri-Minich, N. *New England Journal of Medicine*, 1994, *331*(12) p. 756. Copyright © 1994 Massachusetts Medical Society. All rights reserved.

[a]Defined as spastic quadriplegia, diplegia, or hemiplegia. Two children in each group could not walk.

[b]$p < 0.05$ for the comparison of the three groups by the chi-square test, 2 df.

[c]Rates of visual impairment in at least one eye, without glasses, are based on the study of 48 children in the <750-gram group and 61 children in the 750- to 1,499-gram group. Twenty and four children in the respective groups did not have their vision tested because of poor cooperation or lack of understanding of directions.

[d]Total blindness, unilateral or bilateral.

[e]Rates of hearing impairment are based on the study of 55 children in the <750-gram group, 62 children in the 750- to 1,499-gram group, and 60 children born at term who had their hearing tested.

[f]Denotes unilateral or bilateral hearing loss of more than 25 decibels in at least two frequencies.

[g]More than 2 *SD* below the mean.

adversely affect the developing fetus. In addition, maternal HIV or hepatitis B infection may be transmitted to the fetus or neonate resulting in a serious and potentially lethal chronic health problem.

Maternal Age

High rates of medical problems are found among the newborns of mothers older than 36 and mothers younger than 16 (Rossetti, 1986). Teenage mothers 13–17 years of age have a greater risk of poor outcomes than mothers 20–24 years of age (Fraser, Brockert, & Ward, 1995). Older teenage mothers (18 and 19 years of age) also have a significant increase in these risks. Problems are especially likely if the woman is unmarried and has had previous pregnancies before age 20 (Thurman & Widerstrom, 1990).

The most common correlation between a mother's age and infant status is birth weight, with low birth weight more commonly seen in older and younger mothers than in women ages 20–35 (Holmes, Reich, & Pasternak, 1984). Teenage mothers are more likely to have babies who are premature and have low birth weight (Scholl, Hediger, & Belsky, 1994). The rate of teenage pregnancy is higher among non-Caucasian than Caucasian mothers. In a comparison of adolescent and older mothers, Culp, Appelbaum, Osofsky, and Levy (1988) found significant differences between the two groups in maternal psychosocial characteristics: Adolescent mothers reported being less happy about their pregnancies, having less social support, and receiving less support from the infant's father. Many of these mothers were unmarried, which added to their sense of isolation. All of these factors placed their infants at greater risk.

Adequacy of Prenatal Care

The United States is unique among developed countries of the world in not providing routine prenatal health care to all pregnant women. This fact, together with a general unavailability of maternal and paternal leave following the infant's birth, places a greater burden on low-income parents. In a study reviewing the 1980 National Natality Survey data, only approximately 61% of women received ade-

Alice

Alice had her first baby when she was 16 years old. "Believe it or not, I got pregnant my first time having intercourse, when I was 15 years old. When I found out, I was very angry at myself for being so stupid. I kept thinking, this is not happening to me, but it was. I was scared to tell my parents, and I was worried to death about what my boyfriend would say."

As it turned out, her boyfriend, too, was scared when he found out and stopped seeing Alice, saying he was too young to get married. "He wanted me to have an abortion," Alice said. "But I didn't know where to go or who to talk to about it, and I just couldn't face it alone. By the time my parents found out about the pregnancy, it was too late to think about an abortion. And my mom said she'd help me through having the baby and taking care of it after it was born. And she did. I love my baby and I'm really glad now that I didn't have an abortion."

Alice's baby was born 4 weeks before term and weighed only 4 pounds. "He was kept at the hospital in a special nursery for the first 3 weeks after he was born, until he weighed enough for us to bring him home. He didn't have any serious medical problems, thank goodness. I guess I was lucky. But it was hard to breast-feed him. I had to use a breast pump and take the milk to the hospital for him. They let me visit him every day, though. My dad would drive me over."

Alice is still living at home with her mother and father. She dropped out of school to have the baby and didn't return after the birth. Now she works nights at a fast-food restaurant to help support herself and her 2-year-old son and takes care of him during the day. Her mother has a full-time job during the day, but takes care of the child in the evening and helps Alice on weekends. "I don't know where I'd be if it weren't for Mom and Dad. They've been wonderful to both of us."

quate prenatal care (Kotelchuck, 1994). More Caucasian women than African American women received adequate care. The findings are troubling given the U.S. Surgeon General's call for an increase in services to ensure that 90% of women of all ages, ethnic backgrounds, and income groups receive appropriate prenatal care beginning in the first trimester (Miller, 1989).

Women who receive inadequate prenatal care have a higher risk of premature rupture of amniotic membranes, prematurity, and low birth weight (Gosselink, Ekwo, Woolson, Moawad, & Long, 1993). However, some women do not utilize prenatal care when it is available. Teenagers, unmarried women, women who smoke, and women who have little social support tend to not utilize prenatal care (McCaw-Binns, La Grenade, & Ashley, 1995). Clearly, the management and prevention of teenage pregnancy and availability of prenatal care remain key issues for research and policy development.

Maternal Health Problems

Certain maternal illnesses significantly increase the risk for birth defects and subsequent developmental delay, for example, epilepsy and diabetes. The incidence of birth defects in infants of mothers with epilepsy who are treated with anticonvulsants is two to three times that of mothers without epilepsy (Delgado-Escueta & Janz, 1992). Birth defect syndromes have been described for phenytoin (Dilantin), trimethadione (Tridione), and valproate (Depakene). However, it is not known which of the major anticonvulsants (phenytoin, carbamazepine, valproate, or phenobarbital) is the most likely to cause birth defects (Delgado-Escueta & Janz, 1992). In one study, phenytoin and valproate were the most teratogenic (causing the most birth defects), and phenytoin combined with phenobarbital was more teratogenic than phenobarbital alone (Dravet et al., 1992).

Diabetes is a major complication of pregnancy and is associated with an increased risk for maternal and perinatal morbidity and congenital defects (Reece & Homko, 1993). The infants of mothers with diabetes are five to six times more likely to have a major birth defect compared with mothers who do not have diabetes (Becerra, Khoury, Cordero, & Erickson, 1990; Ramos-Arroyo, Rodriguez-Pinilla, & Cordero, 1992). The absolute risks for central nervous system and cardiovascular defects are 5.3 and 8.5 per 100 live births, respectively (Becerra et al., 1990).

Various sexually transmitted diseases have been associated with preterm birth and low birth weight and thus the risk for later developmental problems. Bacterial vaginosis, ureaplasma, urealyticum, and gonorrhea have been associated with low birth weight and prematurity (Elliott et al., 1990; Eschenbach et al., 1991; McGregor et al., 1994). *Chlamydia trachomatis* can cause infertility, ectopic pregnancy, low birth weight, and infection in the newborn (Much & Yeh, 1991). Chlamydia infects an estimated 4 million people a year (Much & Yeh, 1991). Of note, sexually transmitted diseases are more common in young, non-Caucasian and low-income women.

Human Immunodeficiency Virus Perinatal transmission is the source for nearly 90% of children with human immunodeficiency virus (HIV) infection (Hoernle & Reid, 1995), and the number of women diagnosed with HIV infection has markedly increased (Drake, Youchah, & Damus, 1995). Infants who are born to women with the acquired immunodeficiency syndrome (AIDS) are at higher risk for HIV infection (Abrams et al., 1995). In addition, maternal HIV infection is associated with a significantly lower birth weight and with prematurity (Temmermen et al.,

1994). In general, the rate of mother-to-infant transmission in the United States is 15%–25% (Working Group on Mother-to-Child Transmission of HIV, 1995). The use of zidovudine (AZT) during pregnancy and delivery can significantly reduce the risk of transmission (Connor & Mofenson, 1995; Matheson et al., 1995; Peckham & Gibb, 1995).

The prognosis for perinatal HIV infection is poor. The median age at the onset of any sign of infection is approximately 5 months (Galli et al., 1995), and the median age at the diagnosis of AIDS is 12–24 months (Hoernle & Reid, 1995). The clinical features include pneumocystis pneumonia, cytomegalovirus (CMV) infection, failure to thrive, encephalopathy with developmental delay and apparent spastic cerebral palsy, recurrent bacterial infections, pancreatitis, and hepatitis (Oleske, 1994).

Women infected with HIV are likely to be young, poor, urban, non-Caucasian, and intravenous drug users. A crisis in health care is the effort to provide comprehensive services for HIV-infected infants and their families in a time of lack of federal commitment to such policies as drug abuse prevention and treatment and early intervention.

Hepatitis Hepatitis A is usually a benign, self-limited infection and is an uncommon complication of pregnancy (Simms & Duff, 1993). By contrast, hepatitis B is more common, and infants born to infected mothers are at risk for neonatal hepatitis and chronic liver disease. An estimated 22,000 infants are born each year in the United States to women with chronic hepatitis B infections ("Maternal hepatitis B screening practices," 1994). All pregnant women should be tested for the hepatitis B surface antigen (HbsAg), and all neonates should now receive hepatitis B vaccine. Infants delivered to women with chronic hepatitis B infection should also receive hepatic B immunoglobulin (HBIG) immediately after birth ("Maternal hepatitis B screening practices," 1994).

Hepatitis D is rare and usually occurs as a co-infection with hepatitis B. Immunoprophylaxis of hepatitis B also prevents transmission of hepatitis D (Simms & Duff, 1993). In contrast, hepatitis C is a serious infection that is usually transmitted parenterally, for example, by intravenous drug use. Perinatal transmission of hepatitis C has been reported, particularly in association with maternal HIV infection (Paccagnini et al., 1995; Resti et al., 1995). No immunotherapy is available for infants infected with hepatitis C.

General Health and Nutrition

Poor nutritional intake and inadequate maternal weight gain during the pregnancy are highly associated with low birth weight. In addition, there is now evidence that maternal nutritional status prior to the pregnancy is very important to pregnancy outcome (Crawford et al., 1993). In one study, the majority of both Caucasian and non-Caucasian adolescents had inadequate pre-pregnancy nutritional status based on the weight-for-height ratio (Sargent, Schulken, Kemper, & Hussey, 1994).

Folate as an Important Vitamin Supplementation with multivitamins with folate (a vitamin in the B group) or folate alone for 1 month before conception and during the first trimester can dramatically reduce the incidence of one type of birth defect, neural tube defects, or spina bifida (Czeizel & Dudás, 1992; Wald, Sneddon, Densem, Frost, & Stone, 1991). This major public health breakthrough has led to the recommendation that all women of child-bearing age should take supple-

mental folate ("Recommendations for the use of folic acid," 1992). There has been some reduction in other birth defects (e.g., one type of heart defect), but no consistent effect has been noted for cleft lip and palate (Czeizel, 1995).

Drug Use During Pregnancy

In a survey of 36 hospitals, 11% of women giving birth were found to have been using one or more illicit drugs (Chasnoff, 1989). Other studies report rates of 5%–15% (Chasnoff, Griffith, Freier, & Murray, 1992; Jacobson, Jacobson, & Sokol, 1994; Vega, Kolody, Hwang, & Noble, 1993). In Pinellas County, Florida, the rates were similar in African American and Caucasian women and at public and private clinics (Chasnoff et al., 1992). Other studies have noted higher rates of prenatal drug use in African American women and in urban populations (Forman et al., 1994; Vega et al., 1993). The use of cocaine and other illicit drugs is closely associated with alcohol use and smoking and with prematurity and low birth weight (Kliegman, Madura, Kiwi, Eisenberg, & Yamashita, 1994). The reported effects of any particular drug are compounded by many factors, including use of alcohol and other drugs, including nicotine, postnatal exposure to drugs (e.g., by breast-feeding), difficulties in accurate identification of people who use drugs, and the effects of an inadequate caregiving environment.

Smoking and Nicotine Cigarette smoking is the largest single risk factor for low birth weight according to Chomitz, Cheung, and Lieberman (1995) and other numerous studies since the 1970s. Infants of regular smokers weigh approximately 150–250 grams less at birth than those of nonsmokers (Fried, 1993). There is a substantial reduction in birth weight even for light smokers (Muscati, Gray-McDonald,

& Newson, 1994). Approximately 20% of the births of such infants could be avoided if women abstained from smoking during the pregnancy (Chomitz et al., 1995). In addition, maternal smoking is associated with an increased rate of spontaneous abortion, stillbirth, and perinatal mortality (Finnegan, 1985; Fried, 1993).

Alcohol Excess consumption of alcohol during pregnancy can result in low birth weight, microencephaly (small head size), heart defects, facial dysmorphic features (minor abnormalities in the structure of facial features), poor growth, developmental delay, fine motor impairment, and attention-deficit/hyperactivity disorder (ADHD). The combination of these features is referred to as fetal alcohol syndrome (FAS). This syndrome was first identified in the 1970s (Jones, Smith, Ulleland, & Streissguth, 1973; Shaywitz, Cohen, & Shaywitz, 1978). More recent studies have established that the central nervous system is particularly vulnerable to the effects of alcohol, with the most serious problems occurring during the period of early brain development in the first trimester. Infants born with FAS have been found to be slower to habituate as newborns (Streissguth, Martin, Barr, & Sandman, 1984) and to have poorer ratings on the Neonatal Behavioral Assessment Scales (NBAS) (Brazelton, 1984) as evidenced by poor state regulation and a greater incidence of abnormal reflexes (Coles, Smith, Fernhoff, & Falek, 1985).

Even when the mother stops drinking during the second trimester of pregnancy, the infant is at risk for developmental and behavioral problems. In a study of three groups of pregnant women, those who never drank, those who stopped during the second trimester, and those who drank throughout the pregnancy, Coles, Smith, Lancaster, and Falek (1987) found differences in the infants' motor performance, autonomic regulation, and reflex behavior 1 month after birth. The third group of infants demonstrated the greatest impairments. Only the babies whose mothers never drank had expected performance on the NBAS.

There is no safe amount of alcohol for pregnant women. In one study, the consumption of one or two drinks per day was associated with an increased risk of low birth weight (Mills, Graubard, Harley, Rhoads, & Berends, 1984). However, the evidence for damage to the fetus is much stronger for large amounts of alcohol consumption than for small amounts (Committee on Substance Abuse and Committee on Children with Disabilities, American Academy of Pediatrics, 1993). The label "possible fetal alcohol effects" or "fetal alcohol effects" (FAE) has been applied to children who have some but not all of the characteristics of FAS, when there is a maternal history of moderate alcohol use. FAE is not a specific diagnosis, may not be easily recognized (Olson, Bates, & Bayles, 1984), and, as a label, has been used indiscriminately (Aase, Jones, & Clarren, 1995). The label FAE can provide access to services for some children; however, it can also prevent further evaluation for other potential causes for the child's problems. Some investigators recommend abandoning its use (Aase et al., 1995).

Studies of pregnant women who consume alcohol have revealed that they are also three times more likely than nondrinkers to smoke cigarettes (Coles et al., 1987). This increases the risk to the fetus, particularly for low birth weight and premature infants.

Cocaine and Methamphetamine Marijuana and cocaine are the illicit drugs used most frequently by pregnant women. Early reports on infants exposed to cocaine emphasized the high risk for developmental delay, physical problems, deficits in representational play, and deviant attachment patterns (Howard, 1989; Howard, Beckwith, Rodning, & Kropenske, 1989; Main & Solomon, 1986). Fortunately, recent studies present a somewhat more optimistic picture.

Prenatal cocaine use is definitely associated with low birth weight and decreased length and head circumference (Chasnoff, 1992; Zuckerman & Frank, 1994). Infants exposed to cocaine have neither an increase in the number of minor anomalies nor a birth defect syndrome. However, prenatal cocaine use occasionally has been associated with urogenital anomalies, intestinal atresia, congenital heart defects, limb reduction defects, and cerebral infarctions (Chasnoff, 1992). Cocaine causes vasoconstriction, which can result in disruption of the intrauterine or fetal blood vessels.

Infants exposed to cocaine may have low thresholds for overstimulation and suboptimal performance on the NBAS (Chasnoff, 1992). No significant differences have been found in the performance of children exposed to cocaine and children not exposed to cocaine on the Bayley Scales of Infant Development at 1 and 2 years of age or the Stanford-Binet Intelligence Scale (SBIS) at 3 years of age (Chasnoff et al., 1992; Griffith, Azuma, & Chasnoff, 1994). Children exposed to cocaine scored lower on the SBIS verbal reasoning, and about one third of the group showed delays in language development or problems with attention or self-regulation.

Cocaine and methamphetamine taken during the pregnancy appear to have similar effects on newborns (Dixon, 1989). In one study, 4-year-old children who had been exposed to methamphetamines in utero had slightly lower IQs than the control group, and more were rated as "problem children" (Billing, Eriksson, Steneroth, & Zetterström, 1985).

Infants of mothers who use drugs are at increased risk of abuse. In one study, 23% of the group of infants exposed to cocaine had been maltreated by 24 months of age compared to 4% of the control group (Wasserman & Leventhal, 1993). Physical abuse had occurred in 11% of the cocaine group, but in 2% of the controls. These findings emphasize the importance of providing safe environments and comprehensive family support services for these infants. Infants of mothers using drugs who receive early and regular prenatal care have improved outcomes (Edwards et al., 1994).

Heroin and Methadone Withdrawal symptoms are well known for newborns of mothers who use heroin or methadone. Their infants are also likely to have low birth weight and smaller head circumference. In one study, infants exposed to heroin or methadone in utero were developing within the normal range at 1 year of age, although both groups showed minor motor problems and poor attention span (Wilson, Desmond, & Wait, 1981). Wilson et al. (1981) has also reported that the cognitive performance of a group of children exposed to heroin varied widely over time, suggesting that, at least in part, the changes reflected changes in their home environment.

Marijuana In one study, 49% of women 18–25 years old reported having used marijuana (Richardson, Day, & McGauhey, 1993). Seventy percent of heavy users were still using marijuana during the third month of pregnancy, and 63% were still using at the end of pregnancy (Richardson et al., 1993). No consistent effects have been found for prenatal marijuana use on birth weight or length of gestation. In one study, newborns exposed to marijuana did have suboptimal performance on the NBAS with increased tremors and startles and poor visual habituation (Fried & Makin, 1987); however, other studies have not confirmed this (Fried, 1993). Long-term follow-up studies have generally demonstrated typical development through 5 to 6 years of age (Fried, 1993). In the Ottawa Prenatal Prospective Study, the children of heavy marijuana users scored lower on memory and verbal abilities at 48 months of age (Fried & Watkinson, 1990).

Cynthia

Cynthia had a different experience from Alice's. "I'd been fighting with my mother as long as I could remember. One of my girlfriends had a baby and it seemed like fun. I did drugs by the time I was 10. I started having sex at 11. School was a drag. When you have a baby, you're an adult. Nobody tells you what to do or when to do it. The kid was going to be my road to freedom and ticket to independence. So I quit school and had the kid. But being a mother is hard work. I sure didn't think it would be like this."

Cynthia had her first baby at 14, her second a year later. Neither of the fathers was a good candidate for marriage, being very young, unemployed, and still in school. During the second pregnancy she was using drugs again, mainly amphetamines and alcohol. She smoked quite heavily during both pregnancies and had no prenatal care. Her second child was born preterm with low birth weight and with serious problems. These included respiratory distress, anemia, hyperbilirubinemia, mild mental retardation, and cerebral palsy. "Jamie had to stay in the hospital intensive care nursery for 2 months. It meant I couldn't breast-feed him, which I wanted to do. I couldn't get up to see him very often because I don't have a car, and the buses are practically nonexistent in this town. Besides, I had to take care of Melissa. There's really no one to help me out. My mother and I barely speak to each other any more."

Cynthia manages to support herself and her two children with Aid to Families with Dependent Children (AFDC). Melissa is in kindergarten this year. Jamie is now 3 and attends a special education preschool for children with developmental delays. A bus picks him up three mornings a week and brings him home again. Every other week Cynthia goes with him and spends the morning helping out in the preschool. She enjoys these visits and is thinking about finishing school so she could get a full-time job in a school like Jamie's. "But it's hard to go back to school when you're nearly 19 years old and the oldest person in the class. Besides, what would I do with Melissa and Jamie? I'd sure like to have a job, though."

After Jamie was born Cynthia attended a program at her neighborhood church to try to get off drugs, saying she didn't want to ruin her children's lives. She has managed to quit taking amphetamines and has cut down on her drinking. She has also learned about birth control. "I know it's kinda late, but I'm taking birth control pills. I wish I'd known about it earlier. But then I guess I wouldn't have these two darling children. And I do love them, you know, even though it's hard raising them on my own."

Congenital and Perinatal Infections

The acronym TORCH has been applied to congenital infections: TO for *toxoplasmosis,* R for *rubella,* C for *cytomegalovirus* (CMV) and H for *herpes.* Syphilis also is a significant cause of congenital infections in certain populations, for example, women who use intravenous drugs.

The estimated incidence of congenital infection with *toxoplasmosis* is 1 per 1,000–10,000 live births (Guerina et al., 1994). Most infants with congenital toxoplasmosis are asymptomatic at birth. Routing neonatal screening for toxoplasmosis will identify infants with subclinical infections. There is now strong evidence that early treatment of the infant may reduce the severe ophthalmological and neurodevelopmental sequelae (Guerina et al., 1994)

Maternal rubella has been associated with multiple congenital malformations of the heart, eye, and ear. Among conditions seen in the infants of mothers who contract rubella are congenital heart disease, cataracts, and deafness. Infants prenatally exposed to rubella are also at risk for cerebral palsy. The infant contracts the rubella infection through the mother's placenta. The best prevention is to avoid maternal exposure to the rubella infection.

CMV continues to be the most common of the congenital infections. CMV belongs to the herpes virus group, which also includes herpes simplex virus, varicella-zoster virus (the chickenpox–shingles virus), and the Epstein-Barr virus (the virus that causes infectious mononucleosis). Nearly all adults have been infected with CMV by the time they are age 50 (Bale, Blackman, Murph, & Andersen, 1986).

Although nearly everyone eventually acquires CMV infection, usually in a mild form, pregnant women who previously have not been exposed to the virus (primary infection) are at particular risk. Infection during the first trimester can be devastating to the fetus. The incidence of symptomatic congenital CMV infection in newborns is approximately 1 per 1,000 live births (Gehrz, 1991). However, about 1% of apparently healthy newborns excrete CMV in their urine in the first weeks of life (Gehrz, 1991). Asymptomatic congenital infections that result from primary maternal infection result in significant sequelae in 10%–15% of cases (e.g., sensorineural hearing loss, neurodevelopmental delays). Recurrent infections have a much lower risk of transmission to the fetus and have no long-term sequelae (Gehrz, 1991).

Neonatal herpes simplex virus (HSV) is related to the CMV virus. HSV type 2 is sexually transmitted and can cause very serious problems in the neonate. It is contracted at birth as the neonate passes through a lower genital tract colonized with the virus. Birth by cesarean section is therefore recommended for mothers known to have cervical herpes infections. The effects of HSV can range from simple skin disease to encephalitis and serious neurological damage. Mortality rates have declined in recent years with antiviral drug therapy; however, infants who survive usually experience severe complications such as cerebral palsy, sensory impairment, or mental retardation (Blackman, Andersen, Healy, & Zehrbach, 1985).

Maternal *varicella* (chickenpox) infection in the first 20 weeks of gestation can also result in serious damage to the developing fetus (Enders, Miller, Cradock-Watson, Bolley, & Ridehalgh, 1994); however, the risk for fetal infection is small (Jones, Johnson, & Chambers, 1994). *Parvovirus B19* causes a flu-like illness in older children or adults. However, maternal infection can cause severe anemia in the fetus, birth defects, and fetal death. The risk for maternal infection and the risk of transmission to the fetus appear to be low (Guidozzi, Ballot, & Rothberg, 1994).

PERINATAL FACTORS

Risk factors associated with the perinatal period include medical factors during labor and delivery and those associated with prematurity or low birth weight. In this discussion, *term* and *birth weight* are defined using the criteria of the World

Health Organization. The full-term infant is one born between 37 and 41 weeks' gestation; the preterm infant is born at less than 37 weeks. Similarly, newborns weighing less than 2,500 grams (about 5.5 pounds) are labeled low birth weight. Very low birth weight infants are those weighing less than 1,500 grams (about 3.3 pounds).

Infants born before term are usually also low in birth weight. However, it is important to distinguish between those infants whose birth weight is close to what would be expected, given their early delivery date, and those whose weight is lower than would be expected. The latter group is labeled small for gestational age (SGA) and includes infants whose birth weight is 2 standard deviations below the mean for the gestational age (Bennett, 1987).

Perinatal Asphyxia

Perinatal asphyxia is due to an inadequate supply of oxygen to the brain of the fetus. It can occur antenatally or during labor and delivery and may be chronic or acute. It is manifested by a low Apgar score, irritability and exaggerated responses, or lethargy and low muscle tone or by the occurrence of severe, persistent seizures and coma. The term *hypoxic ischemic encephalopathy* (HIE) refers to the brain damage/dysfunction manifested in these infants. Various causes may be identified as problems with the placenta or umbilical cord or delivery problems, for example, a difficult vaginal delivery of a very large newborn.

Perinatal asphyxia affects both full-term and preterm infants and occurs in approximately 3–9 of every 1,000 births (Thompson, 1994). Usually, infants with evidence of mild HIE do well and infants with severe HIE do not (Robertson & Finer, 1993); they have a high rate of developmental delay and cerebral palsy. The outcome of infants with moderate HIE is more difficult to predict.

Prematurity

Infants born before 37 weeks' gestation are premature. Several methods may be used for calculating gestational age including the obstetric history, mother's self-report of the last menstrual period (LMP), the obstetric examination, and examination of the newborn. Use of only the LMP can be inaccurate. Prenatal ultrasound can be used to confirm the expected date of confinement (EDC). It has also become a valuable tool for the detection of birth defects and the monitoring of fetal growth. The Ballard exam of the newborn is commonly used to calculate the gestational age. It evaluates physical and neurological factors and is based on the assessment developed by Dubowitz and his colleagues (Dubowitz & Dubowitz, 1981; Dubowitz, Dubowitz, & Goldberg, 1970).

Low Birth Weight

Infants weighing less than 2,500 grams are considered to have low birth weight. Very low birth weight infants (VLBW) weigh less than 1,500 grams, and extremely low birth weight (ELBW) infants weigh less than 750 grams. ELBW infants are at high risk for neurodevelopmental sequelae (Hack et al., 1994). In a study of infants born at 25 weeks' gestational age, 79% (31 of 39) of the infants survived, and 69% avoided severe disabilities (Allen et al., 1993).

This category includes infants who are born prematurely with weight appropriate for gestational age (AGA) and infants who are undergrown for their gestational age or are SGA. A variety of factors may contribute to the poor fetal growth of SGA infants including maternal smoking or alcohol use, infection with CMV, placental insufficiency, a chromosomal disorder, or a birth defect syndrome. These infants are at significant risk for subsequent neurodevelopmental problems.

Intraventricular Hemorrhage and Periventricular Echodensities

Intraventricular hemorrhage (IVH) is a frequent finding on cranial ultrasound of premature infants but is rarely found in infants more than 34 weeks' gestational age (Mantovani & Powers, 1991). IVH is most often classified as follows: grade I, germinal matrix hemorrhage only; grade II, IVH without ventricular dilatation; grade III, IVH with ventricular dilatation; and grade IV, IVH with intraparenchymal extension (Papile, Burstein, & Koffer, 1978). Major sequelae are noted in approximately 20% of children with grade I or II hemorrhage (similar to infants of the same birth weight and gestational age without hemorrhage). However, 50%–90% of children with grade III or IV hemorrhage have major deficits at follow-up (Mantovani & Powers, 1991). The primary problems are cerebral palsy and developmental delay or mental retardation.

Periventricular echodensities (PVE) is another pattern of brain damage noted by cranial ultrasound in VLBW infants. PVE is believed to reflect periventricular leukomalacia that results from circulatory insufficiency. PVE that disappears after several weeks and is not associated with ventricular dilatation or cystic change is not likely to lead to significant sequelae (Mantovani & Powers, 1991). However, 90% of infants with PVE that is associated with large bilateral cysts (larger than 3 mm in diameter) in the parietal or occipital regions develop cerebral palsy (Pidcock, Graziana, Stanley, Mitchell, & Merton, 1990).

Respiratory Problems

Respiratory distress syndrome (RDS) is the most important medical problem of the premature infant (Boyle, 1993). Respiratory distress is cause by a lack of surfactant, a chemical that coats the air pockets (alveoli) of the lungs and prevents them from collapsing during normal breathing. Surfactant is not produced in sufficient quantities until approximately 34–36 weeks' gestation. Bronchopulmonary dysplasia (BPD) is the chronic lung disease that develops after the treatment of RDS in some infants.

The treatment of RDS may involve oxygen therapy, continuous positive airway pressure (CPAP), endotracheal intubation, and mechanical ventilation. High-frequency oscillatory ventilation and surfactant therapy have improved the treatment of RDS (Boyle, 1993; Gerdes et al., 1995; Ogawa et al., 1993). Extracorporeal membrane oxygenation (ECMO), or bypassing the lungs, has also been used for selected infants with pulmonary failure. The improvements in the treatment of RDS have not resulted in a change in the neurodevelopmental outcomes of survivors (Boyle, 1993). In a study of VLBW infants with BPD, no significant correlations were found between duration of mechanical ventilation or oxygen therapy and neurodevelopmental outcomes (Luchi, Bennett, & Jackson, 1991); however, IVH and PVE were closely correlated with poor cognitive outcome.

As many as 50% of all preterm newborns experience irregular respiratory patterns, characterized by prolonged pauses in the breathing cycle called *apnea.* Apnea results from an immature or damaged central nervous system. Damage may be due to IVH, infection, or metabolic disorder. Treatment consists of correcting the damaging condition if the etiology is known and, if it is not, the use of tactile stimulation, medication, or CPAP (Ensher & Clark, 1986). Often maturation of the central nervous system is the best solution to the problem of apnea.

Hyperbilirubinemia

Jaundice is the most prevalent problem that pediatricians confront in full-term and preterm newborns (Peabody & Lewis, 1985). Nearly all babies develop some degree of jaundice, and this is due to elevated levels of the chemical bilirubin in their bloodstream. Bilirubin is a yellow pigment that results from the breakdown of red blood cells.

There is a greater risk to premature and low birth weight infants from elevated bilirubin levels, particularly in combination with some medications, infection, and acidosis. This places the infant at risk for cerebral palsy and sensorineural hearing loss (Peabody & Lewis, 1985). Treatment consists of lowering the level of bilirubin in the bloodstream through phototherapy (exposure to fluorescent lights). In severe cases, blood exchange transfusions may be necessary. If brain damage occurs, the neurological disease is known as kernicterus or bilirubin encephalopathy.

Metabolic Problems

Infants with low birth weights and early delivery dates are more susceptible to biochemical and metabolic problems than full-term infants. For example, they may experience a deficiency in glucose, which is essential to brain metabolism. The resulting *hypoglycemia* or low blood sugar may cause brain damage if left untreated. Supplemental glucose and minerals can be provided in the diet of the preterm, usually intravenously, in the intensive care unit. In addition, early feedings immediately following birth have been found to reduce the risk of hypoglycemia (Batshaw & Perret, 1992). Other likely deficiencies include minerals such as calcium, potassium, sodium, phosphorus, iron, and magnesium. In the case of calcium, for example, it has been estimated that 50% of the calcium content of a full-term infant's bones is deposited during the last trimester (Ensher & Clark, 1986). This means that infants born prematurely have lower calcium stores and are susceptible to *hypocalcemia* (calcium deficiency).

Certain metabolic disorders can now be corrected by diet or therapy. Most developed countries now have screening programs for these disorders. The most common are phenylketonuria, galactosemia, and hypothyroidism. *Phenylketonuria* (PKU) is an autosomal recessive disorder resulting from a lack of the enzyme necessary to metabolize the amino acid phenylalanine. Without the enzyme, phenylalanine accumulates in the blood and brain following birth, causing brain damage and severe mental retardation. During the prenatal stage the excess phenylalanine passes across the placental membrane and is metabolized by the mother. Thus, infants with PKU appear normal at birth, only deteriorating without treatment during the first year. Treatment consists of omitting phenylalanine from the diet.

Galactosemia is another autosomal recessive metabolic disorder that manifests in the newborn period without treatment. Infants with galactosemia lack the enzyme necessary to metabolize galactose, a milk sugar, into glucose. Symptoms include an enlarged liver and jaundice, and affected infants are susceptible to cataracts, infections, and mental retardation. Treatment consists of restriction of the sugar lactose in the diet.

A third autosomal recessive disorder is *hypothyroidism*. In this case there is a deficiency in the production of the hormone thyroxine that causes the infant to be small and floppy in tone and that causes mental retardation. Treatment consisting of orally administered thyroxine has been available for more than a century. Hypothyroidism is one of the most commonly occurring metabolic disorders in children. Because of effective screening programs, these three metabolic disorders are now corrected at birth.

The Neonatal Intensive Care Unit Environment

Emphasis on nonmedical aspects of the neonatal intensive care unit (NICU) environment began as professionals from various fields studied the development of babies who had left the NICU. They expressed concern at the great differences between that environment and the one the infants had left too soon, namely, the womb. The NICU is characterized by high levels of noise (70–80 dB, with upper levels reaching to 120 dB, well above the usual conversational speech range of 30–60 dB), bright fluorescent lights unvaried day and night, and people moving about at all hours (Gaiter, 1985).

In addition, studies have shown that newborns receive a great amount of handling during the daily routine, averaging 40–70 contacts per day, reaching as high as 132 contacts for some infants. Furthermore, these contacts are fairly evenly distributed throughout the day and night (Peabody & Lewis, 1985). Contacts tend to come from professional staff rather than parents, despite the open visiting policies of some NICUs, and are usually frequent and of short duration (Gaiter, 1985; Gottfried, Hodgman, & Brown, 1984; Gottfried et al., 1981). The high frequency of handling means that infants in the NICU are allowed little time for uninterrupted sleep. The 29- to 32-week-old fetus sleeps approximately 80% of the time in utero, much of it in REM sleep. It has been postulated by some physiologists that uninterrupted sleep periods are necessary for neuronal maturation (Oswald, 1969). Therefore, infants in the NICU may experience sleep deprivation that affects their cognitive development.

These factors, together with the large amount of technological equipment required for life support, create an environment that is far removed from that of the dark, relatively peaceful womb. Absent also from the NICU is the soothing rocking motion experienced by the fetus as a result of the mother's normal movement and a form of physical stimulation. As Bennett (1987) stated,

> Despite the constant bombardment of visual, auditory, and tactile physical stimulations, the NICU appears to be a startling, nonsocial environment for newborns. Unfortunately, there is also frequently little or no organization, rhythmicity, or developmentally appropriate pattern of either physical or social stimulation incorporated into the treatment plan of newborn intensive care. (p. 89)

As a result of these concerns, practical guidelines have emerged to ensure more positive outcomes for the graduates of intensive care nurseries. They include these measures:

- Recognize the unusual physiological stresses being endured by the premature infant.
- Modify the environment to decrease overstimulation (specifically screen out grossly bombarding and unnecessary sensory stimuli such as handling during periods of quiet sleep).
- Introduce diurnal rhythms to promote behavioral organization.

- Gradually facilitate reciprocal visual, auditory, tactile, vestibular-kinesthetic, and social feedback during alert periods.
- Immediately terminate or alter approaches that produce avoidance responses.
- Educate and assist parents in reading, anticipating, and appropriately responding to their own infant's cues and signals, thus fostering and reinforcing parents' feelings of competence. (Bennett, 1987, p. 108)

The role of parents in the NICU has changed in recent years, due to realization by professional staff that a secure parent–infant attachment is beneficial to infant recovery and that parents' needs for interacting with their infant were not being taken into account in the NICU schedule (Als & Gilkerson, 1995; Gorski, 1983; Gottwald & Thurman, 1990; Minde, Shosenberg, Thompson, & Marton, 1983). Parents in many NICUs are more involved in care and handling of their infant than previously, and support groups are more widely available, including peer-oriented self-help groups (Minde et al., 1983) and groups led by a social worker or other member of professional staff.

The recent trends provide an interesting example of the extent of collaboration currently occurring in the care of infants at risk. The inclusion of educators, psychologists, and therapists on the infant team brings to the NICU a more global view of the infant's development, with concern for cognitive, communicative, physical, and social growth.

A review of 17 neonatal developmental intervention programs that were either infant focused, parent focused, or a combination of the two revealed that, although all the studies reported significantly greater gains by the experimental compared with the control infants, results were mixed and often contradictory (Bennett, 1987). The infant-focused studies were primarily hospital based and consisted of interventions that emphasized auditory, visual, vestibular, and tactile stimulation. The positive effects reported in these studies were generally very short-term, disappearing by 1 year of age. The most positive long-term effects were found in studies that continued the interventions at home following hospital discharge with considerable parent involvement. In fact, interventions that attempt to facilitate effective parenting by focusing on the parent–infant interaction and by incorporating a plan of extended home visitation appear to fit current child development models better than those that are exclusively infant focused. Such models are more useful to families and have a greater likelihood of achieving meaningful results (Bennett, 1987).

POSTNATAL FACTORS

Environmental factors that can affect the infant's risk status following birth include the quality of attachment between parent and infant, the availability of well-baby or hospital-based health care, the socioeconomic status of the family, and the adequacy of the family support network. Biological factors include failure to thrive, seizures, and other serious illnesses such as meningitis, accidental injuries, and nonaccidental injuries (child abuse). In addition, premature infants, especially infants with bronchopulmonary dysplasia, may have frequent respiratory infections. Respiratory synctial virus (RSV) infection can be particularly serious for infants with chronic lung disease. Failure to thrive and seizure disorders are discussed in Chapter 4.

Quality of Attachment

Attachment quality has been found to be a good predictor of both cognitive and social competence. Attachment measured at 13 and 24 months, for example, pre-

Jackie and Fred

Jackie and Fred are the parents of a preterm infant who weighed only 3¼ pounds at birth. Donald was born at 29 weeks' gestation, which means that he was 7 weeks early. He was born with several of the problems common to low birth weight infants, such as respiratory distress, apnea, jaundice, and a very weak suck. Jackie had a difficult labor and a pregnancy marked by infection during the third trimester. She had had excellent prenatal care from her family obstetrician, who decided to induce labor and deliver the baby by cesarean section. Despite labor difficulties, the delivery was uneventful, and the delivery room staff were optimistic about Donald's chances.

Following delivery, Donald was moved to an incubator in the intensive care unit where he was placed on a ventilator and treated with fluorescent lights for jaundice. He was fed through a tube inserted into his nasal cavity and then to his stomach. When attacks of apnea occurred, a NICU nurse would touch him to get him breathing again. Due to this treatment, Donald gradually gained strength, began to breathe without assistance, and began to drink from a bottle.

During these weeks, Jackie and Fred traveled every weekend from their ranch in southern Wyoming to the hospital to visit Donald. Because the ranch was nearly a 4-hour drive from the hospital, daily visits were impossible. But because Donald was their first child, they did not have the needs of other children to consider, and this made weekly visits possible. After Donald's suck became strong enough to take nourishment from a nipple, Jackie brought her refrigerated breast milk with her to the hospital each week, so that she could continue breast-feeding when Donald came home. In the meantime, the nursing staff bottle fed the breast milk to Donald during the week when Jackie could not be there.

The happy event—Donald's homecoming—occurred when he was 8 weeks old and weighed nearly 5 pounds. He was active, alert, eating, and sleeping well, and his respiratory problems seemed to be well under control. Fred and Jackie kept the crib in their own bedroom during the first months after Donald came home, and Jackie says that she hardly slept a wink at first. "I kept getting up to make sure he was breathing. The apnea attacks scared me so much." In fact, Donald did have two episodes of apnea at home, but Jackie and Fred had been instructed at the hospital how to rouse him to get him breathing again. When they realized they were capable of taking care of Donald's problems, both Fred and Jackie became more relaxed parents. "We know he's going to be slower developing than other babies," said Fred, "but we aren't in any hurry. He can take his time. He's already beginning to gain weight, and he's lost that ruddy color he had in the hospital. He's a great looking little guy!"

Jackie says that she is grateful for Fred's close support during and after the ordeal of Donald's birth. "I don't think I could have gone through it alone.

(continued)

(continued)

I don't know how some women do it. And I had the support of my parents and Fred's parents, too. You need all that support when your baby is born with problems and spends 2 months in the hospital. I feel very lucky."

dicted impulse inhibition, school performance, and social behaviors at age 6 (Olson et al., 1984). Attachment quality also predicted later problem-solving skills and social competence (Main & Cassidy, 1988). Research has identified certain factors that affect the quality of attachment between parent and infant (Belsky, Rovine, & Taylor, 1984). These include the infant's temperament, the mother's personality, and environmental influences such as the level of parenting skills, the family's social network, and the quality of the marriage.

Tronick, Ricks, and Cohn (1982) pointed out the necessity of a synchronous interaction between mother and infant to achieve a successful attachment. If either fails to perform, that is, if the infant fails to engage the mother or she fails to respond, a lack of synchrony may lead to a mismatch. Although mismatches can be repaired, it is often difficult to do so because they are due to rather stable factors such as temperament or personality. If the infant fails to engage the mother, other noninteractive behaviors are substituted in the infant's repertoire: gaze aversion, focus on objects instead of on mother, and self-regulatory behaviors such as fist in mouth when distressed.

Depressed mothers, according to Tronick et al. (1982), do not look at or play with their infants as much as other mothers do. Their infants look at and play with objects less than other infants do and look at their mothers less. The mismatched interaction causes the infant to withdraw from exploration of the external world; this in turn adversely affects the infant's development of cognitive, social, communicative, and motor skills.

Differences have been found in the attachment of infants born with disabilities when compared with abused or maltreated infants (Cicchetti & Schneider-Rosen, 1984; Gersten, Coster, Schneider-Rosen, Carlson, & Cicchetti, 1987). Babies with Down syndrome, for example, despite their low affect and passive temperament, which makes them difficult to rouse, are likely to be securely attached to their mothers. Cicchetti (1987) noted that, as a result of their secure attachment, babies with Down syndrome tend to perform language and other symbolic tasks at developmentally appropriate levels. Many also develop mastery, self-esteem, and trust at appropriate mental age levels.

Infants who are abused or maltreated are far less likely to develop secure attachments with their mothers. Cicchetti (1987) estimated that 70% of these infants are insecurely attached at 12, 18, and 24 months and that there is a continuity of maladaptation that leads to increasingly delayed development.

The preceding examples illustrate the growing interest in attachment theory as an important factor in child development. It is part of a more general interest in the interactions between child and parent that may facilitate or hinder optimal development. Study of the atypical or maltreated child has aided our understanding of the attachment process and has demonstrated that insecure attachments may have long-term consequences in behavior and performance.

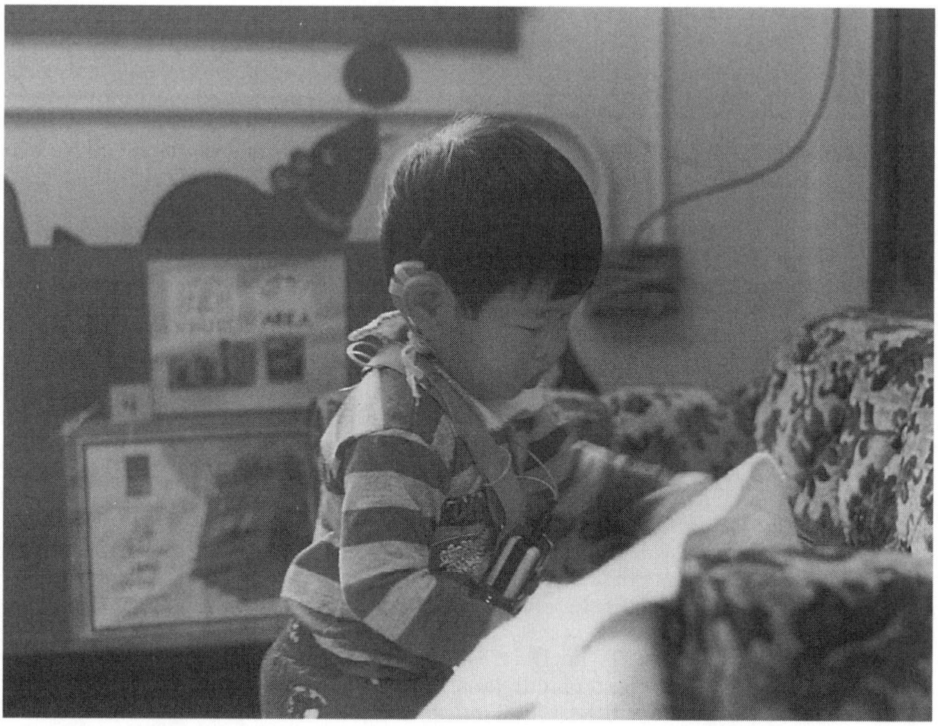

Nonaccidental Injuries

Evidence exists that children with developmental delay (Anastasiow, 1988) and infants of women who use drugs (Wasserman & Leventhal, 1993) are more at risk for child abuse and neglect than typically developing children. A common form of abuse found in young infants is the shaken baby syndrome. The caregiver shakes the baby by the shoulders in an attempt to stop the child from crying and may cause subarachnoid hemorrhage resulting in brain damage. Fragile infants are obviously at greater risk of injury from such treatment.

SUGGESTED READINGS

Batshaw, M.L., & Perret, Y.M. (1992). *Children with disabilities: A medical primer* (3rd ed.). Baltimore: Paul H. Brookes Publishing Co.

Greenspan, S.I., Weider, S., Lieberman, A., Norer, R., Lourie, R., & Robinson, M. (Eds.). (1987). *Infants in multirisk families: Case studies in preventive intervention.* Clinical Infant Report No. 3 of the National Center for Clinical Infant Programs. Madison, WI: International Universities Press.

Harel, S., & Anastasiow, N. (Eds.). (1985). *The at-risk infant: Psycho/socio/medical aspects.* Baltimore: Paul H. Brookes Publishing Co.

Osofsky, J.D. (Ed.). (1987). *Handbook of infant development* (2nd ed.). New York: John Wiley & Sons.

ZERO TO THREE monthly newsletter, National Center for Clinical Infant Programs, Washington, DC.

REFERENCES

Aase, J.M., Jones, K.L., & Clarren, S.K. (1995). Do we need the term "FAE"? *Pediatrics, 95*(3), 428–430.

Abrams, E.I., Matheson, P.B., Thomas, P.A., Thea, D.M., Krasinski, K., Lambert, G., Shaffer, N., Bamji, M., Hutson, D., Grimm, K., & the New York City Perinatal HIV Transmission Collaborative Study Group. (1995). Neonatal predictors of infection status and early death among 332 infants at risk of HIV-1 infection monitored prospectively from birth. *Pediatrics, 96*(3 Pt. 1), 451–458.

Allen, M.C., Donohue, P.K., & Dusman, A.E. (1993). The limit of viability—Neonatal outcome of infants born at 22 to 25 weeks' gestation. *New England Journal of Medicine, 329*(22), 1597–1601.

Als, H., & Gilkerson, L. (1995). Developmentally supportive care in the neonatal intensive care unit. *ZERO TO THREE, 15*(6), 1–10.

Anastasiow, N.J. (1988). Facilitating cognitive development. In E.D. Hibbs (Ed.), *Children and families: Studies in prevention and intervention.* Madison, WI: International Universities Press.

Bale, J.F., Blackman, J.A., Murph, J., & Andersen, R.D. (1986). Congenital cytomegalovirus infection. *American Journal of Diseases of Children, 140,* 128–131.

Batshaw, M.L., & Perret, Y.M. (1992). *Children with disabilities: A medical primer* (3rd ed.). Baltimore: Paul H. Brookes Publishing Co.

Becerra, J.E., Khoury, M.J., Cordero, J.F., & Erickson, J.D. (1990). Diabetes mellitus during pregnancy and the risks for specific birth defects: A population-based case-control study. *Pediatrics, 85*(1), 1–9.

Bee, H.L., Barnard, K.E., Eyres, S.J., Gray, C.A., Hammond, M.A., Spietz, A.L., Snyder, C., & Clark, B. (1982). Prediction of IQ and language skill from perinatal status, child performance, family characteristic, and mother–infant interaction. *Child Development, 53,* 1134–1156.

Belsky, J., Rovine, M., & Taylor, D. (1984). The Pennsylvania Infant and Family Development Project: III. The origins of individual differences in infant–mother attachment: Maternal and infant contributions. *Child Development, 55,* 718–795.

Bennett, F.C. (1987). Infants at biological risk. In M.J. Guralnick & F.C. Bennett (Eds.), *Effectiveness of early intervention for at-risk and handicapped children* (pp. 79–112). New York: Academic Press.

Billing, L., Eriksson, M., Steneroth, G., & Zetterström, R. (1985). Pre-school children of amphetamine-addicted mothers: I. Somatic and psychomotor development. *Acta Obstetricia et Gynecologica Scandinavica, 74,* 179–184.

Blackman, J.A., Andersen, R.D., Healy, A., & Zehrbach, R. (1985). Management of young children with recurrent herpes simplex skin lesions in special education programs. *Pediatric Infectious Disease, 4*(3), 221–224.

Boyle, R.J. (1993). Use of surfactant in premature infants: How it affects health and developmental outcomes. *Infants and Children, 6*(1), 21–25.

Brazelton, T.B. (1984). *Neonatal Behavioral Assessment Scale* (2nd ed.). Clinics in Developmental Medicine, No. 88. Philadelphia: J.B. Lippincott.

Broman, S.H., Nichols, P.L., & Kennedy, W.A. (1975). *Preschool IQ: Prenatal and early development correlates.* Hillsdale, NJ: Lawrence Erlbaum Associates.

Chasnoff, I.J. (1989). Drug use and women: Establishing a standard of care. *Annals of the New York Academy of Science, 562,* 208–210.

Chasnoff, I.J. (1992). Cocaine, pregnancy, and the growing child. *Current Problems in Pediatrics,* 302–321.

Chasnoff, I.J., Griffith, D.R., Freier, C., & Murray J. (1992). Cocaine/polydrug use in pregnancy: Two-year follow-up. *Pediatrics, 89*(2), 284–289.

Chomitz, V.R., Cheung, L.W., & Lieberman, E. (1995). The role of lifestyle in preventing low birth weight. *Future of Children, 5*(1), 121–138.

Cicchetti, D. (1987). Developmental psychopathology in infancy: Illustrations from the study of maltreated youngsters. *Journal of Consulting and Clinical Psychology, 55,* 837–845.

Cicchetti, D., & Schneider-Rosen, K. (1984). Theoretical and empirical considerations in the investigation of the relationship between affect and cognition. In C. Izard, J. Kagan, & R. Zajonc (Eds.), *Emotions, conditions and behavior* (pp. 366–406). New York: Cambridge University Press.

Cicchetti, D., & Toth, S. (1987). The application of a transactional risk model to intervention with multi-risk maltreating families. *ZERO TO THREE, 7,* 1–8.

Coles, C.D., Smith, I.E., Fernhoff, P.M., & Falek, A. (1985). Neonatal neurobehavioral characteristics as correlates of maternal alcohol use during gestation. *Alcoholism, 9,* 454–459.

Coles, C.D., Smith, I.E., Lancaster, J.S., & Falek, A. (1987). Persistence over the first month of neurobehavioral differences in infants exposed to alcohol prenatally. *Infant Behavior and Development, 10,* 23–37.

Committee on Substance Abuse and Committee on Children with Disabilities, American Academy of Pediatrics. (1993). Fetal alcohol syndrome and fetal alcohol effects. *Pediatrics, 91*(5), 1004–1006.

Connor, E.M., & Mofenson, L.M. (1995). Zidovudine for the reduction of perinatal human immunodeficiency virus transmission: Pediatric AIDS clinical trials group protocol 076—results and treatment recommendations. *Pediatric Infectious Disease Journal, 14*(6), 536–541.

Crawford, M.A., Doyle, W., Leaf, A., Leighfield, M., Ghebremeskel, K., & Phylactos, A. (1993). Nutrition and neurodevelopmental disorders. *Nutrition and Health, 9*(2), 81–97.

Culp, R.E., Appelbaum, M.I., Osofsky, J.D., & Levy, J.A. (1988). Adolescent and older mothers: Comparison between prenatal maternal variables and newborn interaction measures. *Infant Behavior and Development, 11*(3), 353–362.

Czeizel, A.E. (1995). Nutritional supplementation and prevention of congenital abnormalities. *Current Opinions in Obstetrics and Gynecology, 7*(2), 88–94.

Czeizel, A.E., & Dudás, I. (1992). Prevention of the first occurrence of neural-tube defects by periconceptional vitamin supplementation. *New England Journal of Medicine, 327*(26), 1832–1835.

Delgado-Escueta, A.V., & Janz, D. (1992). Consensus guidelines: Preconception counseling, management, and care of the pregnant woman with epilepsy. *Neurology, 42*(4 Suppl. 5), 149–160.

Dixon, S. (1989). Effects of transplacental exposure to cocaine and methamphetamine on the neonate. *Western Journal of Medicine, 150,* 436–442.

Drake, K., Youchah, J., & Damus, K. (1995). Human immunodeficiency virus disease in pregnancy. *Journal of the Association for Academic Minority Physicians, 6*(3), 105–111.

Dravet, C., Julian, C., Legras, C., Magaudda, A., Guerrini, R., Genton, P., Soulayrol, S., Giraud, N., Mesdjian, E., Trentin, G., Roger, J., & Ayone, S. (1992). Epilepsy, antiepileptic drugs, and malformations in children of women with epilepsy: A French prospective cohort study. *Neurology, 42*(4 Suppl. 5), 75–82.

Dubowitz, L.M., & Dubowitz, V. (1981). *The neurological assessment of the preterm and full-term newborn infant.* Philadelphia: J.B. Lippincott.

Dubowitz, L.M., Dubowitz, V., & Goldberg, C. (1970). Clinical assessment of gestational age in the newborn infant. *Journal of Pediatrics, 77,* 1–10.

Edwards, C.H., Knight, E.M., Johnson, A.A., Oyemade, U.J., Cole, O.J., Laryea, H., Westney, O.E., & Westney, L.S. (1994). Multiple factors as mediators of the reduced incidence of low birth weight in an urban clinic population. *Journal of Nutrition, 124*(Suppl. 6), 927S–935S.

Elliott, B., Brunham, R.C., Laga, M., Piot, P., Ndinya-Achola, J.O., Maitha, G., Cheang, M., & Plummer, F.A. (1990). Maternal gonococcal infection as a preventable risk factor for low birth weight. *Journal of Infectious Diseases, 161*(3), 531–536.

Enders, G., Miller, E., Cradock-Watson, J., Bolley, I., & Ridehalgh, M. (1994). Consequences of varicella and herpes zoster in pregnancy: Prospective study of 1739 cases. *Lancet, 343*(8912), 1548–1551.

Ensher, G.L., & Clark, D.A. (1986). *Newborns at risk: Medical care and psychoeducational intervention.* Rockville, MD: Aspen Publishers, Inc.

Eschenbach, D.A., Nugent, R.P., Rao, A.V., Cotch, M.F., Gibbs, R.S., Libscomb, K.A., Martin, D.H., Pastorek, J.G., Rettig, P.J., Carey, J.C., & the Vaginal Infections and Prematurity Study Group. (1991). A randomized placebo-controlled trial of erythromycin for the treatment of Ureaplasma urealyticum to prevent premature delivery. *American Journal of Obstetrics and Gynecology, 164*(3), 734–742.

Finnegan, L.P. (1985). Smoking and its effects on pregnancy and the newborn. In S. Harel & N. Anastasiow (Eds.), *The at-risk infant: Psycho/socio/medical aspects* (pp. 127–136). Baltimore: Paul H. Brookes Publishing Co.

Forman, R., Klein, J., Barks, J., Mehta, D., Greenwald, M., Einarson, T., & Koren, G. (1994). Prevalence of fetal exposure to cocaine in Toronto, 1990–1991. *Clinical and Investigative Medicine, 17*(3), 206–211.

Fraser, A.M., Brockert, J.E., & Ward, R.H. (1995). Association of young maternal age with adverse reproductive outcomes. *New England Journal of Medicine, 332*(17), 1161–1162.

Fried, P.A. (1993). Prenatal exposure to tobacco and marijuana: Effects during pregnancy, infancy, and early childhood. *Clinical Obstetrics and Gynecology, 36*(2), 319–337.
Fried, P.A., & Makin, J.E. (1987). Neonatal behavioral correlates of prenatal exposure to marijuana, cigarettes and alcohol in a low risk population. *Neurobehavioral Toxicology Teratology, 6*, 345.
Fried, P.A., & Watkinson, B. (1990). 36- and 48-month neurobehavioral follow-up of children prenatally exposed to marijuana, cigarettes, and alcohol. *Journal of Behavioral and Developmental Pediatrics, 11*, 49.
Gaiter, J.L. (1985). Nursery environments: The behavior and caregiving experiences of term and preterm newborns. In A.W. Gottfried & J.L. Gaiter (Eds.), *Infant stress under intensive care: Environmental neonatology* (pp. 55–81). Baltimore: University Park Press.
Galli, L., De Martino, M., Tovo, P.A., Gabiano, C., Zappa, M., Giaquinto, C., Tulisso, S., Vierucci, A., Guerra, M., Marchisio, P., & Italian Register for HIV Infections in Children. (1995). Onset of clinical signs in children with HIV-1 perinatal infection. *AIDS, 9*(5), 455–461.
Gehrz, R.C. (1991). Human cytomegalovirus: Biology and clinical perspectives. *Advances in Pediatrics, 38*, 203–219.
Gerdes, J., Gerdes, M., Beaumont, E., Cook, L., Dhanireddy, R., Kopleman, A., Jarret, R., & Long, W. (1995). Health and neurodevelopmental outcome at 1-year adjusted age in 508 infants weighing 700 to 1100 grams who received prophylaxis with one versus three doses of synthetic surfactant. *Journal of Pediatrics, 126*(5 Pt. 2), S26–S32.
Gersten, M., Coster, W., Schneider-Rosen, K., Carlson, V., & Cicchetti, D. (1987). The socioemotional bases of communicative functioning: Quality of attachment, language development and early maltreatment. In M. Lamb, A.L. Brown, & B. Rozoff (Eds.), *Advances in developmental psychology* (pp. 306–322). New York: Academic Press.
Gorski, P.A. (1983). Premature infant behavioral and physiological responses to caregiving interventions in the intensive care nursery. In J.D. Call, E. Galenson, & R.L. Tyson (Eds.), *Frontiers in infant psychiatry* (pp. 256–263). New York: Basic Books.
Gosselink, C.A., Ekwo, E.E., Woolson, R.F., Moawad, A., & Long, C.R. (1993). Adequacy of prenatal care and risk of preterm rupture of amniotic sac membranes. *Acta Obstetricia et Gynecologica Scandinavica, 72*(6), 443–449.
Gottfried, A.W., Hodgman, J.E., & Brown, K.W. (1984). How intensive is newborn intensive care? An environmental analysis. *Pediatrics, 72*, 198–202.
Gottfried, A.W., Wallace-Lande, P., Sherman-Brown, S., King, J., Coen, C., & Hodgman, J.E. (1981). Physical and social environment of newborn infants in special care units. *Science, 214*, 637–675.
Gottwald, S.R., & Thurman, S.K. (1990). Parent–infant interaction in neonatal intensive care units: Implications for research and service delivery. *Infants and Young Children, 2*(3), 1–10.
Griffith, D.R., Azuma, S.D., & Chasnoff, I.J. (1994). Three-year outcome of children exposed prenatally to drugs. *Journal of the American Academy of Child and Adolescent Psychiatry, 33*(1), 20–27.
Guerina, N.G., Hsu, H.W., Meissner, H.C., Maguire, J.H., Lynfield, R., Stechenberg, B., Abroms, I., Pasternack, M.S., Hoff, R., Eaton, R.B., & the New England Regional Toxoplasma Working Group. (1994). Neonatal serologic screening and early treatment for congenital toxoplasma gondii infection. *New England Journal of Medicine, 330*(26), 1858–1863.
Guidozzi, F., Ballot, D., & Rothberg, A.D. (1994). Human B19 parvovirus infection in an obstetric population: A prospective study determining fetal outcome. *Journal of Reproductive Medicine, 39*(1), 36–38.
Guyer, B., Strobino, D.M., Ventura, S.J., & Singh, G.K. (1995). Annual summary of vital statistics—1994. *Pediatrics, 92*(6), 1029–1039.
Hack, M., Taylor, G., Klein, N., Eiben, R., Schatschneider, C., & Merguri-Minich, N. (1994). School-age outcomes in children with birth weights under 750 g. *New England Journal of Medicine, 331*(12), 753–759.
Hoernle, E.H., & Reid, T.E. (1995). Human immunodeficiency virus infection in children. *American Journal of Health System Pharmacy, 52*(9), 961–979.
Holmes, D.L., Reich, J.N., & Pasternak, J.F. (1984). *The development of infants born at risk.* Hillsdale, NJ: Lawrence Erlbaum Associates.

Howard, J. (1989, February). *Developmental patterns for infants prenatally exposed to drugs.* Presentation at Perinatal Substance Abuse Educational Forum, California Legislative Ways and Means Committee, Sacramento.

Howard, J., Beckwith, L., Rodning, C., & Kropenske, V. (1989). The development of young children of substance-abusing parents: Insights from seven years of intervention and research. *ZERO TO THREE, 9*(5), 8–12.

Jacobson, J.L., Jacobson, S.W., & Sokol, R.J. (1994). Effects of prenatal exposure to alcohol, smoking and illicit drugs on postpartum somatic growth. *Alcoholism, Clinical and Experimental Research, 18*(2), 317–323.

Jones, K.L., Johnson, K.A., & Chambers, C.D. (1994). Offspring of women infected with varicella during pregnancy: A prospective study. *Teratology, 49*(1), 29–32.

Jones, K.L., Smith, D.W., Ulleland, L., & Streissguth, A.P. (1973). Recognition of the fetal alcohol syndrome in early infancy. *Lancet, 2,* 99–100.

Keogh, B.K., & Kopp, C.B. (1978). From assessment to intervention: An elusive bridge. In F.D. Minifie & L.L. Lloyd (Eds.), *Communicative and cognitive abilities—Early behavioral assessment* (pp. 523–547). Baltimore: University Park Press.

Kliegman, R.M., Madura, D., Kiwi, R., Eisenberg, I., & Yamashita, T. (1994). Relation of maternal cocaine use to the risks of prematurity and low birth weight. *Journal of Pediatrics, 124*(5 Pt. 1), 731–733.

Kotelchuck, M. (1994). The adequacy of prenatal care utilization index: Its U.S. distribution and association with low birth weight. *American Journal of Public Health, 84*(9), 1486–1489.

Littman, G., & Parmalee, A.H. (1978). Medical correlates of infant development. *Pediatrics, 61,* 470–474.

Luchi, J.M., Bennett, F.C., & Jackson, J.C. (1991). Predictors of neurodevelopmental outcome following bronchopulmonary dysplasia. *American Journal of Diseases of Children, 145*(7), 813–817.

Main, M., & Cassidy, J. (1988). Categories of response to reunion with the parent at age 6: Predictable from infant attachment classifications and stable over a 1-month period. *Developmental Psychology, 24,* 15–26.

Main, M., & Solomon, J. (1986). Discovery of an insecure-disorganized/disoriented attachment pattern. In T.B. Brazelton & M.W. Yogman (Eds.), *Affective development in infancy* (pp. 95–124). Norwood, NJ: Ablex.

Mantovani, J.F., & Powers, J. (1991). Brain injury in premature infants: Patterns on cranial ultrasound, their relationship to outcome, and the role of developmental intervention in the NICU. *Infants and Young Children, 4*(2), 20–32.

Maternal hepatitis B screening practices—California, Connecticut, Kansas and United States, 1992–1993. (1994). *Morbidity and Mortality Weekly Report, 43*(17), 311, 317–320.

Matheson, P.B., Abrams, E.J., Thomas, P.A., Hern'an, M.A., Thea, D.M., Lambert, G., Krasinski, K., Bamji, M., Rogers, M.F., Heagarty, M, & the New York City Perinatal HIV Transmission Collaborative Study Group. (1995). Efficacy of antenatal zidovudine in reducing perinatal transmission of human immunodeficiency virus type 1. *Journal of Infectious Diseases, 172*(2), 353–358.

McCaw-Binns, A., La Grenade, J., & Ashley, D. (1995). Under-users of antenatal care: A comparison of non-attenders and late attenders for antenatal care, with early attenders. *Social Science and Medicine, 40*(7), 1003–1012.

McGregor, J.A., French, J.I., Jones, W., Milligan, K., McKinney, P.J., Patterson, E., & Parker, R. (1994). Bacterial vaginosis is associated with prematurity and vaginal fluid mucinase and sialidase: Results of a controlled trial of topical clindamycin cream. *American Journal of Obstetrics and Gynecology, 170*(4), 1048–1060.

Miller, G. (1989). *Giving children a chance: The case for more effective neonatal policies.* Lanham, MD: University Press of America.

Mills, J.L., Graubard, B.I., Harley, E.E., Rhoads, G.G., & Berends, H.W. (1984). Maternal alcohol consumption and birth weight: How much drinking in pregnancy is safe? *Journal of the American Medical Association, 252,* 1875–1879.

Minde, K., Shosenberg, N., Thompson, J., & Marton, P. (1983). Self-help groups in a premature nursery: Follow-up at one year. In J.D. Call, E. Galenson, & R.L. Tyson (Eds.), *Frontiers in infant psychiatry* (pp. 363–378). New York: Basic Books.

Much, D.H., & Yeh, S.Y. (1991). Prevalence of Chlamydia trachomatis infection in pregnant patients. *Public Health Reports, 106*(5), 490–493.

Muscati, S.K., Gray-McDonald, K., & Newson, E.E. (1994). Interaction of smoking and maternal weight status in influencing infant size. *Canadian Journal of Public Health, 85*(6), 407–412.

Ogawa, Y., Miyasaka, Kawano, T., Imura, S., Inukai, K., Okauyama, K., Oguchi, K., Togari, H., Nishida, H., & Mishina, J. (1993). A multicenter randomized trial of high frequency oscillatory ventilation as compared with conventional mechanical ventilation in preterm infants with respiratory failure. *Early Human Development, 32*(1), 1–10.

Oleske, J.M. (1984). The many needs of the HIV-infected child. *Hospital Practice, Hospital Edition, 29*(9), 63–69.

Olson, S.L., Bates, J.E., & Bayles, K. (1984). Mother-infant interaction and the development of individual differences in children's cognitive competence. *Developmental Psychology, 20,* 166–179.

Oswald, I. (1969). Human brain protein, drugs and dreams. *Nature, 233,* 893.

Paccagnini, S., Principi, N., Massironi, E., Tanzi, E., Romano, L.,, Muggiasca, M.L., Ragni, M.C., & Salvaggio, L. (1995). Perinatal transmission and manifestation of hepatitis C virus infection in a high risk population. *Pediatric Infectious Desease Journal, 14*(3), 195–196.

Papile, L., Burstein, R., & Koffer, H. (1978). Incidence and evolution of subependymal hemorrhage: A study of infants with birth weight less than 1500 grams. *Journal of Pediatrics, 92,* 529–534.

Peabody, J.L., & Lewis, K. (1985). Consequences of newborn intensive care. In A.W. Gottfried & J.L. Gaiter (Eds.), *Infant stress under intensive care: Environmental neonatology* (pp. 199–226). Baltimore: University Park Press.

Peckham, C., & Gibb, D. (1995). Mother-to-child transmission of the human immunodeficiency virus. *New England Journal of Medicine, 333*(5), 298–302.

Pidock, F.S., Graziana, L.J., Stanley, C., Mitchell, D.G., & Merton, D. (1990). Neurosonographic features of periventricular echodensities associated with cerebral palsy in preterm infants. *Journal of Pediatrics, 116*(3), 417–422.

Ramey, C.T., Stedman, D.J., Borders-Patterson, A., & Mengel, W. (1978). Predicting school failure from information available at birth. *American Journal of Mental Deficiency, 82*(6), 525–534.

Ramos-Arroyo, M.A., Rodriguez-Pinilla, E., Cordero, J.F. (1992). Maternal diabetes: The risk for specific birth defects. *European Journal of Epidemiology, 8*(4), 503–508.

Recommendations for the use of folic acid to reduce the number of cases of spina bifida and other neural tube defects. [Review] (1992, September). *Morbidity and Mortality Weekly Report, 41*(RR-14), 1–7.

Reece, E.A, & Homko, C.J. (1993). Diabetes-related complications of pregnancy. *Journal of the National Medical Association, 85*(7), 537–545.

Resti, M., Azzari, C., Lega, L., Rossi, M.E., Zammarchi, E., Novembre, E., & Vierucci, A. (1995). Mother-to-infant transmission of hepatitis C virus. *Acta Paediatrica, 84*(3), 251–255.

Richardson, G.A., Day, N.L., & McGauhey, P.J. (1993). The impact of prenatal marijuana and cocaine use on the infant and child. *Clinical Obstetrics and Gynecology, 36*(2), 302–318.

Robertson, C.M., & Finer, N.N. (1993). Long-term follow-up of term neonates with perinatal asphyxia. *Clinics in Perinatology, 20*(2), 483–500.

Rossetti, L.M. (1986). *High risk infants: Identification, assessment, and intervention.* London: Taylor & Francis.

Sameroff, A.J. (1989). Principles of development and psychopathology. In A.J. Sameroff & R.N. Emde (Eds.), *Relationship disturbances in early childhood: A developmental approach.* New York: Basic Books.

Sameroff, A., & Chandler, M. (1975). Reproductive risk and the continuum of caretaking causality. In F.D. Horowitz, M. Hetherington, S. Scarr-Salapatek, & M. Siegel (Eds.), *Review of child development research* (Vol. 4, pp. 187–244). Chicago: University of Chicago Press.

Sargent, R.G., Schulken, E.D., Kemper, K.A., & Hussey, J.A. (1994, Winter). Black and white adolescent females' prepregnancy nutrition status. *Adolescence, 29*(116), 845–858.

Scholl, T.O., Hediger, M.L., & Belsky, D.H. (1994). Prenatal care and maternal health during adolescent pregnancy: A review and meta-analysis. *Journal of Adolescent Health, 15*(6), 444–456.

Shaywitz, S.E., Cohen, D.J., & Shaywitz, B.A. (1978). The expanded fetal alcohol syndrome (EFAS): Behavioral and learning deficits in children with normal intelligence. *Pediatric Research, 12,* 375.

Siegel, L. (1985). Biological and environmental variables as predictors of intellectual functioning at 6 years of age. In S. Harel & N.J. Anastasiow (Eds.), *The at-risk infant: Psycho/socio/medical aspects* (pp. 65–73). Baltimore: Paul H. Brookes Publishing Co.

Simms, J., & Duff, P. (1993). Viral hepatitis in pregnancy. *Seminars in Perinatology, 17*(6), 384–393.

Singer, L.T., Yamashita, T.S., Hawkins, S., Cairns, D., Baley, J., & Kliegman, R. (1994). Increased incidence of intraventricular hemorrhage and developmental delay in cocaine-exposed, very low birth weight infants. *Journal of Pediatrics, 124*(5 Pt. 1), 767–771.

Snyder-McLean, L. (1986). Foreword. In L.M. Rossetti (Ed.), *High risk infants: Identification, assessment and intervention* (pp. xi–xiii). London: Taylor & Francis.

Streissguth, A.P., Martin, D.C., Barr, H.M., & Sandman, B. (1984). Intrauterine alcohol and nicotine exposure: Attention and reaction time in 4-year-old children. *Developmental Psychology, 20,* 533–541.

Temmerman, M., Chomba, E.N., Ndinya-Achola, J., Plummer, F.A., Coppens, M., & Piot, P. (1994). Maternal human immunodeficiency virus-1 infection and pregnancy outcome. *Obstetrics and Gynecology, 83*(4), 495–501.

Thompson, D.G. (1994). Consequences of perinatal asphyxia. *AACN Clinical Issues, 5*(3), 242–245.

Thurman, S.K., & Widerstrom, A.H. (1990). *Infants and young children with special needs: A developmental and ecological approach.* Baltimore: Paul H. Brookes Publishing Co.

Tronick, E., Ricks, M., & Cohn, J. (1982). Maternal and infant affective exchange: Patterns of adaptation. In T. Fields & A . Fogel (Eds.), *Emotion and interaction: Normal and high-risk infants* (pp. 83–100). Hillsdale, NJ: Lawrence Erlbaum Associates.

Vega, W.A., Kolody, B., Hwang, J., & Noble, A. (1993). Prevalence and magnitude of perinatal substance exposures in California. *New England Journal of Medicine, 329*(12), 850–854.

Wald, N., Sneddon, J., Densem, J., Frost, C., & Stone, R. (MRC Vitamin Study Research Group). (1991). Prevention of neural tube defects: Results of the Medical Research Council Vitamin Study. *The Lancet, 338*(8760), 131–137.

Wasserman, D.R., & Leventhal, J.M. (1993). Maltreatment of children born to cocaine-dependent mothers. *American Journal of Diseases of Children, 147,* 1324–1328.

Wilson, G.S. (1989). Clinical studies of infants and children exposed prenatally to heroin. *Annals of the New York Academy of Science, 562,* 183–194.

Wilson, G.S., Desmond, M.M., & Wait, R.B. (1981). Follow-up of methadone-treated and untreated narcotic-dependent women and their infants: Health, developmental, and social implications. *Journal of Pediatrics, 98,* 716–722.

Working Group on Mother-to-Child Transmission of HIV. (1995). Rates of mother-to-child transmission of HIV-1 in Africa, America, and Europe: Results from 13 perinatal studies. *Journal of Acquired Immune Deficiency Syndromes and Human Retrovirology, 8*(5), 506–510.

Zuckerman, B., & Frank, D.A. (1994). Prenatal cocaine exposure: Nine years later. *Journal of Pediatrics, 124,* 731–733.

3 ACTIVITIES

1. Make a chart to summarize the primary risk factors described in this chapter. Make three columns in your chart and label the columns *Prenatal Factors, Perinatal Factors,* and *Postnatal Factors.* List each risk factor under the proper heading. Distinguish between biological risk factors and environmental risk factors.

2. Start a collection of newspaper articles dealing with risk factors in newborns. Include reports of research findings, new drug treatment plans, availability of prenatal care, and other timely topics related to infants at risk.

3. Find out about the availability in your community of health services and treatment facilities for pregnant women addicted to alcohol or other drugs, for low-income pregnant women, and for pregnant teenage girls. If there is a shortage of services, what might you do to advocate for better funding/availability of these services?

CHAPTER 4

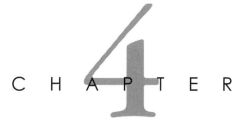

Developmental Disorders in Infancy

Robert E. Nickel and Anne H. Widerstrom

Objectives

- To understand the various genetic and developmental disorders that can occur in young infants, including
  - a. Genetic and chromosomal disorders
  - b. Seizures and seizure disorders
  - c. Hearing and visual disorders, including deafness and blindness
  - d. Neuromotor impairments, such as cerebral palsy or spina bifida
  - e. Mental retardation and autism
  - f. Health problems associated with each of these disorders
- To understand the etiologies of and most current treatments for these genetic and developmental disorders.

This chapter focuses on the concerns and issues in the treatment of infants with disabilities. Genetic and chromosomal disorders, sensory disorders, neuromotor impairments (cerebral palsy and spina bifida), developmental delay and mental retardation, and autism are discussed. Infants with genetic or developmental disorders may experience one or more health problems; for example, a child with cerebral palsy may have associated seizures, failure to thrive (FTT), and developmental delay. The following health problems are reviewed briefly: FTT, oral-motor dysfunction, gastroesophageal reflux, and seizures.

The information contained in this chapter represents important background knowledge for all members of the multidisciplinary team. Although some of it may seem to be specifically the concern of health professionals, psychologists, or physical therapists, it is important that the infant's developmental problems be understood by all team members who provide intervention and that these problems be taken into account when planning the individualized family service plan (IFSP). Sharing developmental and health-related information freely among team members can facilitate the creation of meaningful transdisciplinary team interactions, from which team members and clients alike can benefit.

BIRTH DEFECTS: GENETIC AND CHROMOSOMAL DISORDERS

Major birth defects are diagnosed in about 3%–4% of infants by age 1 (Mili, Edmonds, Khoury, & McClearn, 1991). The incidence of birth defects is closely associated with birth weight. In one study, 16.2% of newborns weighing <1,500 grams had birth defects, yet only 3.2% of newborns weighing 2,500–3,999 grams had birth defects (Mili et al., 1991). Birth defects are now the leading cause of infant mortality (Waitzman, Romano, & Scheffler, 1994).

Birth defects can be caused by teratogens (e.g., alcohol), genetic disorders (e.g., X-linked hydrocephalus), and chromosomal disorders (e.g., Down syndrome). Birth defects can be part of a syndrome that is defined as a recognizable pattern of anomalies that have a known cause or are believed to be causally related (Opitz, 1994). Unfortunately, the cause of some congenital defects is still unknown and may be considered "accidental."

Genetic Disorders

Genes are the basic unit of inheritance. They code for the production of proteins and enzymes and regulate the rate of synthesis of these proteins and enzymes that results in the infant's physical characteristics and biochemical make-up. Genes are made up of nucleotide base pairs, the building blocks of deoxyribonucleic acid (DNA). The human genome contains about 3×10^9 base pairs and an estimated 40,000–100,000 genes (Craig, 1994). Genes are arranged linearly along chromosomes, and each has a particular location on the chromosome.

Each human cell except for the ovum (mother) and the sperm (father) contains 23 pairs or 46 chromosomes (Figure 4.1). One of each pair is from the mother and one from the father. Twenty-two pairs are identical in males and females; these chromosomes are called *autosomes*. The 23rd pair, known as the sex chromosomes, determine the child's sex. This pair consists of two X chromosomes in the female and an X and a Y chromosome in the male. The X chromosome is about three times as large as the Y (Figure 4.1). If the father's chromosomal contribution includes an X chromosome, the infant will be female; if he donates a Y chromosome, the infant will be male. Because the mother can only contribute an X chromosome, the child's sex is determined by the father.

Classically, genetic disorders are caused by an alteration (mutation) in the chemical make-up of a single gene or gene pair. There are four types of Mendelian genetic disorders, depending on whether the gene is located on an autosome or on

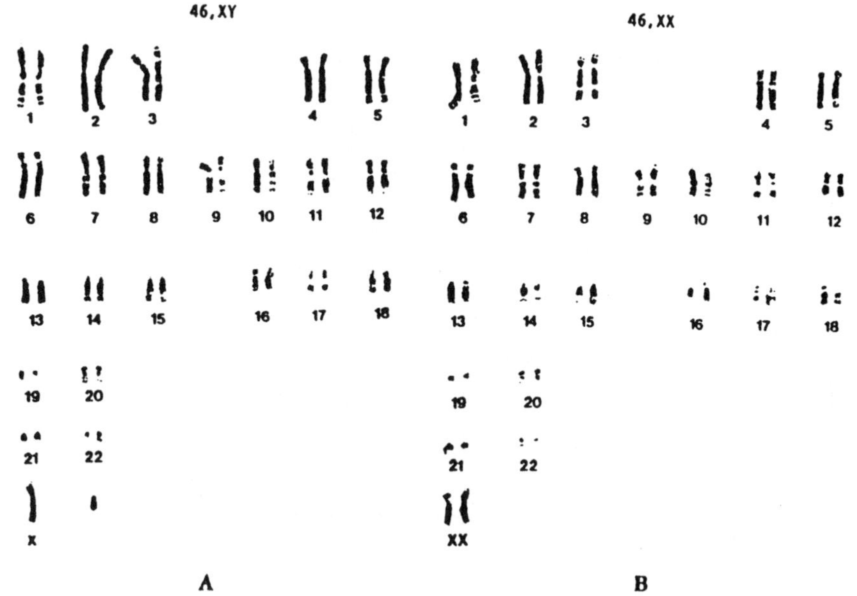

Figure 4.1. Normal chromosome complements: male (A) and female (B). (From Thompson, E.J. [1989]. A genetics primer for early service providers. *Infants and Young Children,* 2[1], p. 39; reprinted by permission, © 1989, Aspen Publishers, Inc.)

the sex chromosome, and whether the gene is dominant or recessive. The four types are known as autosomal dominant, autosomal recessive, X-linked recessive, and X-linked dominant (Figure 4.2). In general, autosomal disorders affect males and females in equal numbers, because the genetic material on the chromosomes is identical. However, X-linked disorders occur with differing frequencies in males and females and fewer X-linked disorders have been identified than autosomal disorders.

Autosomal Dominant Disorders Autosomal dominant disorders are caused by a single altered gene on one of the autosomes. If only one parent carries the gene, there is a 50% risk that it will be passed to the affected person's offspring. Autosomal dominant conditions can be variable in their expression. A parent may show only a few signs of the disorder while the child manifests severe problems. In addition, some cases of autosomal dominant disorders are the result of new mutations. There is also evidence that new dominant mutations may be associated with older paternal age (Skinner, 1990). Two commonly known examples are tuberous sclerosis and neurofibromatosis.

Tuberous sclerosis (TS) is an autosomal dominant disorder with an incidence of approximately 1 per 15,000 in the general population (Al-Gazali et al., 1989). The majority of cases represent new mutations and there can be marked variability in expression in a family. An infant may have severe developmental delay, seizures, brain calcifications, and hypopigmented (white) spots and other characteristic skin findings. The parent may only show a few of the skin lesions.

Neurofibromatosis type 1 (NF-1) is also an autosomal dominant disorder, with 50% of cases representing new mutations and significant variability of expression in affected families (Hofman, Harris, Bryan, & Denckla, 1994). The incidence is at least 1 per 3,000 (Listernick & Charrow, 1990). The characteristic findings include café au

Inheritance Pattern	Characteristics	Examples
Autosomal dominant 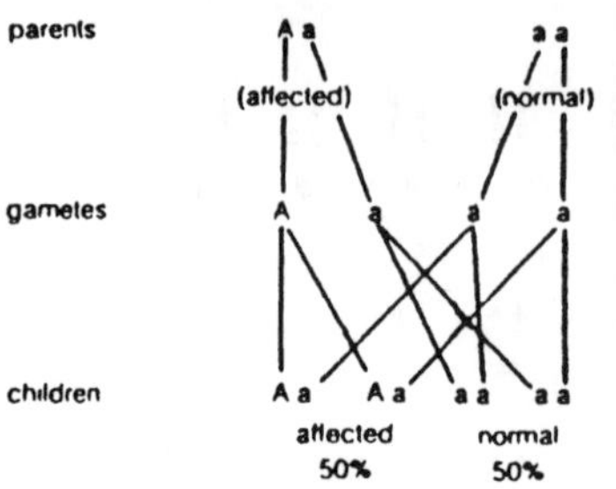	Disorders are caused by a single altered gene on one of the autosomes Either parent may have the gene, or the disorder may be due to a new gene alteration (mutation) If one parent is affected, there is a 50 percent risk of having an affected child (male or female) with each pregnancy	Achondroplasia Huntington disease Tuberous sclerosis Neurofibromatosis Stickler syndrome Myotonic dystrophy
Autosomal recessive 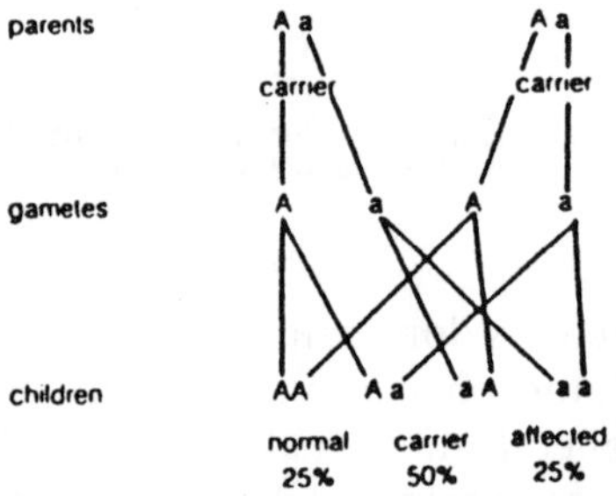	Disorders are caused by a pair of altered genes on the autosomes Both parents are carriers of the altered gene (though they are clinically normal) When both parents are carriers, there is a 25 percent risk of having an affected child (male or female) with each pregnancy	Cystic fibrosis Galactosemia Limb-girdle muscular dystrophy Maple syrup urine disease PKU Sickle cell anemia Tay-Sachs disease
X-linked recessive 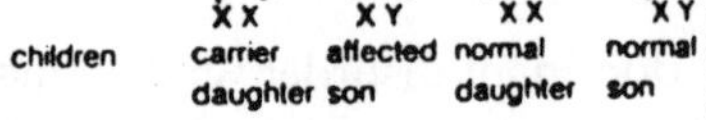	Either parent may have the gene present on the X-chromosome Since females have two X-chromosomes, in order to be affected they must have a pair of altered genes If a woman has an altered gene on only one X-chromosome, she is a carrier (usually not affected) and has a 25 percent risk of having an affected son	Duchenne and Becker muscular dystrophies Hemophilia Hunter syndrome Color blindness Lesch-Nyhan syndrome

(continued)

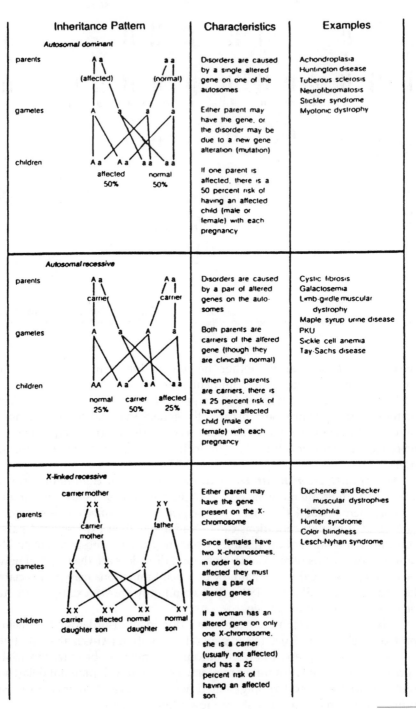

Figure 4.2. Types of single-gene disorders. (From Thompson, E.J. [1989]. A genetics primer for early service providers. *Infants and Young Children,* 2[1], pp. 42–43; reprinted by permission, © 1989, Aspen Publishers, Inc.)

Figure 4.2. *(continued)*

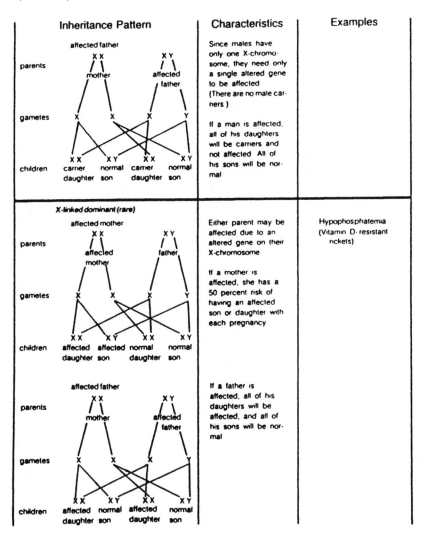

Inheritance Pattern	Characteristics	Examples
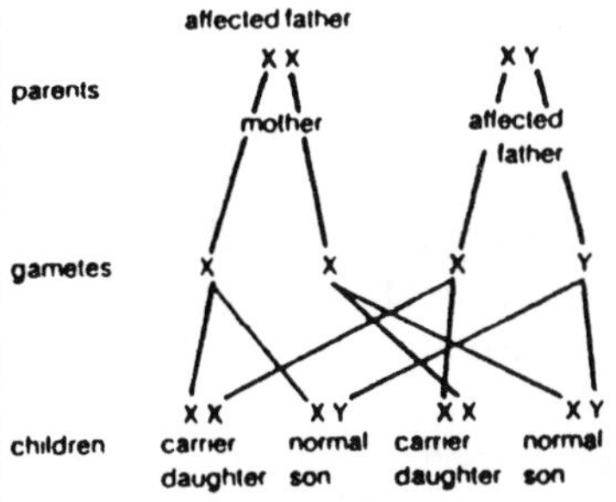	Since males have only one X-chromosome, they need only a single altered gene to be affected (There are no male carriers.) If a man is affected, all of his daughters will be carriers and not affected. All of his sons will be normal	
X-linked dominant (rare) 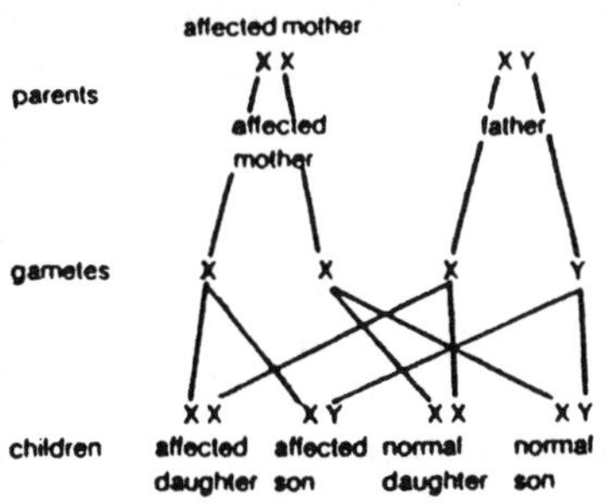	Either parent may be affected due to an altered gene on their X-chromosome. If a mother is affected, she has a 50 percent risk of having an affected son or daughter with each pregnancy	Hypophosphatemia (Vitamin D-resistant rickets)
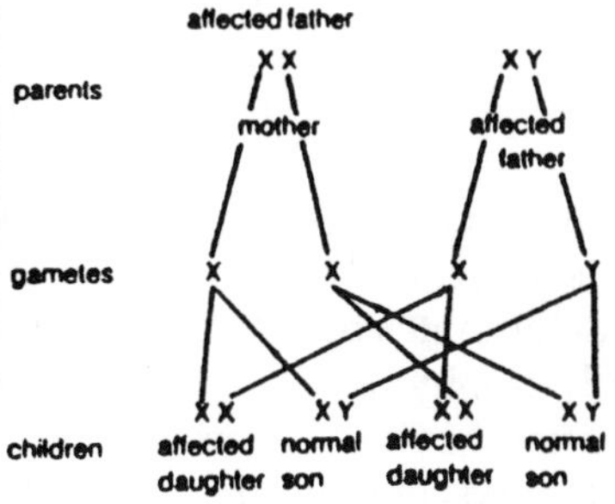	If a father is affected, all of his daughters will be affected, and all of his sons will be normal	

lait spots (irregular, brown spots) on the skin and neurofibromas (small growths) along peripheral nerves. Children with NF-1 have significantly lower IQ and larger head sizes than unaffected siblings (Hofman et al., 1994). They have specific problems with written language and reading. The cranial MRI scan can show a number of small areas of "hyperintensity" that correlate with the child's IQ and less well with motor problems (Hofman et al., 1994). Uncommon but serious problems include plexiform neuromas (large growths that can be disfiguring) and optic gliomas (growths on the optic nerve).

Autosomal Recessive Disorders Autosomal recessive disorders occur when both parents pass the affected gene to their offspring. When both parents are carriers, the risk is 25% of passing the disorder to each offspring. As of the mid-1990s, there are approximately 1,500 known or suspected autosomal recessive disorders (McKusick, 1988), including phenylketonuria and galactosemia.

Phenylketonuria (PKU) is an autosomal recessive metabolic disorder resulting from a lack of the enzyme necessary to break down the amino acid phenylalanine. Without this enzyme, phenylalanine accumulates in the blood and brain, causing brain damage and severe cognitive disabilities. Before birth, the excess phenylalanine from the fetus passes across the placental membrane, where it is metabolized by the normal maternal enzyme. Treatment for PKU consists of a diet with restricted amounts of phenylalanine and limits on high-protein foods such as meat, cheese, and poultry. This disease can be identified through blood and urine tests at birth. This neonatal screening procedure has been available since the 1960s and is now required in every state. As a result, mental retardation from PKU is extremely rare (Thurman & Widerstrom, 1990).

Galactosemia is an autosomal recessive metabolic disorder that is manifested in the newborn resulting in FTT, vomiting, jaundice, and an enlarged liver. Infants with galactosemia lack the enzyme necessary to metabolize galactose, a milk sugar, into glucose. If untreated, they are susceptible to mental retardation, cataracts, and various infections. Newborns are now routinely screened for galactosemia. The cornerstone of treatment is provision of a galactose-free diet (Lewis, Welch, Cherry, Flood, & Marble, 1995).

X-Linked Recessive Disorders X-linked recessive disorders are manifested in males. This is because they have only one X chromosome (the other is Y, inherited from the father) and will manifest the disorder if they inherit a single abnormal gene on the X chromosome. Females have a second X chromosome and must therefore receive an abnormal gene from both father and mother, which is much less likely to occur. If females receive a single altered X chromosome from one parent, they will be "carriers" and will show no or few signs of the disorder. Examples of X-linked recessive disorders include Duchenne and Becker muscular dystrophies, hemophilia, and X-linked hydrocephalus. Color blindness is also caused by an X-linked recessive gene.

Duchenne muscular dystrophy is a generalized muscle disease caused by the lack of the muscle protein dystrophin. It is associated with an increased risk for mental retardation. The child's condition deteriorates over time, often resulting in death in adolescence. Although muscular dystrophy can be diagnosed early in life, it is often not diagnosed until about age 2, after the child begins walking. The diagnosis should be suspected in boys with motor and cognitive delays. The blood level of the enzyme creatine phosphokinase (CPK) is markedly elevated, and the diagnosis is now confirmed by directly testing for the gene mutation.

X-Linked Dominant Disorders X-linked dominant disorders occur more frequently in females; however, such disorders are extremely rare. In general, they will occur twice as often in females as males because females have two X chromosomes. A male will pass the affected gene to all of his daughters (to whom he passes his X chromosome) and none of his sons (to whom he passes his Y chromosome); whereas a female will pass the gene to half of her offspring, whether daughters or sons. An example of an X-linked dominant disorder is vitamin D–resistant rickets.

Recent Advances in Genetics Research studies have clearly demonstrated that many genetic disorders are not explained by classic Mendelian genetics. Mitochondrial inheritance, diparental disomy, and gene expansion are three new mechanisms identified in children with genetic disorders.

Mitochondrial Inheritance It is now known that genetic disorders can be inherited from abnormal genes in the small amount of DNA in the mitochondria of

the cytoplasm of the ovum (mother). This has been referred to as mitochondrial or maternal inheritance. An example of mitochondrial inheritance is Leber hereditary optic neuropathy (LHON) (Larsson, Andersen, Holme, Odfors, & Wahlstrom, 1991). It is a cause of blindness in males due to retinal disease and has been associated with mental retardation, heart defects, and hearing loss in a few cases (Lambert, Kriss, Taylor, Coffey, & Pembrey, 1989).

Diparental Disomy Some genetic disorders are caused by having two copies of apparently normal genes from the same parent rather than one gene from the father and one gene from the mother; this is called diparental disomy. Prader-Willi syndrome can be caused by having the maternal gene on each of the 15th chromosomes (two copies of the maternal gene). Children with Prader-Willi syndrome are hypotonic and short and have a striking eating disorder, and many do not have mental retardation. Of interest, Angelman syndrome can be caused by having two copies of the paternal gene at the same location. Angelman syndrome is characterized by severe mental retardation, dyspraxic (shuffling) gait, and limited, if any, speech development.

Gene Expansion The human genome has many regions of three nucleotide base pair repeating segments of varying size. Some genetic disorders are caused by a gene expanding in size by increasing the number of three nucleotide base pair repeats. When the gene gets too large, it is inactivated or inactivates a neighboring gene and thus causes the disease. *Fragile X syndrome* and myotonic dystrophy are examples of gene expansion syndromes. Typically, the gene "expands" when it is passed from a mother who has the full mutation or who is a "carrier" and has a premutation (the gene is larger, unstable, and prone to "expand").

The three nucleotide base pair repeat in the fragile X gene (FMR-1) is CGG (cytosine-guanine-guanine). The "normal" size of the gene is 50 repeats or fewer. A male or female is a carrier (premutation) when there are 51–200 repeats and manifests the disorder when the number of repeats is >200 (full mutation) (Murphy, 1993). The FMR-1 gene was discovered in 1991 (Hagerman, 1993) and is on the X chromosome; thus, fragile X syndrome is an X-linked disorder. It is the most common inherited cause of mental retardation. It causes mental retardation in approximately 1 in 1,000 males and 1 in 2,000 females (Hagerman, 1993). Only about one third of the females with the full mutation have mental retardation. Boys with fragile X syndrome are hyperactive, anxious, and withdrawn and have developmental delay and speech problems (Simko, Hornstein, Soukup, & Bagamery, 1989). The characteristic physical features of a long face, prominent ears, and large testes are most notable at older ages.

Chromosomal Disorders

Chromosome abnormalities may occur as a result of an abnormal number or an abnormal structure of the chromosomes. Problems of chromosome number include monosomies, trisomies, and mosaicisms. Problems of structure include deletions, additions, inversions, and translocations. Like genetic disorders, chromosome disorders can further be categorized according to whether they involve the autosomes or the sex chromosomes. Most often, chromosome abnormalities are due to *nondisjunction* (lack of separation) of the paired chromosomes during meiosis. When nondisjunction occurs, both members of a chromosome pair go to an individual egg or sperm cell. The result is a cell with either a missing chromosome or one too many. When fertilization occurs, the zygote will have either a *trisomy* (47) or a *monosomy* (45). If the nondisjunction occurs after fertilization during mitotic cell division in the embryo, some cells will be affected and some will not. Thus, this abnormality is labeled *mosaicism.*

Structural chromosome abnormalities also involve the gain, loss, or rearrangement of part of a chromosome. When a chromosome acquires extra genetic material, it is usually called a *duplication, addition,* or a *partial trisomy*. The loss of genetic material is usually referred to as a *deletion* or *partial monosomy.* Additions and deletions occur when a portion of one chromosome breaks off and is lost or becomes attached to another chromosome. An inversion occurs when there are two breaks in a single chromosome followed by reattachment and the section of the chromosome between the breaks becomes inverted. The exchange of chromosome material between two chromosomes is called a *translocation* and may result in either a balanced (no loss of chromosomal material) or unbalanced (associated with deletion or addition) structural rearrangement (Thompson, 1989).

Certain maternal and paternal characteristics are statistically linked to chromosome abnormalities, namely, if the mother or father is older than 35 and if there was a previous birth of a child with a chromosomal disease. If a child has a chromosome disorder with translocation, both parents should be tested to determine if either is a translocation carrier. If one parent is a carrier, the risk for having subsequent children with a chromosome disorder is high.

The most common chromosome anomaly is *Down syndrome* (Figure 4.3), which may occur as either nondisjunction trisomy 21 (95% of cases), translocation (4% of cases), or mosaicism (1% of cases). The characteristics of Down syndrome include

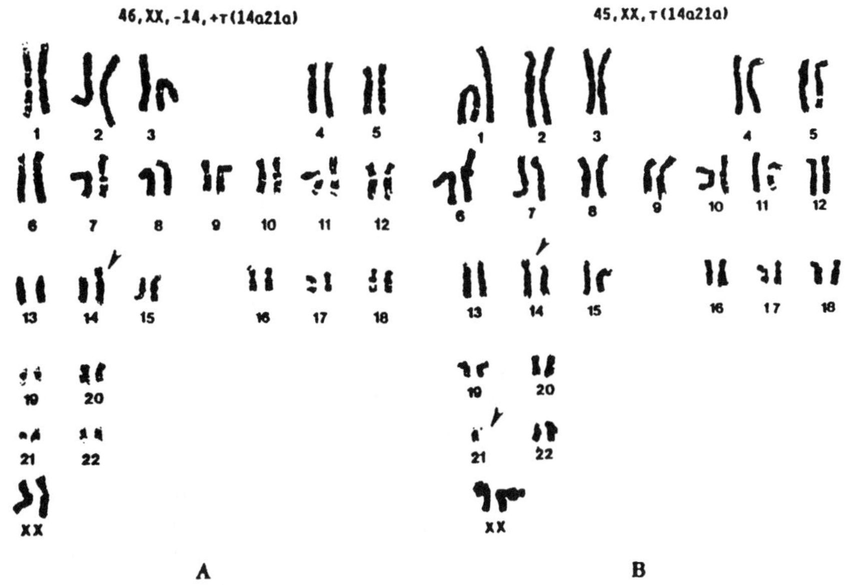

Figure 4.3. (A) Karyotype of translocation trisomy 21 (Down syndrome). An extra number 21 chromosome is attached to the number 14 (arrowhead) chromosome. (B) Karyotype of normal female with balanced translocation. One of the number 21 (arrowhead) chromosomes is attached to the number 14 (arrowhead) chromosome. (From Thompson, E.J. [1989]. A genetics primer for early service providers. *Infants and Young Children,* 2[1], p. 40; reprinted by permission, © 1989, Aspen Publishers, Inc.)

mild to severe cognitive disabilities, hypotonicity (low muscle tone), and certain physical features such as malformation of the ear, eye, and hand. These babies often have congenital heart defects and must often undergo heart surgery. Most children with Down syndrome are now raised at home with the support of early intervention programs and other community services beginning at birth. Many early intervention programs report great success in promoting the development of children with Down syndrome in integrated programs with children without disabilities (Hanson, 1987; Hanson & Harris, 1986; Widerstrom & Goodwin, 1987).

Other autosomal chromosome disorders are trisomies 13 and 18 and cri-du-chat syndrome. In *trisomies 13 and 18,* infants are born with multiple organ malformations that nearly always result in death during the first year. The survivors (20%) manifest severe mental retardation and FTT (Thompson & Thompson, 1986). *Cri-du-chat syndrome* is also known as 5p– syndrome because it is caused by deletion of one portion of the short arm (p) of chromosome 5 (the long arm of a chromosome is referred to as the q arm). Infants with cri-du-chat syndrome are smaller than average at birth and have microcephaly, epithelial folds of the eyelids, poorly formed ears, facial asymmetry, severe cognitive disabilities, and a characteristic cry described as sounding like a mewing cat.

Sex chromosome anomalies include Klinefelter syndrome and Turner syndrome. *Klinefelter syndrome* (XXY) affects 1 in 1,000 males. It is caused by the formation of an extra X chromosome from the mother or father during meiosis. Boys with Klinefelter syndrome have normal intelligence but may have speech problems, are taller than average height, and are infertile. *Turner syndrome* (XO) affects 1 in 2,500 newborn girls. Typically, girls with Turner syndrome have a single X chromosome. Characteristics include puffiness of the hands and feet at birth, a low posterior hairline, and extra skin in the neck region. They may also have a congenital heart defect. Usually they have normal intelligence. As adults, women with Turner syndrome are shorter than average in height. They will not go through puberty unless given hormone treatment and even so are usually infertile (Thompson, 1989).

Microdeletion Syndromes Some infants and children have chromosome disorders due to deletions that are too small to be seen by the light microscope. They can be demonstrated by the use of special probes. These microdeletions involve several genes. They have appeared to be autosomal dominant disorders because the parent with the microdeletion will pass the deletion-bearing chromosome to 50% of his or her children. In addition, like autosomal dominant disorders, the parent may manifest only a few of the clinical problems that the deletion can potentially cause (variable in expression). Therefore, both parents of children with microdeletion disorders should be tested for the deletion. *Velo-cardio-facial syndrome (VCFS)* and *DiGeorge sequence (DGS)* are two examples of microdeletion syndromes.

Both VCFS and DGS appear to be deleted at the same location on the long arm of the 22nd chromosome (22q11 deletion) (Driscoll et al., 1993). Children with VCFS have hypernasal speech, bifid uvula, cleft palate, congenital heart defect, learning disorders or mild cognitive disabilities, and characteristic facial appearance (Goldberg, Motzkin, Marion, Scambler, & Shprintzen, 1993). However, infants with DGS are born with hypocalcemia, thymic hypoplasia (which causes immunodeficiency), congenital heart defect, and minor facial anomalies (Wilson, Burn, Scambler, & Goodship, 1993). These two disorders may be "overlapping gene deletion" syndromes. They may be missing some of the same genes and some different genes. The deletion only appears to be the same in both.

Antenatal Screening and Genetic Counseling Prenatal diagnosis and genetic counseling for parents who are at risk of having an infant with a birth defect or a genetic or chromosomal disorder are important parts of the management of these families. The current procedures for prenatal diagnosis are early amniocentesis (performed prior to 15 weeks' gestation), amniocentesis (performed at 15–16 weeks' gestation), chorionic villus sampling (CVS) (performed at 10–12 weeks' gestation), fetoscopy, and ultrasonography. Diagnostic tests include amniotic fluid alpha-fetoprotein (AFP) and anticholinesterase levels, chromosomal analysis of amniocytes, and tests for specific genetic disorders.

Maternal serum screening tests for Down syndrome in pregnant women under the age of 35 years include alpha-fetoprotein (MSAFP), human chorionic gonadotropin, and estriol levels (triple screen). The use of maternal age and MSAFP levels identifies about 20%–25% of fetuses with Down syndrome, and use of the triple screen increases the detection to approximately 60% (Busch & Himes, 1995). A positive screen does not diagnose a birth defect. These women should be offered diagnostic testing (chromosomal analysis) with CVS or amniocentesis. Most women with positive screen results have unimpaired babies. MSAFP was first developed as a screen for open neural tube defects (spina bifida). Eighty percent to 90% of these defects can be detected by MSAFP screening (Busch & Himes, 1995). Women with positive screen results need diagnostic testing with amniocentesis and ultrasound.

Genetic counseling has evolved from a purely informational service regarding reproductive risk to a diagnostic consultation and case-management approach for providing information, support, and follow-up to families affected by birth defects and genetic disorders (Thompson, 1989). Genetic counselors can provide further information on screening tests for neural tube defects, Down syndrome, and trisomy 18, as well as the availability of prenatal diagnostic tests for specific problems.

When a baby is born with a birth defect or genetic disorder, the genetic counselor can assist the family in obtaining up-to-date information about that problem, refer the family to parent support groups as appropriate, and review local services.

Health-Related Problems

Infants who are at risk due to prematurity or who have disabilities may have difficulty maintaining adequate nutrition. Poor nutritional intake may result in FTT, exacerbate other medical problems (e.g., chronic lung disease), and interfere with developmental progress.

Failure to Thrive Failure to thrive describes infants who, for a number of possible reasons, fail to gain weight or length within the expected range. It occurs predominantly in children less than 18 months of age, with onset usually between the third and fifteenth months. FTT has been classified as either *organic* (has an identified medical cause such as oral-motor dysfunction or gastroesophageal reflux) or *nonorganic.* A number of studies have noted that maternal deprivation and environmental neglect are important factors in nonorganic FTT. A 1993 study, however, has demonstrated that the growth failure in some infants with nonorganic FTT is secondary to a feeding skills disorder (Ramsey, Gisel, & Boutry, 1993).

Oral-Motor Dysfunction Some premature infants have difficulty coordinating oral-motor functions such as sucking, swallowing, and respiration during feeding. Infants with cerebral palsy may have difficulty organizing and moving the food bolus to the back of the mouth and may have an abnormal swallow. Signs of oral-motor dysfunction may include the following:

- Poor sucking
- Feeding that takes too long (45 minutes or longer)
- Abnormal feeding pattern (small frequent feedings with intake less than 1 ounce)
- Crying during a feeding
- Coughing, choking, or gagging during a feeding

Infants who have feeding problems may be at risk for aspiration of formula or food into the lungs and often require evaluation by feeding specialists. Treatment recommendations may include proper positioning during feeding, change in the bottle nipple (to control rate of flow), change in food texture, and adaptations to spoons, cups, and other feeding equipment (Wolf & Glass, 1992).

Gastroesophageal Reflux Gastroesophageal reflux (GER) can complicate the feeding problems of the premature infant and the infant with disabilities. Studies of GER in children with cerebral palsy report significant reflux in 70%–75% of the children (Reyes, Cash, Green, & Booth, 1993). GER occurs when the muscle sphincter of the lower esophagus, which normally prevents food from backing up from the stomach into the esophagus, is weak. The gagging and vomiting that result cause considerable discomfort and may prevent the infant from obtaining adequate nutrition (Orenstein, Whitington, & Orenstein, 1983). GER can lead to FTT, esophagitis, esophageal stricture (scarring), recurrent aspiration, pneumonia, reactive airway disease, apnea, and bradycardia (Wolf & Glass, 1992).

The reflux may manifest as vomiting or be "silent" with no symptoms. Infants with GER and esophagitis may stop feeding after the apparent first ½–1 ounce as a result of pain from the reflux. Table 4.1 presents the characteristic symptoms of GER.

Table 4.1. Symptoms of gastroesophageal reflux (GER)

Recurrent vomiting or spitting up immediately after a feeding, several hours later, or during sleep
Hematemesis (blood in the vomit)
Arching with feedings secondary to esophagitis
Torticollis (wry neck) secondary to esophagitis
Choking
Frequent swallowing
No appetite or refusal of foods
Early satiety
Irritability
Apnea

Infants with mild or moderate oral-motor problems may improve nutrition and growth with the use of high-calorie formulas and specific recommendations to facilitate optimal oral-motor function (e.g., positioning, food texture). GER can be treated by thickening formula and emphasizing solids for feeding and medications. Infants with severe GER may require surgery (antireflux procedure such as the Nissen fundoplication) to "tighten" the lower esophageal sphincter to prevent reflux. Infants with neurodevelopmental problems have a higher risk of complications following antireflux surgery than infants without such impairments (Pearl et al., 1990).

Occasionally infants cannot be fed safely orally due to the risk of aspiration, or they cannot take in sufficient calories to support normal growth. These infants require tube feeding. Nasogastric (nose / stomach) and oral gastric (mouth / stomach) tubes are only short-term solutions. Both of these tubes may also increase the risk of GER. The usual solution is placement of a gastrostomy tube (GT) (Figure 4.4). There are three types of gastrostomy tubes: 1) standard or Stamm, 2) percutaneous endoscopic gastrostomy (PEG), 3) or the "button" (Figures 4.5 and 4.6). If a standard GT is surgically placed, it is usually replaced in several weeks by the button. The button GT is flush with the skin and has a one-way valve to make feeding easy by bolus (all of the feeding in 10–20 minutes) or by continuous drip.

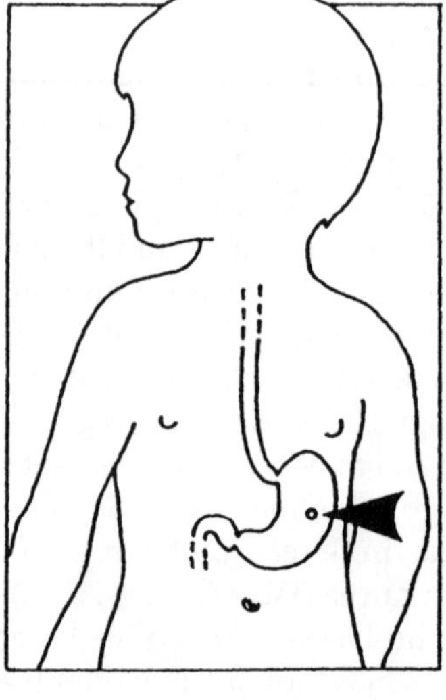

Figure 4.4. The surgically created gastrostomy fistula is usually placed midway between the navel and the left nipple (arrowhead). (From Nelson, C.L., & Hallgren, R.A. [1989]. Gastrostomies: Indications, management, and weaning. *Infants and Young Children, 2*[1], p. 68; reprinted by permission, © 1989, Aspen Publishers, Inc.)

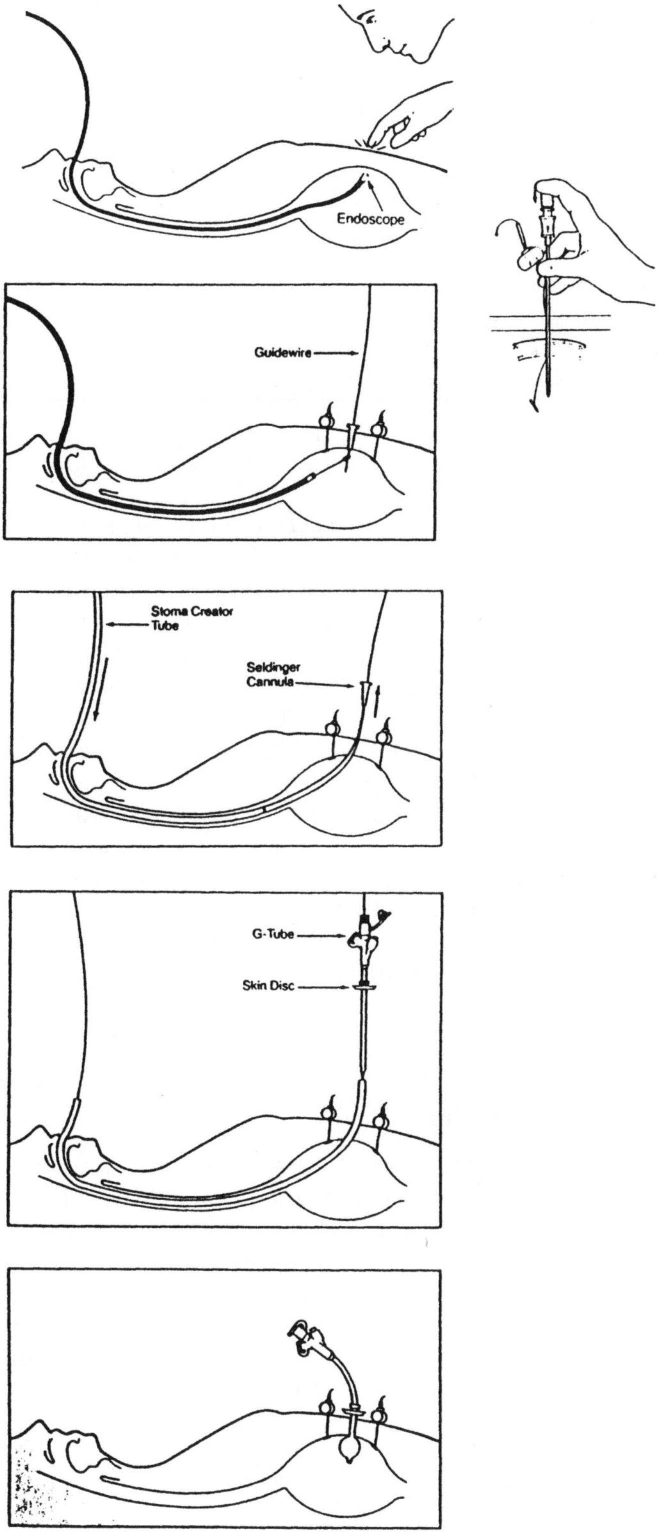

Figure 4.5. Steps in the placement of percutaneous endoscopic gastrostomy. (Adapted from Enteral Feeding Devices, Ross Laboratories, 1993.)

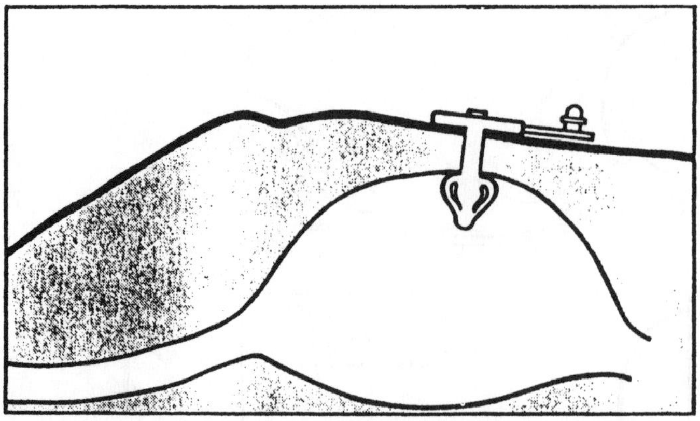

Figure 4.6. The Button gastrostomy tube. This is the Stomate low profile gastrostomy in place, open and ready for placement of feeding tube. (Adapted from Gastrostomy Feeding Devices, Ross Laboratories, 1990.)

The PEG is placed percutaneously (through the skin and into the stomach) with endoscopic guidance (Larson, Burton, Schroeder, & DiMagno, 1987). It does not require surgery; thus it is an appropriate choice for infants who would not tolerate surgery. There is an ongoing difference of opinion regarding when to use a PEG and when to use the standard GT (Albanese, Towbin, Ulman, Lewis, & Smith, 1993). There is also controversy as to when to perform antireflux surgery in conjunction with a GT (Stringel et al., 1989), although children who require placement of a GT and also have significant GER usually have a standard or button GT in conjunction with an antireflux procedure.

Feedings can be given through the GT by a hand-controlled syringe, gravity-controlled bag, open syringe, or mechanical pump. The mechanical pump allows feedings to be given by a continuous drip to avoid problems with gagging and retching that occasionally occur with bolus (by syringe or gravity) feedings. Infants who are safe oral feeders can receive some nutrition orally with supplementation by GT. In addition, infants often achieve rapid catch-up growth with a GT and may experience excessive weight gain if caloric intake and growth are not carefully monitored.

Seizures and Seizure Disorder

The terminology regarding seizure disorders is not the same as some terms still commonly used. Table 4.2 presents the International Classification of Epileptic Seizures (Penry, 1986). The *petit mal seizure* is now classified as *absence seizure*. The *grand mal seizure* is now referred to as *tonic-clonic seizure*, and *psychomotor* or *temporal lobe seizure* is now termed *complex partial seizure*.

Absence Seizures (Petit Mal) Absence seizures occur in 34% of people with seizure disorders (Penry, 1986). They begin abruptly and result in a very brief loss of consciousness (several seconds). They may be associated with subtle motion of the eyelids or chin muscles, dilation of pupils, and facial color change (Penry, 1986). They can be provoked by hyperventilation and may occur in clusters. Classic absence (petit mal) is benign and self-limited and begins in mid-childhood. It is associated with 3-per-second spike and wave discharges on the electroencephalogram (EEG).

Table 4.2. The International Classification of Epileptic Seizures

I. Partial (focal) seizures
  A. Simple partial seizures (consciousness not impaired)
  B. Complex partial seizures (with impairment of consciousness)
  C. Partial seizures evolving to secondary generalized seizures
II. Generalized seizures
  A. Absence seizures
  B. Myoclonic seizures
  C. Clonic seizures
  D. Tonic seizures
  E. Tonic-clonic seizures
  F. Atonic seizures
III. Unclassified epileptic seizures

Adapted from Penry (1986).

Tonic-Clonic Seizures (Grand Mal) Generalized tonic-clonic seizures occur in 4%–10% of all people with epilepsy (Penry, 1986). A tonic-clonic (grand mal) seizure may last several minutes. It consists first of a tonic phase during which the infant loses consciousness and becomes rigid. This is followed by a clonic phase characterized by rhythmic jerking body movements and then by a deep sleep. It is important to differentiate a primary, generalized tonic-clonic seizure from partial seizures that develop into generalized seizures. Different antiepileptic drugs (AEDs) are effective in controlling primary and secondary generalized seizures (Penry, 1986).

Different seizure types can occur at different ages and some children will have a combination of seizure types. Identifying a specific epilepsy syndrome in addition to the seizure type is very important for treatment. Febrile convulsions, neonatal seizures, and infantile spasms are epilepsy syndromes. Children also have a number of paroxysmal nonepileptic events that must be differentiated from seizures (e.g., breath-holding spells, gastroesophageal reflux, paroxysmal vertigo [dizziness]).

Febrile Convulsions Febrile convulsions are seen in children from ages 3 months to 5 years. They occur in approximately 4% of all children (Penry, 1986). Common antecedents are febrile upper respiratory illnesses, ear infections, influenza, roseola, and immunization for diptheria-pertussis-tetanus (DPT) (Hirtz, Ellenberg, & Nelson, 1984). Although most children experience only one episode of febrile convulsions, the risk of having a second is 30%–40%. Only about 10% of children go on to have recurrent seizures, and often these are children with a family history of such disorders suggesting a possible genetic factor (Nelson & Ellenberg, 1981).

The febrile convulsion is typically a generalized tonic-clonic seizure that lasts 5 minutes or less. Treatment is usually not necessary, although the physician may perform a spinal tap to rule out possible meningitis (Gerber & Berliner, 1981).

Neonatal Seizures Seizures in newborns may be subtle and difficult to diagnose. Generalized tonic-clonic seizures are not usually seen. Clinical seizures tend to be focal, clonic (limited to abnormal spasms in a single arm or leg), myoclonic (rapid jerk in one muscle group), or tonic deviation of trunk or eyes. The EEG can help determine what is an electrographic seizure requiring treatment.

Neonatal seizures may be caused by a number of factors, and the prognosis for good recovery depends on the underlying cause. If the seizures are simply the result of depressed levels of calcium (hypocalcemia) or glucose (hypoglycemia), the infant generally recovers quickly following treatment with calcium or glucose. Sick full-term infants, large for gestational age infants, and premature babies who are small for gestational age are at risk for hypoglycemia (Freeman, 1983). More serious and long-term effects may result from neonatal seizures caused by perinatal asphyxia or meningitis. In the case of these potentially serious conditions, the seizure is simply a manifestation of brain damage or dysfunction. Some of these infants will not need AED treatment after discharge from the neonatal intensive care unit (NICU) and other infants will require long-term treatment with AEDs.

Infantile Spasms Infantile spasms (or West syndrome) begin before 12 months of age and resolve by several years of age. They consist of a series of rapid flexion or extension movements in which the body repeatedly jackknifes forward. These episodes may occur as often as every 10 minutes (Freeman, 1983). Approximately half of the children with infantile spasms have other seizure types that may persist after the infantile spasms resolve. The EEG shows a chaotic pattern referred to as hyperarrhythmia. Many children with infantile spasms have a known cause (e.g., Down syndrome, hypoxic ischemic encephalopathy, phenylketonuria). Infantile spasms can be treated effectively by administration of ACTH or oral steroids, and this treatment is usually begun in the hospital. High doses of sodium valproate (an AED) have also been reported to be effective in controlling seizures (Prats, Garaizar, Rua, Garcia-Nieto, & Madoz, 1991). However, 90% of affected infants have mental retardation (Snead, Benton, & Myers, 1983). Infants who have typical development before the seizures and are treated promptly have the best chance for subsequent typical development (Kurokawa et al., 1980).

Treatment

The treatment of seizures in children with disabilities can be a frustrating experience for the family and the physician. The seizure type and syndrome guide the initial choice of an AED. If children rapidly become seizure-free on treatment, they are usually treated for at least 2 years before considering the discontinuance of the AED. A repeat EEG may assist in this decision. In one study, spike discharges on the EEG and a history of mental retardation both significantly increase the risk of seizure recurrence when AEDs were discontinued (Tennison, Greenwood, Lewis, & Thorn, 1994).

The goal of therapy with AEDs is to control the seizures with one drug (monotherapy). If one drug fails, another AED is tried. Only after several AEDs have failed are two or more AEDs used at the same time due to the increased risk of side effects (Penry, 1986). Young children treated with valproate (Depakene) and other AEDs (polytherapy) versus valproate alone have a markedly increased risk of liver toxicity.

A few infants will have very difficult to manage seizures even with optimal use of AEDs. These infants may benefit from treatment with a ketogenic diet. This diet is very high in fat and extremely low in carbohydrates (maximum 19% of the calories) so that the child develops ketosis and acidosis (mimics starvation). This treatment is based on the observation that starvation has an anticonvulsant effect (Withrow, 1980). In one study, seizure control improved in 67% of individuals with the use of a ketogenic diet (Kinsman, Vining, Quaskey, Mellits, & Freeman, 1992). Unfortunately, this diet is difficult to maintain. It also causes high blood cholesterol and lipid levels and increases the risk for atherosclerosis (Withrow, 1980).

New AEDs are becoming available, such as vigabatrin (Sabril) (Chiron et al., 1991). Epilepsy surgery is also available at a number of medical centers for children who continue to have frequent seizures after other treatments. Surgeries include local resection (small area of cortical dysplasia), temporal lobe resection, hemispherectomy, and corpus callostomy (Kotagal & Luders, 1994; Shields, Shewmon, Chugani, & Peacock, 1992). The goal of corpus callostomy is to reduce the number of seizures rather than to eliminate seizures. The goal of other surgeries is to eliminate seizures by resecting the seizure focus. Children referred for consideration of surgery should be carefully selected and receive a comprehensive preoperative evaluation.

SENSORY DISORDERS

Sensory disorders include hearing and visual impairment. The early diagnosis of sensory impairments is critical to the overall success of treatment programs.

Hearing Impairment

Hearing loss in infants is a relatively common disability. Mild to severe sensorineural hearing loss occurs in approximately 1 per 380–750 live births and profound hearing loss in 1 per 1,000 births (Madell, 1988). The incidence in premature infants is higher. Children are usually described as having a mild, moderate, severe, profound, or total hearing loss (see Table 4.3). This is determined by the child's 3-frequency average (500, 1,000, and 2,000 hertz) for the threshold of hearing (measured in decibels [dB]) in the better ear (Gatty, in press).

A child with a mild hearing loss can understand speech when spoken face-to-face but has some difficulty with normal conversations. The child with a moderate loss has difficulty with normal conversations, especially if there is background noise, but can understand amplified speech. The child with a severe loss generally also does well with hearing aids; however, the response to aids is variable in children with profound loss. If the child is totally deaf, he or she will not benefit from a hearing aid (Gatty, in press). Hearing losses are categorized as conductive and sensorineural.

Conductive Hearing Loss Conductive hearing loss can result from congenital defects of the external ear canal or middle ear, damage to the middle ear, and persistent fluid or infections in the middle ear. The persistent middle ear fluid (serous otitis) is caused by blockage of the eustachian tube that prevents fluid from draining from the middle ear. In general, the treatment of conductive hearing loss is highly successful. Medications are used first for serous otitis and acute otitis media. Children with persisting problems may require placement of a tube in the eardrum (tympanic membrane) and adenoidectomy to drain the fluid. Surgery can correct some congenital defects. Bone conduction hearing aids benefit other children.

Table 4.3. Levels of hearing loss

Level of loss	Decibels (dB)
Mild	15–30
Moderate	30–61
Severe	61–90
Profound	91–120
Total	Greater than 120

Sensorineural Hearing Loss Sensorineural hearing loss occurs in the cochlea (part of the inner ear) or the auditory nerve leading to the brain and is a more serious problem. The function of the cochlea is to transform sound waves received from the external and middle ear into electrochemical impulses capable of being processed by the brain. These are sent to the brain by way of the auditory nerve. Sensorineural damage may be caused by illness, high fever, drugs, or congenital birth defects. However, the majority of cases of sensorineural hearing loss are genetic. The use of hearing aids to amplify sound and auditory training is an important part of the infant's treatment, depending on the amount of residual hearing.

A surgical procedure (cochlear implant) has been developed that offers hope to some children and adults with sensorineural hearing losses (Cohen, Waltzman, Fisher, & Department of Veterans Affairs Cochlear Implant Study Group, 1993). The cochlea implant is a device that consists of an electrode array that is surgically implanted into the cochlea. The internal device receives signals (speech information) from a device worn on the outside of the body. The best candidates are children or adults who acquired hearing loss after the development of speech and who receive little or no benefit from hearing aids (Roush, 1990).

Testing for hearing loss can be carried out with great accuracy today for children of all ages. Hearing tests for infants are conducted by means of auditory-brainstem-evoked responses (ABR), in which changes in brain waves are recorded at the same time auditory stimulation is presented to the infant. This method does not depend on conscious response by the infant to auditory input and is very accurate. Many NICUs currently test all children immediately prior to discharge with ABR or with a newly developed test, evoked oto-acoustic emissions (EOAE). EOAE may be useful for screening newborn infants; however, they do have a high false positive rate (Bess & Paradise, 1994). Infants who are 6 months' developmental age and older can be tested with visually reinforced audiometry. For older children (older than age 2) a combination of behavioral and physiological measures is used. The audiologist will observe responses to both noise signal and speech. Testing may be conducted in a play situation, and the child is reinforced visually or with food for responding to test items. An audiogram is plotted for each ear (see Figure 4.7).

The greater the child's hearing loss, the greater will be potential language deficits, such as learning to understand language concepts and to employ the correct language form or structure (grammar or syntax). In addition, due to the inability to hear speech sounds, the child with a severe or profound hearing loss may have little intelligible speech. The choice of a communication program for the infant or young child with a hearing impairment depends on many factors. Different programs emphasize the use of sign language, oral language (speech), or a total communication approach that incorporates elements of both.

Visual Impairment

Objective measurement of visual acuity in infants and young children can be accomplished with three difficult tests: 1) optokinetic nystagmus (OKN)—the infant watches moving stripes of different widths, 2) forced choice preferential looking (FCPL)—the infant chooses between a homogenous field and stripes of different widths, or 3) visual evoked potentials (VEPs)—checkerboard patterns of different sizes are shown to the infant and brain waves are recorded. OKN and FCPL testing indicate a visual acuity of approximately 20/400 in the normal newborn infant

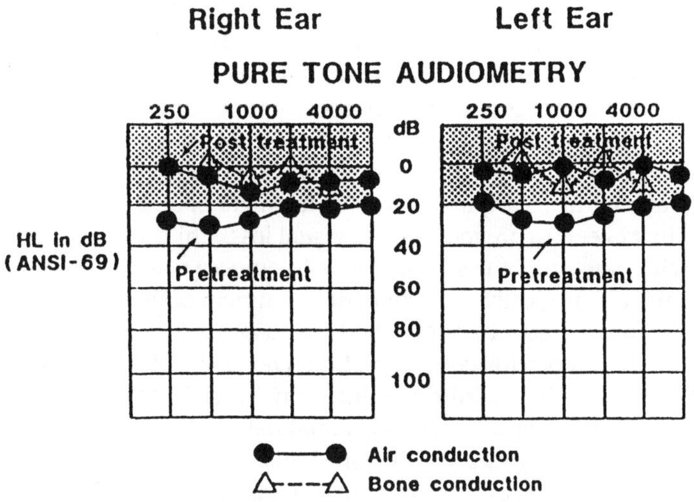

Figure 4.7. Pre- and posttreatment behavioral audiogram from a 6-year-old boy with recurrent otitis media with effusion. This audiogram was obtained by conditioned play audiometry. Pretreatment audiogram shows mild bilateral conductive hearing loss. Following treatment (insertion of pressure-equalizing tubes in the tympanic membrane), the pure tone audiogram is normal (ANSI-69: American National Standards Institute 1969 standard for audiometric normal hearing). (From Hayes, D. [1986]. Audiological assessment. In D.L. Wodrich & J.E. Joy [Eds.], *Multidisciplinary assessment of children with learning disabilities and mental retardation* [p. 123]. Baltimore: Paul H. Brookes Publishing Co.; reprinted by permission.)

(Nelson, Rubin, Wagner, & Breton, 1984). VEP results suggest that by age 1 an infant's vision is 20/20 (the adult standard) (Nelson et al., 1984). The infant's vision can also be assessed clinically by observation of visual fixation and following responses as well as visually directed reaching.

Common visual problems in infancy and childhood include refractive errors, strabismus, and amblyopia. *Refractive errors* include myopia, hyperopia, and astigmatism. The cornea and lens of the eye focus light on the retina. Nearsightedness, or myopia, results when the eye is too long or the refractive power of the cornea and lens is too strong and light is focused in front of the retina. Farsightedness, or hyperopia, results if the eye is too short or the refractive power too weak and the image is focused behind the retina. Astigmatism results when there is irregularity to the shape of the cornea or lens and not all of the image is sharply focused on the retina. The retinoscope is used to determine the presence of refraction errors. Most newborns are hyperopic or farsighted, a condition that gradually improves after age 7. About 25% of newborns are myopic or nearsighted (Nelson et al., 1984). Refractive errors that require glasses are present in approximately 20% of children (Committee on Practice and Ambulatory Medicine, American Academy of Pediatrics, 1986). However, only a few children with refractive errors have significant visual impairments not corrected by glasses.

Strabismus is caused by an imbalance of the eye muscles, which results in the eyes being out of alignment intermittently or all of the time. It is present in 3%–4% of all children; however, it is much more common in children with disabilities (Batshaw & Perret, 1992). The two main types of strabismus are esotropia (turning in of the eye) and exotropia (turning out of the eye). During the first month, most infants show intermittent esotropia and exotropia; however, normal alignment is usually established by 3 months of age. Constant deviation at that age indicates the need for referral to the ophthalmologist (Nelson et al., 1984).

Farsightedness can be a cause of strabismus and is usually treated by glasses. For some children, surgery may be necessary to realign the eyes. When the eyes are not aligned, the visual acuity of the malaligned eye may worsen. This visual change is called *amblyopia*. Amblyopia can also be caused by unequal refractive errors, cataracts, and corneal clouding. Prompt treatment of amblyopia is critical to restore vision in that eye or to prevent further visual loss. Children with strabismus may be treated with patching of the "good" eye to enforce use of the amblyopic eye. The malalignment is surgically corrected after treatment of the amblyopia.

In the United States, blindness and serious visual impairment occur in approximately 64 children per 100,000 population (Davidson, 1983). Blindness is defined in the Individuals with Disabilities Education Act (IDEA) of 1990 (PL 101-476) as a visual acuity of less than 20/200 or a visual field of less than 20 degrees using both eyes with correction by glasses (Bishop, 1991). It can result from illness or injury to the eye, the optic nerve, or the brain. In developing countries, infections and injuries are common causes of blindness. In developed countries, genetic diseases are responsible for a higher proportion of childhood visual loss (Gilbert, Rahi, Eckstein, & Foster, 1995). Cataracts, retinopathy of prematurity, retinal disorders, and glaucoma are common causes of visual impairment in the United States. Central visual inattention or cortical blindness is an important cause of visual impairment in infants who have sustained brain damage (e.g., from intraventricular hemorrhage or hypoxic-ischemic encephalopathy).

A *cataract* is any opacity in the eye's lens. It may or may not lower visual acuity, depending on its size and location. Several types of cataracts are hereditary (e.g., galactosemia), and they may also be associated with trauma, maternal rubella, diabetes mellitus, and Down syndrome. A cataract should be removed as soon as it interferes with vision to avoid amblyopia and permanent visual loss (Batshaw & Perret, 1992). After surgery, the individual can be fitted with a contact lens.

Retinopathy of prematurity (ROP), or retrolental fibroplasia (RFP), results in visual impairment due to retinal scarring and detachment. The administration of oxygen causes abnormal growth of blood vessels in the eyes of some infants, which in turn leads to the scarring and retinal detachment. The incidence of ROP has greatly decreased as hospital staff have learned to carefully monitor the amounts of oxygen administered to infants at high risk. The treatment is regular examination and early laser or cryotherapy (Flage, 1993) to prevent the detachment.

A number of uncommon genetic disorders cause damage or dysfunction to the rods and cones, which are the retinal cells that are sensitive to light. *Retinitis pigmentosa* (RP) is the name given to a group of these disorders associated with progressive visual loss and pigment deposition in the retina (e.g., Usher syndrome [sensorineural hearing loss and RP]). The electroretinogram (ERG), which tests the function of the rods and cones, is used to diagnose these problems.

In young children, *glaucoma* is usually a congenital abnormality. It can also occur secondary to cataracts, infection, trauma, and ROP. Congenital glaucoma is usually caused by genetic disorders or congenital infection (Batshaw & Perret, 1992). Glaucoma causes visual loss through excess accumulation of intraocular fluid, which causes pressure on the retina and damage to the nerve fibers. Primary congenital glaucoma is usually diagnosed early in infancy. It is treated by a combination of medications, lasers, and surgery. The goal of the use of lasers and surgery is to enlarge the channels draining fluid from the eyes.

Cortical blindness, or central visual inattention, results from damage to the visual cortex, usually in association with widespread damage to other parts of the cerebral cortex and is highly associated with other developmental disorders (e.g., developmental delay, cerebral palsy) (Eken, de Vries, van der Graaf, Meiners, & van Nieuwenhuizen, 1995). It reflects an inability to utilize visual sensory information. The prognosis for improvement in vision depends in large part on the rate of overall developmental progress.

The treatment of the infant and young child with visual impairment depends on the degree and cause of visual loss and associated medical and developmental problems. Visual loss alone can affect other areas of development. Blind infants show greater delays in early communication development than deaf infants (Preisler, 1995).

NEUROMOTOR IMPAIRMENTS

Two common neuromotor impairments are cerebral palsy and spina bifida. The motor problems of many children with cerebral palsy relate primarily to spasticity. The motor problems of children with spina bifida relate primarily to weakness and paralysis. Muscle weakness, however, can also be a significant problem for children with cerebral palsy; and spasticity is a problem for some children with spina bifida.

Cerebral Palsy

Cerebral palsy (CP) is a group of disorders rather than a specific disease. It is characterized by a nonprogressive impairment of movement and posture resulting from brain injury or anomaly occurring early in development. The prevalence of moderate and severe CP at school age is about 1.5–2.5 per 1,000 children (Kuban & Leviton, 1994; Paneth, 1986).

CP is classified by the anatomical distribution of the dysfunction and the type of neurological involvement. A child may manifest hemiplegia (one side of the body involved), diplegia (both legs primarily involved or legs more involved than the arms), quadriplegia (total body involvement or arms more involved than legs), triplegia (principal involvement of both legs and one arm), or monoplegia (single extremity involved). The types of neurologic involvement are spastic, extrapyramidal (athetoid, ataxic, dystonic, and atonic), and mixed (spastic-ataxic, spastic-athetoid, and rigid spastic) (Table 4.4).

Most commonly, children with hemiplegia or diplegia manifest spasticity; however, other types of neurological involvement can also be seen (e.g., dystonia) (Scrutton, 1992).

Etiology of Cerebral Palsy The brain insult or anomaly that results in CP may occur prenatally, perinatally, or postnatally (in early childhood). Prenatal factors include chromosomal and genetic causes, isolated brain malformations or birth defect syndromes, and intrauterine ischemic events. Perinatal causes include periventricular leukomalacia (PVL) or intraventricular hemorrhage, perinatal asphyxia, and perinatal infection and hyperbilirubinemia. Postnatal causes include meningitis and head trauma. Preterm infants with PVL represent about 35%–40% of

Table 4.4. Types of cerebral palsy and characteristics

Type	Characteristics
Spastic	
Monoplegia	Single extremity involved
Diplegia	Spasticity and lack of control in both legs and minor motor involvement of arms
Hemiplegia	One side of body involved
Triplegia	Both legs and one arm involved
Quadriplegia	Total body involvement
Extrapyramidal	
Athetoid	Involuntary movements of arms and legs, hypotonia
Ataxic	Difficulty with balance and fine motor control
Dystonic	Rigidity of movements and abnormal postures
Atonic	Markedly low muscle tone
Mixed	Spastic ataxic, spastic athetoid, or rigid spastic

children with CP. In 10% of children with CP, causes were postnatal; in another 5% causes were genetic (Paneth, 1986). There is growing recognition of the importance of prenatal causes of CP for full-term infants and a diminished emphasis on perinatal asphyxia and other perinatal factors (Truwit, Barkovich, Koch, & Ferriero, 1992).

Characteristics of Cerebral Palsy Infants with CP may exhibit mild to severe motor problems. Parents may express concern that their infant is persistently irritable, is difficult to feed, or feels stiff or floppy when they are caring for him or her. They may note that the infant is not developing motor skills as quickly as they expect. They may, however, comment on how early their infant can roll or stand, which may be due to spasticity or use of abnormal motor patterns.

Children with CP are at risk for seizures, feeding problems, speech and language problems, learning disabilities and mental retardation, joint contractures (inability to fully straighten a joint), scoliosis (curvature of the back), and dislocation of the hips.

Treatment of Cerebral Palsy The primary treatment goal is to help the child with cerebral palsy develop to his or her full-potential abilities. Specific treatment goals include to

- Facilitate motor progress during the developmental period
- Improve quality/efficiency of gait
- Improve functional abilities
- Prevent secondary problems (e.g., joint contractures, hip dislocation)
- Facilitate highest possible quality of life (e.g., optimal nutrition and growth, social interaction, relief of pain)

The management program may include physical and occupational therapy; the use of braces, assistive devices, positioning and seating equipment; the use of various medical interventions (e.g., muscle injections of botulinum toxin to treat spasticity) (Cosgrove, Corry, & Graham, 1994); orthopedic surgery; and neurosurgical interventions (e.g., selective dorsal rhizotomy [SDR] [McLaughlin et al., 1994], continuous intrathecal baclofen infusion [CIBI] to treat spasticity [Albright, Barron, Fasick, Polinko, & Janosky, 1993]). Finally, and perhaps most important, the treatment plan should include child and family support services. Treatment recommendations should be based on clearly defined, realistic treatment objectives. Regular physical and occupational therapy services are important components of early intervention programs for these infants.

Table 4.5 reviews indications for the provision of therapy services for a child with cerebral palsy. *Neurodevelopmental treatment* (NDT) (Bobath & Bobath, 1972) is an example of a therapy mode quite comparable with current multidisciplinary team methods of intervention. NDT emphasizes the child's active participation in therapy. It is a hands-on, individually administered treatment, and parents are instructed in handling techniques and exercises to use at home.

Spina Bifida

Another common neuromotor impairment is spina bifida. Spina bifida refers to one type of a neural tube defect (NTD), meningomyelocele (MM). "Meningo" refers to the meninges, which is the covering around the spinal cord and brain; "myelo" refers to the spinal cord; and "cele" refers to the sac-like lesion at the site of the NTD that is often present at birth. The NTDs result from incomplete neural tube closure during early fetal development. They can affect the spinal cord or the brain (anencephaly) and can be "opened" or "closed" (covered by skin). NTDs occur in approximately 1 per 1,500 live births (Busch & Himes, 1995).

Teratogens (e.g., prenatal alcohol or valproic acid exposure), a chromosome disorder (trisomy 18), and a microdeletion syndrome (22q11 deletion) can all cause spina bifida (Nickel et al., 1994). In most children with spina bifida, however, there is not an identifiable cause. Fortunately, periconceptional supplement with folic acid (a B-complex vitamin) and multivitamins has been shown to significantly reduce the occurrence of NTDs in families (Czeizel & Dudás, 1992; MRC Vitamin Study Research Group, 1991). The U.S. Public Health Service recommends that all women of child-bearing age take 0.4 mg of folic acid per day to decrease the risk of having a baby with spina bifida or other NTDs ("Use of Folic Acid," 1991).

Characteristics of Spina Bifida Children with meningomyelocele have varying degrees of muscle weakness and sensory loss depending on the location and size of the NTD. They are generally classified by the level of motor function and spinal innervation as sacral, lumbar, and thoracic. Children with sacral-level injury walk with little need for braces; children with a lumbar-level injury will need more significant braces and adaptive equipment to walk, and many choose to use a wheelchair for part of the day. Finally, children with a thoracic-level injury will use a wheelchair for most of the day. Some of these children can do limited "walking" with a brace such as a reciprocating gait orthosis (RGO), which provides support from the waist to the feet.

These children are at risk for a number of associated medical problems. Almost all have hydrocephalus as well as bowel and bladder incontinence (McLaughlin & Shurtleff, 1979). Many have strabismus, scoliosis, hip dislocation, and other ortho-

Table 4.5. Indications for the provision of therapy services

- Regular therapy throughout the preschool years
- When the child is making rapid changes in motor skills
- When the child has demonstrated the emerging skills of standing and assisted walking
- When there is a high risk of progressive contractures
- Postoperative (i.e., to maintain gains or improve function after release of contractures)
- Other specific situations (e.g., gait training with a new brace or assistive device)
- Cardiovascular and musculoskeletal conditioning program to improve endurance and speed

Margaret

Margaret was born with cerebral palsy. Her pediatrician was unable to tell her parents why this happened, for nothing in her birth history predicted it. The doctor pointed out that in about 40% of cerebral palsy cases there is no known cause.

Margaret has spastic diplegia, which means that movement in both her legs is limited due to spasticity. With spasticity there is an increase in muscle tone with a characteristic clasped-knife quality. When Margaret moves her leg, there is an initial stiff resistance, but it gives way abruptly like a pocket knife closing. Not only is movement difficult under these circumstances, but also Margaret's legs are weak and cannot support her weight. Her arms are less affected than her legs, and so her form of cerebral palsy is called diplegia rather than quadriplegia, which would be the case if all four limbs were spastic.

Margaret wears leg braces and walks fairly well in them by now. She needs help sometimes, though, and tires easily. She used to use a wheelchair most of the day but would like to give it up altogether one day.

When she was 3 years old, her parents enrolled her in a special program at the United Cerebral Palsy Center in her town. Her mother drove her to the program every day. Now she attends a public school class with three other classmates who also previously attended the center. All four of the children are enrolled in a general first-grade class, which has three adults to supervise 27 children. Mr. Johnson, Margaret's teacher, has a degree in elementary education. Mrs. Bacon, his associate in the classroom, is a special education teacher who has had a great deal of experience working with children with motor disabilities. Together with Miss Mallory, a young teaching assistant, the three make a great team in Margaret's opinion, and she never feels scared or neglected at school.

"I can write my name and almost read a book, and I'm learning to feed myself," she says. "Mother says school is very good for me."

pedic problems. A few children will have seizures and some children will require treatment for neurosurgical complications such as tethered cord. Some children have mental retardation; however, the majority of children are of average intelligence (McLaughlin & Shurtleff, 1979). Many children do have a type of learning disability called nonverbal learning disability. These children have problems with attention and organization (executive functions), reading comprehension, math, and social skills (Lollar, 1993; Snow et al., 1994).

Treatment of Spina Bifida The open NTD is generally closed the first day of life and a shunt placed to treat hydrocephalus as needed in the next 2 weeks. Children with spina bifida can generally expect to have at least one surgery to revise the shunt as well as have surgery to correct orthopedic problems, have several urinary tract infections, and will need special programs to manage bladder (e.g., clean intermittent catheterization) and bowel incontinence. Because of the potential for multiple medical and developmental problems, these infants and children are best managed by an experienced team of medical professionals that collaborates closely with early intervention staff. Most infants with spina bifida will require physical and occupational therapy services as part of an early intervention program.

DEVELOPMENTAL DELAY AND MENTAL RETARDATION

Developmental delay is a descriptive term used regarding the skills of infants and young children. It refers to a general delay in skills across all or nearly all developmental domains (e.g., delay in communication, motor, cognitive, adaptive, social/emotional skills). Use of the term *developmental delay* prevents unjustified diagnostic conclusions and inappropriate predictions of future function, because single developmental assessments in early childhood are poorly predictive of later function (Bayley, 1969; McCall, 1971).

The most widely used assessment instrument for measuring the intelligence of infants and toddlers is the *Manual for the Bayley Scales of Infant Development* (Bayley, 1969), which contains scales for assessing both mental and motor functions. It has recently been replaced by the Bayley II (Bayley, 1993). Many more screening and assessment tools also have been developed for children from birth to age 3. These are discussed in Chapter 6.

The American Association on Mental Retardation (AAMR) (1992) published an updated definition of *mental retardation* that is based on both intellectual and adaptive function as well as on age of onset. Mental retardation is characterized by significantly subaverage intellectual functioning existing with related limitations in two or more adaptive skill areas; and it manifests before age 18. Substandard intellectual functioning is defined as an IQ standard score of approximately 70–75 or below. This new definition broadens the concept of mental retardation and avoids sole reliance on the IQ to determine the level of disability.

Classification of Mental Retardation Mental retardation traditionally has been classified as mild, moderate, severe, or profound based on IQ (Table 4.6) (American Psychiatric Association, 1994). These terms are not used as part of the new definition of mental retardation proposed by the AAMR (1992), which focuses on the functional disability and related needs for support. The prevalence of mental retardation in childhood is usually agreed to be approximately 2%–3% of the population (McLaren & Bryson, 1987). About 85% of affected individuals have mild retardation and mild adaptive disability (Batshaw, 1993).

Etiology of Mental Retardation Developmental delay and mental retardation can result from prenatal, perinatal, and postnatal factors. The specific cause cannot be established in as many as 40% of children even after a comprehensive evaluation.

Table 4.6. Classification of mental retardation

Level	IQ range
Mild	55–69 (–2 to –3 *SD*)
Moderate	40–54 (–3 to –4 *SD*)
Severe	25–39 (–4 to –5 *SD*)
Profound	Less than 25 (below –5 *SD*)

Adapted from American Psychiatric Association (1994).

Characteristics of Mental Retardation In general, the more severe the degree of retardation, the earlier the onset and the more striking and generalized the delays in development. Children with mild mental retardation often present with language delay and demonstrate typical or near-typical gross and fine motor development. It may not be identified until 3 or 4 years of age when problems present in preschool or when parents become more concerned about the slow language progress.

Children with moderate mental retardation show more generalized problems with development. They manifest significant delay in the language abilities as well as gross and fine motor and self-help skills. They often have associated hyperactivity and short attention span and are identified by 1 or 2 years of age. In contrast to mild and moderate retardation, the disabilities of children with severe/profound mental retardation are likely to be apparent in the first months of life. These children frequently have associated birth defects and medical problems such as seizures.

Infants and young children with developmental delay or mental retardation have a high incidence of associated problems. The problems include seizures, cerebral palsy, hearing and vision impairment, autism, speech and language disorders, and psychiatric and behavioral problems (e.g., attention-deficit/hyperactivity disorder, self-injurious behaviors). Some 15%–20% of children with mental retardation have seizures (Batshaw, 1993).

Treatment of Mental Retardation Early identification of the developmental delay is essential for effective early intervention services. Some infants and young children also will require medical treatment (e.g., antiepileptic drugs for seizures).

AUTISM AND PERVASIVE DEVELOPMENTAL DISORDERS

Autism is a behavioral syndrome that begins before the age of 3 years and is characterized by impaired social interaction and nonverbal communication and play. Although some early investigators speculated that autism was caused by abnormal parenting, it is now clear that autism is a developmental disorder and has an organic basis. It is diagnosed in approximately 2–13 per 10,000 children (Tsai & Ghaziuddin, 1991).

In 1943, Kanner first used the term "early infantile autism" to describe a group of 11 children with extreme aloofness, inability to develop relationships with people, delayed speech, and repetitive simple play patterns. In 1968, Rutter proposed four essential features for infantile autism:

1. A lack of social interest and responsiveness
2. Impaired language, including peculiar speech patterns or the failure to develop speech
3. Bizarre motor behavior, including limited play patterns and ritualistic and compulsive behavior (e.g., hand-flapping, toe walking)
4. Onset before 30 months of age

Classification of Autism Autism is one subtype of the pervasive developmental disorders (PDDs). Table 4.7 reviews the PDD subtypes from the DSM-IV (American Psychiatric Association, 1994).

Table 4.7. The subtypes of pervasive developmental disorders (PPDs)

Autistic disorder
Rett syndrome
Childhood disintegrative disorder
Asperger syndrome (AS)
Pervasive developmental disorder not otherwise specified (PDD NOS)

Adapted from American Psychiatric Association (1994).

Rett syndrome is a rare progressive neurological disorder with an unknown etiology that affects girls (Perry, 1991). Children with the *childhood disintegrative disorder* develop typically until 2–3 years of age and then regress and manifest severe autistic symptoms (Volkmar, 1992). Children with *Asperger syndrome* (AS) are similar to children with mild or high-functioning autism. In general, children with AS have better language and social skills (Szatmari, 1993). The diagnosis of PDD, not otherwise specified (NOS), is reserved for children with atypical social and communication development who do not fit any of the other subtypes.

Etiology of Autism Autism is a behavioral syndrome that has multiple known causes that represent different genetic mechanisms and types of brain injury. Testing for fragile X syndrome should be considered in all children with suspect autism. However, the majority of infants with autism do not have an identifiable cause. Twin and family studies provide some evidence for genetic factors. Cranial MRI studies have noted differences in the cerebellar vermis and hemispheres (Courchesne et al., 1994). In addition, some individuals with autism have high blood serotonin (a brain neurotransmitter) levels, suggesting a biochemical cause (Ho, Lockitch, Eaves, & Jacobson, 1986).

Table 4.8. Characteristic behaviors of infants and young children with autism

Skills	Characteristic behaviors
Sensory	Appears not to notice voices but overreacts to some sounds
	Refuses food with certain textures
	Has adverse reaction to wool fabrics
	Is sensitive to bright light
	Is preoccupied with watching own hands and fingers
Social	Has no or delayed social smile
	Avoids eye contact when held
	Lacks anticipatory response to being picked up
	Seems not to like being held
	Has little initiative in play (e.g., peekaboo, pat-a-cake, wave bye-bye)
	No shared effect
	No joint attention behavior (e.g., pointing, showing)
	Engages in self-stimulation
	Is preoccupied with spinning objects
	Moves adult's hand like a tool (e.g., to indicate wants)
	Insists on sameness and routines
Language	Has delayed or absent coo
	Fails to imitate words, sounds
	Uses few communicative gestures
	Practices echolalia (repeats words and phrases)
	Practices delayed echolalia unrelated to social situation
	Shows pronoun reversals
	Uses pedantic voice

Table 4.9. Components of effective preschool programs for infants and young children with autism

Curriculum that emphasizes the ability to attend, to imitate, to comprehend and use language, to play appropriately with toys, and to socially interact
Highly supportive teaching environment (initial 1-to-1 to 1-to-2 staff–student ratio)
Recognition of the need for a highly structured environment (predictability and routine)
Use of functional approach to problem behaviors
Facilitation of the transition from preschool to kindergarten or first grade
Involvement of parents in the educational process

Adapted from Dawson & Osterling (1996).

Characteristic Behaviors of Infants and Toddlers An infant with autism may appear to be the perfect baby; he or she may rarely cry and be indifferent to being held. However, some infants with autism may also be persistently irritable, very difficult to console, and rigid when held. Smiling, cooing, and anticipation of feeding may be slow to develop or absent. Older infants and toddlers are delayed in play with toys. They show little or no imitative play, comfort seeking, or empathetic response to another's emotion (Dawson, 1992). They may have a qualitative, not necessarily quantitative, difference in eye contact. Their gaze may be directed to a spot on the parent's forehead or not combined with facial expression and vocalization (Dawson, 1992). Table 4.8 (on p. 115) lists some of the characteristic behaviors of children with autism from birth to 3 years of age.

Some 70%–75% of children with autism have mental retardation, and 25%–30% will have seizures (Tsai & Ghaziuddin, 1991). Children with autism can also have a number of behavioral and psychiatric problems as described for children with developmental delay or mental retardation.

Treatment of Autism The features of effective early intervention programs for infants and young children with autism are reviewed in Table 4.9 (Dawson & Osterling, 1996). Two specific treatment approaches are the structured teaching of the TEACCH program (Schopler, 1994) and intensive behavior modification developed by Lovaas (1987; McEachin, Smith, & Lovaas, 1993). Intensive behavior modification is based on operant conditioning methodology and requires 30–40 hours of one-to-one therapy per week. It has created a controversy in part related to claims of a cure if treatment is started before age 3 years and occasional use of aversives (Buchanan, 1995).

SUMMARY

This chapter has presented a review of the most common developmental disorders that occur during the perinatal period. The most commonly seen genetic and chromosomal disorders and sensory disorders were discussed, as well as cerebral palsy, spina bifida, mental retardation, and early infantile autism. The use of the terms *developmental delay* and *failure to thrive* was explained. Health problems such as oral-motor dysfunction, gastroesophageal reflux, and seizure disorders were reviewed. The chapter discussed the effects of these disorders on young infants as well as information on available treatments.

SUGGESTED READINGS

Batshaw, M.L., & Perret, Y.M. (1992). *Children with disabilities: A medical primer* (3rd ed.). Baltimore: Paul H. Brookes Publishing Co.

Blackman, J. (1990). *Medical aspects of developmental disabilities in children birth to three* (2nd ed.). Rockville, MD: Aspen.
Hanson, M. (Ed.). (1984). *Atypical infant development.* Baltimore: University Park Press.
Thurman, S.K., & Widerstrom, A.H. (1990). *Infants and young children with special needs: A developmental and ecological approach.* Baltimore: Paul H. Brookes Publishing Co.

REFERENCES

Al-Gazali, L.I., Arthur, R.J., Lamb, J.T., Hammer, H.M., Coker, T.P., Hirschmann, P.N., Gibbs, J., & Mueller, R.F. (1989). Diagnostic and counselling difficulties using a fully comprehensive screening protocol for families at risk for tuberous sclerosis. *Journal of Medical Genetics, 26,* 694–703.
Albanese, C.T., Towbin, R.B., Ulman, I., Lewis, J., & Smith, S.D. (1993). Percutaneous gastrojejunostomy versus Nissen fundoplication for enteral feeding of the neurologically impaired child with gastroesophageal reflux. *Journal of Pediatrics, 123*(3), 371–375.
Albright, A.L., Barron, W.B., Fasick, M.P., Polinko, P., & Janosky, J. (1993). Continuous intrathecal baclofen infusion for spasticity of cerebral origin. *Journal of the American Medical Association, 270*(2), 2475–2477.
American Association on Mental Retardation (AAMR). (1992). *Mental retardation: Definition, classification, and systems of supports* (9th ed.). Washington, DC: Author.
American Psychiatric Association. (1994). *Diagnostic and statistical manual of mental disorders* (4th ed.). Washington, DC: Author.
Barakat, A.Y., & Cochran, W.E. (1978). Tuberous sclerosis: Report of nine cases and a review. *Clinical Pediatrics, 17*(12), 875–879.
Batshaw, M.L. (1993). Mental retardation. *Pediatric Clinics of North America, 40*(3), 507–521.
Batshaw, M.L., & Perret, Y.M. (1992). *Children with disabilities: A medical primer* (3rd ed.). Baltimore: Paul H. Brookes Publishing Co.
Bayley, N. (1969). *Manual for the Bayley Scales of Infant Development.* New York: Psychological Corporation.
Bayley, N. (1993). *Bayley Scales of Infant Development—Second Edition Manual.* San Antonio, TX: Psychological Corporation.
Bess, F.H., & Paradise, J.L. (1994). Universal screening for infant hearing impairment: Not simple, not risk-free, not necessarily beneficial, and not presently justified. *Pediatrics, 93*(2), 330–334.
Bishop, V.E. (1991). Preschool visually impaired children: A demographic study. *Journal of Visual Impairment and Blindness, 85,* 69–74.
Bobath, K., & Bobath, B. (1972). Cerebral palsy. In P.H. Pearson & C. Williams (Eds.), *Physical therapy services in the developmental disabilities* (pp. 31–185). Springfield, IL: Charles C Thomas.
Buchanan, S. (1995, Summer). Lovaas revisited: Should we have ever left? *Newsletter of the Indiana Resource Center for Autism, 8*(3), 1–5, 7.
Busch, W., & Himes, P. (1995, December). Maternal serum screening for chromosome disorders and open neural tube defects. *PacNORGG Newsletter, 10*(2&3).
Chiron, C., Dulac, O., Beaumont, D., Palacios, L., Pajot, N., & Mumford, J. (1991). Therapeutic trial of vigabatrin in refractory infantile spasms. *Journal of Child Neurology,* (Suppl. 2), S52–S59.
Cohen, N.L., Waltzman, S.B., Fisher, S.G., & Department of Veterans Affairs Cochlear Implant Study Group. (1993). A prospective, randomized study of cochlear implants. *New England Journal of Medicine, 328*(4), 233–237.
Committee on Practice and Ambulatory Medicine, American Academy of Pediatrics. (1986). Vision screening and eye examination in children. *Pediatrics, 77*(6), 918–919.
Cosgrove, A.P., Corry, I.S., & Graham, H.K. (1994). Botulinum toxin in the management of the lower limb in cerebral palsy. *Developmental Medicine and Child Neurology, 36,* 386–396.
Courchesne, E., Saitoh, O., Yeung-Courchesne, R., Press, G.A., Lincoln, A.J., Haas, R.H., & Schreibman, L. (1994). Abnormality of cerebellar vermian lobules VI and VII in patients with infantile autism: Identification of hypoplastic and hyperplastic subgroups with MR imaging. *American Journal of Radiology, 162,* 123–130.

Craig, I.W. (1994). Organization of the human genome. *Journal of Inherited Metabolic Disease, 17*(4), 391–402.

Czeizel, A.E., & Dudás. (1992). Prevention of the first occurrence of neural-tube defects by periconceptional vitamin supplementation. *New England Journal of Medicine, 327*(26), 1832–1835.

Davidson, P.W. (1983). Visual impairment and blindness. In M.D. Levine, W.B. Carey, A.C. Crocker, & R.T. Gross (Eds.), *Developmental and behavioral pediatrics.* Philadelphia: W.B. Saunders.

Dawson, G. (1992, April). *Educational planning for children with pervasive developmental disorders.* Paper presented at the annual meeting of the Northwest Society for Developmental and Behavioral Pediatrics, Portland, OR.

Dawson, G., & Osterling, J. (1996). Early intervention in autism. In M.J. Guralnick (Ed.), *The effectiveness of early intervention* (pp. 307–326). Baltimore: Paul H. Brookes Publishing Co.

Driscoll, D.A., Slavin, J., Sellinger, B., Budarf, M.L., McDonald-McGinn, D.M., Zackai, E.H., & Emanuel, B.S. (1993). Prevalence of 22q11 microdeletions in DiGeorge and velocardiofacial syndromes: Implications for genetic counselling and prenatal diagnosis. *Journal of Medical Genetics, 30,* 813–817.

Eken, P., de Vries, L.S., van der Graaf, Y., Meiners, L.C., & van Nieuwenhuizen, O. (1995). Haemorrhag-icischaemic lesions of the neonatal brain: Correlation between cerebral visual impairment, neurodevelopmental outcome and MRI in infancy. *Developmental Medicine and Child Neurology, 37*(1), 41–55.

Elliott, G.R. (1993). *Use of medications for patients with autism and other pervasive developmental disorders.* Paper presented at the annual meeting of the American Academy of Child and Adolescent Psychiatry.

Flage, T. (1993). Cryotherapy for retinopathy of prematurity. International perspectives and some recommendations for treatment. *Acta Ophthalmologica Supplement, 210,* 66–67.

Freeman, J. (1983). Neonatal seizures. In F.E. Dreifuss (Ed.), *Pediatric epilestology: Classification and management of seizures in the child.* Boston: John Wright, P.S.G.

Gatty, J.C. (1996). Early intervention and management of hearing in infants and toddlers. *Infants and Young Children, 9*(1), 1–15.

Gerber, M.A., & Berliner, B.C. (1981). The child with a "simple" febrile seizure: Appropriate diagnostic evaluation. *American Journal of Diseases in Children, 135,* 431–433.

Gilbert, C., Rahi, J., Eckstein, M., & Foster, A. (1995). Hereditary disease as a cause of childhood blindness: Regional variation. Results of blind school studies undertaken in countries of Latin America, Asia and Africa. *Ophthalmic Genetics, 16*(1), 1–10.

Goldberg, R., Motzkin, B., Marion, R., Scambler, P.J., & Shprintzen, R.J. (1993). Velo-cardio-facial syndrome, a review of 120 patients. *American Journal of Medical Genetics, 45,* 313–319.

Hagerman, R. (1993). Clinical overview of fragile X syndrome. *Neurogenetic Advances, 2,* 1–2.

Hanson, M.J. (1987). *Teaching the infant with Down syndrome: A guide for parents and professionals* (2nd ed.). Austin, TX: PRO-ED.

Hanson, M.J., & Harris, S.R. (1986). *Teaching the young child with motor delays: A guide for parents and professionals.* Austin, TX: PRO-ED.

Hayes, D. (1986). Audiological assessment. In D.L. Wodrich & J.E. Joy (Eds.), *Multidisciplinary assessment of children with learning disabilities and mental retardation* (pp. 109–131). Baltimore: Paul H. Brookes Publishing Co.

Hirtz, D.G., Ellenberg, J.H., & Nelson, K.B. (1984). The risk of recurrence of nonfebrile seizures in children. *Neurology, 34,* 637–641.

Ho, H., Lockitch, G., Eaves, L., & Jacobson, B. (1986). Blood serotonin concentrations and fenfluramine therapy in autistic children. *Journal of Pediatrics, 180*(3), 465–469.

Hofman, K.J., Harris, E.L., Bryan, R.N., & Denckla, M.B. (1994). Neurofibromatosis type 1: The cognitive phenotype. *Journal of Pediatrics, 124*(4), S1–S8.

Individuals with Disabilities Education Act (IDEA) of 1990, PL 101-476, 20 U.S.C. § 1400 *et seq.*

Kanner, L. (1943). Autistic disturbances of affective contact. *Nervous Child, 2,* 217–250.

Kinsman, S.L., Vining, E.P., Quaskey, S.A., Mellits, D., & Freeman, J.M. (1992). Efficacy of the ketogenic diet for intractable seizure disorders: A review of 58 cases. *Epilepsia, 33*(6), 1132–1136.

Kotagal, P., & Luders, H.O. (1994). Recent advances in childhood epilepsy. *Brain and Development, 16*(1), 1–15.

Kuban, K.C.K., & Leviton, A. (1994). Review article: Cerebral palsy. *New England Journal of Medicine, 330*(3), 188–195.

Kurokawa, T., Goya, N., Fukuyama, Y., Suzuki, M., Seki, T., & Ohtahara, S. (1980). West syndrome and Lennox-Gastaut syndrome: A survey of natural history. *Pediatrics, 65*(1), 81–88.

Lambert, S.R., Kriss, A., Taylor, D., Coffey, R., & Pembrey, M. (1989). Follow-up and diagnostic reappraisal of 75 patients with Leber's congenital amaurosis. *American Journal of Ophthalmology, 107*, 624–631.

Larson, D.E., Burton, D.D., Schroeder, K.W., & DiMagno, E.P. (1987). Percutaneous endoscopic gastrostomy: Indications, success, complications, and mortality in 314 consecutive patients. *Gastroenterology, 93*, 48–52.

Larsson, N., Andersen, O., Holme, E., Odfors, A., & Wahlstrom, J. (1991). Leber's hereditary optic neuropathy and complex I deficiency in muscle. *Annals of Neurology, 30*(5), 701–708.

Lewis, V., Welch, F., Cherry, F., Flood, E., & Marble, M. (1995). Galactosemia: Clinical features, diagnosis and management. A case report. *Journal of the Louisiana State Medical Society, 147*(6), 262–265.

Listernick, R., & Charrow, J. (1990). Neurofibromatosis type 1 in childhood. *Journal of Pediatrics, 116*(6), 845–853.

Lollar, D.J. (1993). Learning among children with spina bifida. *Spotlight* [Pamphlet]. Washington, DC: Spina Bifida Association of America.

Lovaas, O.I. (1987). Behavioral treatment and normal educational and intellectual functioning in young autistic children. *Journal of Consulting and Clinical Psychology, 55*(1), 3–9.

Madell, J.R. (1988). Identification and treatment of very young children with hearing loss. *Infants and Young Children, 1*(2), 20–30.

McCall, R. (1971). New directions in psychological assessment of infants. *Proceedings of the Royal Society of Medicine, 64*, 465–467.

McEachin, J.J., Smith, T., & Lovaas, O.I. (1993). Long-term outcome for children with autism who received early intensive behavioral treatment. *American Journal on Mental Retardation, 97*(4), 359–372.

McKusick, V. (1988). *Mendelian inheritance in man* (8th ed.) Baltimore: Johns Hopkins University Press.

McLaren, J., & Bryson, S.E. (1987). Review of recent epidemiology studies of mental retardation: Prevalence, associated disorders, and etiology. *American Journal on Mental Retardation, 92*(3), 243–254.

McLaughlin, J.F., Bjornson, K.F., Astley, S.J., Hays, R.M., Hoffinger, S.A., Armantront, E.A., & Robert, T.S. (1994). The role of selective dorsal rhizotomy in cerebral palsy: Critical evaluation of a prospective clinical series. *Developmental Medicine and Child Neurology, 36*, 755–779.

McLaughlin, J.F., & Shurtleff, D.B. (1979). Management of the newborn with myelodysplasia. *Clinical Pediatrics, 18*(8), 463–476.

Mili, F., Edmonds, L.D., Khoury, M.J., & McClearn, A.B. (1991). Prevalence of birth defects among low-birth weight infants. A population study. *American Journal of Diseases of Children, 145*(11), 1313–1318.

MRC Vitamin Study Research Group. (1991). Prevention of neural tube defects: Results of the Medical Research Council Vitamin Study. *Lancet, 338*(8760), 131–137.

Murphy, P.D. (1993). Technical aspects of the diagnosis of fragile X syndrome. *Neurogenetic Advances, 2*(2), 2–3.

Nelson, C.L., & Hallgren, R.A. (1989). Gastrostomies: Indications, management, and weaning. *Infants and Young Children, 2*(1), 66–74.

Nelson, K.B., & Ellenberg, J.H. (Eds.). (1981). *Febrile seizures.* New York: Raven Press.

Nelson, L.B., Rubin, S.E., Wagner, R.S., & Breton, M.E. (1984). Developmental aspects in the assessment of visual function in young children. *Pediatrics, 73*(3), 375–381.

Nickel, R.E., Pillers, D.M., Merkens, M., Magenis, R.E., Driscoll, D.A., Emanuel, B.S., & Zonana, J. (1994). Velo-cardio-facial syndrome DiGeorge sequence with meningomyelocele and deletions of the 22q11 region. *American Journal of Medical Genetics, 52,* 445–449.

Opitz, J.M. (1994). Editorial. Associations and syndromes: Terminology in clinical genetics and birth defects epidemiology: Comments on Khoury, Moore, and Evans. *American Journal of Medical Genetics, 49,* 14–20.

Orenstein, S.R., Whitington, P.F., & Orenstein, D.M. (1983). The infant seat as treatment for gastroesophageal reflux. *New England Journal of Medicine, 309,* 760–763.

Paneth, N. (1986). Etiologic factors in cerebral palsy. *Pediatric Annals, 15*(3), 193–201.

Pearl, R.H., Robie, D.K., Ein, S.H., Shandling, B., Wesson, D.E., Superina, R., McTaggart, K., Garcia, V.F., O'Connor, J.A., & Filler, R.M. (1990). Complications of gastroesophageal antireflux surgery in neurologically impaired versus neurologically normal children. *Journal of Pediatric Surgery, 25*(11), 1169–1173.

Penry, J.K. (Ed.). (1986). *Epilepsy: Diagnosis, management, quality of life.* New York: Raven Press.

Perry, A. (1991). Rett syndrome: A comprehensive review of the literature. *American Journal on Mental Retardation, 96*(3), 275–290.

Prats, J.M., Garaizar, C., Rua, M.J., Garcia-Nieto, M.L., & Madoz, P. (1991). Infantile spasms treated with high doses of sodium valproate: Initial response and follow-up. *Developmental Medicine and Child Neurology, 33,* 617–625.

Preisler, G.M. (1995). The development of communication in blind and in deaf infants—Similarities and differences. *Child: Care, Health, and Development, 21*(2), 79–110.

Ramsey, M., Gisel, E.G., & Boutry, M. (1993). Nonorganic failure to thrive: Growth failure secondary to feeding skills disorder. *Developmental Medicine and Child Neurology, 35,* 285–297.

Reyes, A., Cash, A.J., Green, S.H., & Booth, I.W. (1993). Gastroesophageal reflux in children with cerebral palsy. *Child: Care, Health, and Development, 19,* 109–118.

Roush, J. (1990). Acoustic amplification for hearing-impaired infants and young children. *Infants and Young Children, 2*(4), 59–71.

Rutter, M. (1968). Concepts of autism: A review of research. *Journal of Child Psychology and Psychiatry, 9,* 1–25.

Schopler, E. (1994). Behavioral priorities for autism and related developmental disorders. In E. Schopler & G.B. Mesibov (Eds.), *Behavioral issues in autism* (pp. 55–75). New York: Plenum.

Scrutton, D. (1992). The classification of the cerebral palsies. Letter to the editor. *Developmental Medicine and Child Neurology, 34,* 833–837.

Shields, W.D., Shewmon, D.A., Chugani, H.T., & Peacock, W.J. (1992). Treatment of infantile spasms: Medical or surgical? *Epilepsia, 33*(Suppl. 4), S26–S31.

Shorvon, S.D. (1990). Epilepsy octet: Epidemiology, classification, natural history, and genetics of epilepsy. *Lancet, 336,* 93–96.

Simko, A., Hornstein, L., Soukup, S., & Bagamery, N. (1989). Fragile X syndrome: Recognition in young children. *Pediatrics, 83*(4), 547–552.

Skinner, R. (1990). Unifactorial inheritance. In A.E. Emery & D.L. Rimoin (Eds.), *Principles and practice of medical genetics* (Vol. 1, 2nd ed., pp. 95–105). New York: Churchill Livingstone.

Snead, O.C., Benton, J.W., & Myers, G.J. (1983). ACTH and prednisone in childhood seizure disorders. *Neurology, 33,* 966–970.

Snow, J.H., Prince, M., Souheaver, G., Ashcraft, E., Stefans, V., & Edmonds, J. (1994). Neuropsychological patterns of adolescents and young adults with spina bifida. *Archives of Clinical Neuropsychology, 9*(3), 277–287.

Stringel, G., Delgard, M., Guertin, L., Cook, J.D., Maravilla, A., & Worthen, H. (1989). Gastrostomy and Nissen fundoplication in neurologically impaired children. *Journal of Pediatric Surgery, 24*(10), 1044–1048.

Szatmari, P. (1993, October). *Asperger's disorder.* Paper presented at the annual meeting of the American Academy of Child and Adolescent Psychiatry, San Antonio, TX.

Tennison, M., Greenwood, R., Lewis, D., & Thorn, M. (1994). Discontinuing antiepileptic drugs in children with epilepsy, a comparison of a six-week and a nine-month taper period. *New England Journal of Medicine, 330*(20), 1407–1410.

Thompson, E.J. (1989). A genetics primer for early service providers. *Infants and Young Children, 2*(1), 37–48.
Thompson, J.S., & Thompson, M.W. (1986). *Genetics in medicine* (2nd ed.). Philadelphia: W.B. Saunders.
Thurman, S.K., & Widerstrom, A.H. (1990). *Infants and young children with special needs: A developmental and ecological approach* (2nd ed.). Baltimore: Paul H. Brookes Publishing Co.
Truwit, C.L., Barkovich, A.J., Koch, T.K., & Ferriero, D.M. (1992). Cerebral palsy: MR findings on 40 patients. *American Journal of Neuroradiology, 13*, 67–78.
Tsai, L.Y., & Ghaziuddin, M. (1991). Autistic disorders. In J.M. Weiner (Ed.), *Textbook of child and adolescent psychiatry* (pp. 625–641). Washington, DC: American Psychiatric Press.
Use of folic acid for prevention of spina bifida and other neural tube defects: 1983–1991. (1991, August). *Morbidity and Mortality Weekly Report, 40*(30), 513–515.
Volkmar, F.R. (1992). Childhood disintegrative disorder: Issues for DSM-IV. *Journal of Autism and Developmental Disorders, 22*(4), 625–641.
Waitzman, N.J., Romano, P.S., & Scheffler, R.M. (1994). Estimates of the economic costs of birth defects. *Inquiry, 31*(2), 188–205.
Widerstrom, A.H., & Goodwin, L.D. (1987). Effects of an infant stimulation program on the child and family. *Journal of Division for Early Childhood, 11*, 143–153.
Wilson, D.I., Burn, J., Scambler, P., & Goodship, J. (1993). DiGeorge syndrome: Part of CATCH 22. *Journal of Medical Genetics, 30*, 852–856.
Withrow, C.D. (1980). The ketogenic diet: Mechanism of anticonvulsant action. In G.H. Glasser, J.K. Penry, & D.M. Woodbury (Eds.), *Antiepileptic drugs: Mechanisms of action* (pp. 635–642). New York: Raven Press.
Wolf, L., & Glass, R. (1992). *Feeding and swallowing disorders in infancy.* Tucson, AZ: Therapy Skill Builders.

4 ACTIVITIES

1. Name one of each of the following:
   a. A birth defect caused by an autosomal dominant genetic disorder
   b. A birth defect caused by an autosomal recessive genetic disorder
   c. A birth defect caused by an X-linked recessive genetic disorder
   d. A birth defect caused by an X-linked dominant genetic disorder

2. Explain why X-linked recessive disorders are manifested primarily in males.

3. Make a chart that summarizes the major developmental disorders and their characteristics, symptoms, and treatment. Use headings from this chapter to get started.

SECTION III

FAMILY SYSTEMS AND SERVICES

CHAPTER 5

Family Dynamics

Barbara A. Mowder

Objectives

- To understand related topics in parent–infant interaction
- To understand interactions with infants at risk
- To understand issues related to effects of parenting styles on the child

A family is defined as two or more individuals, at least one of whom is an adult and the other a child, who are legally bound to each other through birth, adoption, or legal guardianship (Mowder, 1996). The family represents a complex set of bonds, dynamics, relationships, systems, and subsystems, in which each individual is developing and at the same time interacting with and adjusting to the family.

Typically, at least one individual in the family is the parent. Mowder (1991a, 1991b, 1993) developed the Parent Role Development Model (PRDM), which explains how parents come to perceive and perform the parent role. The PRDM provides professionals with parent role characteristics (see Table 5.1), a model or theory about how parents parent, and therefore affords avenues for communication, consultation, assessment, and intervention (Mowder, Harvey, Moy, & Pedro, 1995; Mowder, Harvey, Pedro, Rossen, & Moy, 1993). Mowder (1993) provided definitions for parenting as well as those involved in parenting activities:

> *Parent Role:* The parent role represents how individuals and societies conceptualize the parent portion of a parent–child relationship and, depending on the culture, typically incorporates the elements of bonding, discipline, education, general welfare and protection, responsivity, and sensitivity.

Table 5.1. Parent role characteristics

Parent role characteristics	Description
1. Bonding	The love and affection that parents feel and demonstrate toward their children
2. Discipline	Establishing parameters, rules, and guidelines for children and ensuring that they are responded to
3. Education	The teaching, guiding, and modeling role that parents play for their children
4. General welfare and protection	Providing children with their basic needs, such as food, clothing, and shelter, and protecting them from harm
5. Responsivity	Being available and responsive to children on a timely basis as their needs arise
6. Sensitivity	The matching of parental responses to the child and the child's perceived needs

> *Parent:* An individual who recognizes, accepts, and performs the parent role.
>
> *Child:* An individual who is a child, the receiver of parenting, in a parent–child relationship. (This definition means that age is not a factor, rather the child is the person who is the recipient of the parent–child interaction.)
>
> *Parenting:* Performing the activities associated with the parent role. Parent role performance does not always reflect individual parent role perceptions. Other factors, beyond parent role perception, also affect parenting, including, for example, additional competing parent responsibilities, exhaustion, motivation, and resource availability. (p. 12)

Nothing influences the infant as significantly as the family. Family interactions, relationships, and the environment it provides affect infants' bonds of affection and development of abilities, interests, language, and skills (Emde & Sameroff, 1989). Families vary in a multitude of ways, including beliefs, education, ethnic background, friends and extended family, geographic location, religion, and values; the complexity of family variables affecting children is further complicated by changes that occur in the family life cycle over time (Terkelson, 1980). Given the possible combinations of characteristics and changes, every family is to some extent unique (Turnbull & Turnbull, 1986).

Early parent–infant family interactions set the stage for each infant's growth and development. The view of the family as the critical element in child development is the foundation for PL 101-476, the Individuals with Disabilities Education Act (IDEA) of 1990, and PL 102-119, the Individuals with Disabilities Education Act Amendments of 1991, and for the provision of services to infants and toddlers at risk for or with disabilities. The assumptions underlying the legislation that guides professional practice in this area hold that families are the primary factor in facilitating children's growth and development. Guralnick (1989) succinctly presented this argument:

> By enhancing natural parenting skills and providing the conditions for families to become more competent and confident in their unique relationship with their children, conditions for optimal child development may well be created. A common element appears to be the child-oriented nature of the relationship, which allows a harmonious, sensitive, and stimulating interactive match to develop. It is important to emphasize that these principles are likely to apply across children's risk or disabilities status. (p. 12)

Parents have not always been viewed as essential, integral, and primary in facilitating children's development. Turnbull and Turnbull (1986) remind us that parents, over time, have assumed or been expected by professionals to assume a

Hallie

Growing up in a family of boys, Gale was surprised at how easy it was having a baby girl. Her brothers had been very demanding in terms of attention required from their parents, and they needed constant physical activity. Their needs generated a good deal of parental frustration, tried their mother's patience, in particular, and created some strained family dynamics.

When Hallie was born, Gale was ready to be a parent. What surprised her after Hallie was born, based on her experience with her demanding siblings, was how easy it was to care for her daughter. Hallie was physically healthy, and breast milk agreed with her. She was responsive to both her parents, and they could figure out her needs and meet them.

Now that Hallie is 2 years old, her needs are changing and their parenting has adjusted accordingly. In particular, because of her increased language skills, she now controls a good deal of their interaction. Hallie enjoys imaginative play, and she and Gale often will host tea parties for Hallie's stuffed animal menagerie. She also needs more social interaction and structured play activities. She has been in play groups and now attends a small nursery school a few mornings a week.

Gale finds parenting an all-consuming activity, adapting to her child's sleeping, eating, and various other changing needs. Gale is struck by how much Hallie establishes and communicates her needs. Hallie knows how to get attention and Gale has learned how much to give and when. Gale is also a working mother, and, besides being sensitive to Hallie's needs, she also balances her child's needs with her own needs to earn a living.

variety of major roles, including source of the child's problem, organization member, service developer, recipient of professionals' decisions, learner and teacher, political advocate, educational decision maker, and family member. Responding to all roles and expectations has been difficult if not impossible for parents. Regardless of specific roles or expectations, however, researchers agree that parents play a tremendous role in infants', toddlers', and children's development. Indeed, an empowerment family-centered model of early intervention service delivery, focused on families' strengths, resources, and concerns, is now a fundamental component of early intervention services (Epps & Jackson, 1991; McLinden & Prasse, 1991). Early interventionists need specific, additional training in order to provide the family-oriented services required by PL 101-476 and PL 102-119 (Bailey, Simeonsson, Yoder, & Huntington, 1990; Hanson & Lovett, 1992; Roberts & Magrab, 1991).

Family dynamics are a particularly important factor when the child in the family is at risk for or has a disabling condition: The family can play a key role in how the disabling condition ultimately affects the child and the child's functioning. This chapter is organized to address family dynamics and infant exceptionality and includes early factors in infant–parent interaction, parenting issues and parent training, attachment and bonding, gender differences in family dynamics, family dynamics and family systems, family interactions with infants at risk for or with disabilities, parenting dynamics and child characteristics, abuse and neglect, and future issues in family dynamics.

PARENT–INFANT INTERACTION

From research we know that spontaneous infant behavior is transformed into interactive behavior by a parent who responds to the infant (Hetherington, 1983). The contingent, interactive parent–infant behavior becomes socialized behavior in the context of the family. The family provides the infant's introduction to cognitive development, social and emotional bonds, language, a sense of security in the world, and skill development. Family interactions lead to relationships that evolve over time and are, at their simplest level, regularities in patterns of interaction (Sroufe, 1989). Relationships characterized by parental attentiveness, responsivity, sensitivity, stimulation, and warmth promote infant, toddler, and child intellectual and social competence (Belsky, Lerner, & Spanier, 1985; Bornstein, 1986; Lamb, 1980; Lamb & Bornstein, 1987).

Early Factors

The early family interactive process, which evolves and develops over time, incorporates three major elements: personality characteristics of the parent, situational influences on the parent, and infant behavioral characteristics (Lamb & Bornstein, 1987). For example, major parental personality traits that contribute to the developing parent–child relationship include adaptability, self-centeredness, sensitivity, and a sense of self as a competent parent (Ainsworth, Blehar, Waters, & Wall, 1978; Lamb & Bornstein, 1987). Situational influences involve parental factors such as parental stress, social support systems, and cross-generational familial expectation. Individual infant characteristics affecting the parent–child relationship include characteristics such as soothability, irritability, and predictability. Together, these three major factors interact and contribute to each individual family's developing interaction patterns.

Family interactions involving a baby typically lead to a strong relationship between parent and child that is unique in its initial asymmetry (Hetherington, 1983; Maccoby, 1992); although the relationship is mutual and interactive, the infant must depend totally on the parent for survival. Parents provide affection, food, clothing, shelter, and warmth to the baby. In addition, parents respond to continuous environmental demands, such as meeting financial obligations, maintaining the home, and meeting family and household needs. Hetherington (1983) found that, although parent characteristics are influenced by the infant's arrival, to a great extent they remain constant. In contrast, the infant makes vast adjustments to the parent and the parent's milieu.

According to many researchers, the parent–infant relationship bond is not present at birth but develops over time. There is considerable research on the specific relationship bond that develops between the infant and the parent. Two separate literatures have evolved regarding the bond—one from the side of the parent, known as *bonding*, and the other from the side of the child, which is referred to as *attachment* (Emde, 1989). Essentially, typically developing newborns and infants give cues such as cooing, crying, cuddling, and smiling, which are signals for parents to respond. As parents respond to their baby's signals and the infant anticipates needs being met, interactions occur that lead to the relationship bond, a bond that is critical to the development of a healthy child.

For parental bonding to occur, Klaus and Kennell (1981; Kennell, Voos, & Klaus, 1979) made the controversial assertion that there is a "sensitive period" immediately after birth. Affectionate attachments or bonds between the parent and infant must be formed at this time; if the bonding is interfered with, aberrant parenting may occur, which, in turn, could affect infant development. De Chateau (1980), too, maintained that fostering early physical contact between the mother and newborn is important and that the effect of early close body contact with infants can be observed in closeness between the two as soon as 1 year after the baby's delivery. However, the importance of close early physical contact is controversial (Lamb & Bornstein, 1987); research evidence fails to support the importance of early contact (Eyer, 1992; Goldberg, 1983; Lamb, 1982; Myers, 1987), and there is little evidence that early contact has significant effects on maternal behavior (Lamb & Hwang, 1982).

Regardless of the merits of a specific sensitive period for bonding, the early close physical contact creates a situation of mutual contingency in which the parent and the newborn continuously adapt to one another's behavior. Behaviors involved in the early interactive process include eye contact, smiling, and vocalizations, which all contribute to the parent–child relationship. Trevarthen (1977) pointed out how these behaviors affect the turn-taking nature of mother–infant interactions, and many researchers (e.g., Papousek & Papousek, 1992; Thoman, 1981) view the interactive process as an early form of communication between parent and infant. Gazing, looking, and mutual visual regard, in particular, appear to contribute substantially to the interaction (Stern, 1974; Stern, Beebe, Jaffe, & Bennett, 1977). Parents agree that bonding is a very important aspect of their parental role when children are infants and toddlers (Mowder et al., 1995).

The relationship that evolves depends not only on what occurs, but how the interaction pattern develops. It is the patterning of a relationship that is closely related to the quality of the interaction, according to Sroufe (1989):

> *Patterning* refers to the timing, sequences, and combinational features of the ongoing interaction. *When* does the caregiver pick up the infant: Is the pickup in response to a gesture by the infant: Is there an ongoing tuning or synchronizing of the behavior of each to the other? Does the infant mold to the caregiver or mix molding with stiffening, squirming, and pushing away?
>
> In one case, an infant's distress may be terminated efficiently and smoothly. The caregiver responds promptly to the infant's cry, bending to pick up the infant and conferring meaning to the cry. Reciprocally, the infant leans or reaches toward the caregiver, yields her body to the pickup, and then actively snuggles into the caregiver's shoulder, both arms wrapped around her neck. The caregiver rocks the infant with a swaying motion, gently pats the infant's back, and whispers in soothing tones. The infant settles, relaxes, and returns to play.
>
> By contrast, in response to the baby's wail, a second caregiver bristles, then after some delay picks him up with a jerky motion. The infant's body stiffens and the crying seems to intensify. The infant shifts from side to side and alternates leaning with pushing away from his mother, whose own irritation and tension show through pats that are too rough and movements that are stiff. The distress persists for several minutes. (p. 89)

During the first year of a baby's life, both the infant and the parents undergo developmental changes. Parents adjust to the infant and the infant's characteristics, interests, and needs in the context of their own personal characteristics and circumstances. Infants develop increasing competence in motor and physical skills, communication abilities, and cognitive growth and development (Papousek & Papousek, 1992) as they respond and interact within the family environment. By approximately 12 months of age, the nature of the infant's attachment to the parent can be assessed. Bowlby (1980) asserted, "Intimate attachments to other human beings are the hub around which a person's life revolves, not only when he or she is an infant or a toddler, but throughout adolescence and the years of maturity as well and on into old age" (p. 442).

Attachment

Attachment is the child's side of the relationship bond that is formed and develops after birth. By the time an infant is 1 year of age, attachment may be reliably measured. Based on parent–infant interactions, through the "strange situation" research method (see Chapter 2), infants are categorized as insecure-avoidant, securely attached, insecure-resistant, or insecure-disorganized/disoriented (Main & Solomon, 1986).

The measurement of attachment, to a great extent, is an indication of how the emerging individual is organizing attitudes, expectations, and feelings. The organization is based on the history and pattern of affective and behavioral regulation that has occurred within the caregiving system (Sroufe, 1989) and has significant implications for the child's future adjustment. For example, infants identified as securely attached are found to be more enthusiastic, affectively positive, and confident in solving problems than infants with histories of avoidant attachment (Arend, 1984; Matas, Arend, & Sroufe, 1978; Sroufe, 1989; Sroufe & Rosenberg, 1980). In addition, securely attached children have greater ego strength at age 3½ (Waters, Wippman, & Sroufe, 1979) and are more resilient at ages 4 and 5 (Arend, Gove, & Sroufe, 1979; Sroufe, 1983). "Thus, young children with histories of secure attachment are seen to be independent, resourceful, curious, and confident in their approach to the environment" (Sroufe, 1989, p. 87).

Avoidant attachment relationships, however, mirror a history of insensitive care and rejection. This pattern of attachment reflects the infant's internalized working model of the caregiver as unavailable and unresponsive to the infant's needs (Sroufe, 1989). Later, these children are characterized as hostile, with displays of unprovoked aggression and generally negative peer interactions (LaFreniere & Sroufe, 1985); in school, they disrupt the classroom routine and engage in deviant or antisocial behavior (Sroufe, 1983). In addition, these children behave in ways that re-create their early relationships, and they often influence their environment to confirm their models of self and others (Sroufe & Fleeson, 1986). Karen (1994) discussed not only how different approaches to mothering are associated with specific infants' behavior but also how negative patterning can be resolved and changed during a person's lifetime.

Attachment has also been considered from a cross-cultural perspective. Sagi (1990), for instance, examined data collected on Israeli kibbutzim as well as samples from different countries. The cross-national analysis suggests that interactive behaviors are similar and thus supports universal aspects of attachment theory. Grossman and Grossman (1990) also found support for attachment theory in that caregivers' responsiveness to infants' signals seems to be the determining factor in infant–parent attachment.

Beckwith (1990) found that one important question in attachment theory and research is how infants integrate attachment relationships, because attachment

security is specific to each infant–parent dyad. Indeed, Main and Weston (1981) found that children can form one type of attachment relationship to one parent and another type of attachment relationship to the other; Barnas and Cummings (1994) documented toddlers' attachment-related behavior toward caregivers in child care. Although the infant–parent attachment tends to be stable over time, the attachment relationship can change due to factors interfering with stability within the family (Shaw & Vondra, 1993; Vaughn, Egeland, Sroufe, & Waters, 1979).

Gender Differences

Most research on family dynamics examining parent–infant interaction focuses on the relationship between the mother and the child. However, since the 1980s, researchers have become increasingly interested in the father's role in the socialization process. The interest stems from two major issues: an increasing consideration of infant sex role development and both parents' influences on such development, and the changing role of women and the impact of that change on child development. The latter issue has been particularly striking as women have moved from care of children and upkeep of the home to a co-equal (or sole) participant in the economic well-being of the family. Mothers' pursuits of economic, educational, and vocational interests have changed dynamics in that the mother is no longer necessarily the sole or primary caregiver (Zigler, 1990). The potential change in the female's role in the family has raised the question of the relative influence of each parent in the infant's development (see the boxed case study on Bill and Sally on p. 132).

Some of the changes in roles have occurred with the birth process itself. It has been only since the mid- to late-1970s that fathers have been involved in the birth process. Now, the expectation for many fathers is that they are present at birth and play an active role in facilitating the birth process. Fathers may even be the first indi-

Bill and Sally

Bill and Sally married when he was in graduate school and she in medical school. They rejected a more traditional marriage, in which the husband works and the wife maintains the home and raises children. Based on the premise of shared commitments and responsibilities, their marriage was up-tempo with the promise of two professional careers ready to unfold.

During her medical residency program, Sally became pregnant with their child, Ann. Sally stayed home with Ann for 4 months and then resumed her residency program. Sally was the only resident intern with an infant, one of very few women in the training program, and she worked under the skeptical eye of senior colleagues who silently questioned her commitment to medicine. Working a 60- to 70-hour-per-week schedule and being on call every third night left little time for her participation in child rearing and child care activities.

What started as a co-equal partnership in marriage quickly became a one-sided arrangement of child care responsibilities, in which Bill, with the more flexible college professor schedule, became the primary parent. His responsibilities included arranging child care during the day; supervising the child care; rearranging his schedule when the child care provider was ill or unavailable; being with Ann in the evening and on weekends; securing diapers, baby food, and clothing; and seeing to all of Ann's other needs. Bill began to feel as if he was in a traditional marriage but with the roles reversed; the traditional child care and home responsibilities were falling on the husband instead of the wife.

As Sally's schedule maintained its excessive time demands and remained inflexible in terms of adaptability, child care, parenting, and marital concerns, a strong relationship formed between Bill and Ann. As Bill supervised child care during the week, cared for Ann at all other times, and included her in all social activities, their relationship became the dominant subsystem in the family. During the times when Sally was home, tensions arose over the unequal distribution of child care responsibilities, questions regarding parental authority, and career demands and frustrations. Over time, the child care issue subsided, but the residual family dynamic concerns awaited resolution.

viduals to hold and cuddle the infant while the mother is still in the final stage of labor, the delivery of the placenta. Research in maternity wards shows that fathers are competent and interested in their newborns and display interaction involvement with the infants (Parke & Tinsley, 1981).

Researchers discern that both males and females play a significant role in infant development, although the specific roles may differ somewhat (Akande, 1994; Hetherington, 1983; Kotelchuck, 1976; Russell & Radojevic, 1992). Studies of early father–infant interaction document the affectionate and nurturant involvement between the father and the newborn (Parke & O'Leary, 1976). Pedersen (1975) also discovered that fathers play both a direct and indirect role in the early parent–child relationship. The direct role involves holding and caring for the infant, whereas the indirect role, in supporting the mother, allows the mother to more effectively interact with the infant.

The relative roles of the mother and father still vary, however. Fathers spend less time with their infants, on the average, than mothers and engage in fewer caregiving activities (e.g., changing diapers, feeding) (Kotelchuck, 1976; Lamb & Bornstein, 1987). Bentley and Fox (1991) found that, although both mothers and fathers are nurturing, mothers obtained higher nurturing scores on an inventory of parental behaviors. Fathers do engage in affectionate behavior and are sensitive and responsive to their infants. Parke and O'Leary (1976), as well as Fagot and Hagan (1991) and Yogman (1982), found that fathers are active with their infants, but in ways that differ from mothers. While mothers engage in more caregiving activities, fathers are involved in more play activities.

The type and relative frequency of activity does not appear to affect infants' attachment to their fathers (Rosenblith & Sims-Knight, 1985). Schaffer and Emerson (1964), for instance, demonstrated that babies cry when their fathers leave and Pedersen and Robson (1969) found that babies display positive greeting behaviors when their fathers appear. Research on father–infant, as well as mother–infant, interaction has been conducted primarily on parents of typically developing infants. Exceptions include Moran, Pederson, Pettit, and Krupka (1992), Niven, Wiszniewkski, and AlRoomi (1993), and O'Connor, Sigman, and Kasari (1992), but there is still a distinct need for researchers to consider father–infant and mother–infant interaction with newborns and infants at risk for or with disabilities.

Role of Child Care

Changing roles within the family and mothers' increasing involvement in the workforce make child care a primary issue of concern. Fishbein (1984) made the point that child care by nonfamily members is not unique in human history; for 99% of human existence, humans lived as hunters and gatherers in close-knit groups in which child rearing was the responsibility of both family and nonfamily group members. For North American and Western industrialized societies, however, child rearing has consistently involved the mother being available to the infant.

With the increasing pattern of mothers working, less availability of extended family members for child care, and the increasing reliance on child care facilities and licensed home-based child care providers, research is beginning to compare home-reared and child care infants. These studies (e.g., Blanchard & Main, 1979; Brookhart & Hock, 1976; Burchinal, Bryant, Lee, & Ramey, 1992; Lamb & Sternberg, 1990; Vaughn, Gove, & Egeland, 1980) showed that there are no persistent or systematic ill effects of child care on infants' attachment behavior.

Zigler (1990) placed tremendous importance on the issue of child care availability and quality. Zigler saw this as the most significant issue regarding children and families and as an issue that will only become more important in the future as even more women enter the workforce and require child care support. He was dismayed over the lack of standards for child care provision, in the light of overwhelming consistency in professional judgment for quality child care. Furthermore, Zigler found troublesome the lack of effort politically in terms of social policy; if children are the primary social resource, we must expend more resources to maintain and enhance that resource (Young & Zigler, 1988).

Family Systems

During the first 2 years of life, if the relationship is going well, caregivers become increasingly sensitive to the individual characteristics of their babies, and a strong, consistent, positive relationship bond becomes established. Infants give signals that elicit parent behavior, parents respond, and a complex set of interactions begins. By the end of the first year, a clear sense of attachment is discerned; and by the end of the second year, the relationship becomes further refined and the infant and parent have developed a highly complex set of interactions forming the basis for the infant's cognitive, emotional, and social development.

Minuchin and his colleagues (Minuchin, 1974, 1980; Minuchin & Fishman, 1981; Minuchin, Montalvo, Guerney, Rosman, & Schumer, 1967; Minuchin, Rosman, Baker, & Liebman, 1978) and Bowen (1978) introduced the ideas and practice of structural family theory and therapy to help describe the family dynamic relationship patterns that evolve as a consequence of parent–child interactions. From this general point of view, individuals are shaped by their own individual characteristics as well as all the various contexts to which the individual is exposed (e.g., peers, school). The most significant factor in individual development from a family systems perspective is the family. The family is made up of dynamics, structures, functions, change mechanisms, and dysfunctions, all of which contribute to the development of the individual (Liebman & Ziffer, 1985).

Minuchin (1974) saw the family structure as, "the invisible set of functional demands that organizes the ways in which family members interact. A family is a system that operates through transactional patterns. Repeated transactions establish patterns of how, when, and to whom to relate, and these patterns underpin the system" (p. 51). Within families, subsystems develop that are formed by interest, generation, sex, or function; they include one, two (a dyad), or more members in roles that may be temporary and changeable (Minuchin et al., 1978).

Typical subsystems include the *spouse dyad* (husband and wife bonds), *parent dyad* (those in parenting roles), and the *sibling subsystem*. The subsystems must have sufficient freedom to function without interference from other subsystems in order to facilitate individual growth and development; for example, children will not learn to resolve their own differences if parents consistently intervene and solve problems for them (Liebman & Ziffer, 1985). There are communication patterns within and between subsystems. Goldstein (1988) examined communication deviance in families, and others considered generational boundaries between parents and children (Kreppner, Paulse, & Schuetze, 1982) and the links between abusive parental histories and child maltreatment (Main, Kaplan, & Cassidy, 1985; Ricks, 1985).

Marital harmony, disharmony, or a dysfunctional relationship can all have significant effects on the baby. Even the lack of an adult relationship can affect the level of stress within the family. Beckman (1983), for example, examined the influence of selected child characteristics on stress in families with infants with disabilities. She reported that the only demographic variable associated with the amount of stress in the home was the number of parents in the home. Single mothers report more stress than do married mothers.

The family system also may involve siblings in terms of sibling–sibling interaction as well as sibling–parent interactions. Stevenson, Leavitt, Thompson, and Roach (1988) introduced a social relations model for understanding interactions between parent–child and sibling play and suggested that adjustments that family members make with one another outweigh family members' general tendencies to act in certain ways. Vandell and Wilson (1987) also explored the issue of sibling interaction and found that infants' turn-taking experiences with their mothers were related to the infants' subsequent interactions with their siblings and peers.

Gibbs, Teti, and Bond (1987) found that infants are more responsive to siblings widely spaced in age than those closely spaced. In addition, siblings who are widely spaced in age direct more social behavior to one another and are involved in more interactive engagements than siblings who are closely spaced in age. Older siblings often act as subsidiary attachment figures, caregivers, and teachers (Stewart, 1983; Stewart & Marvin, 1984).

From the family systems literature, *functional families* are defined as those in which communication, boundaries, hierarchies, and subsystems meet the needs of family members' developmental stages. *Dysfunctional families* suffer when one or more of these factors contribute to the family's failure to meet an individual's developmental needs. Liebman and Ziffer (1985) described five general dysfunctional patterns:

1. *Overprotectiveness:* The tendency of parents to literally hover over the child, perhaps to the point of rarely letting him or her leave the house, except to attend school.
2. *Enmeshment:* An overinvolvement between two or more people resulting in a lack of age-appropriate autonomy, independence, privacy, and peer group relationships for both parties.
3. *Rigidity:* The family's tendency to rely on accustomed usual patterns of transactions when circumstances call for flexibility and change.
4. *Detouring:* A way of avoiding conflict between two people by invoking a third person or situation as the focus of the disagreement.
5. *Disengagement:* The lack of affective bonds, limits, or nurturance between two or more family members. (pp. 185–186)

As a result of dysfunctional family patterns, boundaries may be too permeable, may be not permeable enough, or may have failed altogether. The lack of resolution results in submerged stress, which potentially can create one of five crystallized problematic family types (Liebman & Ziffer, 1985):

1. *Triangulated family system:* Characterized by shifting subsystem coalitions and splitting of the spouse dyad. In this situation, children feel trapped because they cannot agree with one parent without at the same time being perceived as disagreeing with the other.
2. *Detouring protective family system:* Parents superficially present an appropriate nuturant-supportive response to the child; however, there is typically overprotectiveness and enmeshment in these families.
3. *Detouring attacking family system:* Characterized by strength in the spouse dyad, with the parents focusing blame on the child for causing family problems.
4. *Stable coalition family system:* Found with close and constricting relationships between the identified child and one parent. This dyad usually excludes or attacks the other parent.
5. *Disengaged child family system:* The child or adolescent explicitly states his or her disinterest in being involved with the problems of the family.

In summary, parent–child interactions develop over time, as relationship bonds form and patterns of behavior within the family are established. The behavior patterns become family dynamics involving dyads and subsystems. When working well, the family dynamics accommodate the individual, subsystem, and family system developmental changes and needs. When not functioning well, family dynamics lead to patterns of behavior that fail to facilitate the growth and development of one or more family members.

FAMILY INTERACTIONS WITH INFANTS AT RISK FOR OR WITH DISABILITIES

With the addition of any infant to the family, adjustments are made; parents sleep less and are available to their baby at all times of the day and night to provide food, warmth, and shelter. With the birth of a baby at risk for or with disabilities, however, the adjustment is more striking and typically involves more accommodations within the family and the home (Emde & Brown, 1978). For example, there may be additional feeding and caregiving tasks and responsibilities, additional modifications of schedules and activities to meet the medical or related infant needs, adjustments to separation if the infant's medical needs are great and require hospitalization, additional and unforeseen financial obligations, and readjustment of the marital relationship.

Parents with infants in nurseries for babies at risk are often described as angry, emotionally distraught, or shocked (e.g., Damrosch & Perry, 1989; Klaus & Kennell, 1976; Kopf & McFadden, 1974; Pederson, Bento, Chance, Evans, & Fox, 1987; Slade, Redl, & Manguten, 1977). Drotar, Baskiewicz, Irvin, Kennell, and Klaus (1975) described five stages parents pass through in adapting and attaching to their infant with a disability. Initially, parents experience shock and dismay, which gives way to a period of denial. In the third stage, parents express anger, anxiety, and sadness about their baby. In the fourth, there is a gradual adjustment as the parents gain confidence in caring for their infant. Finally, parents accept responsibility for their child and begin to plan for the baby's care and future. This particular set of stages has been questioned in the literature, but it is clear that the birth of a baby with a disability does require a period of parental and familial adjustment (Dyson, 1991; Tangri & Verma, 1992; Tunali & Power, 1993) (see the boxed case study on Mary Kay and Joe on the next page).

Feeding disturbances are common with an infant with disabilities (Klaus & Fanaroff, 1979). This places greater demands on caregivers than with normal babies. Some babies (e.g., premature infants) are alert less and are more difficult to keep alert. Goldberg (1978), for example, found that the cries of premature infants are judged to be more aversive to parents than cries of full-term babies.

Infants at risk may also be less adept at responding to parental cues than typical, full-term babies. Jones (1977), for example, found that infants with Down syndrome engage in less eye contact with their mothers, use fewer "referential" looks, and have poorer vocal turn-taking compared with typical infants. Indeed, preterm infants contribute less to the parent interactive flow than do full-term babies (Brown & Bakeman, 1980). It would be inappropriate, however, to assume that parent–child relationships are necessarily disordered or infants with disabilities have a distorted understanding of themselves, others, or their relationship (Adams & Weaver, 1986; Drotar & Bush, 1985; Drotar, Crawford, & Bush, 1984; Parmalee, 1989). One of the major problems for these relationships may be the difficulties that parents have in gaining confidence in themselves as effective parents and caregivers (Cadman, Boyle, Szatmari, & Offord, 1987).

Factors for infants at risk and infantile impairments can affect the parent–child interaction in two basic ways: 1) by the baby's own behavior in stimulating and

Mary Kay and Joe

Mary Kay and Joe prepared for the birth of their child by attending childbirth classes. In the classes, the instructor posed thought-provoking questions, such as what you would do if your baby had difficulties at delivery. Because they had thought about and discussed such an occurrence, they knew what to do when their daughter was born with problems and after delivery was taken immediately to the intensive care unit. Joe went with baby Katherine to intensive care and was with her during the critical time when she was receiving oxygen and being examined by pediatric specialists. Mary Kay believes that there is a special bond between Joe and Katherine because of the initial period of time they spent with one another.

Although she was born at 38 weeks' gestation, Katherine was a low birth weight baby. She weighed 4 pounds, 13 ounces at birth, exhibited low muscle tone, and had a soft palate cleft and a heart murmur. The physicians did not offer a specific diagnosis of Katherine's difficulties, and as time went on a significant hearing loss also was found. Probably the most difficult physical issue now for Mary Kay and Joe is feeding Katherine. Their strongest feelings of frustration revolve around not being able to help her eat. With much patience and help from professional therapists, they have tried to work with her on sucking and feeding. After much frustration, repeated failures, and a sense that Katherine was losing ground developmentally, they decided to accept physicians' recommendations that a feeding tube be inserted surgically.

As Mary Kay and Joe have adjusted to being new parents and parents of a child with birth difficulties, many issues have emerged. First, they have worked hard to agree about what to do with Katherine and coordinate their ideas on Katherine's needs and her future. This has required that Joe be very supportive of Mary Kay and that their level of communication remain high. Second, issues have emerged regarding grandparents and their expectations for Katherine and, more particularly, for Mary Kay as the mother. The struggle to have the grandparents understand Katherine's needs and be supportive of Joe and Mary Kay as parents has been significant.

Third, many issues have emerged regarding professionals involved in helping Joe, Mary Kay, and Katherine. The speech therapist wanted to come to the home three times during the week. Frequently Katherine would not be awake when the therapist arrived, and the therapist scheduled meetings during the day when Joe could not participate. In addition, coordinating surgery and medical issues has proven to be a major concern; during one month, Katherine had surgery to repair the cleft palate and the next month surgery to insert the feeding tube. It was hard for Mary Kay and Joe to get anyone to coordinate the two surgeries. This was necessary because the proposed nose tube, which was part of the feeding surgery, would interfere with the recently completed cleft palate repair. Because of the hierarchy found in

(continued)

(continued)

traditional medical settings and the apparent inability of physicians to respond to any professional other than another physician, Mary Kay and Joe found coordination of their child's medical needs almost impossible to achieve.

Two other issues that are significant for Mary Kay and Joe are the exhaustion they face and their inability to leave Katherine with anyone who is not specifically trained to care for her needs. Fortunately, Mary Kay's sister lives in their town and is available for child care when Mary Kay and Joe want some relief.

For Joe, there are father–child issues. He feels a strong bond with Katherine and spends a good deal of time holding, cuddling, and talking with her. However, as Katherine has received services, it has been hard for him to keep up with her development. At times, he feels out of the information flow because he is not at home during the day consistently. For him, if therapy schedules could be more flexible, with at least some evening hours, he could feel more involved in her care and development.

Mary Kay, a school psychologist, and Joe, a businessman, believe that it would be extremely hard to be a single parent or to have an uninvolved spouse and still function effectively for a baby with special needs. The need to coordinate activities for the infant is a real priority for intervention to be successful. Both parents believe that parents must be advocates for their children. In their situation, services for Katherine would not be as well coordinated as they are if Mary Kay and Joe were not consistently involved in planning, implementing, and evaluating the service activities.

reacting to the parent or failing to do so, or 2) by parental perceptions and assumptions about what the baby is capable or incapable or perceiving or doing (Hetherington, 1983). In either case, the parent–child interaction and attachment basic to healthy infant development may be at risk. With babies at risk, the signals or cues that typically developing infants give may not be clear or may be distorted (Yoder, 1987); consequently, parents may respond inadequately or not at all to their baby's needs.

The birth of an infant with a disability also appears to affect parents' perceptions of the infant's competence and development. As a whole, Goldberg's (1978) analysis demonstrated that mothers of preterm infants speak with them less, engage in less gazing and looking behavior, vocalize less, and smile and touch less than parents of full-term infants. The results reported by Goldberg, however, are not universal. Yoder and Feagans (1988) reported that some mothers of babies with severe disabilities identify as many cues as mothers of infants with mild disabilities. Some mothers seem to adapt to their infant's disabilities by becoming adept at interpreting their baby's behavior. The PRDM would help explain parents' responses to their infants.

The PRDM (Mowder, 1993; Mowder et al., 1993, 1995) posits that parents' perceptions of the parent role is developmental in nature; individuals have cognitive conceptions of what it means to be a parent and those ideas are modified based on parents' experience and knowledge. As parents adjust their parenting views to their developing child, a number of factors influence parent role development. The factors include individual parent characteristics, child factors, the parent–child relationship that forms, family dynamics, and social-cultural factors. Therefore, parents of children with disabilities would tend to modify their perceptions of how important certain parent role dimensions (i.e., bonding, discipline, education, general welfare and protection, responsivity, sensitivity) are as their child exhibits certain needs and parents respond to their own concerns, family matters, and their social-cultural context. Parenting perceptions guide parenting activities and behavior. For example, the parent of a child with a disability may spend more time on general welfare and protection, if the parent perceives the child to be medically at risk, than on parent–child bonds, discipline, or education.

The obvious question is what the effect is of a potentially different pattern of parent–infant interaction on the development of attachment. Beckwith (1984) reported that medical problems with infants do not adversely affect mother–infant interaction. This issue was considered in a comparison of attachments in infants who did not have disabilities and those who had physical disabilities when infants with facial or orthopedic anomalies were compared with typically developing infants in a variant of the strange situation procedure; infants at high and low risk did not differ in attachment. Responsivity, availability, and positive affect all contributed to measured attachment, but risk and the risk interaction factors did not (Wasserman, Lennon, Allen, & Shilansky, 1987). Wills (1979) also found that, except in the most extreme circumstances, parents adjust and attach to their infant.

Although further research is necessary on the interaction between parents and infants at risk for or with disabilities, it seems clear that attachments can be and are formed. There is a risk, however, that parents may not be sufficiently sensitive to their infant's cues and that infants with early developmental difficulties may be at risk for developing normal attachment behaviors. For example, in recent research on the development of affective expression in typically developing infants and infants with physical disabilities, Wasserman (1986) found that developmentally, over time, infants with disabilities are increasingly unwilling to engage a stranger in a positive affective exchange. In addition, they show a delay, compared with typically developing infants, in their ability to control distress during maternal separation. This gives some indication of possible early diminishment in sociability among infants with physical disabilities and potential eventual difficulties.

PARENTING STYLES AND THEIR INFLUENCE ON THE CHILD

Regardless of whether or not an infant or toddler has a disabling condition, parenting functions must be carried out. Radke-Yarrow and Kuczynski (1983) presented the range of parenting functions:

- Providing physical care, physical protection, and psychological support
- Controlling, motivating, and regulating children's behavior
- Teaching and providing knowledge and skills
- Providing an affective environment
- "Investing" in and identifying with their children
- Facilitating their children's interaction with their physical and interpersonal environments

Parenting functions and the way they are carried out affect infants and toddlers and how they develop. Martin (1981), for example, distinguished between mothers in terms of their involvement, employing the concepts of involvement with the infant versus being autonomous and focused on self.

Much of the parenting dynamics literature has focused on parents' control and regulation of their children's behavior (Fine, 1989). In the early studies of parenting dynamics, techniques of discipline tended to be categorized under two major classifications: 1) *power-assertive discipline*, including forceful commands, punishment, shouting, threats, and yelling; and 2) *love-oriented discipline*, including contingent giving of affection, isolation, reasoning, showing disappointment, and withdrawal of love (Hetherington, 1983).

Baumrind (1966, 1967, 1968, 1970, 1971, 1991a, 1991b, 1991c) is a significant researcher in this area. She has considered parenting in terms of parental demandingness and parental responsiveness. Baumrind identified clusters of parenting behaviors:

- *Authoritarian parenting* is characterized by attempting to control and shape child attitudes and behaviors according to an absolute set of standards; valuing obedience, the preservation of order, and the respect for authority; and discouraging mutual verbal interaction between parent and child. Their research shows that socially withdrawn and unhappy preschool children tend to have parents who fit this parenting pattern.
- *Indulgent-permissive parenting* is characterized by parents who have an accepting attitude, are tolerant, and use little punishment. These parents tend to make few behavioral demands and let children regulate their own behavior. As preschoolers, children raised in this parenting manner tend to lack impulse control, self-reliance, social responsibility, and independence.
- *Authoritative parenting*...includes the following characteristics: expectations for mature behavior, clear standard setting, firm enforcement of rules and standards, encouragement of independence, open communication between children and parents, and a recognition of children's and parents' rights. Preschool children raised in this parenting style tend to act cooperatively, behave in a socially responsible manner, and be independent.
- *Indifferent-uninvolved parenting*...is characterized as an indifference to the developing child. This parenting style refers to parents who are to a great extent uninvolved and uninterested in their children. The children who receive this type of parenting have various problems, ranging from severe behavioral difficulties to withdrawn social behavior. (1967)

Research in the area of parenting dynamics and consequent child characteristics has been dominated by work with parents of children who do not have disabilities, and thus generalizations regarding the research are necessarily limited.

Additional parenting dynamics have also been explored (e.g., the PRDM [Mowder et al., 1995]), including multicultural issues (Darling & Steinberg, 1993) and the effects of socioeconomic factors. Multicultural issues influence parenting in a number of ways. Sameroff (1989) discussed differing cultural codes, including customs, beliefs, and patterns of control and support, which influence parent–child interactions. For example, parents who do not participate in school activities do not necessarily care any less about their children than those who do. They may simply be reflecting cultural norms regarding interactions with school officials (Turnbull & Turnbull, 1986).

Parenting has also been explored in the context of socioeconomic status (SES) factors, including level of education, parent occupation, and income level. Researchers have found that higher-SES families have more resources available to cope with disabling conditions and a higher level of education and thus more knowledge about impairments; however, a higher SES does not necessarily lead to better coping skills or parenting behaviors (Turnbull & Turnbull, 1986). It is clear that a child born to a family that is economically disadvantaged, from a nondominant culture and language, and with few social support systems will experience an environment very different from that of the baby born to an economically stable family, from the dominant culture, with many extensive social support systems.

Optimum parenting dynamics include the competent performance of parenting activities and responsibilities, combined with parent–child interactions that are sensitive, responsive, and warm. Many children, however, experience less than optimum parenting behaviors. In some cases, the parenting dynamics are so problematic that they result in child abuse and neglect.

CHILD ABUSE AND NEGLECT

When parenting dynamics become dysfunctional, the situation may lead to abuse and neglect. Estimates of abuse and neglect vary, but Harrison and Edwards (1983) estimated that approximately 20% of all children may be neglected or emotionally, physically, or sexually abused by their parents. Even though abuse reporting may have increased, McCurdy and Daro (1994) found that child maltreatment as well as deaths due to abuse or neglect have increased steadily since the mid-1980s. The Children's Defense Fund (1994) reported that 2.9 million cases were brought to juvenile authorities in 1992. Abuse occurs in all cultural groups, across all socioeconomic levels, typically with younger parents and with parents who have few friends and sources of social support (Embry, 1980; Knutson, 1995). Table 5.2 lists some of the characteristics of abused and neglected children.

Table 5.2. Characteristics of abused and neglected children

Abused or neglected children are likely to share some of the following characteristics:

1. They appear to be different from other children in physical and emotional make-up, or their parents describe them as being different or bad.
2. They seem afraid of their parents.
3. They may bear bruises, welts, sores, or other skin injuries which seem to be untreated.
4. They are given inappropriate food, drink, or medication.
5. They are left alone with inadequate supervision.
6. They are chronically unclean.
7. They exhibit extremes in behavior: cry often or cry very little and show no real expectation of being comforted; they are excessively fearful or seem fearless of adult authority; they are unusually aggressive or extremely passive or withdrawn.
8. They are wary of physical contact, especially with an adult. They may be hungry for affection yet have difficulty relating to children and adults. Based on their experiences, they feel they cannot risk getting close to others.
9. They exhibit a sudden change in behavior, exhibit regressive behavior, such as wetting their pants or bed, thumb-sucking, whining, or becoming uncommonly shy or passive.
10. They have learning problems that cannot be diagnosed. Their attention wanders and they easily become self-absorbed.
11. They are habitually truant or late to school. Frequent or prolonged absences from school may result from the parents' keeping an injured child at home until the evidence of abuse disappears. Or they may arrive at school early and remain after classes instead of going home.
12. They are tired and often sleep in class.
13. They are not dressed appropriately for the weather. Children who wear long sleeves on hot days may be dressed to hide bruises or burns or other marks of abuse, or they may be dressed inadequately and suffer frostbite or illness from exposure to the weather.

From Harrison, R., & Edwards, J. (1983). *Child abuse* (p. 65). Portland, OR: Ednick Publications; reprinted by permission.

Child abuse appears to be more frequent with children with disabilities (Ammerman, Lubetsky, & Drudy, 1991). Estimates range from 8% to 55% of abused children exhibiting intellectual or physical impairment (Frodi, 1981). Turnbull and Turnbull (1986) are quick to point out that just because a large percentage of abused children have exceptionalities does not mean that a large number of children with disabling conditions are abused. Indeed, the majority of parents with children who do have disabilities do not abuse their children (Embry, 1980).

The incidence of child abuse can be explained by the work of Sroufe and Fleeson (1986), who maintained that relationships have four primary characteristics: 1) relationships are wholes; 2) relationships have continuity and coherence; 3) individuals internalize whole relationships, not simply roles; and 4) early relationship patterns are incorporated into later close relationships. The abusive parent has internalized an abusing role from his or her own parents and carried it forward to a present parent–child relationship (Egeland, Jacobvitz, & Sroufe, 1988). From this point of view, the insecurely attached infant internalizes a relationship model that sets the stage for subsequent maltreatment of his or her own child (Lamb & Bornstein, 1987). From a social learning perspective, the relationship the child learned at home through modeling and imitation, enhanced through direct and vicarious reinforcement, leads to the transmittal of abusive behavior to the next generation (Patterson, 1982).

FAMILY ASSESSMENT AND INTERVENTION

Bailey and Simeonsson (1988) developed a rationale and model for family assessment in early intervention. To a great extent, their rationale rested on the imperatives from PL 99-457, in which parents of infants and toddlers are directed to develop an individualized family service plan (IFSP) with a multidisciplinary team. Their model rests on a goodness-of-fit concept in which goals and services are appropriate only if they match with parents' perception of the need for such services.

Assessment

Bailey and Simeonsson's (1988) assessment model is driven by their model for a family-focused intervention. In this model, family needs are assessed, a focused interview conducted, follow-up assessments made, an IFSP meeting held, services implemented, and an evaluation plan carried out. They suggested assessing child characteristics, parent–child interaction, family stress and needs, critical events in the family's life, family roles and support systems, and family environments. With the assessment data, interventions are planned, implemented, and evaluated (see also Chapter 7). Bagnato, Neisworth, and Munson (1993) suggested a combination of approaches to assess infants, toddlers, and their families. They recommended that initial assessments of most infants and toddlers be conducted in the home and that a number of methods be used to foster family self-appraisals (e.g., interviews, rating scales). Krauss and Jacobs (1990) recommended that the core dimensions in family assessment include parental and familial stress (i.e., the perception of demands exceeding available resources to meet demands), coping strategies and resources (i.e., available psychological and social support to manage the stress), and characteristics of the family environment (i.e., how the family operates as a unit).

Bailey and Henderson (1993) reported that family assessment has its roots in three distinct but overlapping traditions: research, clinical, and support. The three

traditions have led to diverse assessment functions, goals, and strategies. In order to develop family assessments consistent with the goals and traditions of early intervention, they state that effective family assessment

1. recognizes the importance of individual perceptions of events and the likelihood that different individuals will have different perspectives;
2. is an ongoing process taking many forms;
3. requires reflective thinking centered around an inquiry-oriented approach; and
4. may function as an intervention, with potentially negative and positive implications. (p. 128)

In other words, Bailey and Henderson (1993) found that effective assessments incorporate a number of important dimensions. First, the early intervention professional tries to understand the family's value system and their own views of their concerns, priorities, and resources. Second, the assessment process takes many forms and is ongoing in nature. The three primary strategies they support include person-to-person communications (e.g., informal conversations, formal interviews), paper and pencil measures (e.g., surveys and questionnaires like the Family Needs Scale), and direct observation (e.g., parent–child and family interactions). Third, reflective thinking and inquiry suggests that professionals adhere to the following:

- Ask a set of basic questions regarding a family.
- Gather information regarding the questions.
- Reflect on the information gathered.
- Generate hypotheses about the questions asked and information obtained.
- Attempt to validate potential hypotheses.

Fourth, family assessments are events that communicate information and messages to families and may have diverse consequences (e.g., informational, emotional) for the families involved in the process.

A hidden factor in the assessment process may be stress in families of children at risk. Hutliner (1988) found that the effects of stress in families with very young children with disabilities are often pervasive, multiple, and sometimes unsuspected. She suggested the implementation of stress reduction strategies that build on family strengths. In addition, medical stabilization should be pursued and the families provided with social and economic stability. Often, stress is related to the amount of support available to the family. Beckman and colleagues (Beckman, 1983; Beckman & Pokorni, 1988) found that stress in families with 3-month-old babies was significantly negatively related to the amount of formal family support. The extent to which families adapt to the needs of their children determines how well the family functions as a unit promoting both the family's and the child's well-being (Bailey & Henderson, 1993). Able-Boone, Sandall, Loughry, and Frederick (1990) found that parents want to become knowledgeable about their child and available services. They emphasized the importance of professionals' relaying information and fostering families' decision-making roles.

Winton and Bailey (1988) cautioned professionals that what they might see as parents' denial of their child's disability may well be an effective family coping mechanism. Bailey and Henderson (1993), too, found that professional preoccupation with whether parents are accepting or denying their child's disability is unlikely to lead to productive communication between early interventionists and the families they serve.

Intervention

Many intervention programs involving families have been developed (see also Chapters 9 and 10). For example, Rosenberg and Robinson (1985) considered the impact of training on mothers' interactional skills with their infants or toddlers. The results indicated that training focused on interaction strategies enhances maternal abilities to interact with their babies. Other researchers, too, found that mother–child interaction patterns differ among families with children who are at risk for or who have develpmental delays (Holaday, 1987; Kysela & Marfo, 1983) and that parents' interaction skills are enhanced with professional support (Crnic, Greenberg, & Slough, 1986).

Mahoney and Powell (1988) described a transactional intervention program designed to modify the interaction patterns between parents and their children with disabilities from birth to age 3. This home-based intervention program results in decreased parent interactional dominance and frequency of directives, increased parent responsiveness, and relative developmental gains for the infants and toddlers.

Beyond the interaction issue, parents can be taught skills in handling their babies (Satterfield & Yasumura, 1987). Professional and social support stand out as important resources in fostering positive family dynamics (Crnic, Greenberg, Robinson, & Ragozin, 1984; Crockenberg, 1985). Beyond professional support, Weinraub and Wolf (1983) found that optimum interaction within two-parent families is associated with fewer stressful life events, satisfaction with emotional support, and the availability of household help.

Dyson's (1991) research emphasized the need for family interventions to address the issue of parental stress and for intervention programs to emphasize family strengths. Mahoney, O'Sullivan, and Dennebaum (1990b) developed a scale to assess family-focused interventions; they found (1990a) that the most common family intervention services involve providing parents information and assisting families to become involved in early intervention systems. They also found that the need for family services was greater than those being received.

In the future, family systems theory may be taught to parents in parent education programs (Getz & Gunn, 1988) or to counselors for use in training teachers to work more effectively with parents (Berry, 1987). Minuchin (1985) recommended the use of systems theory to study parent–child interactions. Wendt and Zake (1984) made the case for a family systems perspective in school psychological services, and a family systems approach has also been stressed by many in the provision of psychological services for children and families (e.g., Anderson, 1983; Pfeiffer & Tittler, 1983). Most programmatic developments for infants at risk and with disabilities focus on the family.

The professional literature on family dynamics and research with infants, toddlers, and their families make it clear that services need to be developed and delivered within the family context. Ecological and social systems perspectives are increasingly dominating family studies and affecting the conceptualization and delivery of early intervention services (Marfo, 1991). These changing perspectives emphasize the need for new models of professional involvement (Roberts & Magrab, 1991). Consultation models and skills, for instance, implied in most of the early intervention literature, have yet to address treating parents as partners in the early intervention enterprise (Mowder, 1994). Furthermore, cultural differences in families need to be understood, addressed, and respected in early intervention service provision (Roberts & Magrab, 1991).

Parent education programs are becoming increasingly important (Fine, 1989), and family supports are important family-centered components of service delivery options. Respite services as well as material, emotional, and informational support should be available to families (Bryant & Graham, 1993). Parent empowerment and parent–professional collaboration are hallmarks of early intervention programming (Healy, Keesee, & Smith, 1989). Families must be encouraged to make crucial decisions for their children.

FAMILY–PROFESSIONAL RELATIONSHIPS

Historically, the family–professional relationship has been an uneven one whenever an infant or toddler at risk for or with a disability is involved. In some relationships, family decision making and empowerment have been valued, facilitated, and fostered; in others, families have been made to believe that they are at the root of their child's difficulties or are impediments to their child's growth and development. Fortunately, the implementation of PLs 99-457 and 102–119 have strengthened the assumption that parents are the primary decision makers in their child's developmental assessment and intervention.

To some extent, establishing parents as the primary decision makers is difficult for both parents and professionals. Parents are socialized to seek, respect, and follow professional advice; professionals are trained to deliver, advise, and anticipate adherence to their prescriptions. Therefore, it will take time, training, and practice for parents and professionals to learn to work together as effective partners in efforts to facilitate infants' and toddlers' growth and development.

SUMMARY

The general consensus is that parents and families play an enormous role in children's development. In order to discuss the issues surrounding family dynamics, however, it is important to define what a family is, what makes individuals parents, what consitutes parenting, and what children's needs are. This chapter has examined these issues and, further, discussed parent–infant interactions, family systems, and family interactions with infants who are at risk for or who have disabilities. New models, such as the PRDM, offer professionals, as well as parents, new ways of thinking about parenting and how parenting responds to children's development and individual needs. Family dynamics are essential to appreciate since they are so influential in children's lives and necessary to appreciate for professionals serving young children who are at risk for or who have disabilities and their families.

SUGGESTED READINGS

Bornstein, M.H. (1995). *Handbook of parenting.* Hillsdale, NJ: Lawrence Erlbaum Associates.
Cole, R.E., & Reiss, D. (Eds.). (1993). *How do families cope with chronic illness?* Hillsdale, NJ: Lawrence Erlbaum Associates.
Correa, V.I., & Weismantel, J. (1991). *Multicultural issues related to families with an exceptional child.* Brandon, VT: Clinical Psychology Publishing Co.
Doll, B., & Bogler, M.W. (1991). The family with a young developmentally disabled child. In M.F. Fine (Ed.), *Collaboration with parents of exceptional children* (pp. 183–199). Brandon, VT: Clinical Psychology Publishing Co.
Fine, M. (1991). *Collaboration with parents of exceptional children.* Lawrence, KS: Clinical Psychology Publishing Co.
Marfo, K. (1991). *Early intervention in transition: Current perspectives on programs for handicapped children.* New York: Praeger.

REFERENCES

Able-Boone, H., Sandall, S., Loughry, A., & Frederick, L.L. (1990). An informed, family-centered approach to Public Law 99-457: Parental views. *Topics in Early Childhood Special Education, 10,* 100–111.
Ainsworth, M.D.S., Blehar, M.C., Waters, E., & Wall, S. (1978). *Patterns of attachment.* Hillsdale, NJ: Lawrence Erlbaum Associates.
Adams, J.A., & Weaver, S.J. (1986). Self-esteem and perceived stress of young adolescents with chronic disease: Unexpected findings. *Journal of Adolescent Health and Care, 7,* 173–177.

Akande, A. (1994). What meaning and effects does fatherhood have in child development? *Early Child Development and Care, 101,* 51–58.
Ammerman, R.T., Lubetsky, M.J., & Drudy, K.F. (1991). Maltreatment of handicapped children. In R.T. Ammerman & M. Hersen (Eds.), *Case studies in family violence* (pp. 209–230). New York: Plenum.
Anderson, C. (1983). An ecological developmental model for a family orientation in school psychology. *Journal of School Psychology, 21,* 179–189.
Arend, R. (1984). *Preschoolers' competence in a barrier situation: Patterns of adaptation and their precursors in infancy.* Unpublished doctoral dissertation, University of Minnesota.
Arend, R., Gove, F.L., & Sroufe, L.A. (1979). Continuity of individual adaptation from infancy to kindergarten: A predictive study of ego-resiliency and curiosity in preschoolers. *Child Development, 50,* 950–959.
Bagnato, S.J., Neisworth, J.T., & Munson, S.M. (1993). Sensible strategies for assessment in early intervention. In D.M. Bryant & M.A. Graham (Eds.), *Implementing early intervention: From research to effective practice* (pp. 148–156). New York: Guilford Press.
Bailey, D.B., & Henderson, L.W. (1993). Traditions in family assessment: Toward an inquiry-oriented, reflective model. In D.M. Bryant & M.A. Graham (Eds.), *Implementing early intervention: From research to effective practice* (pp. 124–147). New York: Guilford Press.
Bailey, D.B., & Simeonsson, R.J. (1988). *Family assessment in early intervention.* Columbus, OH: Charles E. Merrill.
Bailey, D.B., Simeonsson, R.J., Yoder, D.E., & Huntington, G.S. (1990). Preparing professionals to serve infants and toddlers with handicaps and their families: An integrative analysis across eight disciplines. *Exceptional Children, 57,* 26–35.
Barnas, M.V., & Cummings, E.M. (1994). Caregiver stability and toddlers' attachment-related behavior towards caregivers in day care. *Infant Behavior and Development, 17,* 141–147.
Baumrind, D. (1966). Effects of authoritative parental control on child behavior. *Child Development, 37,* 887–907.
Baumrind, D. (1967). Child care practices anteceding three patterns of preschool behavior. *Genetic Psychology Monographs, 75,* 43–88.
Baumrind, D. (1968). Authoritarian vs. authoritative parental control. *Adolescence, 3,* 256.
Baumrind, D. (1970). Socialization and instrumental competence in young children. *Young Children, 26*(2), 104–119.
Baumrind, D. (1971). Current patterns of parental authority. *Developmental Psychology Monographs, 4*(1, Pt. 2).
Baumrind, D. (1991a). Effective parenting during the early adolescent transition. In P.A. Cowan & E.M. Hetherington (Eds.), *Family transitions* (pp. 111–163). Hillsdale, NJ: Lawrence Erlbaum Associates.
Baumrind, D. (1991b). Parenting styles and adolescent development. In R.M. Lerner, A.C. Peterson, & J. Brooks-Gunn (Eds.), *Encyclopedia of adolescence* (pp. 56–95). New York: Gardner.
Baumrind, D. (1991c). The influence of parenting style on adolescent competence and substance use. *Journal of Early Adolescence, 11,* 56–95.
Beckman, P.J. (1983). Influence of selected child characteristics on stress in families of handicapped infants. *American Journal of Mental Deficiency, 88,* 150–156.
Beckman, P.J., & Pokorni, J.L. (1988). A longitudinal study of families of preterm infants: Changes in stress and support over the first two years. *Journal of Special Education, 22*(1), 55–65.
Beckwith, L. (1984). Parent interaction with their preterm infants and later mental development. *Early Child Development and Care, 16,* 27–40.
Beckwith, L. (1990). Adaptive and maladaptive parenting: Implications for intervention. In S.J. Meisels & J.P. Shonkoff (Eds.), *Handbook of early childhood intervention* (pp. 53–77). Cambridge, England: Cambridge University Press.
Belsky, J., Lerner, R., & Spanier, G. (1985). *The child in the family.* Reading, MA: Addison-Wesley.
Bentley, K.S., & Fox, R.A. (1991). Mothers and fathers of young children: Comparison of parenting styles. *Psychological Reports, 69,* 320–322.
Berry, J.O. (1987). A program for training teachers as counselors of parents of children with disabilities. *Journal of Counseling and Development, 65,* 508–509.

Blanchard, M., & Main, M. (1979). Avoidance of the attachment figure and social-emotional adjustment in day care infants. *Developmental Psychology, 14,* 445–446.
Bornstein, M.H. (1986). *The multivariate model of the interaction effects in human development: Categories of caretaking.* Unpublished manuscript, New York University.
Bowen, M. (1978). *Family therapy in clinical practice.* New York: J. Aronson.
Bowlby, J. (1980). *Attachment and loss: Vol. 3. Loss, sadness and depression.* New York: Basic Books.
Brookhart, J., & Hock, E. (1976). The effects of experimental context and experiential background on infants" behavior toward their mothers and a stranger. *Child Development, 47,* 333–340.
Brown, J.V., & Bakeman, R. (1980). Relationships of human mothers with their infants during the first year of life: Effects of prematurity. In R.W. Bell & W.P. Smotherman (Eds.), *Maternal influences and early behavior.* Holliswood, NY: Spectrum.
Bryant, D.M., & Graham, M.A. (Eds.). (1993). *Implementing early intervention: From research to effective practice.* New York: Guilford Press.
Burchinal, M.R., Bryant, D.M., Lee, M.W., & Ramey, C.T. (1992). Early day care, infant–mother attachment, and maternal responsiveness in the infant's first year. *Early Childhood Research Quarterly, 7,* 383–396.
Cadman, D., Boyle, M.M., Szatmari, P., & Offard, D.R. (1987). Chronic illness, disability and mental and social wellbeing: Findings of the Ontario Child Health Study. *Pediatrics, 79,* 805–813.
Children's Defense Fund. (1994). *The state of America's children: Yearbook 1994.* Washington, DC: Author.
Crnic, K.A., Greenberg, M.T., Robinson, N.M., & Ragozin, A.S. (1984). Maternal stress and social support: Effects on the mother–infant relationship from birth to eighteen months. *American Journal of Orthopsychiatry, 54*(2), 224–235.
Crnic, K.A., Greenberg, M.T., & Slough, N.M. (1986). Early stress and social support influences on mothers' and high risk infants' functioning in late infancy. Special issue: Social support, family functioning, and infant development. *Infant Mental Health Journal, 7*(1), 19–33.
Crockenberg, S. (1985). Professional support and care of infants by adolescent mothers in England and the United States. *Journal of Pediatric Psychology, 10*(4), 413–428.
Damrosch, E., & Perry, L. (1989). Self-reported adjustment, chronic sorrow, and coping of parents with Down syndrome. *Nursing Research, 38,* 25–30.
Darling, N., & Steinberg, L. (1993). Parenting styles as context: An integrative model. *Psychological Bulletin, 113,* 487–496.
de Chateau, P. (1980). Parent–neonate interaction and its long-term effects. In E.C. Simmel (Ed.), *Early experiences and early behavior: Implications for social development.* New York: Academic Press.
Drotar, D., Baskiewicz, B.A., Irvin, N., Kennell, J., & Klaus, M. (1975). The adaptation of parents to the birth of an infant with a congenital malformation: A hypothetical model. *Pediatrics, 56*(5), 710–717.
Drotar, D., & Bush, M. (1985). Mental health issues and services. In N. Hobbs & J.M. Perrin (Eds.), *Issues in the care of children with chronic illness: A source book on problems, services and policies.* San Francisco: Jossey-Bass.
Drotar, D., Crawford, T., & Bush, M. (1984). The family context of childhood chronic illness: Implications for psychosocial intervention. In M.G. Eisenberg, L.C. Suttin, & M.A. Jansen (Eds.), *Chronic illness and disability through the lifespan: Effects on self and family* (pp. 103–129). New York: Springer-Verlag.
Dyson, L.L. (1991). Families of young children with handicaps: Parental stress and family functioning. *American Journal on Mental Retardation, 95,* 623–629.
Egeland, B., Jacobvitz, D., & Sroufe, L.A. (1988). Breaking the cycle of abuse: Relationship predictors. *Child Development, 59,* 1080–1088.
Embry, L.H. (1980). Family support for handicapped preschool children at risk for abuse. In J.J. Gallagher (Ed.), *New directions for exceptional children* (pp. 29–57). San Francisco: Jossey-Bass.
Emde, R. (1989). The infant's relationship experience: Developmental and affective aspects. In A.J. Sameroff & R.N. Emde (Eds.), *Relationship disturbances in early childhood: A developmental approach* (pp. 33–51). New York: Basic Books.

Emde, R.N., & Brown, C. (1978). Adaptation to the birth of a Down's syndrome infant: Grieving and maternal attachment. *Journal of the American Academy of Child Psychiatry,* 299–323.

Emde, R.N., & Sameroff, A.J. (1989). Understanding early relationship disturbances. In A.J. Sameroff & R.N. Emde (Eds.), *Relationship disturbances in early childhood: A developmental approach* (pp. 3–14). New York: Basic Books.

Epps, S., & Jackson, B.J. (1991). Professional preparation of psychologists for family-centered service delivery to at-risk infants and toddlers. *School Psychology Review, 20,* 498–509.

Eyer, D.E. (1992). *Mother–infant bonding: A scientific fiction.* New Haven, CT: Yale University Press.

Fagot, B.I., & Hagan, R. (1991). Observations of parent reactions to sex-stereotyped behaviors: Age and sex effects. *Child Development, 62,* 617–628.

Fine, M.J. (1989). *The second handbook on parent education: Contemporary perspectives.* San Diego: Academic Press.

Fishbein, H.D. (1984). *The psychology of infancy and childhood: Evolutionary and cross-cultural perspectives.* Hillsdale, NJ: Lawrence Erlbaum Associates.

Frodi, A.M. (1981). Contribution of infant characteristics to child abuse. *American Journal of Mental Deficiency, 85,* 341–349.

Getz, H., & Gunn, W.B. (1988). Parent education from a family-systems perspective. *School Counselor, 35,* 331–336.

Gibbs, E.D., Teti, D.M., & Bond, L.A. (1987). Infant–sibling communication: Relationships to birth-spacing and cognitive and linguistic development. *Infant Behavior and Development, 10*(3), 307–323.

Goldberg, S. (1978). Prematurity: Effects on parent–child interaction. *Journal of Pediatric Psychology, 3,* 137–144.

Goldberg, S. (1983). Parent-to-infant bonding: Another look. *Child Development, 54,* 1355–1382.

Goldstein, M. (1988). The family and psychopathology. *Annual Review of Psychology, 39,* 283–299.

Grossman, K.E., & Grossman, K. (1990). The wider concept of attachment in cross-cultural research. *Human Development, 33,* 31–47.

Guralnick, M.J. (1989). Recent developments in early intervention efficacy research: Implications for family involvement in PL 99-457. *Topics in Early Childhood Special Education, 9,* 1–17.

Hanson, M.J., & Lovett, D. (1992). Personnel preparation for early interventionists: A cross-disciplinary survey. *Journal of Early Intervention, 16*(2), 123–135.

Harrison, R., & Edwards, J. (1983). *Child abuse.* Portland, OR: Ednick Publications.

Healy, A., Keesee, P.D., & Smith, B.S. (1989). *Early services for children with special needs: Transactions for family support.* Baltimore: Paul H. Brookes Publishing Co.

Hetherington, E.M. (1983). Socialization in the context of the family: Parent–child interaction. In P.H. Mussen (Ed.), *Handbook of child psychology: Vol. IV. Socialization, personality, and social development.* New York: John Wiley & Sons.

Holaday, B. (1987). Patterns of interaction between mothers and their chronically ill infants. *Maternal Child Nursing Journal, 16*(1), 29–45.

Hutliner, P. (1988). Stress: Is it an inevitable condition for families of children at risk? *Teaching Exceptional Children, 20,* 36–39.

Individuals with Disabilities Education Act (IDEA) of 1990, PL 101-476, 20 U.S.C. § 1400 *et seq.*

Individuals with Disabilities Education Act Amendments of 1991, PL 102-119, 20 U.S.C. § 1400 *et seq.*

Jones, O.H.M. (1977). Mother–child communication with prelinguistic Down's syndrome and normal infants. In H.R. Schaffer (Ed.), *Studies in mother–infant interaction* (pp. 379–401). New York: Academic Press.

Karen, R. (1994). *Becoming attached: Unfolding the mystery of the infant–mother bond and its impact on later life.* New York: Warner Books.

Kennel, J.H., Voos, D.K., & Klaus, M.H. (1979). Parent–infant bonding. In J.D. Osofsky (Ed.), *Handbook of infant development.* New York: John Wiley & Sons.

Klaus, M.H., & Fanaroff, A.A. (1979). *Care of the high-risk neonate* (2nd ed.). Philadelphia: W.B. Saunders.

Klaus, M.H., & Kennell, J.H. (1976). *Maternal–infant bonding.* St. Louis: C.V. Mosby.

Klaus, M.H., & Kennell, J.H. (1981). *Parent–infant bonding*. St. Louis: C.V. Mosby.
Knutson, J.F. (1995). Psychological characteristics of maltreated children: Putative risk factors and consequences. *Annual Review of Psychology, 46*, 401–431.
Kopf, R.C., & McFadden, E.L. (1974). Nursing intervention in the crisis of new born illness. *Journal of Nursery Midwifery, 16*, 629–636.
Kotelchuck, M. (1976). The infant's relationship to the father: Experimental evidence. In M.E. Lamb (Ed.), *The role of the father in child development* (pp. 329–344). New York: John Wiley & Sons.
Krauss, M.W., & Jacobs, F. (1990). Family assessment: Purposes and techniques. In S.J. Meisels & J.P. Shonkoff (Eds.), *Handbook of early childhood intervention* (pp. 428–444). Cambridge, England: Cambridge University Press.
Kreppner, K., Paulse, S., & Schuetze, Y. (1982). Infant and family development: From triads to tetrads. *Human Development, 25*, 373–391.
Kysela, G.M., & Marfo, K. (1983). Mother–child interactions and early intervention programs for handicapped infants and young children. *Educational Psychology, 3*(3–4), 201–212.
LaFreniere, P., & Sroufe, L.A. (1985). Profiles of peer competence in the preschool: Interrelations between measures, influence of social ecology, and relation to attachment history. *Developmental Psychology, 21*, 58–68.
Lamb, M.E. (1980). The development of parent–infant attachments in the first year of life. In F.A. Pedersen (Ed.), *The father–infant relationship observational studies in a family setting.* New York: Praeger Special Studies.
Lamb, M.E. (1982). Early contact and mother–infant bonding: One decade later. *Pediatrics, 70*, 763–768.
Lamb, M.E., & Bornstein, M.H. (1987). *Development in infancy: An introduction.* New York: Random House.
Lamb, M.E., & Hwang, C.P. (1982). Maternal attachment and mother–neonate bonding: A critical review. In M.E. Lamb & A.L. Brown (Eds.), *Advances in developmental psychology* (Vol. 2, pp. 1–39). Hillsdale, NJ: Lawrence Erlbaum Associates.
Lamb, M.E., & Sternberg, K.J. (1990). Do we really know how day care affects children? *Journal of Applied Developmental Psychology, 11*, 351–379.
Liebman, R., & Ziffer, R.L. (1985). Case consultation within a family systems framework. In R.L. Ziffer (Ed.), *Adjunctive techniques in family therapy.* New York: Grune and Stratton.
Maccoby, E.E. (1992). The role of parents in the socialization of children: An historical overview. *Developmental Psychology, 28*, 1006–1017.
Mahoney, G., O'Sullivan, P., & Dennebaum, J. (1990a). A national study of mothers' perceptions of family-focused early intervention. *Journal of Early Intervention, 14*, 133–146.
Mahoney, G., O'Sullivan, P., & Dennebaum, J. (1990b). Maternal perceptions of early intervention services: A scale for assessing family-focused intervention. *Topics in Early Childhood Special Education, 10*, 1–15.
Mahoney, G., & Powell, A. (1988). Modifying parent–child interactions: Enhancing the development of handicapped children. *Journal of Special Education, 22*(1), 82–96.
Main, M., Kaplan, N., & Cassidy, J. (1985). Security in infancy, childhood and adulthood: A move to the level of representation. In I. Bretherton & E. Waters (Eds.), Growing points of attachment theory and research. *Monographs of the Society for Research in Child Development, 50*(1–2, Serial No. 209).
Main, M., & Solomon, J. (1986). Discovery of an insecure-disorganized/disoriented attachment pattern. In T.B. Brazelton & M.W. Yogman (Eds.), *Affective development in infancy.* Norwood, NJ: Ablex.
Main, M., & Weston, D. (1981). The quality of the toddler's relationship to mother and father: Related to conflict behaviors and the readiness to establish new relationships. *Child Development, 52*, 932–940.
Marfo, K. (Ed.). (1991). *Early intervention in transition: Current perspectives on programs for handicapped children.* New York: Praeger.
Martin, J.A. (1981). A longitudinal study of the consequences of early mother–infant interaction: A microanalytic approach. *Monographs of the Society for Research in Child Development, 46*(3, Serial No. 190).
Matas, L., Arend, R., & Sroufe, L.A. (1978). Continuity of adaptation in the second year. The relationship between quality of attachment and later competent functioning. *Child Development, 49*, 547–555.

McCurdy, K., & Daro, D. (1994). Child maltreatment: A national survey of reports and fatalities. *Journal of Interpersonal Violence, 9*, 75–94.

McLinden, S.E., & Prasse, D.P. (1991). Providing services to infants and toddlers under PL 99-457: Training needs of school psychologists. *School Psychology Review, 20*, 37–48.

Minuchin, P. (1985). Families and individual development: Provocations from the field of family therapy. *Child Development, 56*, 289–302.

Minuchin, S. (1974). *Families and family therapy.* Cambridge, MA: Harvard University Press.

Minuchin, S. (1980). *Structural family therapy: Activating alternatives within a therapeutic system.* Philadelphia: Smith, Kline & French Laboratories Report #3.

Minuchin, S., & Fishman, H.C. (1981). *Family therapy techniques.* Cambridge, MA: Harvard University Press.

Minuchin, S., Montalvo, B., Guerney, B., Rosman, B., & Schumer, F. (1967). *Families of the slums.* New York: Basic Books.

Minuchin, S., Rosman, B.L., Baker, L., & Liebman, R. (1978). *Psychosomatic families: Anorexia nervosa in context.* Cambridge, MA: Harvard University Press.

Moran, G., Pederson, D.R., Pettit, P., & Krupka, A. (1992). Maternal sensitivity and infant–mother attachment in a developmentally delayed sample. *Infant Behavior and Development, 15*, 427–442.

Mowder, B.A. (1991a, June). *Working with parents: Challenges and opportunities.* Keynote presentation to the New York City Board of Education's District IV Staff Development Conference, Brooklyn, NY.

Mowder, B.A. (1991b, July). *Parent role development.* Paper presented at the annual meeting of the International School Psychology Association, Braga, Portugal.

Mowder, B.A. (1993, November). *Educators and parents: Communication chasm or opportunity?* Invited presentation at Teachers College, Columbia University, New York.

Mowder, B.A. (1994). Consultation with families of young, at-risk, and handicapped children. *Journal of Educational and Psychological Consultation, 5*, 309–320.

Mowder, B.A. (1996). *Parent development.* Submitted for publication.

Mowder, B.A., Harvey, V.S., Moy, L., & Pedro, M. (1995). Parent role characteristics: Parent views and their implications for school psychologists. *Psychology in the Schools, 32*, 27–37.

Mowder, B.A., Harvey, V.S., Pedro, M., Rossen, R., & Moy, L. (1993). Parent Role Questionnaire: Psychometric qualities. *Psychology in the Schools, 30*, 205–211.

Myers, B.J. (1987). Mother–infant bonding: The status of this critical-period hypothesis. In M.H. Bornstein (Ed.), *Sensitive periods in development: Interdisciplinary perspectives.* Hillsdale, NJ: Lawrence Erlbaum Associates.

Niven, C., Wiszniewkski, C., & AlRoomi, L. (1993). Attachment (bonding) in mothers of preterm babies. *Journal of Reproductive and Infant Psychology, 11*, 175–185.

O'Connor, M.J., Sigman, M.D., & Kasari, C. (1992). Attachment behavior of infants exposed prenatally to alcohol: Mediating effects of infant affect and mother–infant interaction. *Development and Psychopathology, 4*, 243–256.

Papousek, H., & Papousek, M. (1992). Beyond emotional bonding: The role of preverbal communication in mental growth and health. *Infant Mental Health Journal, 13*, 43–53.

Parke, R.D., & O'Leary, S.E. (1976). Family interaction in the newborn period: Some findings, some observations and some unresolved issues. In K.F. Riegel & J.A. Meacham (Eds.), *The developing individual in a changing world: Vol. 2. Social and environmental issues* (pp. 653–663). The Hague: Mouton.

Parke, R.D., & Tinsley, B.R. (1981). The father's role in infancy: Determinants of involvement in caregiving and play. In M.E. Lamb (Ed.), *The role of the father in child development* (2nd ed.). New York: John Wiley & Sons.

Parmalee, A.H. (1989). The child's physical health and the development of relationships. In A.J. Sameroff & R.N. Emde (Eds.), *Relationship disturbances in early childhood: A developmental approach* (pp. 145–162). New York: Basic Books.

Patterson, G.R. (1982). *Coercive family process.* Eugene, OR: Castalia Publishing.

Pedersen, D.R., Bento, S., Chance, G.W., Evans, B., & Fox, A.M. (1987). Maternal emotional responses to preterm birth. *American Journal of Orthopsychiatry, 57*, 15–21.

Pedersen, F.A. (1975). Mother, father, and infant as an interactive system. In J. Belsky (Ed.), *In the beginning: Readings on infancy.* New York: Columbia University Press.

Pedersen, F.A., & Robson, K.S. (1969). Father participation in infancy. *American Journal of Orthopsychiatry, 39*, 466–472.

Pfeiffer, S., & Tittler, B.I. (1983). Utilizing the multidisciplinary team to facilitate a school-family systems orientation. *School Psychology Review, 12,* 168–173.

Radke-Yarrow, M., & Kuczynski, L. (1983). Conceptions of environment in childbearing interactions. In D. Magnusson & V.L. Allen (Eds.), *Human development: An interactional perspective.* New York: Academic Press.

Ricks, M.H. (1985). The social transmission of parental behavior: Attachment across generations. In I. Bretherton & E. Waters (Eds.), Growing points of attachment theory and research (pp. 211–227). *Monographs of the Society for Research in Child Development, 50*(1-2, Serial No. 209).

Roberts, R.N., & Magrab, P.R. (1991). Psychologists' role in a family-centered approach to practice, training, and research with young children. *American Psychologist, 46*(2), 144–148.

Rosenberg, S., & Robinson, C. (1985). Enhancement of mothers' interactional, skills in an infant education program. *Education and Training of the Mentally Retarded, 20*(2), 163–169.

Rosenblith, J.F., & Sims-Knight, J.E. (1985). *In the beginning: Development in the first two years.* Monterey, CA: Brooks/Cole.

Russell, G., & Radojevic, M. (1992). The changing role of fathers? Current understandings and future directions for research and practice. *Infant Mental Health Journal, 13,* 296–311.

Sagi, A. (1990). Attachment theory and research from a cross-cultural perspective. *Human Development, 33,* 10–22.

Sameroff, A.J. (1989). Principles of development and psychopathology. In A.J. Sameroff & R.N. Emde (Eds.), *Relationship disturbances in early childhood: A developmental approach* (pp. 17–32). New York: Basic Books.

Satterfield, M.J., & Yasumura, K. (1987). Facilitating the high risk neonate's head control: Effect of teaching method on mother's performance. *International Journal of Rehabilitation Research, 10*(1), 55–62.

Schaffer, H.R., & Emerson, P.E. (1964). The development of social attachments in infancy. *Monographs of the Society for Research in Child Development, 29*(e, Serial No. 94).

Shaw, D.S., & Vondra, J.I. (1993). Chronic family adversity and infant attachment security. *Journal of Child Psychology and Psychiatry and Allied Disciplines, 34,* 1205–1215.

Slade, C.I., Redl, O.J., & Manguten, H.H. (1977). Working with parents of high-risk newborns. *Journal of Obstetric and Gynecologic Nursing, 6,* 21–26.

Sroufe, L.A. (1983). Infant–caregiver attachment and adaptation in the preschool: The roots of competence and maladaptation. In M. Perlmutter (Ed.), *Development of cognition, affect, and social relations* (pp. 41–81). Hillsdale, NJ: Lawrence Erlbaum Associates.

Sroufe, L.A. (1989). Relationships, self, and individual adaptation. In A.J. Sameroff & R.N. Emde (Eds.), *Relationship disturbances in early childhood: A developmental approach* (pp. 70–94). New York: Basic Books.

Sroufe, L.A., & Fleeson, J. (1986). Attachment and the construction of relationships. In W. Hartup & Z. Rubin (Eds.), *Relationships and development.* Hillsdale, NJ: Lawrence Erlbaum Associates.

Sroufe, L.A., & Rosenberg, D. (1980, March). *Coherence of individual adaptation in lower SES infants and toddlers.* Paper presented at the International Conference on Infant Studies, Providence, RI.

Stern, D.N. (1974). Mother and infant at play: The dyadic interaction involving facial, vocal and gaze behaviors. In M. Lewis & L.A. Rosenblum (Eds.), *The effect of the infant on its caregiver.* New York: John Wiley & Sons.

Stern, D.N., Beebe, B., Jaffe, J., & Bennett, S.L. (1977). The infant's stimulus world during social interaction: A study of caregiver behaviors with particular reference to repetition and timing. In H.R. Schaffer (Ed.), *Studies in mother–infant interaction.* London: Academic Press.

Stevenson, M.B., Leavitt, L.A., Thompson, R.H., & Roach, M.A. (1988). A social relations model analysis of parent and child play. *Developmental Psychology, 24*(1), 101–107.

Stewart, R.B. (1983). Sibling interaction: The role of the older child as teacher for the younger. *Merrill Palmer Quarterly, 29*(1), 47–68.

Stewart, R.B., & Marvin, R.S. (1984). Sibling relations: The role of conceptual perspective-taking in the ontogeny of sibling caregiving. *Child Development, 55*(4), 1322–1332.

Tangri, P., & Verma, P. (1992). A study of social burden felt by mothers of handicapped children. Special series III: Mental and physical handicap. *Journal of Personality and Clinical Studies, 8,* 117–120.

Terkelson, K.G. (1980). Toward a theory of family life cycle. In E. Carter & M. McGoldrick (Eds.), *The family life cycle: A framework of family therapy* (pp. 21–52). New York: Gardner Press.

Thoman, E.B. (1981). Affective communication as the prelude and context for language learning. In R.L. Schiefelbusch & D. Bricker (Eds.), *Early language: Acquisition and intervention.* Baltimore: University Park Press.

Trevarthen, C. (1977). Descriptive analyses of infant communicative behavior. In H.R. Schaffer (Ed.), *Studies in mother–infant interaction.* New York: Academic Press.

Tunali, B., & Power, T.G. (1993). Creating satisfaction: A psychological perspective on stress and coping in families of handicapped children. *Journal of Child Psychology and Psychiatry and Allied Disciplines, 34,* 945–957.

Turnbull, A., & Turnbull, H.R. III. (1986). *Families, professionals, and exceptionality: A special partnership.* Columbus, OH: Charles E. Merrill.

Vandell, D.L., & Wilson, K.S. (1987). Infant's interactions with mother, sibling, and peer: Contrasts and relations between interaction systems. *Child Development, 58*(1), 176–186.

Vaughn, B., Egeland, B., Sroufe, L.A., & Waters, E. (1979). Individual differences in infant–mother attachment at twelve and eighteen months: Stability and change in families under stress. *Child Development, 50,* 971–975.

Vaughn, B.E., Gove, F.L., & Egeland, B. (1980). The relationship between out-of-home care and the quality of infant–mother attachment in an economically disadvantaged population. *Child Development, 51,* 1203–1214.

Wasserman, G.A. (1986). Affective expression in normal and physically handicapped infants: Situational and developmental effects. *Journal of the American Academy of Child Psychiatry, 25*(3), 393–399.

Wasserman, G.A., Lennon, M.C., Allen, R., & Shilansky, M. (1987). Contributors to attachment in normal and physically handicapped infants. *Journal of the American Academy of Child and Adolescent Psychiatry, 26*(1), 9–15.

Waters, E., Wippman, J., & Sroufe, L.A. (1979). Attachment, positive affect, and competence in the peer group: Two studies in construct validation. *Child Development, 50,* 821–829.

Weinraub, M., & Wolf, B.M. (1983). Effects of stress and social support on mother–child interactions in single-parent and two-parent families. *Child Development, 54,* 1297–1311.

Wendt, R.N., & Zake, J. (1984). Family systems theory and school psychology: Implications for training and practice. *Psychology in the Schools, 21,* 204–210.

Wills, D.M. (1979). The ordinary devoted mother and her blind baby. *Psychoanalytic Study of the Child, 34,* 31–49.

Winton, P.J., & Bailey, D.B. (1988). The family focused interview: A collaborative mechanism for family assessment and goal-setting. *Journal of the Division for Early Childhood, 12*(3), 195–207.

Yoder, P.J. (1987). Relationship between degree of infant handicap and clarity of infant cues. *American Journal of Mental Deficiency, 91*(6), 639–641.

Yoder, P.J., & Feagans, L. (1988). Mothers' attributions of communication to prelinguistic behavior of developmentally delayed and mentally retarded infants. *American Journal on Mental Retardation, 93*(1), 36–43.

Yogman, M.W. (1982). Development of the father–infant relationship. In H.E. Fitzgerald, B.M. Lester, & M.W. Yogman (Eds.), *Theory and research in behavioral pediatrics* (Vol. 1, pp. 221–279). New York: Plenum.

Young, K.T., & Zigler, E.F. (1988). Infant and toddler day care: Regulation and policy implications. In E.F. Zigler & M. Frank (Eds.), *The parental leave crisis: Toward a national policy* (pp. 120–140). New Haven, CT: Yale University Press.

Zigler, E. (1990, January). *Child care and children at risk.* Keynote address at the annual Queens College School Psychology Conference, Queens, NY.

5 ACTIVITIES

1. What role does patterning take in the bonding/attachment relationship?
2. Describe the outcomes of children with histories of secure attachment and avoidant attachment relationships.
3. Describe the roles of the subsystems within the family structure.
4. Describe the family dynamics that may occur with infants at risk for and with disabilities.
5. Explain the effects of parenting styles on children's social development.
6. Describe three types of intervention for families in crisis.

CHAPTER 6

The Family Service Team

Susan R. Sandall

Objectives

- To understand various team models and the impact of the roles and relationships of the team members on team functioning
- To recognize the importance of interagency collaboration as an important feature of successful and effective early intervention
- To appreciate the value of service coordination for young children and their families

Early intervention services and supports are provided by groups of people. How these people come together to form teams for the purposes of maximizing a young child's development and learning, as well as family functioning, is discussed in this chapter. The roles, responsibilities, and qualifications of the professional team members are also considered, and the roles that families may take on the early intervention team and strategies that can be used to optimize meaningful family involvement with the team are discussed.

There is a great deal of variability in terms of how early intervention services are managed and delivered. The stories of Michael and Sonja provide just two examples: Michael and his mother are involved with at least three agencies (the community health program that employs his nurse, the clinic where he receives physical therapy, and the medical center where he goes to a follow-up clinic) and at least eight professionals who provide direct service and consultation. In contrast, Sonja's early intervention services are provided by a single agency, and most of her direct services are provided by her teachers

Michael

Michael, 8 months old, has been home for about 2 months. Michael was born 13 weeks early and weighed less than 2 pounds. He was on a ventilator for several weeks and experienced numerous health crises in the hospital. He spent his first 4 months at a large regional medical center, followed by 3 weeks in the community hospital near his home. Home is his grandmother's house where Michael's mother moved after her marriage broke up during Michael's hospital stay. Michael's uncle also lives there. A developmental nurse makes home visits once a week, and Michael goes to physical therapy at a local clinic once a week. In addition to the well-baby care provided by his pediatrician, Michael goes to a follow-up clinic on a regular schedule. There, he is seen by a pediatrician, nutritionist, physical therapist, speech therapist, psychologist, and social worker. Michael's mother accompanies him on most of these visits. Because she works part time, Michael's grandmother and uncle share caregiving responsibilities. Michael's mother often remarks that her baby is only 8 months old but she already has a file drawer full of reports and records. She prides herself on her organizational skills and wonders how others keep track of everything.

and two therapists. Regardless of the organizational structure, collaboration within and among agencies and providers is essential to effective early intervention. Interagency relationships, another contexual layer within which early intervention takes place, are discussed, including some of the challenges of interagency work and strategies for achieving interagency collaboration.

The "glue" for keeping all of the many parts of early intervention working together for any family is their service coordinator. This chapter concludes with historical background on service coordination, the responsibilities and functions of the service coordinator, and a discussion of the interplay of the service coordinator with the team and with other agencies.

GUIDING PRINCIPLES

In their compilation of recommended practices, Odom and McLean (1993) cited a team approach as one of the established standards for evaluating other recommended practices in early intervention. They wrote that "practices should involve the efforts of members of various disciplines working as a team rather than as individual professionals" (p. 5). That is, it has become accepted that early intervention is appropriately and effectively provided through a team approach. Ideally, the team consists of individuals who are knowledgeable and skillful in their own area of expertise, and in group dynamics and who possess a sensitive and respectful family orientation.

The team approach is decreed in Part H of IDEA, PL 101-476 (Individuals with Disabilities Education Act [IDEA] of 1990), in its direction to states to develop and implement a comprehensive, coordinated, multidisciplinary, interagency program of early intervention services. It was recognized that no single agency or profes-

Sonja

Sonja and her father drive to the child care center every morning. Sonja, 14 months old, was born with Down syndrome. She is the youngest of four children in a family of half-siblings that includes three teenagers. Both of her parents work full time outside the home. They feel very fortunate that one of the service options presented to them when Sonja was a newborn was a child care center that includes children with and without disabilities and provides educational, therapeutic, and health services to the children. Her parents placed Sonja on the waiting list, and when Sonja's mother returned to work Sonja began attending the center. She is in a classroom with 12 children. The classroom is staffed by a lead teacher and two assistant teachers. The program staff also includes a speech therapist and an occupational therapist who come into the classroom to work with Sonja and other children who need their services. A school nurse and a social worker are also on the staff. Sonja's parents are delighted with this arrangement, and Dad reports that Sonja is all smiles when she sees her teachers in the morning.

sional discipline can meet the diverse, individual, and often complex needs of infants and toddlers with disabilities or other special needs and their families. Thus, a team approach to planning and implementing early intervention is warranted.

TEAMS AND TEAMWORK

In early intervention, groups of individuals come together to plan for and provide services and supports for young children and their families. This section describes the various team models as well as the roles and relationships of team members.

Team Models

There are at least three team models common to early intervention: multidisciplinary, interdisciplinary, and transdisciplinary (Allen, Holm, & Schiefelbusch, 1978; McGonigel & Garland, 1988). These team models are described in Table 6.1.

Multidisciplinary Team Multidisciplinary teams are groups of professionals representing several different disciplines who work on different facets of the same family situation; the professionals work independently. They assess and provide services directly to the child or family, with little active or planned coordination among the members of the team. When a child and family visit a child development clinic for a comprehensive assessment and are scheduled for separate consecutive appointments with the various specialists, they are experiencing the multidisciplinary team approach.

Interdisciplinary Team More planned communication and coordination occurs in an interdisciplinary team. In this model, the professional members of the team may conduct assessments and provide services separately but they come together to review their findings, share information, and plan. This means that team meetings are scheduled with sufficient time for sharing, members of the team pos-

Table 6.1. Early intervention team models

Model	Description	Conducting assessments	Implementing intervention
Multidisciplinary	Professionals from a variety of disciplines work independently. Families generally meet with team members separately by discipline.	Team members conduct separate assessments by discipline.	Team members develop separate plans for their disciplines. Team members implement the part of the service plan related to their discipline.
Interdisciplinary	Professionals from a variety of disciplines may work independently but come together for planning and sharing. Families generally meet with team or a team representative. Families' roles on the team vary.	Team members conduct separate assessments by discipline and share results.	Team members share their separate plans with one another. Team members implement their section of the plan and incorporate other sections where possible.
Transdisciplinary	Professionals from a variety of disciplines work together actively planning, sharing, problem solving, teaching, and learning across disciplines. Families are full team members with decision-making authority.	The team, including the family, participates in an arena-style assessment, observing and recording across disciplines.	The team, including the family, develops a plan based on family priorities, concerns, and resources. The primary service provider implements the plan with the family and with support of team.

Adapted from McGonigel & Garland (1988).

sess a willingness to share and cooperate, and members have a commitment to group decision making.

Transdisciplinary Team The extent of communication, collaboration, and shared responsibility increases in the transdisciplinary team. The boundaries between disciplines are somewhat blurred. Each team member teaches other team members some of the skills from his or her discipline and also shares information and knowledge. Individual team members must commit to teaching and learning from each other and to assuming somewhat interchangeable roles and responsibilities. In this way, one team member can serve as the primary interventionist with the child and family *with* support and consultation from the other members of the team. This model requires trust, respect for other team members, open communication, and acceptance of role release. This model does not rule out individual or specialized interventions when needed nor does it negate the specialized expertise of individual team members, but it does emphasize the sharing of professional skills and knowledge.

Just as the role of the professionals differs from model to model, so does the role of the family. In the multidisciplinary model, the family is frequently the recipient of information. In the interdisciplinary model, the role of the family varies. There are usually more opportunities for participation than in the multidisciplinary approach. A goal of the transdisciplinary approach is to involve families as full members of the team and to allow the needs of the child and family to guide the team. Families may be active participants at all levels of team functioning and decision making on the transdisciplinary team.

Nash (1990) outlined strategies to facilitate family participation on teams. First, the team must be available to the families so that they can actually participate. This means that team meetings are scheduled at convenient times and places. Team members can enable family members to define their role as a team member. This may mean that professional team members need to reconsider the value they place on parenting and caregiving and the expertise that family members bring to the team. When family members become active contributors during early intervention activities (e.g., assessment), they will have additional information to share at team meetings. All team members need to learn to develop goals and outcomes in a collaborative way (Bailey, 1987). In this way, the family's goals can be the team's goals. Some other practices that promote family participation include using a common language, clarifying the decision-making process, communicating openly, allowing disagreements, and using effective conflict management. All team members should participate in training activities that help them be better team members.

Effective Teams

The teams described previously have evolved over the history of early intervention and other human services. At present, the transdisciplinary model is considered recommended practice because it represents a whole child and whole family approach (McWilliam & Strain, 1993). It is an approach that is incompatible with fragmented services and practices. It allows one team member to be the primary interventionist with the family and reduces the number of professionals with whom the child and family need to relate. This approach is guided by respect for families. This means that families choose the extent and nature of their involvement with the team. The approach also offers benefits to professionals. They have opportunities to expand their own knowledge and skills through association with other team members and to become more capable with a wide range of children and families.

However, for the transdisciplinary model to work in this optimal fashion the commitment of the team members and the agencies involved is absolutely critical. This means that time must be available and scheduled for team members to meet, to train each other, to share information, and to receive consultation. Teams do not just coalesce when people are assigned to work together. Sufficient time and ongoing support must be given to the process of team development.

It must also be noted that, although the transdisciplinary model may be considered optimal by early interventionists, this model may not fit the needs or expectations of a family or a particular circumstance. A family-centered approach to early intervention means that the way in which planning, assessment, and intervention are provided considers the individual family circumstance. Sometimes, alternative team approaches or delivery models may be more appropriate.

Regardless of the team model that is used, there are certain features of the transdisciplinary approach that will maximize the effectiveness of early intervention and the family friendliness of the process. These include respect among all members of the team, sharing of information, and opportunities for teaching and learning.

Team Development

Teams go through stages of development (Brill, 1976; Tuckman, 1965). Various names and descriptions are used for these stages. It may be easier to remember the stages when they are referred to as forming, storming, norming, and performing.

Forming Forming is the first stage of the team's development. During this orientation stage, the team will determine its rules, methods of functioning, and expectations. Individual team members are generally looking for guidelines and direction.

Storming The second stage of the team's development is called storming because this is frequently a period of conflict, resistance, and crises. Resistance to other team members' ideas, roles, or assigned tasks may appear. It is during this stage that team members are trying to come to grips with their identity as individuals and their identity as a team.

Norming During the third stage of the team's development, norming, a sense of cohesion develops. There is a sense of team spirit and an enthusiasm for the work involved in making the team succeed. The team establishes its own norms for how to interact, how to divide tasks, and how to make decisions. Trust and open communication characterize this stage.

Performing The fourth stage of the team's development is called performing. The team's purpose and working relationships are established. Now that procedural issues have been dealt with, the work of the team can be accomplished. But team development is a continuing endeavor. Conflicts can recur when faced with new challenges. Changes in team membership can also upset the team balance and process. Thus, it is important to recognize the dynamic character of teamwork.

Given that teams do not just happen, that they develop over time, the significance of ongoing support for teamwork should be obvious. Unfortunately, many agencies and organizations do not provide adequate time for team development and maintenance. Team development requires constant commitment from team members and administrators. Characteristics of effective teams and effective team process include the following:

- Organizational support
- Clear roles including the leadership/facilitator role
- Clear goals
- Shared norms including a common language
- An understanding and appreciation for each other's values
- Clear decision-making process
- Open communication
- Creative conflict management
- A plan for monitoring, discussing, and adjusting team process and structure (Nash, 1990)

Team Members

The members of the team are the family and service providers from several disciplines who work cooperatively for the benefit of the child and family. Team members may also include family friends or advocates and representatives from agencies or community groups. Each family's team will vary somewhat in order to meet the needs and concerns of that family. For example, we met Michael in an earlier vignette. Michael's mother has become close with another mother who was assigned to her through a parent-to-parent support program. At the mother's request, this woman attends many of Michael's planning meetings.

The number of professional disciplines represented in an early intervention program varies according to the children and families served, the approach taken,

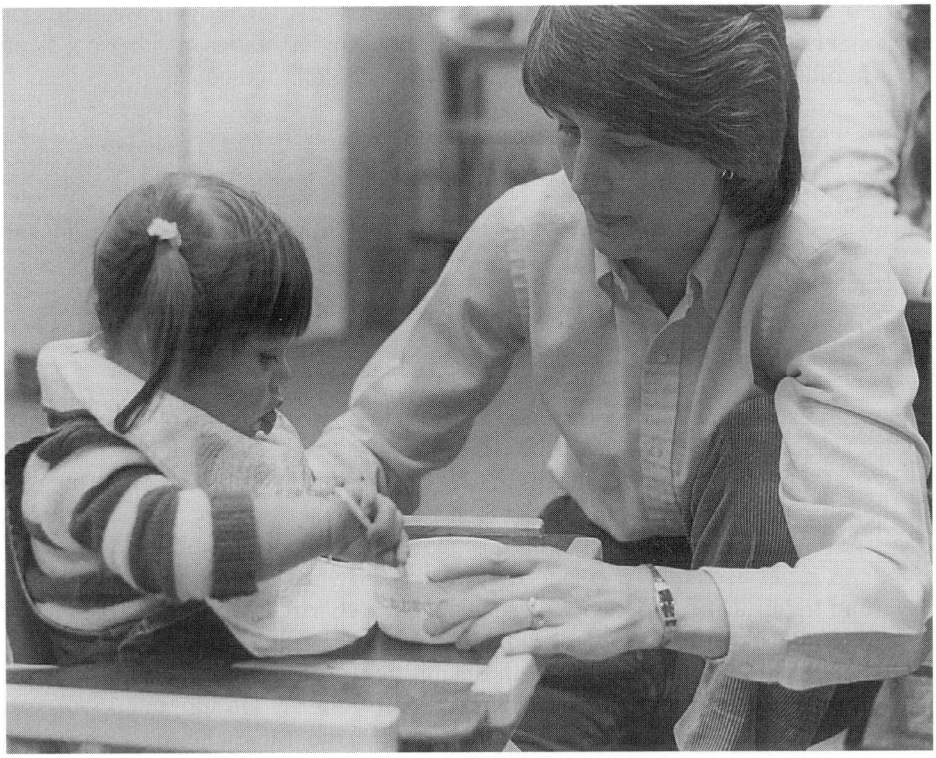

financial considerations, and community resources (Mowder, Widerstrom, & Sandall, 1989). Nevertheless, certain services are identified under Part H along with the admonition that these services are to be provided by qualified personnel. The professional service providers include the special educator, speech-language pathologist, audiologist, occupational therapist, physical therapist, psychologist, social worker, nurse, nutritionist, physician, family therapist, and orientation and mobility specialist. The roles and functions of these providers are described in Chapter 1.

Knowledge, Skills, and Standards

What does it mean to be appropriately qualified to provide early intervention services? Working with infants and toddlers with disabilities and other special needs and their families requires special knowledge and skills. A number of professionals have described this knowledge base and the corresponding competencies (Bailey, 1989b; Bailey, Farrel, O'Donnell, Simeonsson, & Miller, 1986; Bricker & Slentz, 1988; Fenichel & Eggbeer, 1990; McCollum & Maude, 1994; Thorp & McCollum, 1988).

Fenichel and Eggbeer (1990) provided the following seven knowledge areas that they believed were required for working with infants, toddlers, and their families:

> 1) endowment, maturation, and individual differences in the first three years of life; 2) the power of human relationships; 3) transactions between the child and environment; 4) parenthood as a developmental process; 5) developmental processes and their interrelationship; 6) risk, coping, adaptation, and mastery; and 7) the helping relationship. (p. 5)

In addition to a strong and comprehensive knowledge base, skills that are essential for working with young children with disabilities or other risks and their families could be added. These skills include the following:

1. Working with young children and families
2. Doing assessments
3. Developing IFSPs
4. Planning, implementing, and evaluating interventions, treatments, and supports
5. Coordinating transition planning
6. Evaluating programs
7. Interacting with other professionals

To be appropriately qualified to provide early intervention services means that a person has the knowledge and skills in the areas described. It also means that the professional is certified, licensed, or registered (depending on the profession and requirements of the state) within their professional discipline. This ensures that the individual has met the basic requirements for their profession including schooling and supervised field experience. It does not always ensure that the individual has had training and experience with very young children, families, and teams (Bricker & Widerstrom, 1996). Other professionals have a great deal of knowledge and experience with young children with disabilities and their families, but they lack the appropriate certification (Bailey, Simeonsson, Yoder, & Huntington, 1990).

The hiring process is another important part of the challenge of ensuring qualified early intervention team members. Job descriptions should adequately detail the multiple roles and responsibilities of early interventionists. To complement this, practices such as role playing, multiple interviews, and responses to hypothetical situations may yield information about the prospective early interventionist's skills, knowledge, experiences with young children and families, and attitudes. Such personal characteristics as flexibility, maturity, initiative, a willingness to share, and tolerance for change are necessary to function successfully as an early interventionist and as a member of a team (Thorp & McCollum, 1988).

Preparation and Training Issues

A number of factors such as the age of the children served, the pivotal role of families, and the need for teamwork and collaboration all point to the need for specialized preparation of early interventionists (Bailey, Palsha, & Simeonsson, 1991; Thorp & McCollum, 1988). As Thorp and McCollum have written, early interventionists need a strong knowledge base and clinical skills within their own professional discipline, and they need skills in working as members of a team and forming a relationship with families. This requires cross-disciplinary training experiences as well as within-discipline experiences. It is often difficult to provide sufficient and productive team training experiences at the preservice level. However, such experiences in the form of interdisciplinary course content and field settings are important and needed. This need has been acknowledged by professionals across the disciplines involved in early intervention (Bricker & Widerstrom, 1996). This acknowledgment stems from the belief that early intervention is most effective if the approaches to intervention used by the various members of the team are integrated and mutually supportive.

Another important element in the preparation of early interventionists is the meaningful involvement of family members throughout the process (Able-Boone, Sandall, & Loughry, 1989). Parents and other family members can serve as mentors, assist in the development of courses and field experiences, and assist in teaching courses. When family members personally communicate their concerns, needs, feelings, and reactions, the value of their input moves far beyond what is gained from simply reading about families. Furthermore, several experiences with families are necessary to demonstrate the diversity of family experiences in early intervention.

However, given the personnel shortages in the field (Hebbeler, 1994) and the position of early intervention as an emerging field in which current practices may not match recommended practices, ongoing professional development is also critical. Early intervention services continue to change in quality and quantity. Within this context of change, professional development (in-service education and technical assistance) plays an important role in improving the capabilities of those who provide early intervention services (Trohanis, 1994). Preparation of teachers, therapists, and others does not end with attainment of a certification or license. Rather, ongoing program refinement is supported, at least in part, by organized and goal-directed professional development activities that are aimed at changing and upgrading skills, knowledge, and attitudes.

Finally, a reflective orientation may be particularly important for professionals in early intervention, a field that is young, dynamic, and relationship based (McCollum, Rowan, & Thorp, 1994). Preservice and in-service activities should encourage early interventionists to stop, think, and reflect on what they are doing and learning to enhance their understanding of the professional self and their relationships with families and team members. They, too, should study experiences of families to understand the diversity of family experiences in early intervention.

INTERAGENCY COLLABORATION

Thus far, this chapter has focused on the interactions among individuals. Effective teamwork is a complex process that requires a range of skills and a strong commitment. Another level of teamwork is required to achieve successful and efficient early intervention. This level requires that the various agencies involved with young children and their families work together.

Congress, in framing PL 99-457, the Education of the Handicapped Act Amendments of 1986, made interagency collaboration a primary feature. The task for states was to plan, develop, and implement an *interagency* program of early intervention services. The history of human services in general and children's services in particular had been one of independent, specialized, and often disjointed programs that were unwieldy, expensive, and frustrating. Direct service providers told stories of some families who managed to collect multiple services and resources while other families had none. Families reported their frustrations with figuring out a system that often was not a system at all but separate programs with separate policies and practices. Experiences such as these, coupled with the vision of certain policy makers, provided the push for greater coordination of human services during the 1970s and 1980s. The rationale that developed recognized that interagency collaboration could result in improved services, decreased duplication of services, comprehensive services (e.g., elimination of service gaps, increased accessibility), and reduced costs (Hanson & Lynch, 1995).

PL 99-457 was groundbreaking legislation in that it required a coordinated interagency effort that involved multiple disciplines, multiple agencies, and multiple sources of financial support. In the years since the passage of the law, we have seen that interagency collaboration (like teamwork) is a challenging and complex process. It remains a worthwhile goal.

In reviewing the interagency literature and analyzing the legal ramifications of PL 99-457, Peterson (1991) clarified the terms *cooperation, coordination,* and *collaboration.* She wrote that cooperation among agencies refers to facilitating each other's activities. However, local, state and federal agencies remain autonomous in terms of specification of goals, planning, and decision making. Coordination among agencies extends the working relationship and means that two or more agencies may coordinate such tasks or activities as schedules, events, or services. However, goals and decision making are still fairly autonomous. Collaboration refers to a more intensive and continuous relationship among agencies. It refers to shared goals, joint planning, and shared decision making. Interagency collaboration requires a common set of implementation strategies that guide these shared activities. By its very nature, collaboration necessitates that individual agencies must adapt some policies and practices and relinquish some autonomy. Peterson concluded that collaboration requires both cooperation and coordination. However, cooperation or coordination may be strategies that are used without or before moving on to true collaboration.

The law emphasizes that all relevant agencies should be involved in the planning process, in developing the statewide system of services, in coordinating payment for services, and in actually delivering services. One of the mechanisms for collaboration is the Interagency Coordinating Council (ICC) mandated in each state as part of the Part H requirements. Another mechanism is service coordination, which is described later in this chapter. A third mechanism that has become increasingly important is writing formal interagency agreements.

The Interagency Coordinating Council

The ICC consists of parents, representatives from public and private providers of early intervention, representation from the state legislature, representation from institutions of higher education, and representatives from the appropriate state agencies involved in the provision of or payment for early intervention services. Thus, at the direction of the law, a state-level council is in place appointed by the governor, to advise and assist in planning, developing, and implementing a coordinated, comprehensive interagency program of early intervention services. Many states have extended the concept to the development of local or community ICCs.

Interagency Agreements

Interagency agreements are formal, written agreements that specify the working arrangements that are intended to put collaboration into practice. These agreements detail the purpose of the agreement, tell what each agency will do and how, and provide the terms and limits of the agreement. Formal agreements are important for lasting relationships. Examples of formal, interagency agreements are those that have been developed by Head Start and local education agencies (LEAs) to ensure collaboration between the two agencies in serving young children with disabilities

(Hanson & Widerstrom, 1993). A written agreement often is the difference between an interagency arrangement that only works while certain individuals are doing the work, and an arrangement that is integrated into the organizational structures and persists even when staff come and go.

Interagency Collaboration and the Team

What is the impact of interagency collaboration on the early interventionist or on the family? From an ecological perspective (Bronfenbrenner, 1979), the linkages and relationships among agencies and groups are influential.

Early intervention takes place within a larger context. These contexts include the family, community, clinics, schools, and centers. Governmental and nongovernmental agencies and the relationships among these various systems represent the broader context for early intervention. Thus, cooperation, coordination, and collaboration at federal, state, and local levels will facilitate the provision of effective early intervention for an individual child and family.

Interagency collaboration means that services, supports, and resources are available, coordinated, and accessible; or, if gaps do exist, then action is taken to reduce these gaps. From the family's perspective, this means that they are more likely to obtain the type of help they need to meet the concerns they feel and the challenges they face in caring for their young child with a disability or special need.

The availability of help is also important to early interventionists. Neither a single interventionist working in isolation nor a single service program can be expected to meet the needs of every child and family. Collaboration at the various organizational and administrative levels sets the stage for early interventionists, at the local program level, to work collaboratively to maximize their mutual efforts. Again, the examples of Michael and Sonja help to illustrate the effects of collaborative work.

SERVICE COORDINATION

Part H of IDEA (PL 101-476) recognizes the need for coordinated services for young children with disabilities and their families. This recognition grew out of the experiences of both families and service providers. Thus, service coordination is a service under the law and each family is to be provided with a service coordinator. In the

Michael *(continued)*

Michael's developmental nurse, Alma, is employed by a community agency that provides early intervention services to infants and toddlers and their families. She also participates in a task force at the medical center. The primary purpose of the task force is to plan, develop, and implement early intervention services for children who are living in the neonatal intensive care unit (NICU) and graduates of the unit as they move home. Similarly, the medical center has a representative on the state's ICC so that the center's planning is coordinated with state efforts as well as community efforts.

Sonja *(continued)*

At first glance, Sonja's early intervention program may appear to be so comprehensive that it addresses all the concerns of the child and family. However, the child care center cannot provide a full array of family support and educational services. Through information shared between Sonja's care providers and the family, Sonja's parents have found a parent education program that provides them with the child-rearing information they wanted. Sonja's brothers and sisters have also participated in sibling support groups that were offered as a service by another agency. The director of Sonja's child care center is a member of the local ICC. The members of the local ICC are on each other's mailing lists so that they receive newsletters and other updated material. These are ways that the program director finds out about other services and resources and shares this information with her staff and the families.

original version of the law, the terms *case manager* and *case management* were used. We had forgotten, but families quickly reminded us of what Hobbs (1984) had told us, that families do not view themselves as cases nor do they want to be managed. (In presenting the historical antecedents to service coordination, we use the term *case management.*)

According to Dunst and Trivette (1989), three historical approaches to case management may be identified: role-focused approaches; resource procurement approaches, which emphasize the case manager's role in helping clients obtain what they need to function successfully; and client empowerment approaches, in which the case manager focuses on enhancing the clients' abilities to procure their own resources and services. The first two of these approaches originated early in the century as responses in the field of social work to the need for service coordination, accountability, and nonduplication of services. With the growing urbanization of American society and the proliferation of programs to address economic, social, and health care problems, coordination among diverse service providers became a necessity; at the same time, program accountability became important. Gradually, these two functions were placed under the rubric of case management. Finally, as client advocacy emerged as an issue, it was added to the case manager's responsibilities (Weil & Karls, 1985). The deinstitutionalization movement for people with mental retardation and people with mental illness in the 1960s led to an increased need for case managers and a review of then-existing case management practices.

Much of the history of case management is rooted in service systems focused on individuals who, for various reasons (e.g., mental illness, mental retardation), were perceived as requiring considerable assistance in obtaining needed services. Deficit models of case management have emphasized the dependence and reduced capability of clients and have utilized role-focused or resource procurement approaches. Such approaches place the case manager in the position of primary decision maker regarding services. This has often resulted in case management practices that do not empower the individuals receiving services, but rather foster dependence and perceptions of inadequacy and dysfunction (Bailey, 1989a; Dunst,

1989). In contrast, the empowerment approach assumes that clients have the current or potential ability to manage their own affairs, participate in the process, and make their own decisions.

The early intervention field has generally embraced the empowerment approach to case management. This certainly reflects the family-centered spirit of Part H. The change in terminology to service coordination also reflects this spirit.

The Empowerment Model

The empowerment model supports families in maintaining or building upon their own capabilities. It is a model that fosters active participation and views the family as competent. The birth or identification of a child with special needs does not alter the family's basic capacity to make and implement decisions. However, the birth or identification of a child with special needs may necessitate the acquisition of new knowledge and skills, and the mobilization of resources in different ways. The empowerment model of service coordination is dedicated to supporting families as they obtain skills in acquiring and activating resources, services, and supports in a confident and competent manner. Service coordination services are themselves individually tailored, in recognition of the changing capacities of families.

Dunst and Trivette (1989) further define the empowerment model as effective helping. It is the act of enabling families to become better able to solve their own problems, meet their own needs, or achieve their aspirations by promoting the acquisition of competencies that develop a greater sense of control over the intervention process. In this model, effective helping consists of providing contingent helping, enabling experiences, and fostering a sense of empowerment.

The notion of *contingent helping* is that help must be provided to clients contingent upon their behavior. That is, people acquire resources when they are actively involved in solving their own problems. If people perceive that help will be given no matter what they do, a sense of helplessness and dependence results. If, however, families perceive that the help is contingent upon their own behavior, and they have control over whether they receive that help or not, they feel a greater sense of control over the process. For example, a young mother who is dependent on illegal drugs is offered the opportunity to enroll her child in an extended child care and intervention program contingent upon her entry into a drug treatment program. She is offered the services of a home health visitor on a regular basis if she will take the initiative to schedule the visits in advance. This is just one example. Contingent helping is an individualized process.

Enabling experiences are those that afford individuals opportunities to learn new competencies that strengthen their functioning as parents and independent citizens. They are experiences that allow active participation on the part of families in decisions that affect them. They increase the family's sense of control over future events. For example, parents of an infant with multiple disabilities may set goals for their child and other family members, decide which professionals with whom they want to work and for how long, and then evaluate the effectiveness of their early intervention program. They may participate in a parent support group in which they learn to share ideas with other parents who are less experienced.

Empowerment implies that the family already has many competencies that may previously have gone unrecognized by either themselves or the professionals, that what is seen as poor family functioning is really the result of the existing social

structure or a lack of resources, and that new competencies are best learned in the context of daily living.

Desired family outcomes for the service coordination process include an enhanced sense of personal control, an increased belief in each family member's own ability to make things happen, and a sense of participatory competence on the part of the family. *Participatory competence* means that family members see themselves as able to take effective action on their own behalf. Empowered families take the initiative, find meaningful services and supports, reject or change those that are not helpful, and decide how to allocate their resources. Effective service coordination means that families take a meaningful role in the coordination of their service plan.

Responsibilities of the Service Coordinator

What then are the responsibilities of the service coordinator? First, we look at the definition of service coordination according to the regulations that accompany Part H of IDEA (PL 101-476). Service coordination means activities are carried out to assist and enable a child and the child's family to receive the rights, procedural safeguards, and services that are authorized to be provided under the state's early intervention program (CFR 303.6[a][1]).

Service coordination is flexible. It can be carried out in a variety of ways that are still consistent with the law and regulations. Service coordination continues throughout the early intervention process. It is not something that occurs only at intake or only at the individualized family service plan (IFSP) meeting.

Key service coordination activities are listed in the regulations. These include the following:

Michael *(conclusion)*

The service coordinator for Michael and his family is his developmental nurse, Alma. The family was referred to Alma's agency while Michael was still in the medical center. Alma was assigned as the interim service coordinator and visited Michael, his mother, and the hospital's social worker on a visit to the medical center. She kept in contact with them by telephone. When Michael was transferred to the community hospital, Alma began regular visits and worked with the nurse and Michael's mother and grandmother as they prepared for discharge. Physical therapy was recommended for Michael; Alma provided the family with the names of therapists and agencies who could provide this service. At about this time, a meeting was held to revise Michael's IFSP. Alma explained that a new service coordinator could be selected. Because Michael's mother was satisfied with the program and services, she asked that Alma continue as their service coordinator. Alma receives consultation from a speech therapist and a psychologist at her agency. Alma and Michael's mother have decided that a good way for Alma and the physical therapist to keep in contact with each other is for Alma to attend a therapy appointment about once a month in place of her home visit. They also decided that Alma would receive a copy of the reports from Michael's visits to the follow-up clinic.

1) coordinating the performance of evaluations and assessments;
2) facilitating and participating in the development, review, and evaluation of IFSPs;
3) helping families identify available service providers;
4) coordinating and monitoring the delivery of available services;
5) informing families of the availability of advocacy services;
6) coordinating with medical and health providers;
7) facilitating the development of a transition plan to preschool services, if appropriate. (CFR 303.6[b])

This list of activities suggests a role-focused approach to service coordination. In contrast, the definition of service coordination uses the phrase "to assist and enable." These contrasting views of "doing for" the client versus enabling the client to "do for him- or herself" occur repeatedly in the literature. This means that service coordinators, other members of the early intervention team, and early intervention agencies must clearly articulate their model of service coordination and regularly review their practices to see that their actions match their model and family needs.

The regulations also describe the qualifications of the service coordinator. A service coordinator must have demonstrated knowledge and understanding about the following:

1) infants and toddlers who are eligible;
2) Part H of the act and the regulations in this part; and
3) the nature and scope of services available under the state's early intervention program, the system of payments for services in the State, and other pertinent information. (CFR 303.6[d])

Sonja *(conclusion)*

Sonja's family has had two service coordinators. Shortly after Sonja was born, the family was referred to a county office that oversees early intervention services. Marco, a psychologist, worked with Sonja's family during the intake process and determination of eligibility, provided the family with information on programs in their community, and put them in touch with a parent group. Sonja's family decided to wait until her mother returned to work before enrolling Sonja in an early intervention program. Marco served as the family's service coordinator for the first 6 months and helped them develop the first IFSP. He also participated in the IFSP process when Sonja enrolled in the child care center. At the meeting to update Sonja's IFSP (when she was 7 months old), Sonja's parents were given the opportunity to select a new service coordinator from among three staff members at the child care center who were available. They selected Terri, the speech therapist. Terri is in regular contact with Sonja's family to fulfill her responsibilities of coordinating, informing, and advocating. Terri is also a member of the classroom team in Sonja's class. That team is responsible for planning, implementing, and monitoring activities for all the children in the classroom.

The law and regulations provide a framework for the provision of service coordination. States may expand on this to meet the particular needs of their population. Similarly, there are a variety of local models of service coordination. For example, one program may have a staff member such as the social worker who is the designated service coordinator for the enrolled families. (However, this model limits family choice.) Another program may be able to allow families to choose their service coordinator from the staff and, thus, all staff members may potentially serve as service coordinators. Another option used in some locations uses service coordinators who are employed by a human services agency rather than the local early intervention program. In some states, parents may be their own service coordinator. In others, experienced parents may serve as service coordinators. Regardless of how the service is delivered, it is essential that those who serve in the role of service coordinator receive adequate training and continuing education so that they have the most current information about services and resources for families.

The Service Coordinator and the Team

The relationship between the service coordinator and the other professional members of the team will vary. This variability is due in part to the other responsibilities and obligations of the service coordinator. As described previously, the service coordinator may be a direct service provider, a designated service coordinator, or a parent. The service coordinator may be employed and supervised by the same agency as the other team members or by some other agency. Because working relationships are so potentially varied, it increases the importance of sharing a purpose, communicating, and appreciating and learning from the other members of the team. The stories of Michael and Sonja continue to show two different working relationships.

SUMMARY

Effective early intervention requires a team approach. Productive and valued team members are knowledgeable and skillful in their own area of expertise and capable in team process. Teams do not just happen; they develop over time. The need for ongoing support for teamwork is substantial. Organizations and agencies must recognize the importance of teamwork by actions and policies that support teams. Effective early intervention also requires another kind of teamwork at the agency level. Multiple agencies must collaborate to achieve comprehensive, coordinated, interagency early intervention systems.

SUGGESTED READINGS AND RESOURCES

Bailey, D., McWilliam, P.J., Winton, P., & Simeonsson, R.J. (1992). *Implementing family-centered services in early intervention: A team-based model for change.* Cambridge, MA: Brookline Books.

Garland, C., Frank, A., Buck, D., & Seklemian, P. (1992). *Skills inventory for teams (SIFT): A resource for teams.* Lightfoot, VA: Child Development Resources.

Mile High Down Syndrome Association. (1990). *Taking charge: Family-centered case management* [Videotape]. Littleton, CO: Author.

Project Copernicus. (1992). *Train-the-trainer series in family-centered service delivery.* St. Paul, MN: Pathfinder Resources, Inc.

Virginia Institute For Developmental Disabilities. (1991). *Interdisciplinary teamwork: A team in name only* and *Becoming an effective team* [Videotapes]. Van Nuys, CA: Child Development Media, Inc.

Zipper, I.N., Hinton, C., Weil, M., & Rounds, K. (1993). *Service coordination for early intervention: Parents and professionals.* Cambridge, MA: Brookline Books.

REFERENCES

Able-Boone, H., Sandall, S., & Loughry, A. (1989). Preparing family specialists in early childhood special education. *Teacher Education and Special Education, 12*(3), 96–102.

Allen, K.E., Holm, V.A., & Schiefelbusch, R.L. (Eds.). (1978). *Early intervention: A team approach.* Austin, TX: PRO-ED.

Bailey, D.B. (1987). Collaborative goal-setting with families: Resolving differences in values and priorities for services. *Topics in Early Childhood Special Education, 7*(2), 59–71.

Bailey, D.B. (1989a). Case management in early intervention. *Journal of Early Intervention, 13*(2), 120–134.

Bailey, D.B. (1989b). Issues and directions in preparing professionals to work with young handicapped children and their families. In J. Gallagher, P. Trohanis, & R. Clifford (Eds.), *Policy implementation and PL 99-457: Planning for young children with special needs* (pp. 97–132). Baltimore: Paul H. Brookes Publishing Co.

Bailey, D.B., Farrel, A., O'Donnell, K., Simeonsson, R., & Miller, C. (1986). Preparing infant interventionists: Interdepartmental training in special education and maternal and child health. *Journal of the Division for Early Childhood, 11*(1), 67–77.

Bailey, D.B., Palsha, S.A., & Simeonsson, R.J. (1991). Professional skills, concerns, and perceived importance of work with families in early intervention. *Exceptional Children, 58*(2), 152–165.

Bailey, D.B., Simeonsson, R.J., Yoder, D.E., & Huntington, G.S. (1990). Preparing professionals to serve infants and toddlers with handicaps and their families: An integrative analysis across eight disciplines. *Exceptional Children, 57*(1), 26–35.

Bricker, D., & Slentz, K. (1988). Personnel preparation: Handicapped infants. In M. Wang, H. Walberg, & M. Reynolds (Eds.), *The handbook of special education: Research and practice* (Vol. 3, pp. 319–345). Elmsford, NY: Pergammon.

Bricker, D.D., & Widerstrom, A.H. (Eds.). (1996). *Preparing personnel to work with infants and young children and their families: A team approach.* Baltimore: Paul H. Brookes Publishing Co.

Brill, N. (1976). *Teamwork.* Philadelphia: J.B. Lippincott.

Bronfenbrenner, U. (1979). *The ecology of human development: Experiments by nature and design.* Cambridge, MA: Harvard University Press.

Dunst, C.J. (1989, October). *Case management practices in early intervention.* Presentation at the International Conference on Children with Special Needs, Division for Early Childhood, Minneapolis, MN.

Dunst, C.J., & Trivette, C.M. (1989). An enablement and empowerment perspective of case management. *Topics in Early Childhood Special Education, 8*(4), 87–102.

Education of the Handicapped Act Amendments of 1986, PL 99-457, 20 U.S.C. § 1400 *et seq.*

Fenichel, E.S., & Eggbeer, L. (1990). *Preparing practitioners to work with infants, toddlers, and their families: Issues and recommendations for educators and trainers.* Washington, DC: National Center for Clinical Infant Programs.

Hanson, M.J., & Lynch, E.W. (1995). *Early intervention* (2nd ed.). Austin, TX: PRO-ED.

Hanson, M.J., & Widerstrom, A.H. (1993). Consultation and collaboration: Essentials of integration efforts for young children. In C.A. Peck, S.L. Odom, & D.D. Bricker (Eds.), *Integrating young children with disabilities into community programs: Ecological perspectives on research and implementation* (pp. 149–168). Baltimore: Paul H. Brookes Publishing Co.

Hebbeler, K. (1994). *Shortages in professions working with young children with disabilities and their families.* Chapel Hill, NC: National Early Childhood Technical Assistance System.

Hobbs, N. (Ed.). (1984). *Strengthening families.* San Francisco: Jossey-Bass.

Individuals with Disabilities Education Act (IDEA) of 1990, PL 101-476, 20 U.S.C. § 1400 *et seq.*

McCollum, J.A., & Maude, S.P. (1994). Early childhood special educators as early interventionists: Issues and emerging practice in personnel preparation. In P.L. Safford, B. Spodeck, & O.N. Saracho (Eds.), *Yearbook in early childhood education: Early childhood special education* (Vol. 5). New York: Teachers College Press.

McCollum, J.A., Rowan, L.R., & Thorp, E.K. (1994). Philosophy as training in infancy personnel preparation. *Journal of Early Intervention, 18*(2), 216–226.

McGonigel, M.J., & Garland, C.W. (1988). The individualized family service plan and the early intervention team: Team and family issues and recommended practices. *Infants and Young Children, 1*(1), 10–21.

McWilliam, R.A., & Strain, P.S. (1993). Service delivery models. In Division for Early Childhood (Ed.), *DEC recommended practices: Indicators of quality in programs for infants and young children with special needs and their families* (pp. 40–46). Reston, VA: Council for Exceptional Children.

Mowder, B.A., Widerstrom, A.H., & Sandall, S.R. (1989). School psychologists serving at-risk and handicapped infants, toddlers, and their families. *Professional School Psychology, 4*(3), 159–171.

Nash, J.K. (1990). Public Law 99-457: Facilitating family participation on the multidisciplinary team. *Journal of Early Intervention, 14*(4), 318–326.

Odom, S.L., & McLean, M.E. (1993). Establishing recommended practices for programs for infants and young children with special needs and their families. In Division for Early Childhood (Ed.), *DEC recommended practices: Indicators of quality in programs for infants and young children with special needs and their families* (pp. 1–10). Reston, VA: Council for Exceptional Children.

Peterson, N.L. (1991). Interagency collaboration under Part H: The key to comprehensive, multidisciplinary, coordinated infant/toddler intervention services. *Journal of Early Intervention, 15*(1), 89–105.

Thorp, E., & McCollum, J.A. (1988). Defining the infancy specialization in early childhood special education. In J. Jordan, J. Gallagher, M. Karnes, & P. Hutinger (Eds.), *Early childhood special education: Birth–3* (pp. 147–162). Reston, VA: Council for Exceptional Children.

Trohanis, P.L. (1994). Planning for successful inservice education for local early childhood programs. *Topics in Early Childhood Special Education, 14*(3), 311–332.

Tuckman, B.W. (1965). Developmental sequence in small groups. *Psychological Bulletin, 63*(6), 384–399.

Weil, M., & Karls, J.M. (1985). *Case management in human service practice.* San Francisco: Jossey-Bass.

6 ACTIVITIES

1. Contact the lead agency for the Part H program in your state. Get information about attending a state or local ICC meeting. Attend a meeting and report to the class.

2. Interview a service coordinator. Ask what the service coordinator believes are the benefits of service coordination for children and families. Ask about training or other requirements for being a service coordinator.

3 Make of list of your experiences with early intervention teams, as an observer or as a participant. What are your strengths as a team member? What would make you a better team member?

4. Make a list of your experiences with families in early intervention. Share your list with classmates. Use your discussion with classmates and your own thinking to make a list of experiences you would like to have, and indicate why these experiences are important to you.

CHAPTER 7

Ethical Issues in Family-Centered Neonatal Care

Helen Harrison

Objectives

- To increase awareness of the complexity of issues surrounding treatment of premature and low birth weight infants in the neonatal intensive care unit (NICU)
- To increase understanding of parents' viewpoints concerning NICU treatment and the need for full participation by parents in treatment decisions
- To become familiar with the Principles for Family-Centered Neonatal Care developed by parents and professionals to increase the parents' participation in their infant's neonatal intensive care

Advances in medical technology allow neonatologists to save the lives of many premature infants who previously would have died at birth. However, intensive neonatal treatment, particularly for infants born at the margins of viability, involves prolonged pain and stress, exposure to poorly validated therapies, great expense, and the high risk of an extended dying process or of survival with serious disability.

The burdensome, costly, and uncertain nature of neonatal intensive care raises ethical issues and the need for parental decision making. However, parents have been barred from their traditional roles as decision makers for their infant because of legal ambiguities created by "Baby Doe" legislation and because of the strong commitment of many neonatologists to provide aggressive treatment to all potentially viable infants. Unfortunately, society does not always demonstrate a similar high level of commitment to the ongoing care of children who survive with disabilities.

This chapter begins with three vignettes that illustrate ethical problems inherent in the present structure of neonatal decision making. The chapter goes on to argue for a treatment protocol that places medical and ethical decision making firmly in the hands of well-informed parents. The chapter concludes with a statement of principles for family-centered care developed by parents of premature infants in collaboration with neonatal professionals.

Neonatal Care

Sarah, a social worker in Minnesota, was employed finding foster placements for disabled survivors of neonatal intensive care units (NICUs) when, ironically, she found herself in the midst of a high-risk triplet pregnancy. In labor at 21 weeks' gestation (19 weeks from term), she and her husband Bob asked the perinatologist about their options. "You have no options," the doctor replied.

Sarah's pregnancy was prolonged several weeks with tocolytics, but her triplets were still born extremely prematurely. Within 24 hours of delivery, one of the babies was hemorrhaging severely into his lungs and brain. Sarah then approached the doctor and asked the question she thought any responsible, loving parents would ask: "At what point do we say enough is enough for this little boy?" The neonatologist replied, "You don't make those decisions! We do!"

Soon all three boys had suffered severe brain hemorrhages. When Sarah and Bob asked what this meant for their children's future, they were given falsely optimistic information. When they discovered the truth about their sons' prognoses, they asked to speak to the hospital ethics committee to request that aggressive treatment be discontinued. Their request to meet with the committee was denied.

When Sarah expressed her concerns about bringing home three medically fragile babies, the neonatologist told her, "If you can't manage, you can put them in foster care." This response, says Sarah, showed the doctor to be not only shockingly insensitive, but also shockingly ignorant about the world outside the NICU. "As a county social worker," she explained, "I had spent the better part of the previous year developing a placement for a youngster whose problems weren't nearly as serious as those of my children. This placement outside an institutional setting was so unique it made the local papers. It also cost $300 a day."

The triplets survived with major health problems and disabilities including cerebral palsy, mental retardation, hydrocephalus, seizure disorders, chronic lung disease, and blindness. They are cared for at home by their parents between their numerous rehospitalizations.

(continued)

Mary Ann and Charles, a couple in New Jersey, watched helplessly as doctors administered a series of aggressive treatments to their newborn son, only to have it all end in death half a year later. "What my son went through in 6 months," Mary Ann wrote, "I will **never** forget as long as I live. It was torture, cruel and inhumane, all for a terrible proposed outcome."

Wanda and Keaton, a couple in Wisconsin, discovered by surreptitiously reading the medical chart that their infant son, born at 23 weeks' gestation, had suffered a severe brain hemorrhage and that a likely outcome was a persistent vegetative state. This information directly contradicted optimistic statements they had been given by their son's physicians. The parents requested that their son be taken off life support. The neonatologists refused. With the help of a support group, the parents found an attorney who directed them to a neonatologist at a neighboring hospital. *This* neonatologist believed the request to remove life support was reasonable. Only after the new neonatologist agreed to take the baby as a transfer to his unit did the original neonatologist relent and allow the infant to be removed from the respirator. The baby died quickly and peacefully in his parents' arms.

These accounts are taken from letters written to the author of this chapter by parents whose children were treated in NICUs. Their views and experiences reflect those of a growing number of parents who have come to understand the short- and long-term suffering that can accompany the attempted high-technology medical rescue of marginally viable infants. Parents who do not want this treatment for their extremely premature or critically ill infants all too often find themselves in ethical and legal conflicts with neonatal staff who feel obligated to administer intensive care (Alecson, 1995b; Halpern, 1989; Kolata, 1991; Roan, 1993; Stein, 1994; Stinson & Stinson, 1983).

Parents who *do* want intensive care for their premature babies have also expressed dissatisfaction with aspects of neonatal care that they consider to be unethical or insufficiently sensitive to the needs of the baby and family. Problems identified by both groups of parents include difficulties obtaining accurate information about their babies' conditions, treatments, and prognoses; parental exclusion from medical and ethical decision making; overtreatment of marginally viable infants; undertreatment of infant pain; exposure of infants to a stressful and developmentally inappropriate nursery environment; questions about the safety and efficacy of neonatal therapies; unnecessary impediments to parental nursing and nurturing in the NICU; poor discharge planning; and inadequate or nonexistent follow-up programs and services for the survivors of the NICU (Harrison, 1993).

ETHICAL ISSUES IN TREATMENT OF PREMATURE INFANTS

Technological innovations since the 1960s have dramatically improved the survival of premature infants. However, the arduous, poorly validated treatments used by neonatal caregivers and the high rate of disability among survivors raise ethical questions: When is aggressive life-saving treatment too costly, too painful, or too experimental? And who should make such decisions?

"Costs" of Treatment

Respirator care for infants has had its largest impact on the survival of very low birth weight (VLBW) infants—babies born before the 32nd week of gestation with birth weights less than 1,500 grams (3 lbs., 5 oz.). Before the use of respirators, most such infants died (Paneth, 1995). Today, more than 80% survive (Hack et al., 1995). However, this survival has come at great human and financial cost. Initial life-saving treatment typically involves months of difficult and painful intensive care. Disabling conditions, serious enough to be diagnosed in infancy or early childhood, have been found in 25% of VLBW survivors (Escobar, Littenberg, & Pettiti, 1991). By school age, an additional 20%–40% are diagnosed with significant intellectual or academic disabilities (Bennett, 1988; Hunt, Cooper, & Tooley, 1988). Persistent stress has been documented among families of surviving VLBW children, with negative impacts reported on sibling and parental well-being, ability to work, financial and marital stability, and future childbearing (Cronin, Shapiro, Casiro, & Cheang, 1995).

The monetary cost of treating VLBW infants is difficult to determine because of the high degree of fragmentation in neonatal care and billing, but the burdens to family and society are thought to be substantial (Lewit, Baker, Corman, & Shiono, 1995). Medical costs in the first year of life for low birth weight infants have been conservatively estimated at $4 billion per year (Lewit et al., 1995). The costs of treatment of ongoing health and developmental problems among VLBW children is even more difficult to quantify, but a conservative estimate of the total annual cost of care for infants and children born at low birth weight is $6 billion, exceeding the annual cost of AIDS (Lewit et al., 1995).

As birth weight and gestational age decline, mortality, morbidity, and cost of treatment increase sharply. Of particular concern to parents, physicians, and ethicists are babies who weigh less than 800 grams at birth, or babies who are born before the 26th week of gestation (American Academy of Pediatrics Committee on Fetus and Newborn, 1995; Tyson, 1995). More than 85% of these extremely low birth weight survivors are left with some degree of functional limitation resulting from chronic illness, sensory deficits, physical disabilities, behavioral problems, and cognitive disorders (Saigal et al., 1994). One half to two thirds of these infants have disabilities that are classified as moderate or severe (Hack et al., 1994; Johnson, Townshend, Yudkin, Bull, & Wilkinson, 1993). The average cost for the initial treatment of such an infant (in 1992 dollars) has been estimated at $363,000, with individual costs for the smallest of these infants often exceeding $1 million (Pomerance, Pomerance, & Gottleib, 1993).

As mortality has decreased among extremely low birth weight babies, researchers have noted an increase in the severity and complexity of ongoing problems among survivors (Hoffman & Bennett, 1990; Tyson, 1995). The evolution of this new morbidity is well described by Dr. James Thullen, a neonatologist in Raleigh, North Carolina, who directs the follow-up clinic at Wake Medical Center:

> In my earlier years, running the [follow-up] clinic was a gratifying experience as most babies had normal catch-up growth, development and behavior. Of the handicapped survivors, most had spastic diplegia, unassociated with mental

> retardation, which was amenable to early intervention. Fifteen years later, the complexity of medical and psychosocial problems has increased...the children are fragile and the families severely stressed. (Thullen, 1992)

The new morbidities include poor growth; multiple disabilities besides cerebral palsy; visual, auditory, and mental disabilities; chronic lung disease; and dependency on tracheostomies, oxygen, and continuous feedings via infusion pumps. "Our society seems determined to treat almost every newborn with the most sophisticated technology at our disposal. [Yet] our federal and state commitment to the long term care of these babies and families is negligible" (Thullen, 1992).

Institutional and foster care placements have not kept pace with the increasing numbers of children who leave the NICU with severe disabilities or the need for continued life support technology (Trost, 1989). Adequate funding and support is often unavailable to families who wish to care for their children with severe disabilities at home (American Academy of Pediatrics Special Report, 1989; Bergman & Simpson, 1991; Morris, 1987).

Educational and developmental services for premature infants at risk are offered in many communities under Part H of the Individuals with Disabilities Education Act (IDEA) of 1990 (PL 101-476), but some states are backing away from providing services due to the costs involved (see Chapter 1). How best to serve infants with or at risk for disabilities is also becoming increasingly unclear. Results of a large, multicenter study raise doubts about the ability of early intervention to enhance intellectual functioning of VLBW children (Brooks-Gunn et al., 1994). Other studies have failed to demonstrate benefits of physical therapy for children with or at risk for cerebral palsy (Palmer et al., 1988; Rothberg, Goodman, Jacklin, & Cooper, 1991). How current developmental and family support programs will fare under managed health care and proposed governmental budget cuts remains to be seen.

In countries such as Sweden and England, initial neonatal care is much less aggressive than in the United States, but the societal commitment to those infants who survive the NICU with disabilities is far greater (Thullen, 1992; Young, 1984). Finding a compassionate and rational policy that can balance neonatal lifesaving, the preferences of families, and the need to provide ongoing care for infants with disabilities remains an important ethical challenge for families, caregivers, and policy makers in this country.

Pain and Suffering

The pain of infant intensive care presents serious ethical dilemmas for families and caregivers. In the mid-1980s, parents brought the issue of infant pain to public attention after Jill Lawson, a mother in Silver Spring, Maryland, went to *The Washington Post* with the discovery that her premature infant son (without her knowledge or consent) had undergone major unanesthetized surgery (Rovner, 1986). Within months, *Lancet* and *The New England Journal of Medicine* published articles confirming the widespread practice of withholding anesthesia and analgesia from premature infants during painful procedures including major surgery (Anand & Hickey, 1987; Anand, Sippel, & Aynsley-Green, 1987). The authors of these articles challenged the then-common medical assumption that premature infants do not feel pain. The authors presented strong evidence that mortality and morbidity among premature infants is increased by the stress of unrelieved pain. The American Academy of Pediatrics Committee on Fetus and Newborn (1987) then issued a statement

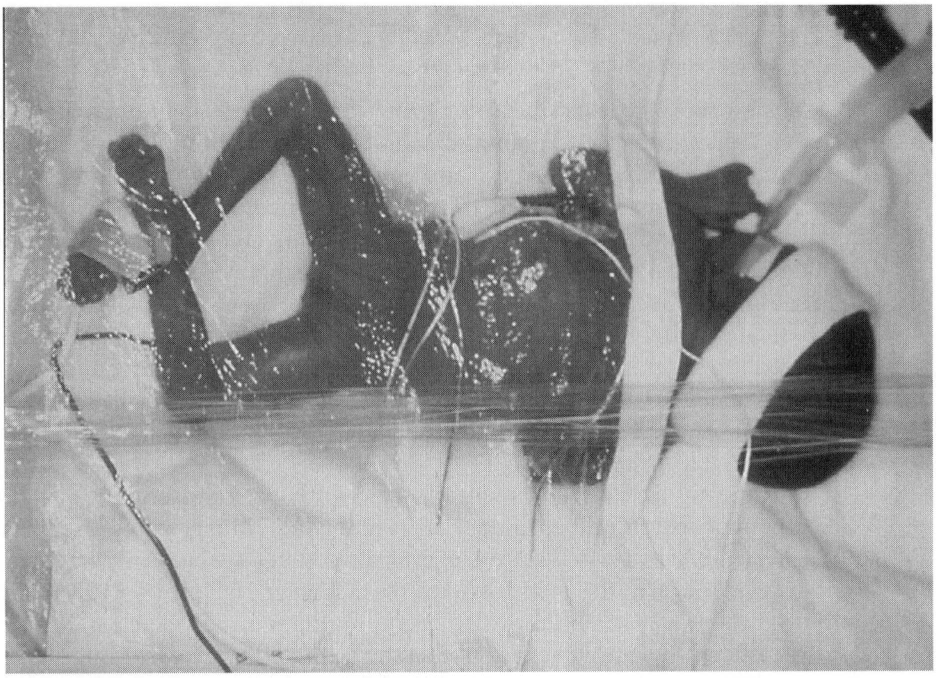

urging greater attention to pain and advocating the use of anesthesia in neonatal surgery based on the same medical criteria used for older patients.

Since the academy statement was issued, anesthesia has become more widely used in neonatal surgery. However, surveys continue to show that premature babies are greatly undermedicated for pain compared to older patients (Anand, Selanikio, & the SOPAIN Study Group, 1996; Bauchner, May, & Coates, 1992), and physicians continue to express doubts that pain relief can be safely and effectively administered to all infants (Rogers, 1992), particularly to those who are extremely sick and/or extremely premature (Campbell, 1989).

According to Dr. William Silverman, one of the founding fathers of neonatal intensive care, the issue of neonatal pain (and the failure of physicians to discuss this issue with parents) has significant ethical ramifications. At a parent–physician conference in 1992, Silverman made the following statement: "As a matter of common decency, parents *must* be informed that at the present time neonatologists do not know how to control much of their babies' pain. Parents *must* be told about this deficit in medical knowledge if they are to participate in the process of informed consent…the pain these babies (and families) suffer is the most important issue" ("Intensive concern," 1992, p. 147).

Many families would agree with Silverman. They see pain as a moral as well as a medical issue, and they want to be the ones to decide how much medically inflicted pain their babies must endure (Harrison, 1993; "Intensive concern," 1992).

Closely related to concerns about pain are worries about the adverse effects of the stressful hospital environment. In the NICU, infants are subjected, day and night, to intense fluorescent light, loud noise, frequent handling, sleep deprivation, and many invasive procedures (Avery & Glass, 1989). Fluorescent lighting exposure in the NICU is thought by some researchers to play a role in the development of retinopathy of prematurity and other eye disorders in premature infants (Aleff, 1991; Avery & Glass, 1989; Fielder, Robinson, Shaw, & Moseley, 1992; Glass et al., 1985). Stress from environmental input and from routine handling and treatment procedures has been shown to reduce oxygen levels in the blood and increase the risk of such serious complications as chronic lung disease and intraventricular hemorrhage (Als et al., 1994; Avery et al., 1987; Long, Philip, & Lucey, 1980a, 1980b; Martin, Herrell, Rubin, & Fanaroff, 1979).

Premature infants who are extremely small and ill are the most vulnerable to the deleterious effects of environmental stress (Avery & Glass, 1989). They may also be the least able to tolerate anesthesia or analgesia to alleviate the pain of their illnesses and treatments (Campbell, 1989). Yet these are precisely the infants who must endure the most pain and stress from prolonged, highly intensive neonatal treatment. NICU nurse Joy Penticuff (1992) described how she and many of her coworkers feel about subjecting fragile babies to neonatal intensive care:

> Most experienced nurses believe that intensive care is inherently damaging for infants, in that there is infliction of pain without the ability to comfort the baby adequately.... It is the nurses who must frequently carry out the routine painful, invasive procedures—starting intravenous [lines], sticking heels for blood sampling, inadvertently peeling off the skin when removing monitor leads—required by current neonatal technology....Procedures performed day in and day out... include emergency chest tube insertions to reinflate collapsed lungs—usually done without benefit of anesthesia, analgesia, or sedation—needle puncture of arteries...again usually without benefit of pain relief...and countless episodes of endotracheal tube suctioning which clears the infant's airway, but induces significant momentary discomfort....[There are also] prolonged periods of sleep interruption, periods of anxiety caused by acute air hunger, and other discomforts. The sicker the infant, the longer the NICU stay, the more damaging the physical and emotional cumulative effects of these experiences. (pp. 273–275)

In the words of one NICU mother, "We are torturing people to life the way we used to torture them to death" (Lieberman, 1984).

The Experimental Nature of Care

Ethical issues are also raised by the poorly validated nature of many of the therapies used in neonatology. Most treatments in neonatal care were adapted from adult medicine and hastily introduced into the NICU without controlled trials to determine their safety and efficacy in infants. The result has been a high level of iatrogenic (treatment-caused) death and disability (Silverman, 1980; Stahlman, 1990). Treatment regimens vary widely from physician to physician, and many questions remain about "established" but largely untested neonatal therapies (Hack et al., 1992; Investigators of the Vermont-Oxford Trials Network Data Base Project, 1993; National Institute of Child Health and Human Development [NICHD], 1985).

In 1985, the NICHD described neonatal care as "often based on limited knowledge of new modalities not subjected to critical studies prior to introduction and acceptance... [where] therapeutic interventions may change within months before adequate studies of safety and efficacy are initiated much less completed" (p. 2).

A 1992 survey compared data about caregiving and outcomes from a network of hospitals established by the NICHD around the United States. The researchers found important intercenter variations in approaches to care; in philosophies of care; and in prevalence of serious morbidity, including chronic lung disease, necrotizing enterocolitis, sepsis, intraventricular hemorrhage, and periventricular leukomalacia. The authors of the survey concluded that "the variability of care provided in neonatal centers...raises important questions about current regimens of neonatal care...[which] remains in part an art rather than an exact science" (Hack et al., 1992, pp. 588, 595).

Relatively few survivors of the NICU receive comprehensive, long-term follow-up to determine the outcomes of neonatal treatment (Escobar, 1992). Most existing follow-up studies have been criticized for the small numbers of infants followed, the short duration of follow-up, inconsistencies in reporting and defining disabilities the absence of control groups, and the many children who are "lost to follow-up"—all factors that tend to bias outcome statistics toward optimism (Aylward, Hatcher, Stripp, Gustafson, & Leavitt, 1985; Collin, Halsey, & Anderson, 1991; Escobar, 1992; Gross, Slagle, D'Eugenio, & Mettleman, 1992; Wariyar & Richmond, 1989). Nevertheless, the reported rate of impairment is high, particularly in the United States. A recent meta-analysis of English language follow-up studies revealed an *overall* rate of serious disability of 25% among VLBW survivors, with a 30% rate reported in U.S. studies and a 20.5% rate reported in studies from English-speaking countries outside the United States (Escobar et al., 1991). The differing rates may reflect the more aggressive neonatal treatment policies in the United States.

Noting the high, and probably underestimated, rate of disability among survivors, neonatologist Jeffrey Maisels (quoted in Browne, 1993) bluntly described neonatal intensive care for VLBW infants as "a vast and uncontrolled experiment undertaken without informed consent and with possibly undesirable results" (p. 1).

THE ROLE OF THE PARENTS

One of the most distressing areas of ethical concern about treatment of very low birth weight infants is the frequent exclusion of parents from decisions about the child's medical care. The three case examples recounted earlier in this chapter are clear examples of the disdain with which some medical providers approach parental participation. The following sections examine several areas in which parents typically express frustration in their relations with medical providers.

Lack of Information and Informed Consent

Parents are at a disadvantage in understanding treatment alternatives or in challenging physicians' decisions because of limited parental access to medical, ethical, and legal information (Rottman, 1985). Researchers who have studied parent–staff relationships in the NICU have found that the information given parents in the NICU is often communicated in euphemisms, vague statements, and half-truths and that parents are often shielded from information about uncertainties or controversies surrounding their baby's treatments (Anspach, 1993; Bogdan, Brown, & Foster, 1982; Frohock, 1986; Guillemin & Holmstrom, 1986; Rottman, 1985). "Miracle baby" and "miracle therapy" stories in the media may also promote optimistic (and unrealistic) expectations among parents. Stahlman (1990) has written, "We [neonatologists] have allowed the media to publicize our successes widely, and have minimized our failures to the public" (p. 167).

Caregiver attitudes that interfere with the ability to communicate honestly and openly with parents include fears that parents are too upset to assimilate information and make rational decisions (Anspach, 1993; Frohock, 1986; Guillemin & Holmstrom, 1986), fears that information about treatment complications and outcomes will upset parents and interfere with the "bonding" process (Anspach, 1993; Bogdan et al., 1982; Klaus & Kennell, 1982), fears that parents will feel guilt if involved in decision making (Anspach, 1993), and the perceived need for staff to suppress professional disagreements among themselves and present a united front to parents (Anspach, 1993; Guillemin & Holmstrom, 1986). Professionals may also find it difficult to acknowledge the pain and poor outcomes of NICU treatment to themselves, much less to the parents (Cunningham, 1993; Perrotta, 1995).

Families who object to treatment or who simply ask "too many" questions may find themselves characterized by the staff as psychologically disturbed, "troublemakers," "bad parents," or even potential child abusers (Anspach, 1993; Bogdan et al., 1982; Eikner, 1986; Lawson, 1986; Stinson & Stinson, 1983). They may be threatened with legal proceedings, public notoriety, and the loss of custody of their children (Harrison, 1986, 1987; "Intensive concern," 1992). Few parents have the emotional resources to resist a determined staff or the financial and legal resources to engage in a courtroom battle.

In the absence of accurate and complete information and treatment choices, parents may sign consent documents, but they are not participating in a process of genuine informed consent. This is true whether the issue is a life-or-death decision or a facet of daily caregiving.

Exclusion from Decision Making

In delivery room and NICU decisions, parents and babies are largely at the mercy of a rapidly expanding life-support technology and their physicians' personal philosophies and motives determining its use (Anspach, 1993; Guillemin & Holmstrom, 1986; Gustaitis & Young, 1986; Harrison, 1986; Kolata, 1991; Lyon, 1985; Stinson & Stinson, 1983; Tyson, 1995). Physicians' decisions may be influenced by such factors as legal fears (Kopelman, Irons, & Kopelman, 1988), reimbursement patterns (Associated Press, 1991; International Medical News Service, 1984; Stahlman, 1990), institutional obligations (Perrotta, 1995), research interests (Harrison, 1986), and differing interpretations of the "mission" of neonatology (Kolata, 1991; Perrotta, 1995; Stahlman, 1990; Stein, 1994).

Philosophies concerning the use of neonatal care and the role of parents as caregivers and decision makers in the NICU can vary significantly among practitioners and hospitals (Carter, 1993; Tyson, 1995), as exemplified in the vignette describing Wanda and Keaton's experiences (see p. 177). Because of the emergency nature of most preterm deliveries, parents have little ability to "comparison shop" for neonatologists who share the family's preferences and philosophy.

Legal Ambiguity

The law has traditionally allowed parents a wide range of discretion in making medical and ethical decisions on behalf of their children. A report by the President's Commission for the Study of Ethical Problems in Medicine (1983) upheld this tradition and advocated the right of parents to make treatment decisions for their infants whenever the benefits of proposed treatments were "ambiguous or uncertain" (p. 218).

However, in 1984, a contradictory standard was established with the enactment of the Federal Child Abuse Amendments (FCAA), also known as the "Baby Doe" regulations in reference to the infant with Down syndrome whose death created the controversy that led to the legislation (Clark, 1994). Baby Doe was born in 1982 in Bloomington, Indiana, with Down syndrome, esophageal atresia, a tracheal-esophageal fistula, and a suspected heart defect (Pless, 1983). The child's parents denied permission for the series of difficult operations necessary to attempt reconstruction of the esophagus. They were supported in that decision by their personal physician, the Superior Court of Monroe County, and the Indiana Supreme Court. The child died of pneumonia before the case could be appealed to the U.S. Supreme Court (Harrison, 1986; Merrick, 1992; Pless, 1983).

Prompted by complaints from pressure groups, then-President Ronald Reagan instructed the Department of Health and Human Services (DHHS) to mandate regulations, under Section 504 of the Rehabilitation Act of 1973 (PL 93-112), for hospitals that receive federal aid, declaring the act of withholding treatment based on an infant's disabilities unlawful (Merrick, 1992). Medical groups mounted a legal challenge, and in 1986 the Supreme Court set aside the DHHS regulations on the grounds that the "Rehabilitation Act's ban on discrimination against the handicapped does not permit intervention by federal officials into medical treatment decisions traditionally left by state law to concerned parents of handicapped infants" (quoted in Merrick, 1992, p. 54). The court further reaffirmed the parental decision-making role, stating, "The decision to provide or withhold medically indicated treatment is, except in highly unusual circumstances, made by the parents or legal guardian" (Nelson, 1990, p. 57).

However, before the "Baby Doe" regulations were invalidated by the Supreme Court, Congress passed amendments to the Federal Child Abuse Act (FCAA) that incorporated much of the language of the DHHS regulations. Withdrawal of infant life support was, with rare exceptions, now defined as child abuse. The few exceptions to mandatory treatment—when an infant is in an "irreversible coma" or when treatment is "virtually futile"—are so difficult to interpret in the context of neonatal care as to be meaningless (Kopelman, Kopelman, & Irons, 1992; Penticuff, 1992).

The FCAA has never been interpreted at the appellate court level, nor has it been directly challenged in court, but clarifications offered by DHHS and the 1989 Civil Rights Commission maintain that under the FCAA "quality of life" is never to be considered in the provision of medical care and that even inhumane treatment is mandated unless it is "virtually futile" (Clark, 1994; DHHS, 1985; U.S. Commission on Civil Rights, 1989). The FCAA thus establishes a standard far stricter than that of the Roman Catholic Church, which permits patients (or their surrogates) to refuse "burdensome" life-saving treatment (Oskandy, 1985).

In the absence of a definitive court interpretation, many physicians have been inclined to "play it safe" by treating every infant as aggressively as possible, despite the wishes of the family or the suffering of the infant (Kopelman, Irons, & Kopelman, 1988). As a result, the FCAA, which was passed to protect the rights of marginally viable infants and infants with disabilities, may actually discriminate against these infants by denying them the legal right granted all other incompetent patients to refuse treatment through a surrogate (Angell, 1986). Furthermore, it has been suggested that the FCAA may actually be "the instrument of child abuse...[by] prolonging dying under conditions of a brutal intensive care from which there is no escape" (Penticuff, 1992, p. 273). It is also ironic that legislation designed to affect the treatment of children with disabilities such as Down syndrome and spina bifida has had its greatest impact on the treatment of extremely premature infants. The major outcome of the law, writes ethicist Arthur Caplan (1992), is that extremely premature infants "wind up getting full-press aggressive intervention with less choice being given to their parents. Experimentation...[has] flourished with respect to premature infants" (p. 114).

A poll in *The New England Journal of Medicine* showed one third of responding neonatologists felt required by the FCAA to administer treatment they personally believed was not in the baby's best interest, and two thirds of the neonatologists believed the law failed to consider the suffering of infants or the rights of parents (Kopelman et al., 1988).

Although the FCAA has encouraged physicians to provide more aggressive treatment with little or no parental input, a different legal standard has been emerging from the state courts. Frank Clark, an attorney and neonatologist, examined all court cases since 1984 that involved withdrawal of life support from infants or children. In all six such cases, the courts affirmed the rights of parents to refuse life-sustaining treatment for their children based on quality of life criteria. In Dr. Clark's view, two competing legal standards now exist: 1) the FCAA standard in which the physician is the decision maker and quality of life is not to be considered, and 2) the standard of the state court rulings in which parents are the decision makers who may take quality of life and other subjective factors into account in their decision making. Physicians, in Dr. Clark's view, must choose between the two standards and take their chances (Clark, 1994).

In 1995, Dr. Clark and Jesuit bioethicist Father John Paris served as expert witnesses for the defense in the trial of Dr. Gregory Messenger of East Lansing, Michigan. Dr. Messenger had been charged with manslaughter for removing his own extremely premature newborn son from life support after the child had been intubated contrary to the wishes of Dr. Messenger and his wife (*People v. Messenger*, 1995). During the legal proceeding, the Messenger family (personal communication, 1995) received more than 1,000 letters of support, many from other parents of premature babies (Miner, 1995). Dr. Messenger was acquitted on the first jury ballot.

EMPOWERMENT THROUGH FAMILY-CENTERED CARE

The ethical issues discussed in this chapter—especially those related to overtreatment of infants who are medically fragile and to the exclusion of parents from information-sharing and decision-making processes—demand a shift toward family-centered care in neonatal medical provision. The importance of family-centered care for children with special medical needs has been recognized by support organizations and disability law (Bishop, Woll, & Arango, 1992; Education of the Handicapped Act Amendments of 1986 [PL 99-457], 1986; Shelton, Jeppson, & Johnson, 1987). The family-centered concept acknowledges that the parents are the child's primary caregivers. A family-centered philosophy supports parent–professional collaboration at all levels of health care and promotes the sharing of unbiased and complete information with parents. It stresses family individuality, respect for different methods of coping, and responsiveness to family needs (Shelton et al., 1987). To quote Suzanne Smith-Sharp of Colorado Consortium of Intensive Care Nurseries,

> Family-centered care is the compassionate, open, total inclusion of the family in the care and decision-making process for their baby. In order to accomplish this, a great deal of information must be provided and education must occur, not only

> regarding medical facts, but also about rights, values, priorities, expectations and needs of the family. The goal is to *leave the power with the family*—that is, never take it away in the first place, necessitating "empowering" the family at a later date. (Browne & Smith-Sharp, 1995, p. 19)

Although programs for parent–professional collaboration on caregiving issues and nursery policies are currently being introduced into NICUs across the United States (Browne & Smith-Sharp, 1995; Johnson, 1995; Wyly & Allen, 1995), ethical decision making and other important, but controversial, ethical issues are not usually mentioned in the context of these collaborations. Nevertheless, the spirit of family-centered care would seem to support the emerging legal standard that reaffirms parents as the medical and ethical decision makers for their infants, and it would seem to encourage parental involvement in other areas of ethical controversy as well.

In 1992 in Burlington, Vermont, a group of parents of prematurely born children met with a group of distinguished neonatal and perinatal professionals to apply the philosophy of family-centered care to ethical problems in neonatology ("Intensive concern," 1992). As a result of this conference, a document was drafted by the parents entitled "The Principles for Family-Centered Neonatal Care." The Principles were published a year later in *Pediatrics* (Harrison, 1993). The following is a list of the Principles and commentary adapted from the *Pediatrics* article:

1. *Family-centered care should be based on open and honest communication between parents and professionals on medical and ethical issues.*
   Comment: No rationale, no matter how well-intentioned, justifies the withholding of important clinical information about a child's condition or prognosis from his or her family. Parents should have access to complete, specific, detailed, and meaningful information about their baby's condition, treatment, and prognosis. Parents should be informed about relevant differences of medical and ethical opinions among hospital professionals or within the medical community in general, and they should be encouraged to share their own ethical views and caregiving preferences with the staff.

   The views of nurses, who provide most of the "hands-on" care to the baby, can be particularly valuable and should be freely available to the parents.

   To ensure that parents come to the NICU with a basic level of understanding, discussions of the medical and ethical implications of prematurity and other perinatal problems should be offered as part of the high school health curriculum and as a standard feature of all prenatal care. The media should also be encouraged to avoid sensationalism and present a more balanced and realistic view of medical advances.

   Courses in communication should become an important part of the medical school curriculum and should encourage sharing the complete, honest, unbiased information with families in a humane and respectful manner.
2. *To work with professionals in making informed treatment choices, parents must have available to them the same facts and interpretation of those facts as the professionals, including medical information presented in meaningful formats, information about uncertainties surrounding treatments, information from parents whose children have been in similar medical situations, and access to the chart and rounds discussions.*
   Comment: Under the doctrine of informed consent, physicians are obliged to discuss the risks and benefits of performing a given procedure as well as the risks and benefits of alternative procedures (Applebaum, Lidz, & Meisel, 1987).

In the NICU, informed consent would need to involve disclosing whether a given procedure has been clinically evaluated in controlled trials and whether reasonable practitioners elsewhere use different treatments. In cases in which the burdens of treatment equal or outweigh the benefits, the physician should also discuss the option of foregoing the treatment altogether.

Parents must have free access to relevant information from a variety of formats and sources such as medical books and journal articles, books and articles from the lay press, videotapes or audiotapes, as well as contact with families whose children have experienced similar conditions. The family pediatrician can provide significant help to parents in their search for information and understanding.

Systematic investigations should be undertaken into the issue of how families with differing needs can best be served through various formats and sources of information.

Parents in other countries are routinely given copies of the obstetric and pediatric charts (Young, 1991). Copies of obstetric, neonatal, and pediatric charts (or free and complete access to these charts) should be offered to all NICU parents. In addition, parents should be invited to record their own observations, concerns, and questions in the chart and to participate in rounds discussions concerning their baby.

3. *In medical situations involving very high mortality and morbidity, great suffering, and/or significant medical controversy, fully informed parents should have the right to make decisions regarding aggressive treatment for their infants.*

   Comment: Whenever the chance for a bad outcome (mortality combined with moderate to severe morbidity) equals or exceeds the chance for intact survival, especially when the purposed course of treatment involves significant pain or medical controversy, parents should have the right to determine issues of obstetrical management, resuscitation, and intensive care.

   Current areas of poor outcomes and medical controversy include intensive treatment for babies less than 750–800 grams birth weight and/or 26 weeks' gestational age (American Academy of Pediatrics Committee on Fetus and Newborn, 1995; Tyson, 1995). A growing number of physicians and ethicists support parental decision making for these infants (GUIDe Neonatal Intensive Care Subcommittee, 1994; Peabody, 1995; Thullen, 1992; Tyson, 1995; Young & Stevenson, 1990)

   With babies of higher gestational ages and birth weights, parents should have the option of declining intensive care if a serious complication (e.g., severe intraventricular hemorrhage) makes intact survival of the child unlikely. When intensive care is declined by the parents, supportive care provided by the family and staff would be seen as a valid alternative to aggressive treatment.

   The right of parents to make quality-of-life–based nontreatment decisions on behalf of their marginally viable newborns has been upheld by recent state court decisions (Clark, 1994) and is supported by strong majorities in public opinion polls (Abrams, Cargo, Foss, & Mashow, 1988; Taylor, 1990).

4. *Expectant parents should be offered information about adverse pregnancy outcomes and be given the opportunity to state in advance their treatment preferences if their baby is born extremely prematurely and/or critically ill.*

   Comment: Families should have the chance to make their wishes known to caregivers through advance treatment directives, filled out during the prenatal period, in which parents state what they want done (or not done) in the event of the birth of a critically ill or extremely premature baby. The use of advance directives would help parents clarify their own views, understand their ethical options, and choose neonatal caregivers whose philosophies most closely resemble their own (Veatch, 1995). A parent–professional collaborative effort is currently underway to draft such a neonatal advance directive (Alecson, 1995a; Perrotta, 1995).

5. *Parents and professionals must work together to acknowledge and alleviate the pain of infants in intensive care.*

   Comment: Discussions of pain management with parents should be routine and ongoing and should include attention not only to acute pain from procedures but also to chronic pain from illness and treatment side effects (e.g., kidney stones from diuretic administration, fractures due to rickets, postoperative pain, hypoxemia from chronic lung disease) (Scanlon, 1991).

   If medication cannot be given to an infant for the effective relief of serious acute or chronic pain, the physician should share this information with the parents who would then have the option of seeking another medical opinion or of refusing the burdensome course of treatment altogether.

   The Roman Catholic Church with its strong right-to-life ethic nevertheless maintains that "burdensome" treatment can be justifiably declined by a patient or the patient's surrogate, even if the alternative is death. Examples of burdensome treatment cited by Roman Catholic ethicists and scholars include unanesthetized surgery (Oskandy, 1985). Parents must have the right to refuse such treatment on behalf of their children.

   Research into the effects of infant pain and the safety and efficacy of analgesics and anesthetics should have a high priority in pediatric research.

6. *Parents and professionals must work together to ensure an appropriate environment for babies in the NICU.*

   Comment: A growing body of evidence strongly suggests that providing premature infants with individualized developmentally appropriate care reduces immediate and long-term morbidity, shortens hospital stays, and reduces costs. Parents and primary care nurses trained in the developmental needs of premature infants can best provide the baby with consistent, individualized caregiving. Training in developmental care is currently available in the form of the Newborn Individualized Developmental Care and Assessment Program (NIDCAP) developed by Heidelise Als and her colleagues. NIDCAP training provides a systematic method for the detailed observation of infant behavior and for the use of each infant's unique behavioral cues as a guide to caregiving. Developmental caregiving also involves protecting the baby as much as possible from environmental sources of stress such as bright light, loud noise, excessive handling, uncomfortable positions, sleep disruptions, and invasive treatments (Als & Gilkerson, 1995; Als et al., 1994; Buehler, Als, Duffy, McAnulty, & Liederman, 1995).

   Potentially harmful aspects of the nursery environment and of caregiving routines deserve thorough investigation. In the meantime, *suspected* hazards (e.g., short wavelength fluorescent light) (Aleff, 1991; Fielder et al., 1992) should be eliminated from the nursery until safety has been established.

7. *Parents and professionals should work together to ensure the safety and efficacy of neonatal treatments.*

   Comment: New treatments should be introduced into neonatal care only in the context of properly controlled trials. Controlled trials should also be used to investigate therapies currently in use in the NICU that have never been adequately studied for safety and efficacy.

Parents whose children were treated in NICUs should have a voice in determining the research agenda, establishing outcomes of interest, and educating other parents about the need for ethically and scientifically sound neonatal research.

8. *Parents and professionals should work together to develop nursery policies and programs that promote parenting skills and encourage maximum involvement of families with their hospitalized infant.*

   Comment: In a family-centered NICU, professionals should recognize parents as their infant's primary caregivers and as essential partners of the staff. Families should be encouraged to provide daily caregiving for their infant and to participate in policy development and program planning, in peer support groups, in staff in-service training, and in other collaborative activities (Browne & Smith-Sharp, 1995; Johnson, 1995).

   Facilities should be available for parents to "room-in" with their child before discharge for as much time as necessary to establish breast-feeding and to become comfortable with all important aspects of the baby's care.

   Breast-feeding has been shown to have significant positive effects on the health and development of premature babies (Lucas, Morley, Cole, & Gore, 1994; Lucas, Morley, Cole, Lister, & Leeson-Payne, 1992). Mothers should be informed of the research on the benefits of breast-feeding and strongly encouraged to provide breast milk and nurse their babies. They should be helped in their efforts by a committed staff, peer support, and trained lactation counselors. Kangaroo care, in which the baby is kept warm, not by the incubator, but by skin-to-skin contact with the parent (Ludington-Hoe & Golant, 1993) should be encouraged along with other forms of close parent–infant contact.

9. *Parents and professionals must work together to promote meaningful long-term follow-up for all high-risk NICU survivors.*

   Comment: The following recommendations are adapted from Escobar et al., 1991:

   a. Evaluation of infants and other survivors of the NICU who are at high risk for disabilities should be a pediatric research priority.
   b. Minimum standards should be developed for the design, conduct, and reporting of follow-up studies.
   c. Geographically based birth weight– and gestational age–specific morbidity databases should be established.
   d. Outcome studies should be prospective, use impartial observers, include full-term infants as controls, and include the views and experiences of the families of NICU survivors.
   e. Consistent outcome measures should be developed so that studies can be compared.
   f. Sufficient funding must be made available for follow-up, especially for multicenter and geographically based studies.
   g. The period of follow-up should extend into adolescence and, ideally, into adulthood.

10. *Parents and professionals must acknowledge that critically ill newborns can be harmed by overtreatment as well as by undertreatment, and we must insist that our laws and treatment policies be based on compassion. We must work together to promote awareness of the needs of NICU survivors with disabilities to ensure adequate support for*

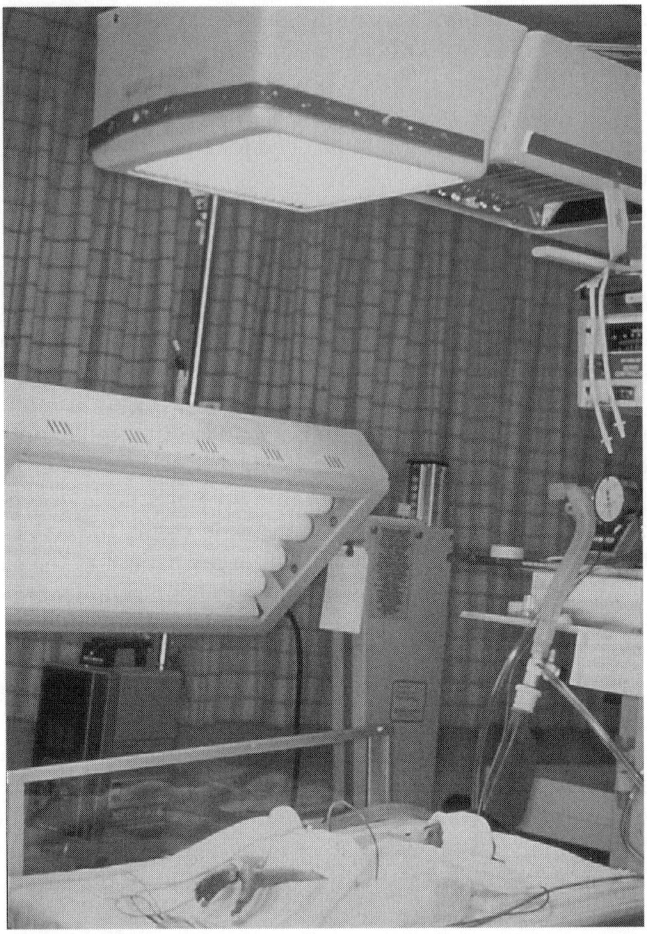

them and their families. We must work together to decrease disability through universal prenatal care.

Comment: Without the parental right to refuse excessively painful, burdensome, and unproven neonatal therapies, infants can become the unprotected targets of an unthinking medical activism. Laws and policies that promote overtreatment and rob parents of their rights and responsibilities should be repealed or revised. Medical treatment of critically ill newborns should be driven by compassion and dedication to the welfare of these babies and their families, not by fear of politically motivated and poorly drafted laws.

Physicians who care for imperiled newborns must recognize the life-long impact of their treatment decisions on infants and their families. They must understand the resources that are (and are not) available to these children and families. The presence or absence of such resources should not be irrelevant to treatment decisions in the NICU.

Physician training should include rotations providing care in the community for children or adults with disabilities. Professionals should work with parents to ensure the availability of ongoing care and services for children and adults with disabilities. To the greatest extent possible, disability should be prevented through universal prenatal care.

SUMMARY

The problems described in this chapter are not, for the most part, unique to neonatology. Overtreatment, pain, use of directives, and the rights of patients and families have also been identified as important issues in the care of critically ill adults (SUPPORT Principle Investigators, 1995). The family-centered approach to the resolution of these problems is also not unique. Instead it reflects the growing partnership between consumers and providers throughout the health care system to make medicine more responsive to the needs of patients, families, and society; to encourage informed medical decision making among health care consumers; and to encourage wise and compassionate use of our awesome life-support technology (Abrams et al., 1988; Browne & Smith-Sharp, 1995; Gianelli, 1994; GUIDe Neonatal Intensive Care Subcommittee, 1994; Johnson, 1995; Winslow, 1992; Wyly & Allen, 1995).

The publication of the principles has elicited many supportive letters and statements from professionals, parents, and parent groups around the world. The principles have been widely reprinted and cited in support of collaborative programs in NICUs, as well as regional efforts to develop guidelines for intensive care and research proposals to study developmental care, NICU outcomes, physician training, parent–professional communication, and ethical issues. The worldwide response to the principles suggests that the problems identified are of universal concern and that the family-centered approach to their solution has universal appeal and relevance.

REFERENCES

Abrams, F.R., Cargo, R.A., Foss L.L., & Mashaw, R. (1988). *Colorado speaks out on health: The final report of a two-year educational program and study of public opinion on critical care issues.* (Available from Campus Box 133, 1200 Larimer Street, Denver, CO 80204: Colorado Speaks Out on Health, 7–8.)

Alecson, D.G. (1995a). Letter to the editor. *Journal of Perinatology, 15*(6), 520–522.

Alecson, D.G. (1995b). *Lost lullaby.* Berkeley: University of California Press.

Aleff, H.P. (1991). Baby blinding retinopathy of prematurity and intensive care nursery lighting. *Iatrogenics, 1*(2), 68–85.

Als, H., & Gilkerson, L. (1995). Developmentally supportive care in the neonatal intensive care unit. *Zero to Three, 15*(6), 1, 3–10.

Als, H., Lawhon, G., Duffy, F.H., McAnulty, G.B., Gibes-Grossman, R., & Blickman, J.G. (1994). Individualized developmental care for the very low-birth-weight preterm infant. *Journal of the American Medical Association, 272*(11), 853–858.

American Academy of Pediatrics Committee on Fetus and Newborn, American College of Obstetricians and Gynecologists Committee on Obstetric Practice. (1995). Perinatal care at the threshold of viability. *Pediatrics, 96*(5), 974–976.

American Academy of Pediatrics Committee on Fetus and Newborn, Committee on Drugs, Section on Anesthesiology, Section on Surgery. (1987). Neonatal anesthesia. *Pediatrics, 80*(3), 446.

American Academy of Pediatrics Special Report. (1989). *Barriers to care.* Elk Grove Village, IL: American Academy of Pediatrics.

Anand, K.J.S., & Hickey, P.R. (1987). Pain and its effects on the human neonate and fetus. *New England Journal of Medicine, 317*(21), 1321–1329.

Anand, K.J.S., Selanikio, J.D., & the SOPAIN Study Group (1996). Routine analgesic practices in 109 neonatal intensive care units (NICUs). *Pediatric Research, 39*(4), 192A.

Anand, K.J.S., Sippel, W.G., & Aynsley-Green, A. (1987). Randomised trial of fentanyl anaesthesia in preterm babies undergoing surgery: Effects on the stress response. *Lancet, 1* (852,4), 61–66.

Angell, M. (1986). The Baby Doe rules. *New England Journal of Medicine, 314*(10), 642–644.
Anspach, R.R. (1993). *Deciding who lives: Fateful choices in an intensive care nursery.* Berkeley: University of California Press.
Applebaum, P.S., Lidz, C.W., & Meisel, A. (1987). *Informed consent: Legal theory and clinical practice.* New York: Oxford University Press.
Associated Press. (1991, December 18). Study ties hospital care of newborns to coverage. *New York Times*, p. A-26.
Avery, G.B., & Glass, P. (1989). The gentle nursery: Developmental interventions in the NICU. *Journal of Perinatology, 9*, 204–206.
Avery, M.E., Tooley, W.H., Keller, J.B., et al. (1987). Is chronic lung disease preventable? A survey of eight centers. *Pediatrics, 79*(1), 26–30.
Aylward, G.P., Hatcher, R.P., Stripp, B., Gustafson, N.F., & Leavitt, L.A. (1985). Who goes and who stays: Subject loss in a multicenter, longitudinal follow-up study. *Developmental and Behavioral Pediatrics, 6*(1), 3–8.
Bauchner, H., May, A., & Coates, E. (1992). Use of analgesic agents for invasive medical procedures in pediatric and neonatal intensive care units. *Journal of Pediatrics, 121*(4), 647–649.
Bennett, F.C. (1988). Neurodevelopmental outcome in low-birthweight infants: The role of developmental intervention. In R.D. Guthrie (Ed.), *Neonatal intensive care* (pp. 221–249). New York: Churchill Livingstone.
Bergman, A.I., & Simpson, J. (1991, January/February). Health care industry forces family impoverishment: UCPA witness testifies on access to health insurance. *Exceptional Parent*, U7–U8.
Bishop, K.K., Woll, J., & Arango, P. (1992). *Family/professional collaboration for children with special health care needs.* Burlington: University of Vermont, Department of Social Work.
Bogdan, R., Brown, M.A., & Foster, S.B. (1982). Be honest but not cruel: Staff/parent communication on a neonatal unit. *Human Organization, 41*(1), 6–16.
Brooks-Gunn, J., McCarton, C.M., Casey, P.H., et al. (1994). Early intervention in low-birthweight premature infants. *Journal of the American Medical Association, 272*(16), 1257–1262.
Browne, J.V., & Smith-Sharp, S. (1995). The Colorado consortium of intensive care nurseries: Spinning a web of support for Colorado infants and families. *Zero to Three, 15*(6), 18–23.
Browne, S.J. (1993, January). Neonatal intensive care: Life at what cost? *Pediatric News*, 1, 26.
Buehler, D.M., Als, H., Duffy, F.H., McAnulty, G.B., & Liederman, J. (1995). Effectiveness of individualized developmental care for low-risk preterm infants: Behavioral and electrophysiologic evidence. *Pediatrics, 96*(5), 923–932.
Campbell, N. (1989). Infants, pain and what health care professionals should want to know—A response to Cunningham Butler. *Bioethics, 3*(3), 200–210.
Caplan, A.L. (1992). Hard cases make bad law. In A.L. Caplan, R.H. Blank, & J.C. Merrick (Eds.), *Compelled compassion* (pp. 105–122). Totowa, NJ: Humana Press.
Carter, B.S. (1993). Neonatologists and bioethics after Baby Doe. *Journal of Perinatology, 13*(2), 144–150.
Clark, F.I. (1994). Intensive care treatment decisions: The roots of our confusion. *Pediatrics, 94*(1), 98–101.
Collin, M.F., Halsey, C.L., & Anderson, C.L. (1991). Emerging developmental sequelae in the "normal" extremely low birth weight infant. *Pediatrics, 88*(1), 115–120.
Cronin, C.M.G., Shapiro, C.R., Casiro, O.G., & Cheang, M.S. (1995). The impact of very low-birth-weight infants on the family is long lasting. *Archives of Pediatrics and Adolescent Medicine, 149*, (2) 151–158.
Cunningham, N. (1993). Moral and ethical issues in clinical practice. In K.J.S. Anand & P.J. McGrath (Eds.), *Pain in neonates* (pp. 255–273). New York: Elsevier.
Department of Health and Human Services. (1985, April 15). 45 CFR Part 1340, Child Abuse and Neglect Prevention and Treatment Program; Final Rule. *Federal Register, 50*(72), 14879.
Education of the Handicapped Act Amendments of 1986, PL 99-457, 20 U.S.C. § 1400 *et seq.*
Eikner, S. (1986). Dealing with long term problems: A parent's perspective. *Neonatal Network, 5*(1), 45–49.
Escobar, G.J. (1992). Prognosis of surviving very low birthweight infants: Still in the dark. *British Journal of Obstetrics and Gynaecology, 99*(1), 1–3.

Escobar, G.J., Littenberg, B., & Pettiti, D.B. (1991). Outcome among surviving very low birthweight infants: A meta-analysis. *Archives of Disease in Childhood, 66*(2), 203–211.

Fielder, A.R., Robinson, J., Shaw, D.E., & Moseley, M.J. (1992). Light and retinopathy of prematurity: Does retinal location offer a clue? *Pediatrics, 89*(4), 648–653.

Frohock, F.M. (1986). *Special care: Medical decisions at the beginning of life.* Chicago: University of Chicago Press.

Gianelli, D.M. (1994). Getting a better fix on futility. *American Medical News, 37*(3), 14–16.

Glass, P., Avery, G.B., Subramanian, K.N.S., Keys, M.P., Sostek, A.M., & Friendly, D.S. (1985). Effect of bright light in the hospital nursery on the incidence of retinopathy of prematurity. *New England Journal of Medicine, 313*(7), 401–404.

Gross, S.J., Slagle, T.A., D'Eugenio, D.B., & Mettleman, B.B. (1992). Impact of a matched term control group on interpretation of developmental performance in preterm infants. *Pediatrics, 90*(5), 681–687.

GUIDe Neonatal Intensive Care Subcommittee. (1994). *GUIDe, 1*(1), 6. (Newsletter available from Guidelines for the Use of Intensive Care in Denver, 1801 High Street, Denver, CO 80218.)

Guillemin, J.H., & Holmstrom, L.L. (1986). *Mixed blessings: Intensive care for newborns.* New York: Oxford University Press.

Gustaitis, R., & Young, E.W.D. (1986). *A time to be born, a time to die.* Reading, MA: Addison-Wesley.

Hack, M., Horbar, J.D., Malloy, M.H., Tyson, J.E., Wright, E., & Wright L. (1992). Very low birth weight outcomes of the National Institute of Child Health and Human Development Neonatal Network. *Pediatrics, 87*(5), 587–597.

Hack, M., Taylor, H.G., Klein, N., Eiben, R., Schatschneider, C., & Mercuri-Ninich, N. (1994). School-age outcomes in children with birth weights under 750 g. *New England Journal of Medicine, 331*(12), 753–759.

Hack, M., Wright, L.L., Shankaran, S., et al. (1995). Very low birth weight outcomes of the National Institute of Child Health and Human Development Neonatal Network, November 1989 to October 1990. *American Journal of Obstetrics and Gynecology, 172*(2), 457–464.

Halpern, S. (1989, September). Miracle baby. *Ms, 18*(3), 56–64.

Harrison, H. (1986). Neonatal intensive care: Parents' role in ethical decision making. *Birth, 13*(3), 165–175.

Harrison, H. (1987). Commentary on the special report "Changes in the delivery room care of the extremely small infant (<750 g): Effects on morbidity and outcome" by Maureen Hack and Avroy A. Fanaroff in *The New England Journal of Medicine.* 1986; *314*; 660–664. In M. Klaus & A.A. Fanaroff (Eds.), *Yearbook of perinatal and neonatal medicine.* Chicago: Yearbook Publishers.

Harrison, H. (1993). The principles for family-centered neonatal care. *Pediatrics, 92*(5), 643–650.

Hoffman, E.L., & Bennett, F.C. (1990). Birth weight less than 800 grams: Changing outcomes and influences of gender and gestation number. *Pediatrics, 86*(1), 27–34.

Hunt, J.V., Cooper, B.A.B., & Tooley, W.H. (1988). Very low birth weight infants at 8 and 11 years of age: Role of neonatal illness and family status. *Pediatrics, 82*(4), 596–603.

Individuals with Disabilities Education Act (IDEA) of 1990, PL 101-476, 20 U.S.C. § 1400 *et seq.*

Intensive concern: Parents and physicians discuss neonatology—conference transcript. (1992). A Special Ross Conference. June 28–29, 1992, Burlington, Vermont. (Transcript available from Helen Harrison, 1144 Sterling Avenue, Berkeley, CA 94708.)

International Medical News Service. (1984). Advises complying if parents want severely ill neonate treated. *Pediatric News, 18*(1), 55.

Investigators of the Vermont-Oxford Trials Network Data Base Project. (1993). The Vermont-Oxford Trials Network: Very low birth weight outcomes for 1990. *Pediatrics, 91*(3), 540–545.

Johnson, A., Townshend, P., Yudkin, P., Bull, D., & Wilkinson, A.R. (1993). Functional abilities at age 4 years of children born before 29 weeks of gestation. *British Medical Journal, 306*(6894), 1715–1718.

Johnson, B.H. (1995). Newborn intensive care units pioneer family-centered change in hospitals across the country. *Zero to Three, 15*(6), 11–17.

Klaus, M.H., & Kennell, J.H. (1982). *Parent–infant bonding* (2nd ed.). St. Louis, MO: Mosby Yearbook.
Kolata, G. (1991, September 30). Parents of tiny infants find care choices are not theirs. *The New York Times*, pp. A-1, A-12.
Kopelman, L.M., Irons, T.G., & Kopelman, A.E. (1988). Neonatologists judge the "Baby Doe" regulations. *New England Journal of Medicine, 318*(11), 677–683.
Kopelman, L.M., Kopelman, A.E., & Irons, T.G. (1992). Neonatologists, pediatricians, and the Supreme Court criticize the "Baby Doe" regulations. In A.L. Caplan, R.H. Blank, & J.C. Merrick (Eds.), *Compelled compassion* (pp. 237–266). Totowa, NJ: Humana Press.
Lawson, J.R. (1986). Letter to the editor. *Perinatal Press, 9*(9), 141–142.
Lewit, E.M., Baker, L.S., Corman, H., & Shiono, P.H. (1995). The direct cost of low birth weight. *The Future of the Children, 5*(1), 35–56.
Lieberman, A. (Producer). (1984, November 20). Better off dead? *Frontline.*
Long, J.G., Philip, A.G., & Lucey, J.F. (1980a). Excessive handling as a cause of hypoxemia. *Pediatrics, 65*(1), 203–207.
Long, J.G., Philip, A.G., & Lucey, J.F. (1980b). Noise and hypoxemia in the ICN. *Pediatrics, 65*(1), 143–145.
Lucas, A., Morley, R., Cole, T.J., & Gore, S.M. (1994). A randomised multicentre study of human milk versus formula and later development in preterm infants. *Archives of Disease in Childhood, 70*(2), F141–F146.
Lucas, A., Morley, R., Cole, T.J., Lister, G., & Leeson-Payne, C. (1992). Breast milk and subsequent intelligence quotient in children born preterm. *Lancet, 339*(8788), 261–264.
Ludington-Hoe, S.M., & Golant, S.K. (1993). *Kangaroo care.* New York: Bantam Books.
Lyon, J. (1985). *Playing God in the nursery.* New York: W. W. Norton & Company.
Martin, R.J., Herrell, N., Rubin, D., & Fanaroff, A. (1979). Effect of supine and prone positions on arterial oxygen tension in the preterm infant. *Pediatrics, 63*(4), 528–531.
Merrick, J.C. (1992). Conflict, compromise and symbolism: The politics of the Baby Doe debate. In A.L. Caplan, R.H. Blank, & J.C. Merrick (Eds.), *Compelled compassion* (pp. 35–72). Totowa, NJ: Humana Press.
Miner, B.J. (1995, February 5). Messengers receive flood of support. *Lansing State Journal,* A1, A4.
Morris, M.W. (1987, July). Health care: Who pays the bills? *Exceptional Parent*, 38–42.
National Institute of Child Health and Human Development. (1985). Request for Cooperative Agreement Applications RFA-NICHD-85. Title: Cooperative Multicenter Network of Neonatal Intensive Care Units (NICUs). Application receipt date: June 14.
Nelson, L.J. (1990). And the truth shall set you free: The case of Baby Boy Cory. In C.M. Culver (Ed.), *Ethics at the bedside* (pp. 40–69). Hanover, NH: University Press of New England.
Oskandy, D.L. (1985). *Severely defective newborns: The Catholic physician's dilemma.* St. Louis, MO: The Catholic Health Association of the United States.
Palmer, F.B., Shapiro, B.K., Wachtel, R.C., et al. (1988). The effects of physical therapy on cerebral palsy: A controlled trial in infants with spastic displegia. *New England Journal of Medicine, 318*(13), 803–808.
Paneth, N.S. (1995). The problem of low birth weight. *The Future of Children, 5*(1), 19–34.
Peabody, J.L. (1995, Spring). Who controls the plug? *Periscope, 6,* 3–6.
Penticuff, J.H. (1992). The impact of the Child Abuse Amendments on nursing staff and their care of handicapped newborns. In A.L. Caplan, R.H. Blank, & J.C. Merrick (Eds.), *Compelled compassion* (pp. 267–284). Totowa, NJ: Humana Press.
People v. Messenger. (1995). Ingham County (Michigan) Circuit Court, Judge Harrison, File No. 94-67694-FH.
Perrotta, L. (1995). Letter to the editor. *Journal of Perinatology, 15*(6), 519–520.
Pless, J.E. (1983). The story of Baby Doe. *New England Journal of Medicine, 309*(11), 664.
Pomerance, J.J., Pomerance, L.J., & Gottleib, J.A. (1993). Cost of caring for infants weighing 500–749 g at birth. *Pediatric Research, 23*(4), 231 A.
President's Commission for the Study of Ethical Problems in Medicine. (1983). *Deciding to forego life-sustaining treatment.* Washington, DC: U.S. Government Printing Office.
Rehabilitation Act of 1973, PL 93-112, 29 U.S.C. § 701 *et seq.*
Roan, S. (1993, December 26). Heroics and heartbreak. *Los Angeles Times,* pp. E1, E6.

Rogers, M.C. (1992). Do the right thing: Pain relief in infants and children. *New England Journal of Medicine, 326*(1), 55–56.
Rothberg, A.D., Goodman, M., Jacklin, L.A., & Cooper, P.A. (1991). Six year follow-up of early physiotherapy intervention in very low birth weight infants. *Pediatrics, 88*(3), 547–552.
Rottman, C.J. (1985). *Ethics in neonatology: A parents' perspective.* Unpublished thesis, Case Western Reserve University, School of Applied Social Sciences, Cleveland, OH.
Rovner, S. (1986, August 12). Surgery without anesthesia: Can preemies feel pain? *The Washington Post, Healthtalk,* pp. 7–8.
Saigal, S., Rosenbaum, P., Stoskopf, B., Hoult, L., Furlong, W., Feeny, D., Burrows, E., & Torrance, G. (1994). Comprehensive assessment of the health status of extremely low birth weight children at eight years of age: Comparison with a reference group. *Journal of Pediatrics, 125*(3), 411–417.
Scanlon, J.W. (1991). Appreciating neonatal pain. In L.A. Barness, D.C. DeVivo, G. Morrow, F.A. Oski, & A.M. Randolph (Eds.), *Advances in pediatrics* (pp. 317–333). Chicago: Yearbook Medical Publishers.
Shelton, T.L., Jeppson, E.S., & Johnson B.H. (1987). *Family centered care for children with special health care needs* (2nd ed.). Washington, DC: Association for the Care of Children's Health.
Silverman, W.A. (1980). *Retrolental fibroplasia: A modern parable.* New York: Grune & Stratton.
Stahlman, M.T. (1990). Ethical issues in the nursery: Priorities versus limits. *Journal of Pediatrics, 116*(2), 167–170.
Stein, S. (1994, December 11). The cruelest choice. *Chicago Tribune Magazine,* 16–22.
Stinson, R., & Stinson, P. (1983). *The long dying of Baby Andrew.* Boston: Little, Brown.
SUPPORT (The Study to Understand Prognoses and Preferences for Outcomes and Risks of Treatments) Principle Investigators. (1995). A controlled trial to improve care for seriously ill hospitalized patients. *Journal of the American Medical Association, 274*(20), 1591–1598.
Taylor, H. (1990). Withholding and withdrawal of life support from the critically ill. *New England Journal of Medicine, 322*(26), 1891–1892.
Thullen, J.D. (1992, April 13). *Moral and ethical dilemmas at the onset of life: A pediatric perspective.* Presented at the School of Medicine, Center for Ethical Development, Newberry College, South Carolina.
Trost, C. (1989, November 13). Prisoners of technology. *Wall Street Journal,* p. R25.
Tyson, J. (1995). Evidence-based ethics and the care of premature infants. *The Future of Children, 5*(1), 197–213.
U.S. Commission on Civil Rights. (1989). *Medical discrimination against children with disabilities.* Washington, DC: U.S. Government Printing Office.
Veatch, R.M. (1995). Abandoning informed consent. *Hastings Center Report, 25*(2), 5–12.
Wariyar, U.K., & Richmond, S. (1989). Morbidity and preterm delivery: Importance of 100% follow-up. *Lancet, 1*(8634), 387–388.
Wegman, M.E. (1994). Annual summary of vital statistics—1993. *Pediatrics, 94*(6), 792–803.
Winslow, R. (1992, February 25). Videos, questionnaires aim to expand role of patients in treatment decisions. *Wall Street Journal,* pp. B1, B3.
Wyly, V., & Allen J. (1995). Early intervention and the NICU health professional: An interdisciplinary model. *Zero to Three, 15*(6), 30–35.
Young, D. (1991). Who should hold the medical record: Provider, parents or both? *Birth, 18,* 2–4.
Young, E.W.D. (1984). *Societal provision of the long-term needs of the disabled in Britain and Sweden relative to decision making in neonatal intensive care units.* New York: World Rehabilitation Fund, International Exchange of Experts and Information in Rehabilitation.
Young, E.W.D., & Stevenson, D.K. (1990). Limiting treatment for extremely premature low-birth-weight infants (500 to 750 g). *American Journal of Diseases in Children, 144*(5), 549–552.

7 ACTIVITIES

1. Interview several parents of preterm and/or low birth weight infants who spent time in the NICU to gain their perspectives on the experience.

2. As part of class discussion, hold a formal debate on the ethical issues raised in this chapter. For example, take the parent viewpoint outlined in the chapter to construct arguments for a primary role for parents in decisions affecting their infants. Classmates should present opposing views, arguing for exclusive professional responsibility for decision making.

3. Observe procedures in a NICU. Interview the staff to learn how much and what kind of parent participation takes place.

CHAPTER 8

Ethics in Early Intervention

Harriet Able-Boone

Objectives

- To become aware of how professional values and biases can influence intervention recommendations and services offered to families
- To develop a sensitivity to individual families' values and priorities and how to consider those in the early intervention decision-making process
- To become aware of how to consider the early interventionist's obligations to the child, family, and professional in the intervention decision-making process
- To become familiar with a value framework focused on enhancing the community, as well as strengthening the family, that can be used in early intervention decision making

This chapter explores the ethical dimensions of early intervention services from policy choices to decisions regarding direct services for young children and their families. Strategies for achieving a more responsive service system congruent with individual family's values, priorities, and concerns are proposed.

The Individuals with Disabilities Education Act Amendments of 1990 (PL 102-119) has shifted the focus of intervention efforts from a strict child orientation to a focus on interventions for both the child and family, recognizing that any long-lasting impact on the child must consider the family system. The intent of IDEA is to design and implement policies and programs for families and young children that are respectful of and responsive to individual family concerns and priorities for their child. Because early childhood services and policies have adopted an ecological or systems perspective (Bronfenbrenner, 1979), the ethical dimensions of intervention commonly range from policy choices regarding who should receive services (Paul, Kern-Dunlap, & Falk, 1993) to parent–professional value conflicts regarding interventions and supports for individual children. The importance of policy makers, program administrators, and direct service providers understanding the role of values in early intervention is paramount. Early interventionists should examine their own personal and professional values before intervening in the lives of families and young children.

The very nature of early intervention implies a change in a young child's life that has immediate implications for the child and family. The change may affect the child's developmental progress or overall physical health. The change also may affect the parents by altering their parenting styles, attitudes, or knowledge. Thus, intervention without a consideration of individual family concerns and priorities can be viewed as an active intrusive process (Bricker, 1993).

The changes promoted in early intervention efforts often are based on the interventionist's values regarding how things ought to be. The values of intervention are expressed by what is viewed as good for the child and family or what the child and family should do. For example, the interventionist's values are reflected in his or her recommendations to the family regarding a child's developmental course. The implication is that the early interventionist or expert knows what is best for the child and family.

The major actors in the intervention process are the givers, or helpers, and the receivers, or ones to be helped. This relationship is characterized by instability and inequality (Pinker, 1973). Often, the very nature of our human services transactions makes families dependent on our services (Maroney, 1986). For example, in families' transactions with a babysitter or child care provider, the service or dependency is temporary and ends with a payment. However, in families' transactions with the early intervention system, the relationship usually lasts longer and often creates dependency on the professional or early intervention system.

Professionals have been defined as "technical rationalists" having the expertise and power to identify their clients' problems as well as identify solutions (Schon, 1983). Professionals are thus placed in a very powerful paternalistic position at the onset of the intervention relationship. The early interventionist is presented to the individual family as an expert with knowledge, skills, and values that influence the family. The family, for their part, comes to the interventionist for information, advice, support, and direction.

DEFICIT ORIENTATION TO INTERVENTION

Given this paternalistic or authoritative view of intervention, our efforts have been characterized by a deficit or "fix it" orientation. This has been referred to as the treatment focus to intervention, emphasizing the child's and family's needs (Sokoly & Dokecki, 1992). The deficit orientation is reflected in the tendency to label young children. Research has informed us that labeling a child inevitably lowers teachers' expectations, which ultimately influences the adult–child relationship and may lead to differential treatment (Haring et al., 1992). This is of particular concern with young children because they are strongly influenced by adults, whether they be parents or teachers. Also, intervention efforts undoubtedly have been influenced by the deficit orientation prevalent in family research, which has primarily focused on the negative impact on the family of the child with special needs (Turnbull, Blue-Banning, Behr, & Kerns, 1986). This is a concern because the research that informs intervention practices also provides empirical information derived from the professional's world view, values, or biases.

The deficit orientation to intervention is admittedly value-laden, reflecting professional biases. The professional's bias is evident in terms of the desire to fix or make the child and family better. However, the child's family may have an entirely different orientation toward their child and his or her concerns. For example, when faced with an infant with severe developmental delays, the interventionist may advise the parents to enroll their child in an infant program providing comprehensive therapeutic and developmental services. However, the parents may disagree with the professional's recommendation, wanting their 20-month-old to remain at home with the mother like their other children did until age 5.

The dominant perspective driving human services practice has been the medical model (Harry, 1992). This model has purported the idea that the child has an intrinsic deficit that should be corrected and can be treated within the parameters of systematic intervention. Dissonance between the family and professional can arise when the family takes a different view of the child's disability. For instance, in some rural Native American communities in the southwestern United States, families who have a child with a special need view that child as a blessing. They believe the child born with a disability has fewer gifts or talents because that child's gifts and talents are given to the other children in the family. Thus, the other children have more abilities or talents because of their sibling's special need. This value base is markedly different from the value base reflected in our intervention efforts.

VALUE-BASED INTERVENTION DECISIONS

Early intervention is influenced by the interventionist's world view—the values or theories he or she espouses. Examples of value-based intervention decisions are evident from the policy level to direct service level of intervention. Policy makers often make decisions regarding where society's scarce resources should be spent. The early intervention administrator decides what service options are available for individual children and families, and the direct service provider recommends particular intervention strategies for the child. All of these decisions are value laden and may not reflect the values of the families being served.

A policy maker's philosophical framework, knowledge base, and self-interest can be an ethical matter (Paul et al., 1993). A policy maker may value inclusion above all else in early intervention. Thus, only inclusive center-based programs for young children will receive sufficient funds. This type of policy decision may create conflict for families whose child is chronically ill and cannot tolerate an inclusive setting or for families who prefer that their young child be served in the home rather than in an inclusive center.

Similarly, a program director's or administrator's allegiance to a particular program certainly influences his or her decision making. For instance, in a community interagency consortium, program directors or policy makers may decide which child and family will receive what type of services in a community. If the local developmental child care center has the most slots available for young children with developmental delays, the majority of referrals may be made to this center regard-

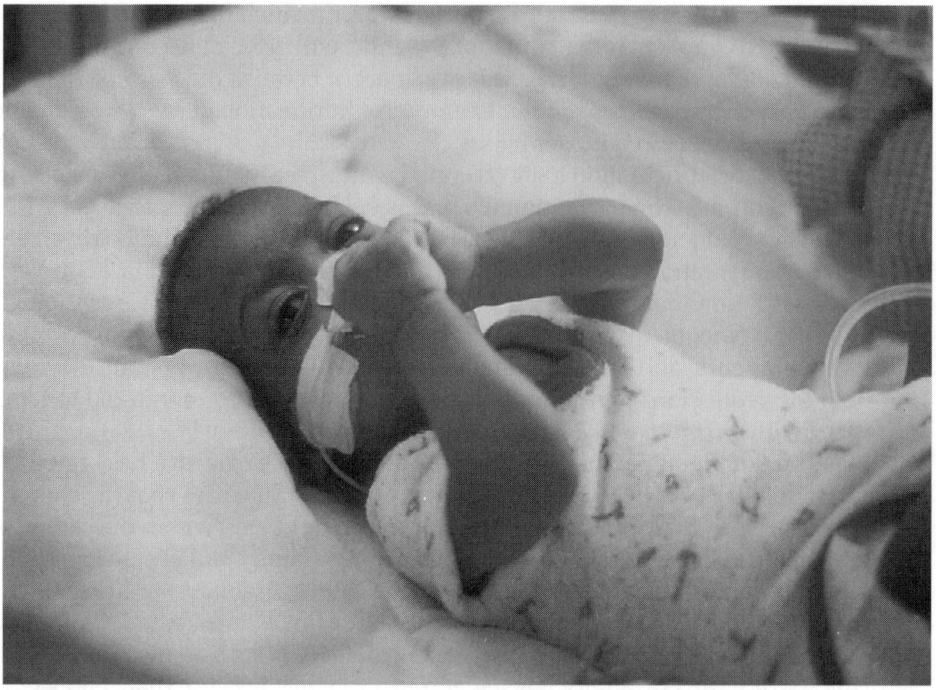

less of individual children's needs for home-based intervention or for a more inclusive setting. In an interview study, an early interventionist described this situation as follows: "We were serving a child with spina bifida who was typically developing except for his physical needs. His mother was single and working full time, so our program for young children with developmental disabilities provided him with the therapy and transportation services he needed because we had the slots available even though this child needed to be in a mainstreamed setting with his typically developing peers" (Able-Boone, 1995).

Parent–professional partnerships, advocated by IDEA, have often led to value conflicts between early interventionists and parents. For example, a mother of a young child with multiple physical needs told her child's physical therapist who had provided home-based intervention for 9 months that she had seen no progress in her child's motor skills and had consulted with a chiropractor specializing in craniosacral therapy. The chiropractor told the mother he could help her child learn to walk. Thus, the mother told the physical therapist she no longer needed her services. The physical therapist was in a quandary about how to use her professional knowledge regarding recommended practices for this child while respecting the culture and values of this mother (Able-Boone, 1995). Should she impose her own values on the mother about what is right for this child, or should she respect this mother's concern for her child? Professional codes of ethics often provide limited guidance in certain circumstances.

In the health care arena, the effects of high technological medicine on infants with chronic illnesses and disabilities raise many ethical dilemmas. Although neonatology can save younger and sicker newborns, a high degree of disabilities or illnesses result from the treatment. In a review of 142 infants born at 22–25 weeks' gestation, it was found that only 2% of infants born at 23 weeks' gestation escaped disabilities, compared with 21% born at 23 weeks' and 69% born at 25 weeks' (Allen, Donohue, & Dusman, 1993).

In addition to the effects on the infant's quality of life, the psychological, social, and economic effects on the family are important ethical considerations as well. Without a supportive and caring community and service system, the family and child may suffer from a lack of responsive resources in the community. The Child Abuse Amendments of 1984 mandate the treatment of all premature newborns except under extreme conditions. If medical treatment is mandated for these infants, responsive policies and programs providing support and assistance to families for their children's health care and rehabilitation would help alleviate some of the burden that families encounter.

Value-based decisions affecting the lives of young children and their families are made on a daily basis by policy makers, program directors, and direct service providers in early intervention. For interventionists, it is impossible not to let our personal values and biases influence the recommendations made to parents. It is important, however, to consider the parents' values and biases in any decision made for the child and family in order to realize the true family-centered intent of IDEA.

RELATIONSHIP-FOCUSED INTERVENTIONS

A family's interpretation of their child's disability or special need demands understanding and respect from the professional. In order to achieve this understanding and respect, a trusting and equitable relationship between the family and professional should be established. The importance of professional–client relationships has been emphasized as determining the nature and outcome of interventions. Kalmanson and Seligman (1992) asserted that "the success of all interventions will rest with the quality of provider–family relationships" (p. 48). Our current emphasis in early intervention has moved from an "us–them" orientation to a "we" orientation in which parents and professionals are viewed as equal members of a team.

This "we" orientation requires the early intervention professional to be a reflective practitioner encompassing such characteristics as caring and prudence (Sokoly & Dokecki, 1992). In an interview study of parents of young children, parents reported that their expectations of professionals were "understanding, respect for my child and family, and a sense of humor" (Able-Boone, Sandall, Loughry, & Fredrick, 1990, p.106). These traits are not skills necessarily taught in a preservice preparation program. Rather, these are characteristics of the professional requiring him or her to be a reflective and caring practitioner respectful of differing values and priorities for families and children.

In order to achieve this respectful approach, the early interventionist's challenge is to consider the perspective of the recipient of intervention (Darling, 1989; Turnbull, Turnbull, & Blue-Banning, 1994) in the decision making for children and families. Until the 1990s, most interventions have been professionally defined. Assessment and intervention strategies have been professionally based, typically on the professional's definition of an improved life quality for the family and child. Unfortunately, most of the training in the human services professions has been focused on this professionally defined orientation in which families and children must fit into predefined clinical categories and interventions have been designed accordingly (Darling, 1989). Instead, in order to be responsive and respectful of individual children and their families, the professional's assessment and intervention efforts should include developing an understanding of the client's or family's definition of the situation or concern regarding their child (Darling, 1989). Thus, interventions become more congruent with the family's values and expectations. For instance, in serving rural Native American communities in the southwestern United States, interventions may focus on the sibling interactions with the child with disabilities, reflecting the belief these families have that their other children have received more abilities as mentioned previously.

PARENTS' PERSPECTIVE

A focus on the parents' perspective also requires interventionists to consider the consumer's rights. Thus, in intervention planning and implementation efforts, the rights of both the parent(s) and child must be considered. The child's rights include receiving quality interventions in a timely manner (Paul, Gallagher, Kendrick, Thomas, & Young, 1992). Parents and professionals, however, have reported long waiting lists to receive early intervention services and the fact that that all families do not have equal access to services (Able-Boone, 1995). This concern has been expressed by a father of one child: "We need to make sure that all families have equal access to services so we don't just serve families who are middle class, educated advocates for their child. I am concerned that we don't serve the families who don't have the knowledge or financial resources to access the early intervention system" (Able-Boone, 1995).

The family's right to self-determination and self-actualization requires the professional to encourage and support the family in an informed decision-making process (Bryant, Lyons, & Wasik, 1990). In order to achieve this, the family has a right to be educated about all the options available for services. Often, however, this is not the case. For instance, in an interview study of parents' perceptions of services, a major concern of parents was expressed as, "I want to know what type of services are out there for my child and family so I can decide what is best for us" (Able-Boone et al., 1990).

In addition, parents need to be informed of what the intervention will not do (Bryant et al., 1990). Families need to be reminded that there are limits to the interventionist's knowledge and efforts. Thus, parents have a right to say "no" to those services. For instance, the mother who wanted her child to be able to walk, as described previously, had false expectations of physical therapy and its effects on her child's physical development. Based on this mother's view, physical therapy was not meeting her child's need so she questioned why she should continue the service. Thus, this mother's right to discontinue services may need to be respected except in cases of extreme neglect. Clearly, no one intervention or interventionist can be all things to a family.

Families certainly have a right to confidentiality. With the focus on determining families' priorities and concerns for their child as a component of the individualized family service plan (IFSP) process, families can be vulnerable because of the information they are asked to provide. The professional needs to assure the parents that the information is confidential as well as to let the parents know who will have access to their child's records and the information provided.

Another primary focus in our early intervention efforts is a focus on parent–professional collaboration. Families have a right to be treated as equal and respected members of the early intervention team. In order to achieve this, parents need full information regarding their child's abilities and special needs and the services and supports available to facilitate their child's development. An example of parent empowerment in intervention is to give parents access and control of their child's records (Beatty, 1993). Several studies in the health care literature have suggested

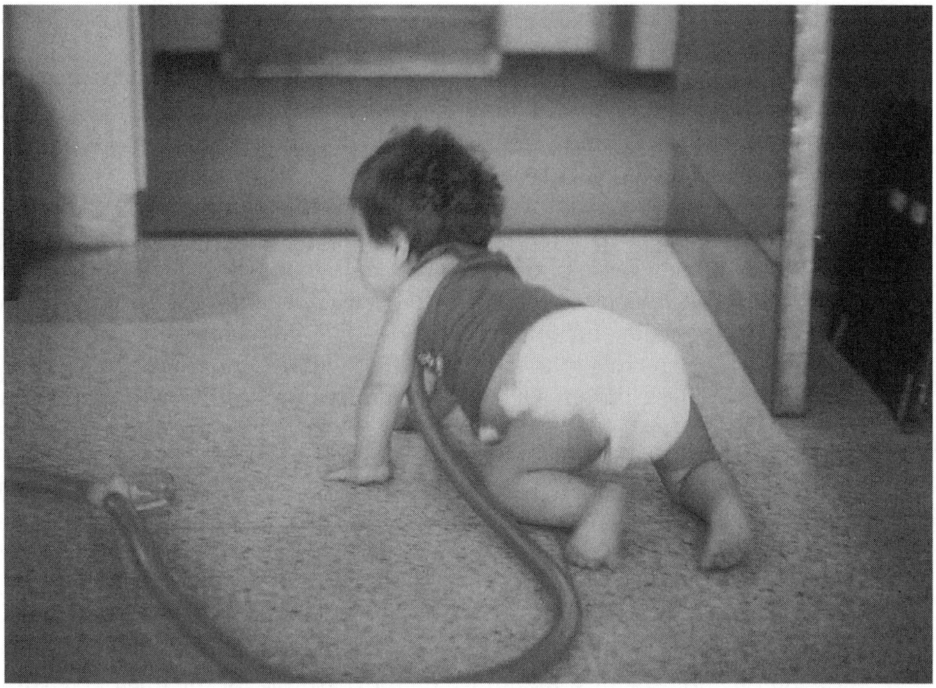

that an open sharing of records resulted in a shift of power from the physician to client, creating a more trusting and equitable relationship between physician and parent (Greene & MacFarlane, 1985; MacFarlane, 1992). Parent-held records as well as parent participation in child assessment encourage parents to take a more active role in their child's health and development. Empowerment of parents has been stressed by practitioners in the field: "We have a tendency to do a lot of hand-holding and coddling of our parents. Instead, we need to help parents deal with their own issues more by giving them information on how to access services on their own" (Able-Boone, 1995).

ETHICAL SOLUTIONS TO CONFLICTS

There undoubtedly will be conflicts between parents and professionals in the early intervention enterprise. The first step in resolving the conflict must be the acknowledgment and acceptance of differences and the need for a shared decision-making process.

The relationship perspective toward the intervention process is important in arriving at shared decision making between parents and professionals. Ethical decision making has been referred to as a distinct form of human conversation requiring two virtues (Kipinis, 1987). The first virtue is a willingness to accept values and priorities that may be different from one's own. The second virtue is a commitment to collaborative decision making for an improved quality of life for the family and child.

This decision-making process requires "systematic critical reflection about our obligations" (Kipinis, 1987, p. 26). Interventionists need to ask themselves what they should do to consider all the viewpoints. The child, the family, and professional obligations to the field all must be considered.

Dokecki (1983) provided a *value framework* for early childhood services useful for analyzing the different perspectives in the intervention process. This framework is based on the premise that all interventions should enhance human development through community. Thus, an ideal intervention would be enhance community, strengthen families, enable parents, and enhance and protect each family member (Dokecki, 1983; Hobbs et al., 1984; Kaiser & Hemmeter, 1989).

The first component of this framework asks the question, *Does the intervention enhance community?* Early interventionists should consider if their interventions are inclusive, creating a sense of community for all young children and their families. The practice of inclusion has been viewed from a relationship perspective as including three components (Turnbull et al., 1994). The first is the physical component, referring to the principle that young children with disabilities belong in the same places as all young children such as community or private child care centers. Second, inclusive interventions should promote mutually satisfying and reciprocal relationships for all young children and families. Thus, young children and their families should not be singled out for separate therapy or support sessions. Third, the inclusive community is characterized by an emotional belonging of all members exemplified by mutual affection and concern.

The second component of the value framework asks the question, *Does the intervention strengthen the family?* In other words, do early intervention programs enable families to raise their children in congruence with their own values and priorities? Early interventionists must relinquish their expert role for the role of consultant or "broker of services." Thus, the interventionist should avoid giving specific recommendations for achieving goals, but rather provide parents with options for services—not just those the interventionist believes would be more effective (Leviton, Mueller, & Kauffman, 1992; Sontag & Schacht, 1994). This may, under certain conditions, require the early interventionist to go against his or her professional judgment, which inevitably will create some conflict. The collaborative goal-setting or decision-making strategy as defined by Bailey (1987) provides a framework for resolving such conflicts.

The third component concerns the question, *Does the intervention enable parents to do their jobs well?* Early interventionists must ensure that interventions do not cause undue stress or burden on the child or family. Often, early intervention services are based on the interventionist's perception of family and child priorities and what he or she thinks can be done to make their lives better (Bailey, 1987). Instead, the expert model of intervention can be replaced with the role of facilitator and intermediary with the interventionist becoming an advocate for the child and family (Maroney & Dokecki, 1984). This would require the interventionist to be sensitive to the individual family concerns as well as knowledgeable about community resources. The ultimate goal would be to give parents full autonomy in the decision making for their child. Thus, the early interventionist's role is to empower parents in becoming informed consumers for their child and family.

The fourth component asks, *Does the intervention enhance individual development and protect the rights of individual family members?* This implies that early intervention efforts should benefit all family members, not only the child (Kaiser & Hemmeter, 1989). The end result of interventions would be to create mutually satisfying relationships between the young child and his or her family members. For instance, in teaching parents correct positioning techniques with their infant with cerebral palsy, a more satisfying relationship between the parent and child is encouraged.

SUMMARY

The major premise of the value framework is that all interventions should be proactive with the ultimate goal of strengthening families (Kaiser & Hemmeter, 1989). This would create increased informed parental decision making, which ultimately will require the service system to become more flexible and responsive to individual family concerns and priorities. The early interventionist's values may influence the choices offered to families, but if early interventionists examine their values within this context, they should become better facilitators of family choices and preferences.

REFERENCES

Able-Boone, H. (1995, November). Early intervention ethical decision making: Value conflicts in services and supports. Presentation at the National Division for Early Childhood Conference, Orlando, FL.

Able-Boone, H., Sandall, S.R., Loughry, A., & Fredrick, L. (1990). An informed, family-centered approach to Public Law 99-457: Parental views. *Topics in Early Childhood Special Education, 10*(1), 100–111.

Allen, M.C., Donohue, P.K., & Dusman, A.K. (1993). The limit of viability: Neonatal outcomes of infants born at 22 to 25 weeks' gestation. *New England Journal of Medicine, 329*(1), 1597–1601.

Bailey, D.B. (1987). Collaborative goal setting with families: Resolving differences in values and priorities for services. *Topics in Early Childhood Special Education, 7*(2), 59–71.

Beatty, C. (1993). Access and control of the child's record in family-centered services. *Infant Toddler Intervention, 3*(1), 73–83.

Bricker, D.A. (1993). A rose by any other name, or is it? *Journal of Early Intervention, 17*(2), 89–96.

Bronfenbrenner, U. (1979). *The ecology of human development: Experiments by nature and design.* Cambridge, MA: Harvard University Press.

Bryant, D., Lyons, C., & Wasik, B. (1990). Ethical issues involved in home visiting. *Topics in Early Childhood Special Education, 10*(4), 92–107.

Child Abuse Amendments of 1984, PL 98-457, 42 U.S.C. § 1752 *et seq.*

Darling, R.B. (1989). Using the social system perspective in early intervention: The value of a sociological approach. *Journal of Early Intervention, 13*(1), 24–35.

Dokecki, P.R. (1983). The place of values in the world of psychology and public policy. *Peabody Journal of Education, 60*(3), 108–125.

Greene, A., & MacFarlane, A. (1985). Parent-held child record cards: A comparison of types. *Health Visitor, 58*, 14–16.

Haring, K., Lovett, D.L., Haney, K.F., Algozzine, B., Smith, D.D., & Clarke, J. (1992). Labeling preschoolers as learning disabled: A cautionary position. *Topics in Early Childhood Special Education, 12*(2), 151–173.

Harry, B. (1992). Developing cultural self-awareness: The first step in values clarification for early interventionists. *Topics in Early Childhood Special Education, 12*(3), 333–350.

Hobbs, N., Dokecki, P.R., Hoover-Dempsey, K.V., Moroney, R.M., Shayne, M.W., & Weeks, K.H. (1984). *Strengthening families.* San Francisco: Jossey-Bass.

Individuals with Disabilities Education Act Amendments of 1991, PL 102-119, 20 U.S.C. § 1400 *et seq.*

Kaiser, A.P., & Hemmeter, M.L. (1989). Value-based approaches to family intervention. *Topics in Early Childhood Special Education, 8*(4), 72–86.

Kalmanson, B., & Seligman, S. (1992). Family-provider relationships: The basis of all interventions. *Infants and Young Children, 4*(4), 46–52.

Kipinis, K. (1987). How to discuss professional ethics. *Young Children, 42*(4), 26–30.

Leviton, A., Mueller, M., & Kauffman, C. (1992). The family-centered consultation model: Practical applications for professionals. *Infants and Young Children, 4*(3), 1–8.

MacFarlane, A. (1992). Personal child health records held by parents. *Archives of Disease in Childhood, 67*(5), 571–572.

Maroney, R.M. (1986). Family care: Toward a responsive society. In P.R. Dokecki & R.M. Zaner (Eds.), *Ethics of dealing with persons with severe handicaps: Toward a research agenda* (pp. 217–232). Baltimore: Paul H. Brookes Publishing Co.

Maroney, R.M., & Dokecki, P.R. (1984). The family and the professions: Implications for public policy. *Journal of Family Issues, 5*(2), 224–238.

Paul, J.L., Gallagher, J.J., Kendrick, S.B., Thomas, D.D., & Young, J.F. (1992). *Handbook for ethical policy making.* Chapel Hill, NC: Frank Porter Graham Child Development Center.

Paul, J.L., Kern-Dunlap, L., & Falk, G.D. (1993). Ethical issues in providing services for families: Policy and clinical considerations. In J.L. Paul & R.J. Simeonsson (Eds.), *Children with special needs: Family, culture, and society* (pp. 279–294). Orlando, FL: Harcourt Brace Jovanovich.

Pinker, R. (1973). *Social theory and social policy.* London: Heinemann Educational Books.

Schon, D.A. (1983). *The effective practitioner: How professionals think in action.* New York: Basic Books.

Sokoly, M.M., & Dokecki, P.R. (1992). Ethical perspectives in family-centered early intervention. *Infants and Young Children, 4*(4), 23–32.

Sontag, J.C., & Schacht, R. (1994). An ethical comparison of parent participation and information needs in early intervention. *Exceptional Children, 60*(5), 422–433.

Turnbull, A.P., Blue-Banning, M., Behr, S., & Kerns, G. (1986). Family research and intervention: A value and ethical examination. In P.R. Dokecki & R.M. Zaner (Eds.), *Ethics of dealing with persons with severe handicaps: Toward a research agenda* (pp. 119–140). Baltimore: Paul H. Brookes Publishing Co.

Turnbull, A.P., Turnbull, H.R., & Blue-Banning, M. (1994). Enhancing inclusion of infants and toddlers with disabilities and their families: A theoretical and programmatic analysis. *Infants and Young Children, 7*(2), 1–14.

8 ACTIVITIES

1. Consider the various scenarios presented in the chapter exemplifying a value conflict. How would you resolve these conflicts considering your obligations to the child, family, and your profession?

2. Consider the three most important values you espouse regarding early intervention services. Think of a family you have worked with and have disagreed with regarding services and supports for their child. What do you suppose were the family's values and priorities? How might you have dealt with the situation differently, if at all?

SECTION IV

ASSESSMENT

CHAPTER 9

Developmental Assessment in Early Intervention

Susan R. Sandall

Objectives

- To understand the rationale for family-directed assessments and the importance of family participation
- To appreciate the value of theoretical and practical knowledge of child development and learning as a basis for assessing and understanding young children
- To be able to link assessment practices with specific and valid uses
- To understand the assessment process in early intervention

When designing and implementing assessment procedures for identification of and intervention with infants and toddlers with disabilities or other special needs, the early intervention team must consider a number of issues and concerns. One of these issues is the specification of the purpose of the assessment. Assessment is pivotal to the effectiveness of early intervention efforts. It is also time consuming and potentially stressful. Thus, assessment should be done with a clear purpose in mind. Assessment strategies and procedures must be selected that will help meet that purpose. Assessment should yield information about the young child's abilities, strengths, and needs and the family's concerns. It is important to recognize that assessment and intervention are both early intervention services and that they are intertwined services that depend on each other. This chapter offers guidelines for assessment with the recognition that the process should be individualized for each child and family.

Family members are key participants in the assessment process. They guide the process by determining their own priorities and preferences for involvement. Family members remind other team members of the purpose of the assessment and identify their own concerns, interests, and resources for their child and family.

Family participation is the central ingredient of a family-centered approach to early intervention. That is, assessment practices must recognize families as the constant in the child's life, recognize and support families as partners in the process, and respond to individual families' strengths and priorities. This is consistent with the assessment requirements of Part H of the Individuals with Disabilities Education Act (IDEA) of 1990 (PL 101-476). Family participation optimizes the validity of the assessment results and the intervention outcomes and procedures. Family participation during the assessment process sets the stage for effective communication and collaboration among family members and the professional members of the early intervention team.

IMPORTANT CONSIDERATIONS

Assessment of infants and toddlers is both challenging and exciting. It is different from the assessment of older children and adults. Accurate assessments require that the assessor be patient, creative, observant, and energetic. The behavior of very young children is highly variable. Such factors as temperament, state, physical comfort, and health will influence the assessment. In addition, between the developmental ages of about 7 and 18 months, young children may demonstrate anxious or wary behavior toward strangers or unfamiliar adults, including assessors.

Rogers (1982) described five important characteristics of an effective assessor of young infants and toddlers:

- Truly enjoys young children
- Has a strong knowledge of child development
- Has experience with young children
- Is able to read the young child's signals and match his or her interactive style
- Reads the parent's signals and is able to ease his or her anxiety

The effective assessor must also possess and use sound professional judgment. The selection and use of appropriate procedures and the careful observation of the child's interactions with materials and people require professional knowledge and clinical skill. That is, the assessment of a child is never the simple administration of a test. It involves the considered use of many methods of assessment and the thoughtful interpretation of the child's responses and interactions to better understand the child.

DEFINITION OF TERMS

Any discussion of the assessment of young children requires the knowledge of terms used to describe the characteristics of tests, test development, and measurement. Definitions of terms used in this chapter are provided in Table 9.1.

RECOMMENDED PRACTICES AND GUIDING PRINCIPLES

A number of professional organizations have published formal policy statements regarding appropriate practices and procedures for the assessment of very young

Table 9.1. Test and measurement terminology

Term	Definition
Validity	The extent to which the measure fulfills the purpose for which it is intended
Content validity	The extent to which the measure covers a representative sample of the behaviors it supposedly samples
Criterion-related validity	The correspondence between test scores and present (concurrent) or future (predictive) performance as measured in another way
Construct validity	An indicator of how well the test actually measures the theoretical construct such as cognition, creativity, or intelligence
Reliability	The consistency with which a test measures what it is supposed to measure
Test–retest reliability	The correlation between two administrations of the same test to the same individual on two occasions
Alternative-form reliability	The correlation between scores from two forms of a test given at essentially the same time
Interrater reliability	The extent to which two or more scorers are consistent in their judgments
Standardized test	A measure with fixed procedures of administration and scoring; standard materials, stimulus items, and instructions; empirical testing of the items; and norms
Norm-referenced test	A test in which an individual child's performance is compared with a normative group, usually of others of the same age
Criterion-referenced test	A test in which an individual child's performance is compared to a standard of mastery or sequence of skills
Curriculum-referenced measure	A measure in which an individual child's performance is compared with a sequence of curricular objectives

Adapted from Anastasi (1982) and Goodwin & Driscoll (1980).

children. The following themes emerge from these policy statements: 1) assessments should be family directed, 2) the assessment process and the resultant information must be useful, 3) the assessment procedures must have social validity, 4) the assessment procedures must include and value multiple sources and types of information, and 5) assessment is an ongoing process (American Speech-Language-Hearing Association [ASHA], 1990; DEC Task Force on Recommended Practices, 1993; Greenspan & Meisels, 1994; National Association for School Psychologists [NASP], 1991).

A conceptual framework for useful, valid, valuable, respectful, family-directed assessments is provided by the *Zero to Three Work Group on Developmental Assessment* (Greenspan & Meisels, 1994). Their vision of appropriate developmental assessment is built upon current, comprehensive knowledge of child development and an alliance with families. The process is guided by a quest to understand the child, the child's capacities and resources, and the caregiving and learning environments that will best support the child's development. Observation and sharing are key elements. Specialized or structured tests or procedures are used only if needed. This chapter describes observation and interview methods and lists available tests. The early intervention team needs to know a variety of methods to answer the critical questions and to gain understanding of the child within the caregiving context.

CONDUCTING ASSESSMENTS

The word assessment comes from the Latin *assidere,* which means "to sit beside." Although the word *assessment* may conjure up the picture of a structured setting with a child sitting across the table from a tester, interaction, communication, and flexibility are actually fundamental to the gathering of assessment information.

Identifying Family's Role

Sometimes lost in the rush to ensure family participation in assessment and intervention is the important notion that family involvement can take a variety of forms and that families should be presented with options from which to choose. Another important component of family involvement is that a family's form of involvement may change over time. Cripe (1993) identified at least seven roles for families in the assessment process: colleague, informant, assistant, facilitator, observer and validator, assessor, and guide. Families must be provided with opportunities to choose the extent of their involvement as well as their role. Families must also have the opportunity to adjust the role and level of involvement.

Optimizing Child's Performance

Most young children do best when they are with their parents or familiar caregivers in familiar or comfortable settings, with familiar and interesting materials. To increase the validity of assessments, these factors should be incorporated into assessment practices.

Home and play settings are appropriate contexts for assessments. Parents or caregivers should be present and should be allowed to interact with their child. This means that assessments must be scheduled for convenient, unhurried times. The toys and materials should be interesting and accessible.

Play-based, arena-style assessments provide an effective and naturalistic alternative to traditional assessment approaches that involve multiple appointments with one professional at a time. Arena assessments involve multiple professional disciplines and simultaneous assessment across developmental domains (Child Development Resources, 1992; Linder, 1993; Wolery & Dyk, 1984). Typically, the parent or one of the professionals interacts with the child and guides the child through play activities and routines (e.g., eating). Meanwhile, the other team members record their observations and may score portions of assessment tools based on their observations. Periodically, team members may suggest specific tasks. Parents (or caregivers) are present throughout to provide information, to validate the child's responses, and, in some situations, to interact with their child.

This assessment procedure increases efficiency, reduces the number of professionals who must handle the child and whom the child must get to know, provides team members with observations of the child across developmental domains, and should result in more team consensus for intervention planning.

Collecting Information

Assessment information should be gathered from multiple sources, using multiple methods and employing multiple measures. As mentioned previously, some important sources of information include parents, other family members and caregivers, and professionals. Similarly, multiple methods should be used to ensure a comprehensive and integrated assessment of the child. Possible methods include observations, interviews, direct testing, and records review.

Observations Observations can be done by a professional, a family member, or the team. As noted previously, it is preferred that the settings and situations for observations be as natural as possible in order to reduce stress and optimize the child's performance. The observer(s) records various behaviors, dimensions of behaviors (e.g., frequency, intensity, duration, latency), and environmental factors that influence the child's performance. Methods and guidelines for observing young children are presented in Table 9.2. The observers may use their knowledge of child development and developmental checklists to guide their observations. The *Assessment, Evaluation, and Programming System* (AEPS) (Bricker, 1993) and *Transdisciplinary Play-Based Assessment* (TPBA) (Linder, 1993) are just two examples of useful formats for observing the young child.

Interviews Another method for gathering information is through interviews. Parents and other caregivers are the usual informants. They provide their perceptions and recollections of the child's capabilities as well as their concerns. They can also provide a developmental history. Interviews provide important insights into the child's and family's experience. Conducting comfortable and useful interviews requires skill. Guidelines for conducting conversational but focused family interviews in early intervention are described by Winton and Bailey (1988). In the focused interview, the interviewer provides a moderate degree of structure by specifying topics to be covered and by using an interview guide. The interviewer has flexibility in the order and manner in which topics are discussed. A format that allows families to tell their own story establishes a foundation for an exchange of concerns, questions, and information. Important interview techniques are outlined in Table 9.3

Direct Testing Sometimes it will be necessary to use direct testing to gather information about the young child when the professional wants to know how the child will respond to a specific set of materials, requests, or instructions. It is important to remember that infants and toddlers, quite naturally, may not be able to comprehend the cues used in direct testing. Thus, failure to perform may not mean an inability to perform. However, through direct testing, a skilled examiner is often able to elicit child behaviors that have not been observed in play or caregiving routines. The AEPS is an example of an assessment tool that incorporates multiple methods including direct testing.

Review of Records Another method for gathering information is to review health records, records from previous assessments, and developmental records from

Table 9.2. Methods for observing infants and toddlers

Term	Description
Narratives	Diary description—a chronological record of an individual child's behavior, made after the behavior occurs
	Anecdotal record—a descriptive narrative, recorded after the behavior, visit, or session occurs
	Running record—a sequential record over a given time, recorded while the behavior is occurring
Time sampling	Record of the frequency of occurrence of a selected behavior, recorded while the behavior is occurring for a given period of time
Event sampling	Record of an event that has been defined in advance, recorded while it is taking place
Checklist	Record of presence or absence of selected behaviors
Rating scales	Record of the quality of selected behaviors

Adapted from Hills (1992).

Table 9.3. Interview techniques

Create a warm atmosphere.
Explain the purpose of the interview.
Confirm the time allotted. Parents should not feel rushed.
If the child is present, provide toys and tell the parents that it is okay for the child to play while the adults talk.
Identify in advance the broad topics to be covered.
Use both open- and close-ended questions.
Listen.
Use clear, jargon-free, respectful, and honest language.
Express appreciation for the parents' participation in the interview and make plans.

Adapted from Ulrey & Rogers (1982) and Winton & Bailey (1988).

early intervention programs or child care experiences. Of course, this requires the parents' permission. Records are reviewed with the intention of gaining perspective on the child's history and previous experiences. Records review may also decrease the possibility of repeated testing or using ineffective methods.

A family-directed, developmental assessment is multifaceted. The guidelines for assessment and evaluation, as required by Part H of IDEA (PL 101-476) and supported by recommended practices, incorporate multiple sources, use multiple methods, and seek to understand the child's development, health, and caregiving contexts.

THE ASSESSMENT PROCESS IN EARLY INTERVENTION

The early intervention assessment process is a series of recurring questions. Once the question is posed, information is gathered and interpreted, and decisions are made. In Table 9.4, we outline the types of questions and decisions that are made in early intervention: identification, screening, in-depth assessment, assessment for program planning, monitoring change, and evaluating program effectiveness.

Assessment refers to the process of gathering information for the purpose of making a decision. By gathering and integrating information from observations, interviews, tests, and records, decisions can be made regarding the appropriate services and supports for a child and family. But, assessment is a continuing process.

Table 9.4. The early intervention assessment process

Step	Description
Identification	The process of locating those infants and toddlers and their families who might be eligible for early intervention
Screening	The process of identifying those infants and toddlers in need of further in-depth assessment
In-depth assessment	The process of conducting in-depth assessments to verify a developmental problem, to determine the nature of the problem, and to determine the types of appropriate services
Assessment for planning intervention	The process of gathering information to determine the child's current level of functioning, to identify strengths and weaknesses, to determine intervention outcomes and objectives, and to identify useful intervention strategies
Monitoring change	The process of keeping track of the infant's or toddler's progress and determining the effectiveness of intervention strategies and activities
Program evaluation	The process of gathering information to determine the effectiveness of the program for infants, toddlers, and their families

Decisions should be evaluated regularly as child and family concerns change and as new information is gathered.

Identification

Identification is the process of locating infants and toddlers and their families who might be eligible for early intervention. Identification involves a variety of activities related to defining the target population, increasing public awareness of services, encouraging referrals, and canvassing the community for children and families who may be in need of services (Peterson, 1987).

Many different types of activities are used to locate and identify young children with special health or developmental concerns. For example, public service announcements are used to educate and alert the public to risks and warning signs of health or developmental problems. Other awareness activities include distribution of informational materials about early intervention services, hotlines, and support groups. Awareness materials and activities are often targeted at locations where young children and their families can be found, such as physician's offices, health clinics, community centers, and child care centers. These activities need to be repeated periodically to maintain awareness and to gain referrals for screening.

A state's comprehensive Child-Find system is one mechanism for identifying children with disabilities. Explicit in the Part H guidelines is the requirement for coordination of Child-Find activities for infants and toddlers with existing Child Find and early identification activities that have been undertaken to meet the requirements of other legislation (e.g., PL 94-142, the Education for All Handicapped Children Act of 1975; Early and Periodic Screening, Diagnosis, and Treatment [EPSDT]) and local initiatives.

Screening

Screening is the process of identifying those children in need of further in-depth assessment. Using procedures that are quickly and easily administered, those children who do not fall within the expected ranges of development are identified. Screening does not specify the nature of the problem, or the reasons for its existence. Screening informs us of the suspected presence of developmental problems. Further and more complete assessment is then done to confirm or disconfirm the presence of a developmental delay or disability.

The scope of screening programs varies. For example, the Apgar Scoring System (Apgar, 1953) is typically administered by medical personnel in the delivery room within minutes after birth. The Apgar measures muscle tone, heart rate, reflex to stimulation, appearance, and respiratory effort. The score helps to identify newborns in immediate need of special care and treatment. Other newborn screening tests are available to determine the absence or presence of disorders such as phenylketonuria (PKU), galactosemia, and cystic fibrosis. A screening program for older children might be offered by a public agency. For example, a school district may offer screening to all infants and toddlers in the community two or three times a year. These screenings might be conducted by trained volunteers and supervised by an early intervention team. As another example, the national program for EPSDT typically includes a pediatric examination, a developmental history provided by the family, a family report of special problems or concerns, and an assessment of the child's developmental status using a screening instrument. EPSDT serves children who are eligible for Medicaid.

As with all assessment activities, several sources of information should be used during screening. In particular, family input is crucial. Families have a rich history of observations and experiences with their infant and can provide a more complete picture of their child than can be gleaned from a single visit to a screening program or clinic. To increase the accuracy of family input, it is important that the family members know in advance the purpose and limitations of screening and that the professionals be skilled in interview techniques.

The results of the screening should be shared with the family as soon as possible. The family's need for information should be responded to quickly and as comprehensively as possible (Hanson & Lynch, 1995). As Meisels and Provence (1989) have stated, screening should be viewed as a service. For many families it is their introduction to the early intervention system. Screening can be a helpful service that provides families with an initial response to their concerns, information about child development and developmental services, and a link to community-based resources and programs.

Multiple sources of information should be included in the screening procedure. Several screening instruments are available (see Table 9.5), and the child's performance on such an instrument can contribute valuable information to the decision-making process. The selection of screening instruments should be done with care and caution. A particular test must be used for its intended purpose. It must be empirically valid and reliable and the characteristics of the standardization sample considered. The users of the test should be well trained. Although attempts have been made in the 1980s and 1990s to address potential cultural bias of tests, care should be taken in using and interpreting test results in order to reduce the risk of confusing cultural differences with developmental difficulties.

It should be noted that some children with established conditions will bypass the screening step and proceed to in-depth assessment and program planning. For those children who do participate in screening, the child's behavior or development may be viewed as questionable or significantly different from expectations. The next step in the assessment process is a referral for comprehensive assessment. However, families of children who are not referred should be provided with general information on child development and community resources. Screening programs should offer periodic screenings for children during tho early years of life (Meisels & Provence, 1989).

In-Depth Assessment

The next step in the assessment process is a comprehensive assessment to verify the presence of a disability or delay, to describe the nature and extent of the disability or delay, and to determine if the child is eligible for services or programs. This step in the assessment process is sometimes called diagnosis. The term *diagnosis* as used by the health profession refers to the determination of the cause of a disease or physical disorder to prescribe treatment leading to a cure. In early intervention, however, the cause of a developmental problem may be unknown or difficult to determine. This step should provide a fairly complete description of the child's capabilities as well as developmental concerns and the extent of those concerns. This description can then be used to determine eligibility and appropriate services. Determination of eligibil-

Table 9.5. Selected screening instruments

Name	Author(s) (Date)	Age range	Description	Content
Ages & Stages Questionnaires (ASQ): A Parent-Completed Child-Monitoring System	Bricker, Squires, and Mounts (1995)	4–48 months	Set of 11 developmental questionnaires periodically sent to parents of children at risk	Gross and fine motor, communication, personal-social, problem solving
Battelle Developmental Inventory Screening Test	Newborg, Stock, Wnek, Guidubaldi, and Svinicki (1984)	Birth–8.5 years	Subset of items from the Battelle; administered by a professional	Personal-social, adaptive, motor communication, cognition
Denver Developmental Screening Test	Frankenburg et al. (1990)	Birth–6 years	Designed to screen for developmental delays; administered by professional or other trained person	Personal-social, fine motor-adaptive, language, gross motor, test behavior ratings
Developmental Activities Screening Inventory (DASI–II)	Fewell and Langley (1984)	1–60 months	Designed to provide early detection of developmental disabilities; administered by a professional; some flexibility in instructions	Cognition, academic, perceptual motor, foundational skills
Developmental Profile–II	Alpern, Boll, and Shearer (1980)	Birth–12 years	Designed to assess a child's functional, developmental age level; parent interview	Physical, self-help, social, academic, communication
Early Language Milestone Scale (2nd ed.)	Coplan (1993)	Birth–36 months	Designed to assess speech and language development during infancy and early childhood; administered by a professional	Auditory expressive, auditory receptive, visual

> **Corinna**
>
> Corinna's parents have become more and more concerned about her development. She is a 1-year-old who has not achieved the expected developmental milestones. After discussions with their pediatrician, Corinna's parents contacted the local early intervention program to which he referred them. A child development specialist from the center spoke to them on the phone and made a home visit to meet Corinna and her family. Today, Corinna and her mother and aunt have come to the center, where several professionals will observe Corinna while she plays, interacts with her mother, and eats.

ity is called evaluation in the Part H (PL 101-476) guidelines. The story of Corinna shows her and her family participating in an in-depth assessment or evaluation.

Eligibility Issues Eligibility issues and criteria for early intervention services were described in Chapter 1. Harbin and colleagues (Harbin, Danaher, & Derrick, 1994; Harbin, Gallagher, & Terry, 1991) have described some of these eligibility concerns in relation to Part H services and the fact that states have latitude in determining their own criteria. Although federal law allows the use of confirmed presence of an established condition or clinical judgment in making eligibility decisions, some infants and toddlers must meet some quantitative criteria, such as 1.5 or 2.0 standard deviations below the mean as measured by a standardized, norm-referenced device, or 25% delay in one or more areas of development as determined by assessment results. Thus, direct testing is often used to determine eligibility despite the disadvantages that are discussed in this chapter.

To make decisions about eligibility, the child and family are entitled to an assessment that involves qualified personnel who represent multiple disciplines and to an evaluation and assessment of the child's current level of functioning in the following domains of development: cognition, communication, social and emotional, adaptive behavior, and physical development, including vision and hearing. No single test, instrument, or procedure may be used in isolation to make an eligibility decision.

Strategies and Techniques Planning for the strategies and techniques of the assessment process involves introducing family members to the process and its purpose, enabling families to participate in meaningful ways, and selecting assessment strategies that will yield the desired information about the young child's developmental concerns and eligibility. This step in the assessment process may be conducted by a multidisciplinary team as a series of separate sessions with professionals; however, it may be unduly taxing for the child and family. In a 1996 study, Myers, McBride, and Peterson found that arena-style, play-based assessments are accurate, valid, and less time-consuming than traditional multidisciplinary assessments.

Observations of the child in arena-style assessments will provide valuable information. Additional information can be gathered through direct testing. A number of tests are available for use in an in-depth assessment. Because standardized measures are often required by programs or funding agencies as part of the eligibility determination, some of the issues and concerns for their use are discussed.

Standardization refers to uniformity of procedure in administering and scoring the test (Anastasi, 1982). Uniformity in administration requires that the test include specific instructions that may consist of exact test materials, verbal directions, procedures for demonstrations, numbers of trials or opportunities, and time limits. Detailed instructions for scoring of individual items as well as the overall test must also be provided.

In addition, the establishment of norms is another step in the standardization of a test (Anastasi, 1982). A *norm* is the normal or average performance. To establish norms, the test is given to a large, representative sample of individuals for whom the test is designed. Norms permit the comparison of an individual's position relative to the normative or standardization sample. Very often children with disabilities or other special needs are not included in the standardization sample. Users should be cautious in interpreting test results for children who are substantially different from the standardization sample.

In evaluating the usefulness of such a test, reliability and validity are also considered. *Reliability* refers to the consistency of the test in repeated administrations. *Validity* refers to the degree to which the test actually measures what it was designed to measure (see Table 9.1). Many sourcebooks review standardized tests that may be used with very young children. Just a few of these tests are described here and others are listed in Table 9.6.

Standardized Tests Standardized tests may be used in assessing infants and children. The Bayley Scales of Infant Development (BSID) (Bayley, 1969, 1993) are among the most widely used infant tests. There are three scales: 1) the Mental Scale includes items that assess memory, habituation, problem solving, early number concepts, generalization, classification, vocalizations, language, and social skills; 2) the Motor Scale assesses control of the gross and fine muscle groups; and 3) the Behavior Rating Scale measures the qualitative aspects of the child's test session behavior

Table 9.6. Selected measures for in-depth assessment

Name	Author(s) (Date)	Age range	Description	Content
Assessing Linguistic Behavior (ALB)	Olswang, Stoel-Gammon, Coggins, and Carpenter (1987)	Birth–24 months	Assessment of early language learning and linguistic skills; observation and direct administration	Cognitive antecedents to word meaning, play, communication intention, language comprehension, language production
Battelle Developmental Inventory Screening Test	Newborg, Stock, Wnek, Guidubaldi, and Svinicki (1984)	Birth–8.5 years	Comprehensive assessment for identifying child's strengths and weaknesses and planning intervention; observation, direct testing, report	Personal-social, adaptive, motor, communication, cognition
Bayley Scales of Infant Development–Second Edition	Bayley (1993)	1–42 years	Designed to provide a basis for early diagnosis of developmental delay; direct testing by trained professional	Mental, motor, behavior rating
MacArthur Communicative Development Inventories (CDI)	Fenson et al. (1993)	8–30 months	Designed to assess young child's comprehension and production vocabularies by parent report	Words and gestures, actions and gestures, words and sentences, sentences and grammar
Peabody Developmental Motor Scales	Folio and DuBose (1983)	Birth–83 months	Designed to assess young child's gross and fine motor development; direct testing and observation	Gross and fine motor
Preschool Language Scale–3 (PLS–3)	Zimmerman, Steiner, and Pond (1992)	Birth–6 years, 11 months	Designed to identify children who have specific language problems; direct testing and observation	Auditory comprehension, expressive communication
Receptive-Expressive Emergent Language (REEL) Scale–2	Bzoch and League (1971)	Birth–3 years	Designed to assess young child's expressive and receptive language; parent interview	Receptive and expressive language
Sequenced Inventory of Communication Development (SICD)	Hedrick, Prather, and Tobin (1975)	4 months–4 years	Diagnostic instrument to assess the communication abilities of young children; direct testing and interview	Receptive and expressive language
Toddler and Infant Motor Evaluation (TIME)	Miller and Roid (1994)	4 months–3.5 years	For diagnostic assessment of children who are suspected to have motor delays or deviations and for development of treatment plans; observation, direct testing, partnership with parents	Mobility, stability, motor organization, social-emotional, functional performance

such as motor quality, attention/arousal, emotional regulation, and orientation/engagement. The BSID–II is used for children from 1 to 42 months of age.

The original version of the test was considered outstanding among infant tests in terms of the technical quality of the test construction procedures (Anastasi, 1982). The revised version, in 1991, went through a considerable development and field-testing phase and was published with acceptable levels of reliability and validity and new norms. The revised version covers an extended age and provides some new items and test materials. The most frequent use of the BSID–II is to diagnose children who have developmental delays. This test should be administered by well-trained, experienced individuals who are qualified to use, score, and interpret the test.

The Battelle Developmental Inventory (BDI) (Newborg, Stock, Wnek, Guidubaldi, & Svinicki, 1984) may be used with children from birth through 8 years of age. It provides a comprehensive assessment of the child's performance in five areas of development: personal-social, adaptive, motor, communication, and cognition. The BDI was designed for assessing children with and without disabilities. Adaptations in administration for children with disabilities are provided. The wider age range is one of the advantages of the BDI. Although it correlates well with the BSID (Boyd, Welge, Sexton, & Miller, 1989), some researchers find that it takes longer to administer and scoring may be more difficult (McLean, McCormick, Bruder, & Burdg, 1987).

Assessors must recognize some of the potential limitations of standardized tests. Such tests may restrict the child's performance because of the reliance on motor responses. These tests often rely on visual and auditory stimuli, and this may also restrict the performance of some young children. When used by a skilled assessor, these tests can be one way of gathering information. The skilled assessor views the whole child, watches for the child's efforts, and looks for the child's capabilities rather than focusing exclusively on the child's response to discrete test items. As part of the in-depth assessment, hearing and vision must also be assessed.

Assessment of Vision One of the important ways to identify young children with visual disorders or difficulties is to be alert for warning signs. Such warning signs as well as significant birth events or early history (e.g., very low birth weight) warrant a visit to an ophthalmologist who is comfortable with examining very young children. The ophthalmological examination includes examination of the eyes, assessment of visual function, and developmental history. It may include more extensive laboratory tests.

It can be difficult to assess the visual acuity of very young children. The Snellen chart that is used with older children and adults requires literacy skills. Observation and description of the young child's fixation, tracking, and visually directed reaching are part of the assessment.

Specialized techniques are available, but all have disadvantages as well as advantages. Teplin (1995) described several of these including the optokinetic nystagmus method, visually evoked potential, and preferential looking.

Forced preferential looking is based on the premise that an infant who is shown a blank target and a patterned target will prefer to look at the patterned target (Fantz, 1958). During testing, the infant is shown a number of presentations of gratings of varying stripe widths, with the left–right placement of the grating varied from one presentation to the next. The examiner uses the infant's eye and head movements to make a judgment on each trial as to the infant's preference. In this way, the infant's visual acuity is determined. The procedure has been used in research as well as in clinical practice (Dobson, 1994).

Assessment of vision should not be limited to acuity. The infant's functional vision must also be assessed. This usually requires careful observation over an extended period of time using a variety of materials. Teachers of children with visual impairments as well as other child development specialists who know the child well are often the best people to assess the child's visual function (i.e., use of vision in everyday activities). Descriptions of methods and materials are provided by Baird and Hemming (1982) and Langley (1980).

Assessment of Hearing Advances in the assessment of hearing and the field of audiology have improved the ability to identify very young children with hearing impairments (Kramer & Williams, 1993). *Auditory brain-stem response* (ABR) has become a routine procedure that can be used with newborns, including those who are premature, and infants younger than 6 months. It can also be used with older children who are uncooperative or who have difficulty with the tasks typically used to assess older children. ABR involves taping electrodes to the forehead and behind each ear. A series of clicking sounds is delivered via earphones and a burst of neural activity results. A computer averages the intensity of the responses, which are presented on a viewing screen in the form of waves. An absence of one or more of the waves suggests an abnormality in the hearing pathways. The rapidity of the conduction of the nerve impulse is also measured. This type of testing does not require active participation by the infant and can be accomplished while the infant sleeps.

A newer technique is called *otacoustic emissions* (OAE) (Lonsbury-Martin, Whitehead, & Martin, 1991). This method does not require attachment of electrodes, and a sleeping infant can be tested more quickly than by ABR. Sensitive microphones are placed at the entrance of the ear canals. Auditory stimuli are presented, and the inner ear emits a subaudible echolike sound. These emissions (or lack of) are recorded, and a computer assists in analyzing the results.

Infants older than 6 months of age may be tested reliably using *visual reinforcement audiometry* (VRA) (Thompson & Wilson, 1984). Depending on the child's developmental skills, the infant sits in an infant seat, on the parent's lap, or in a high chair in a soundproof room. The infant is taught to look at a lighted display when a sound is presented. Then, sounds of varying frequencies are presented; if the infant turns, the display lights up. VRA must be done with earphones in order to get ear-specific information.

Systematic Observations The observations of knowledgeable observers may be the most worthwhile part of the in-depth assessment process. A number of assessment tools rely on systematic observations.

For example, the Neonatal Behavioral Assessment Scales (NBAS) (Brazelton, 1973) were designed as interactive assessments of the newborn's behavioral repertoire (e.g., orientation to visual, auditory, and social stimuli) and neurological responses (e.g., reflexes). The assessment is appropriate for infants (older than 37 weeks' gestation) from the first day of life through the end of the first month. The NBAS conceptualizes the infant as active, competent, and social. The aim is to identify the infant's best performance. The examiner assesses the infant's ability to modulate its own systems in response to external manipulation.

An interesting clinical application of the NBAS is its use as a teaching tool with parents. The examiner assesses the infant in the parents' presence so that the infant's skills and capabilities are demonstrated. By observing methods to comfortably handle and position the baby, strategies to facilitate behaviors, and other responsive techniques, parents are alerted to their infant's own particular signals. This relatively simple intervention may help parents learn that their babies are capable and may also promote significant changes in parenting skills and knowledge of child development (Nugent, 1985; Szajnberg, Ward, Krauss, & Kessler, 1987; Widmayer & Field, 1981). For example, the public health nurse for Orion (see below) is using the NBAS to demonstrate Orion's capabilities to his parents.

The Assessment of Preterm Infants' Behavior (APIB) (Als, Lester, Tronick, & Brazelton, 1982) was designed as a refinement and extension of the NBAS for preterm infants and infants at high risk. It includes many of the NBAS items and presents them in graduated fashion to observe the infant's current level of organization in the presence of varying demands. Five subsystems are observed: physiological, motor, state, interactive and attentional, and self-regulation. A trained examiner utilizes the APIB to assess the very young infant's current status and to identify the amount of support needed to optimize the infant's development and organization.

The Infant Behavioral Assessment (IBA) (Hedlund & Tataka, 1989) is a time sampling of infant communicative behaviors designed for use with infants birth through 6 months of age. It is designed for infants with complex health needs or who are at high risk for developmental difficulties. The user observes the infant (live or videotaped) during a caregiving or developmental task, and then scores the IBA by noting the occurrence of autonomic, motor, state, and attention/interactional behaviors (discrete behaviors are operationally defined). The major uses of the IBA are 1) to provide an objective measure of an infant's neurobehavioral organization, 2) to increase the interventionist's awareness of an infant's communicative behaviors, and 3) to provide a framework for parent support. Specialized training is required to use the IBA.

The Play Assessment Scale (Fewell, 1991) is a useful instrument for assessing the young child's play with toys or objects. The scale consists of 45 behaviors representing typical play behaviors of children from birth to 3 years of age. Readily available toys and objects are the assessment stimuli. Both spontaneous play and facilitated play may be observed. A play age can be determined. The scale is perhaps most useful for describing a child's approach to and use of toys, identifying intervention targets, and understanding the effectiveness and need for assistance or prompting. Additional play measures are described by Fewell and Glick (1993).

TPBA (Linder, 1993) is a functional assessment process designed for young children between the ages of 6 months and 6 years. The process involves observation of the child while the child interacts with a play facilitator (e.g., parent, caregiver, team member, peer). The facilitator follows the child's lead to encourage optimal performance, but also gently leads the child through the play session so that the child's

Orion

Orion is 2 weeks old. He was born early and weighed about 5 pounds. He lives at home with his first-time parents. Today, the public health nurse comes for a visit. One of the things that she does is show Orion's parents how he responds to sounds, how his states change, his reflexes, and his responses to interaction. Orion's parents are fascinated by how many things their little boy can do and how he can communicate with them.

performance across all areas of development may be observed. TPBA includes systematic observation guidelines, worksheets for analyzing observations, and summary sheets.

Criterion-Referenced Measures In contrast to norm-referenced measures, criterion-referenced measures compare a child's performance with a specified level or standard of achievement. *Curriculum-based measures* are a form of criterion-referenced assessment. Curriculum-based measures assess the child's achievements along a continuum of objectives, especially within a developmentally sequenced curriculum (Neisworth & Bagnato, 1988). These sorts of assessment tools may have greater utility than norm-referenced tests for describing the child's capabilities. They are discussed in more detail in the section on assessment for program planning.

Family Participation Family participation in the assessment process has been described in a number of ways already. The in-depth assessment phase may be particularly stressful and emotional for the family because the purpose is to confirm or disconfirm a developmental delay or disability. The professional team members, by their attitude and behaviors, can help families to participate and contribute. They can do this by clearly explaining the assessment process and what to expect. They can encourage family participation by listening to and valuing the family's concerns, by encouraging their participation throughout the process, by sharing their findings, and by following through to ensure a shared understanding of the assessment process and findings.

Assessment of Family Issues As one way of ensuring family involvement in early intervention, Part H guidelines (PL 101-476) provide for a statement of the family's resources, priorities, and concerns. As with any assessment procedure, the purpose of family assessment needs to be carefully considered. In most situations, it will be simply to work with the family to help them pinpoint their strengths and resources as well as their needs and concerns. This can be accomplished through an interview, as previously described.

Sometimes a written needs inventory or specialized assessment scale will help to structure the interview. If the interview is too open ended, a family member may not focus on areas of true concern. Or, without the support of suggestions provided by a scale or skilled interviewer, families may not think of their rich support system of family, friends, and co-workers in relation to their child with disabilities. In a study of parental perspectives on the use of written surveys, Bailey and Blasco (1990) found that such a survey was useful and acceptable, although parents provided a range of individual views. Parents also reported that parental choice in the method for sharing information is critical.

A growing number of specialized scales is available to early intervention teams. These scales, if used at all, should be used judiciously. Some of the available scales were not designed for early intervention purposes and, unfortunately, focus on deficits or negative aspects of family functioning. Such scales are not useful for early intervention teams whose purposes are to identify needs, sources of formal and informal support, other resources, and strategies to obtain or mobilize resources (Slentz & Bricker, 1992). Early intervention teams must clearly recognize their limits and make appropriate referrals when family needs are such that they cannot be met by the early intervention program. Some examples of measures that can help a family identify its strengths, needs, and resources include the following:

- Family Needs Survey (Bailey & Simeonsson, 1985)
- Family Support Scale (Dunst, Jenkins, & Trivette, 1988)

- Family Strengths Scale (Olson, Larsen, & McCubbin, 1983)
- How Can We Help? (Child Development Resources, 1988)
- Personal Network Matrix (Trivette & Dunst, 1988)

Parent–Child Interactions Valuable information can be obtained from observations of parent–child interaction. Interactions between a parent and a young child can be experiences of joy. These interactions set the stage for social, cognitive, and communication development. When the child is at risk for developmental difficulties, these interactions may be jeopardized. The promotion of productive and pleasurable interactions between parent and child is a likely goal of early intervention specialists.

Available measures of parent–child interaction include rating scales that provide somewhat broad categories, such as responsivity and warmth, more narrowly defined coding systems of targeted behaviors, and observational checklists (see Table 9.7). Rosenberg, Robinson, and Beckman (1986) suggested that measures of parent–child interaction should allow for reliable assessments even if a member of the dyad displays ambiguous behavior, should be easily incorporated within an intervention program, and should identify effective intervention strategies. Measures and their guidelines for use should also include instructions for administration and interpretation that incorporate contextual information.

A frequent comment from interventionists as well as from parents is that measures of parent–child interaction, like some family assessment measures, can be intrusive. After all, the parent expects that the child will be observed but usually does not expect that they, the parents, will also be observed. Because many methods rely on videotape, the procedure itself may produce anxiety if not used carefully. It is suggested that such measures be used following a period of trust and rapport building among parents, infants, and professional team members. Observation and taping should take place in a comfortable setting to ensure the family's privacy, whether in the family home, clinic, or other location. Videotaping can be an extremely useful medium for both parents and professionals. Parents often can identify both effective and ineffective interaction strategies upon viewing segments of interaction.

The information gathered from the in-depth assessment is compiled, integrated, and synthesized. If the child is in need of special services, meets the eligibility criteria for Part H services, and the family chooses to enroll their child in such services, an individualized plan is developed. The process for developing the individualized family service plan (IFSP) is described in Chapter 10.

Assessment for Program Planning

The IFSP is the plan to implement the services and supports that the child and family need. Now, the connection between assessment and intervention comes even closer. The IFSP provides direction; however, as intervention in the form of educational and therapy services occurs, more information is gathered, responses to intervention are observed, and the interplay of assessment and intervention is in full swing. Guidelines and strategies for gathering information for program planning will follow; but because this phase of assessment is so closely tied with intervention, this discussion continues in Chapter 11.

The purpose of assessment at this phase is to determine the young child's current level of functioning, to clarify strengths and needs, and to identify intervention

Table 9.7. Selected measures of parent–child interaction

Name	Author(s) (Date)	Focus	Format
ECO	MacDonald and Gillette (1989)	Adult and child variables in the areas of social play, turn-taking, communication, language, and conversational pragmatics	Rating scales scored following observation of play and an interview; linked to intervention program
Maternal Behavior Rating Scale	Mahoney, Finger, and Powell (1985)	Parent variables such as sensitivity, responsiveness, physical handling, warmth	Likert-type rating scale scored following observation of videotaped free play
Nursing Child Assessment Teaching and Feeding Scale	Barnard (1978)	Parent and infant variables such as verbalizations, clarity of cues, responsiveness	Checklist based on observation of short, teaching session, feeding session
Parent Behavior Progression	Bromwich (1981)	Parent variables such as pleasure, variety of stimulation, response to signals	Binary checklist based on observations and conversations
Parent/Caregiver Involvement Scale	Farran, Kasari, Comfort, and Jay (1986)	Parent variables such as responsiveness, control, verbalizations	Rating scale scored following live or taped free play
Social Interaction Assessment/Intervention (SAIA)	McCollum and Stayton (1985)	Parent and infant variables such as turn-taking, imitation, vocalizations	Behavioral count scored from videotaped play interaction
Teaching Skills Inventory	Rosenberg, Robinson, and Beckman (1984)	Parent variables such as clarity of instructions, effectiveness of prompts, task modification	Rating scale scored following observation of videotaped interaction

techniques that can be incorporated into the intervention plan. Some of the assessment tools and procedures described in previous sections may well provide the starting point for planning intervention.

The intervention team attempts to answer many questions. One question is, what can the infant do? Does the child respond to sounds, babble, grasp, and play pat-a-cake? The intervention team is interested not only in what the child does but also in the quality of performance. For example, an infant may bang toys together by holding them securely in each hand and bringing them together at midline, or the infant may brace one toy against a surface and bang another against it. The infant may perform the behavior purposefully and display pleasure in the performance, or the infant may knock the toys together with seeming lack of interest. Interventionists are interested in quantitative and qualitative aspects of the child's behavior.

In addition to determining what the infant does and how, another question is, what are the best ways to support the infant's development and learning? Is the infant demonstrating solid patterns? Does the infant demonstrate clusters of similar skills? Or is the infant displaying isolated or scattered skills? For example, a child may be able to tower blocks but unable to demonstrate other activities requiring eye–hand coordination, such as stacking other objects or dropping pop beads into a bottle.

Interventionists also ask, what is the infant unable to do and why not? For example, a young child with cerebral palsy may not be able to pull a string to get the attached object. Is the child failing to perform the task because of lack of the cognitive requisites or because the child cannot perform the necessary physical movements? Unsuccessful attempts may signal the need for practice or intervention or may signal the need for alternative or adaptive strategies for that child.

A further question is, what contextual variables will best support the child's development and learning? The infant may do best when interacting with a particular person, or in a particular position or setting, or with favorite toys and materials. These factors need to be considered both for assessment and intervention.

Strategies and Techniques As in earlier phases of assessment, the selection of appropriate strategies and techniques is a critical function of the team. Likewise, the family remains involved during this phase to ensure that intervention planning addresses their concerns and uses approaches that fit their child and family.

Curriculum-Based Measures Curriculum-based measures are appropriate tools for identifying outcomes, goals, and objectives. Curriculum-based measures ensure that assessment and intervention are connected. They make assessment directly relevant to program planning and monitoring. A selection of these is provided in Table 9.8. Curriculum-based measures typically use direct observation of the child and may use some direct testing.

In selecting a curriculum-based measure, there are several important characteristics to consider: 1) the format should ensure that children are assessed in familiar settings with familiar people, 2) the measure should accommodate a range of abilities and also allow for adaptations, 3) the measure should include logical developmental sequences of important and functional behaviors, and 4) performance criteria should be stated. In addition, the measure should allow for flexibility in administration such that the assessor can find out what the child can do independently, what the child can do with assistance, and how the child responds to assistance.

Environments Sometimes it will be helpful to assess the child's environments in order to determine if they are facilitating development and learning. Such an assessment can provide information for ways to modify the environment.

The most widely known and frequently used measure of the home environment is the Home Observation and Measurement of the Environment (HOME) (Caldwell & Bradley, 1984). The HOME measures the content, quality, and responsiveness of a young child's home environment. The version for children between birth and 3 years consists of six subscales:

1. Emotional and verbal responsiveness of mother
2. Avoidance of restriction and punishment
3. Organization of physical and temporal environment
4. Provision of appropriate play materials
5. Maternal involvement with child
6. Opportunities for variety in daily stimulation

The HOME is completed by a trained observer during a home visit. Interventionists should use the HOME cautiously. The interventionist's primary goal is to create a positive relationship with the parents so that issues and concerns can be addressed. Sometimes the use of a formal observation tool hinders the formation of such a relationship. Interventionists will also need to examine the HOME (or other measure of home environments) to ensure that the measure is culturally sensitive.

Another environment for many young children is their child care or development center. The Infant-Toddler Environment Rating Scale (ITERS) (Harms, Cryer,

Table 9.8. Selected curriculum-based measures

Name	Author(s) (Date)	Age range	Description	Content
Assessment, Evaluation, and Programming System (AEPS) for Infants and Young Children: Vol. 1. Measurement for Birth to Three Years	Bricker (1993)	Birth–3 years	Designed for assessment to determine goals and objectives, intervention activities, monitor progress; also includes family forms	Fine motor, gross motor, self-care, social-communication, social
Brigance Diagnostic Inventory of Early Development–Revised	Brigance (1991)	Birth–6 years	Assessment of developmental status, targeting objectives, monitoring progress	Psychomotor, self-help, communication, general knowledge, comprehension, social and emotional, readiness, basic reading, writing, math
Callier-Azusa Scale: G Form	Stillman (1978)	Birth–9 years	Assessment of development in children who are deaf-blind, multiply disabled	Motor, perceptual, daily living, socialization, language
The Carolina Curriculum for Infants and Toddlers with Special Needs (2nd ed.)	Johnson-Martin, Jens, Attermeier, and Hacker (1991)	Birth–24 months	Assessment of child's developmental abilities for entry into the curriculum, monitors progress	Cognition, communication, social adaptation, fine motor, gross motor
Early Intervention Developmental Profile	Rogers, D'Eugenio, Brown, Donovan, and Lynch (1981)	Birth–36 months	Comprehensive developmental assessment and program planning	Cognition, fine motor/perceptual, gross motor, self-help, language, personal-social
Hawaii Early Learning Profile (HELP)	Furuno et al. (1979)	Birth–36 months	Assessment of a child's strengths and weaknesses; provides activities, charts progress	Cognition, language, gross motor, social-emotional, self-help
Learning Accomplishment Profile for Infants, Revised (Early LAP)	Glover, Preminger, and Sanford (1978)	Birth–36 months	Designed to provide a profile of overall development of the young child	Fine and gross motor, social, self-help, language, cognition
Transdisciplinary Play-Based Assessment: A Functional Approach to Working with Young Children (Rev. ed.)	Linder (1993)	6 months–6 years	Designed to provide a comprehensive, integrated view of the child's development, style, interaction patterns; includes worksheets and summary sheets	Cognition, social-emotional, communication and language, sensorimotor

& Clifford, 1990) is designed to assess the quality of care for children under 30 months of age. Subscales of this measure include personal care routines, furnishings and displays for children, listening and talking skills, learning activities, interaction skills, program structure, and adult needs. A comparable scale is the Family Day Care Rating Scale (FDCRS) (Harms & Clifford, 1990) for assessing family child care environments. Again, the purpose of environmental assessments is to gain information that can be useful for determining the match between the child and the environment and for planning changes if needed. Environments are complex and dynamic; multiple measures and methods should be used as in all phases of assessment.

SUMMARY

This chapter provided information on a family-directed, developmental framework for assessment in early intervention. This framework requires comprehensive knowledge of child development, formation of partnerships with families, and an understanding of contextual influences on development and learning. Carefully linked with the assessment of the child is the identification of the family's resources, concerns, hopes, and dreams. An overriding goal of assessment is to figure out the best ways to support the infant's or toddler's development and learning within the family and community. Chapter 11 examines those strategies and methods that can provide this support in greater detail.

REFERENCES

Alpern, G., Boll, T., & Shearer, M. (1980). *Developmental Profile II.* Aspen, CO: Psychological Development Publications.

Als, H., Lester, B.M., Tronick, E.C., & Brazelton, T.B. (1982). Towards a research instrument for the assessment of preterm infants' behavior (APIB). In H.E. Fitzgerald, B.M. Lester, & M.W. Yogman (Eds.), *Theory and research in behavioral pediatrics* (Vol. 1, pp. 1–35). New York: Plenum.

American Speech-Language-Hearing Association (ASHA). (1990). *Guidelines for practices in early intervention.* Rockville, MD: Author.

Anastasi, A. (1982). *Psychological testing* (5th ed.). New York: Macmillan.

Apgar, V. (1953). A proposal for a new method of evaluation of the newborn infant. *Current Researches in Anesthesia and Analgesia, 32*(4), 260–267.

Bailey, D.B., & Blasco, P.M. (1990). Parents' perspectives on a written survey of family needs. *Journal of Early Intervention, 14*(3), 196–203.

Bailey, D.B., & Simeonsson, R.J. (1985). *Family Needs Survey.* Chapel Hill: University of North Carolina, Frank Porter Graham Child Development Center.

Baird, A.S., Hemming, A.M. (1982). Neonatal vision screening. *Journal of Visual Impairment and Blindness, 76*(5), 182–185.

Barnard, K. (1978). *Nursing Child Assessment Teaching and Feeding Scale.* Seattle: University of Washington.

Bayley, N. (1969). *Bayley Scales of Infant Development.* New York: Psychological Corporation.

Bayley, N. (1993). *Bayley Scales of Infant Development—Second Edition.* San Antonio, TX: Psychological Corporation.

Boyd, R.D., Welge, P., Sexton, D., & Miller, J.H. (1989). Concurrent validity of the Battelle Developmental Inventory: Relationship with the Bayley Scales in young children with known or suspected disabilities. *Journal of Early Intervention, 13*(1), 14–23.

Brazelton, T.B. (1973). *Neonatal Behavioral Assessment Scales.* Philadelphia: J.B. Lippincott.

Bricker, D. (Ed.). (1993). *Assessment, Evaluation, and Programming System (AEPS) for infants and young children: Vol. 1. Measurement for birth to three years.* Baltimore: Paul H. Brookes Publishing Co.

Bricker, D., Squires, J., & Mounts, L. (1995). *Ages & Stages Questionnaires (ASQ): A parent-completed child-monitoring system.* Baltimore: Paul H. Brookes Publishing Co.
Brigance, A.H. (1991). *Brigance Diagnostic Inventory of Early Development–Revised.* North Billerica, IL: Curriculum Associates.
Bromwich, R. (1981). *Working with parents and infants: An interactional approach.* Baltimore: University Park Press.
Bzoch, K., & League, R. (1971). *Receptive-Expressive Emergent Language (REEL) Scale–2.* Austin, TX: PRO-ED.
Caldwell, B., & Bradley, R. (1984). *Home Observation for Measurement of the Environment (HOME).* Little Rock: University of Arkansas at Little Rock, Center for Research on Teaching and Learning.
Child Development Resources. (1988). *How can we help?* Lightfoot, VA: Author.
Child Development Resources. (1992). *Transdisciplinary arena assessment process viewing guide.* Lightfoot, VA: Author.
Coplan, J. (1993). *Early Language Milestone Scale* (2nd. ed.). Austin, TX: PRO-ED.
Cripe, J.W. (1993). *Developing a linked system approach to early intervention.* Unpublished manuscript.
DEC Task Force on Recommended Practices. (1993). *DEC recommended practices: Indicators of quality in programs for infants and young children with special needs and their families.* Reston, VA: Council for Exceptional Children.
Dobson, V. (1994). Visual acuity testing by preferential looking techniques. In S.J. Isenberg (Ed.), *The eye in infancy* (2nd ed.). St. Louis: C.V. Mosby.
Dunst, C.J., Jenkins, V., & Trivette, C.M. (1988). Family Support Scale. In C.J. Dunst, C.M. Trivette, & A.G. Deal (Eds.), *Enabling and empowering families: Principles and guidelines for practice* (pp. 155–157). Cambridge, MA: Brookline Books.
Education for All Handicapped Children Act of 1975, PL 94-142, 20 U.S.C. § 1400 *et seq.*
Fantz, R. (1958). Pattern vision in young infants. *Psychological Record, 8*(2), 43–49.
Farran, D., Kasari, C., Comfort, M., & Jay, S. (1986). *Parent/Caregiver Involvement Scale.* Greensboro: University of North Carolina, Continuing Education.
Fenson, L., Dale, P., Reznick, J.S., Thal, D., Bates, E., Hartung, J., Pethick, S., & Reilly, J. (1993). *MacArthur Communicative Development Inventories (CDI).* San Diego: Singular Publishing Co.
Fewell, R.R. (1991). *Play Assessment Scale.* Miami, FL: University of Miami.
Fewell, R.R., & Glick, M.P. (1993). Observing play: An appropriate process for learning and assessment. *Infants and Young Children, 5*(4), 35–43.
Fewell, R.R., & Langley, M.B. (1984). *DASI–II: Developmental Activities Screening Inventory.* Austin, TX: PRO-ED.
Folio, M., & DuBose, R.F. (1983). *Peabody Developmental Motor Scales.* Allen, TX: Teaching Resources.
Frankenburg, W.K., Dodds, J., Archer, P., Bresnick, B., Mashka, P., Edelman, N., & Shapiro, H. (1990). *Denver Developmental Screening Test (Denver–II).* Denver, CO: Denver Developmental Materials, Inc.
Furuno, S., O'Reilly, A., Hosaka, C.M., Inatsuka, T.T., Allman, T.L., & Zelsloft, B. (1979). *The Hawaii Early Learning Profile.* Palo Alto, CA: Vort Corp.
Glover, M.E., Preminger, J.L., & Sanford, A.R. (1978). *Learning Accomplishment Profile for Infants (Early LAP).* Winston-Salem, NC: Kaplan School Supply.
Goodwin, W.L., & Driscoll, L.A. (1980). *Handbook for measurement and evaluation in early childhood education.* San Francisco: Jossey-Bass.
Greenspan, S.I., & Meisels, S.J. (1994). Toward a new vision for developmental assessment of infants and young children. *Zero to Three, 14*(6), 1–8.
Hanson, M.J., & Lynch, E.W. (1995). *Early intervention: Implementing child and family services for infants and toddlers who are at risk or disabled.* Austin, TX: PRO-ED.
Harbin, G., Danaher, J., & Derrick, T. (1994). Comparison of eligibility policies for infant/toddler programs and preschool special education programs. *Topics in Early Childhood Special Education, 14*(4), 455–471.
Harbin, G., Gallagher, J., & Terry, D. (1991). Defining the eligible population: Policy issues and challenges. *Journal of Early Intervention, 15*(1), 13–20.
Harms, T., & Clifford, R.M. (1990). *The Family Day Care Rating Scale.* New York: Teachers College Press.

Harms, T., Cryer, D., & Clifford, R.M. (1990). *Infant/toddler environment rating scale.* New York: Teachers College Press.

Hedlund, R., & Tataka, M. (1989). *Infant Behavioral Assessment (IBA) training manual.* Seattle, WA: Child Development and Mental Retardation Center.

Hedrick, D.L., Prather, E.M., & Tobin, A.R. (1975). *Sequenced Inventory of Communication Development (SICD).* Seattle: University of Washington Press.

Hills, T.W. (1992). Reaching potentials through appropriate assessment. In S. Bredekamp & T. Rosegrant (Eds.), *Reaching potentials: Appropriate curriculum and assessment for young children* (Vol. 1, pp. 43–63). Washington, DC: National Association for the Education of Young Children.

Individuals with Disabilities Education Act (IDEA) of 1990, PL 101-476, 20 U.S.C. § 1400 *et seq.*

Johnson-Martin, N.M., Jens, K.G., Attermeier, S.M., & Hacker, B.J. (1991). *The Carolina Curriculum for infants and toddlers with special needs* (2nd ed.). Baltimore: Paul H. Brookes Publishing Co.

Kramer, S.J., & Williams, D.R. (1993). The hearing-impaired infant and toddler: Identification, assessment, and intervention. *Infants and Young Children, 6*(1), 35–49.

Langley, M.B. (1980). *Functional vision inventory for the multiple and severely handicapped.* Chicago: Stoelting.

Linder, T.W. (1993). *Transdisciplinary play-based assessment: A functional approach to working with young children* (Rev. ed.). Baltimore: Paul H. Brookes Publishing Co.

Lonsbury-Martin, B., Whitehead, M., & Martin, G. (1991). Clinical applications of otoacoustic emissions. *Journal of Speech and Hearing Research, 34*(5), 964–981.

MacDonald, J., & Gillette, Y. (1989). *ECO: A partnership program.* Chicago: Riverside Publishing.

Mahoney, G., Finger, I., & Powell, A. (1985). The relationship of maternal behavioral style to the development of organically impaired mentally retarded infants. *American Journal of Mental Deficiency, 90*(3), 296–302.

McCollum, J., & Stayton, V. (1985). Infant/parent interaction: Studies and intervention guidelines based on the SIAI model. *Journal of the Division for Early Childhood, 9*(2), 125–135.

McLean, M., McCormick, K., Bruder, M.B., & Burdg, N. (1987). An investigation of the validity and reliability of the Battelle Developmental Inventory with a population of children younger than 30 months with identified handicapping conditions. *Journal of the Division for Early Childhood, 11*(3), 238–246.

Meisels, S., & Provence, S. (1989). *Screening and assessment: Guidelines for identifying young disabled and developmentally vulnerable children.* Washington, DC: National Center for Clinical Infant Programs.

Miller, L., & Roid, G. (1994). *Toddler and Infant Motor Evaluation (TIME).* San Antonio, TX: Psychological Corporation.

Myers, C.L., McBride, S.L., & Peterson, C.A. (1996). Transdisciplinary, play-based assessment in early childhood special education: An examination of social validity. *Topics in Early Childhood Special Education, 16*(1), 102–126.

National Association for School Psychologists (NASP). (1991). *Position statement on early childhood assessment.* Bethesda, MD: Author.

Neisworth, J.T., & Bagnato, S.J. (1988). Assessment in early childhood special education: A typology of dependent measures. In S.L. Odom & M.B. Karnes (Eds.), *Early intervention for infants and children with handicaps* (pp. 23–49). Baltimore: Paul H. Brookes Publishing Co.

Newborg, J., Stock, J.R., Wnek, L., Guidubaldi, J., & Svinicki, J. (1984). *Battelle Developmental Inventory.* Allen, TX: Teaching Resources.

Nugent, J.K. (1985). *Using the NBAS with infants and their families.* White Plains, NY: March of Dimes.

Olson, D.H., Larsen, A.S., & McCubbin, H.I. (1983). Family strengths. In D.H. Olson, H.L. Muxen, & M.A. Wilson (Eds.), *Families: What makes them work?* (pp. 261–262). Beverly Hills: Sage Publications.

Olswang, L., Stoel-Gammon, C., Coggins, T., & Carpenter, R. (1987). *Assessing Linguistic Behavior.* Seattle: University of Washington Press.

Peterson, N. (1987). *Early intervention for handicapped and at-risk children.* Denver, CO: Love Publishing.

Rogers, S.J. (1982). Techniques of infant assessment. In G. Ulrey & S.J. Rogers (Eds.), *Psychological assessment of handicapped infants and young children* (pp. 59–64). New York: Thieme-Stratton.

Rogers, S.J., D'Eugenio, D.B., Brown, S.L., Donovan, C.M., & Lynch, E.W. (1981). *Early Intervention Developmental Profile.* Ann Arbor: University of Michigan Press.

Rosenberg, S., Robinson, C., & Beckman, P. (1984). Teaching skills inventory: A measure of parent performance. *Journal of the Division for Early Childhood, 8*(2), 107–113.

Rosenberg, S.A., Robinson, C.C., & Beckman, P.J. (1986). Measures of parent–infant interaction: An overview. *Topics in Early Childhood Special Education, 6*(2), 32–43.

Slentz, K., & Bricker, D. (1992). Family-guided assessment for IFSP development: Jumping off the family-assessment bandwagon. *Journal of Early Intervention, 16*(1), 11–19.

Stillman, R. (Ed.). (1978). *The Callier-Azusa Scale.* Reston, VA: Council for Exceptional Children.

Szajnberg, N., Ward, M.J., Krauss, A., & Kessler, D.B. (1987). Low birth-weight prematures: Preventive intervention and maternal attitude. *Child Psychiatry and Human Development, 17*(3), 152–165.

Teplin, S.W. (1995). Visual impairment in infants and young children. *Infants and Young Children, 8*(1), 18–51.

Thompson, G., & Wilson, W. (1984). Clinical application of visual reinforcement audiometry. In J. Northern & W. Perkins (Eds.), *Seminars in hearing: Early identification of hearing loss in infants* (Vol. 5[1], pp. 85–99). New York: Thieme-Stratton.

Trivette, C.M., & Dunst, C.J. (1988). Personal network matrix: A system for assessing family needs and support. In C.J. Dunst, C.M. Trivette, & A.G. Deal (Eds.), *Enabling and empowering families: Principles and guidelines for practice* (pp. 165–174). Cambridge, MA: Brookline Books.

Ulrey, G., & Rogers, S.J. (1982). *Psychological assessment of handicapped infants and young children.* New York: Thieme-Stratton.

Widmayer, S., & Field, T. (1981). Effects of Brazelton demonstrations for mothers on the development of preterm infants. *Pediatrics, 67*(5), 711–714.

Winton, P.J., & Bailey, D.B. (1988). The family focused interview: A collaborative mechanism for family assessment and goal-setting. *Journal of the Division for Early Childhood, 12*(3), 195–207.

Wolery, M., & Dyk, L. (1984). Arena assessment: Description and preliminary social validity data. *Journal of The Association for the Severely Handicapped, 9*(3), 231–235.

Zimmerman, I., Steiner, V., & Pond, R. (1992). *Preschool Language Scale–3 (PLS-3).* San Antonio, TX: Psychological Corporation.

9 ACTIVITIES

1. Talk with some early interventionists about the assessment procedures and methods they use in their programs or practices. Ask them how satisfied they are with the procedures and methods. Ask how useful they are for planning intervention activities.

2. Practice your observation skills. Develop or locate a simple observation tool. Visit an early intervention program, child care center, or play group. Observe at least two children for a minimum of 15 minutes each. What have you observed? How useful was your observation method? What else could you learn from doing observations?

3. Select a partner for a role play in which one of you is the parent and the other is an early interventionist. Role play the following situation: The early interventionist telephones the parent in preparation for a clinic visit. The purpose of the clinic visit will be an assessment of this parent's 6-month-old child to determine eligibility for early intervention services. After the role play, discuss it in terms of the family-centered principles that you have read about thus far.

4. Locate an early intervention program that uses play-based, arena-style assessment procedures. Obtain permission to observe an assessment. Write a critique.

CHAPTER 10

The Individualized Family Service Plan

Susan R. Sandall

Objectives

- To understand the components and requirements for the individualized family service plan (IFSP)
- To recognize the importance of planning and participating in the IFSP process

A major requirement and a guiding feature of early intervention services, as outlined in Part H of IDEA (PL 101-476) is the individualized family service plan (IFSP). The IFSP includes specific expected outcomes and serves as the plan of action for achieving those outcomes. The IFSP venture involves family and early intervention professionals working together to develop a plan that describes the services and supports that will enhance the development of the child and the capacity of the family to meet the special needs of the child (*Federal Register,* 1989). The law and regulations that provide guidance for developing IFSPs recognize the family as the central focus of early intervention policies and practices. That is, families are the context within which early intervention efforts take place.

The NEC*TAS Expert Team for the IFSP, a national task force, developed the following set of principles to guide the IFSP process:

- Infants and toddlers are uniquely dependent on their families for their survival and nurturance. This dependence necessitates a family-centered approach to early intervention.

Alicia

Alicia is a 15-month-old girl with myelomeningocele. She lives at home with her mother, father, and two older brothers (James, 6, and Mark, 5).

Alicia was born by planned cesarean section following prenatal diagnosis. The lesion (located in the lumbar area) was surgically closed shortly after birth. After 5 days in the hospital, Alicia joined her family at home.

Alicia wore a hip splint during the neonatal period. She had a shunt inserted at 6 months of age to prevent hydrocephalus. At 8 months of age, she had surgery on her feet and ankles and was in casts for about 6 weeks. She now wears plastic ankle / foot orthoses.

Alicia's family, the Bensons, live in a neighborhood of houses and apartment buildings in a large city. Alicia's health care is provided by a team at a local health maintenance organization (HMO). During her first 3 months of life, Alicia received outpatient physical therapy through the HMO. For a variety of reasons, the Bensons then enrolled Alicia in a center-based early intervention program. At the center, Alicia receives services from a teacher, physical therapist, and speech therapist. There is also a social worker on the team. Over the past year, the frequency and intensity of services have changed depending on Alicia's needs, family requests, and scheduling issues. At the present time, Alicia attends the center twice a week. In the first session, she is seen individually by the teacher and physical therapist. The second session is conducted as an integrated play group with three other children. The speech therapist and teacher facilitate this session. In addition, the teacher makes a home visit about once a month, usually in the early evening.

Both Mr. and Mrs. Benson work full time outside the home. Finding suitable child care has always been a problem. Currently the boys go to an after-school child care center. A woman in the neighborhood cares for Alicia and transports her to the early intervention center. This will soon end, however, as the woman plans to return to other work.

Mrs. Benson is able to attend Alicia's sessions by scheduling her lunch break at the same time. Mr. Benson's work schedule doesn't allow this on a regular basis, although he has attended a few times. Evening home visits allow Alicia's father and brothers to participate and learn more about her intervention program. It is now time for Alicia, her family, and the other members of the team to develop a new IFSP.

- States and programs should define "family" in a way that reflects the diversity of family patterns and structures.
- Each family has its own structure, roles, values, beliefs, and coping styles. Respect for and acceptance of this diversity is a cornerstone of family-centered early intervention.
- Early intervention systems and strategies must honor the racial, ethnic, cultural, and socioeconomic diversity of families.

- Respect for family autonomy, independence, and decision making means that families must be able to choose the level and nature of early intervention's involvement in their lives.
- Family/professional collaboration and partnerships are the keys to family-centered early intervention and to successful implementation of the IFSP process.
- An enabling approach to working with families requires that professionals reexamine their traditional roles and practices and develop new practices when necessary—practices that promote mutual respect and partnerships.
- Early intervention services should be flexible, accessible, and responsive to family-identified needs.
- Early intervention services should be provided according to the normalization principle—that is, families should have access to services provided in as normal a fashion and environment as possible and that promote the integration of the child and family within the community.
- No one agency or discipline can meet the diverse and complex needs of infants and toddlers with special needs and their families. Therefore, a team approach to planning and implementing the IFSP is necessary. (McGonigel, 1991, p. 9)

Alicia *(continued)*

Alicia is being reassessed to evaluate her progress, to update her IFSP, and to identify new intervention targets and other outcomes. The early intervention center uses a transdisciplinary model and arena assessment. The team consists of Alicia's parents, teacher, physical therapist, speech therapist, and social worker. The physical therapist is the service coordinator. About a week ago, Mr. and Mrs. Benson and the service coordinator talked about priorities and concerns for this reassessment. These included a request for more information on Alicia's progress toward walking with assistance and talking and a need for alternative child care. The early intervention program typically uses the Assessment, Evaluation, and Programming System (AEPS) (Bricker, 1993) for reassessments. It was decided that the AEPS, along with an evaluation by the physical therapist, observation of play and eating, and a focused interview with the social worker, would fulfill the purposes identified by the family and the other members of the team. It was also decided that the assessment could be accomplished during Alicia's usual individual session by extending the time a bit.

The session was structured as follows: 20 minutes free play with mother; 20 minutes with the physical therapist to check reflexes, reactions, and quality of movement; snack with mother; and mother's interview with the social worker while Alicia played with the other members of the team. When the team set up this schedule they noted that, because language was a priority, the speech therapist should interject suggestions as needed to encourage communicative behavior. The team also noted that the times were only approximate and that they would follow Alicia and her mother's lead.

Because Alicia was familiar with the playroom and was used to adults being present, very little warm-up time was needed. During the play time,

(continued)

(continued)

the physical therapist sat near Mrs. Benson. The other team members sat away from the play area. Each team member had a copy of the AEPS. Their primary responsibility was to complete "their" section (e.g., the teacher completed the cognitive section). In addition, team members recorded their observations across domains. The speech therapist also collected a communication sample by writing down Alicia's communicative intents as they occurred and noting the form (gestural or verbal).

The social worker used the Bensons' priority concerns as topics during the interview. She also asked Mrs. Benson if she would like to look at or complete the Family Support Scale. She suggested that this might help their discussion of child care options. Mrs. Benson willingly completed the scale.

As the interview drew to a close, the other team members joined Mrs. Benson and the social worker. The team took this time to discuss their observations and initial results. Mrs. Benson shared her impressions of Alicia's behaviors that day and compared them with what she is able to do at home. The service coordinator suggested that in the time before the IFSP meeting, Mr. and Mrs. Benson might want to write down their observations and any concerns about Alicia. Mrs. Benson thought this was a good idea and suggested that the babysitter could add her observations also. At this point, the team made plans for a meeting to revise the IFSP.

COMPONENTS OF THE IFSP

The law specifies that the IFSP shall include the following:

1. A statement of the infant's or toddler's present levels of physical development (including vision, hearing, and health status), cognitive development, communication development, social or emotional development, and adaptive development, based on acceptable, objective criteria.
2. A statement of the family's resources, priorities, and concerns relating to enhancing the family's capacity to meet the developmental needs of their infant or toddler with a disability.
3. A statement of the major outcomes expected to be achieved for the infant or toddler and family, and the criteria, procedures, and time lines to be used to track progress and to determine whether modifications or revisions of the goals or services are necessary.
4. A statement of specific early intervention services necessary to meet the needs of the infant or toddler and the family and of the necessary frequency, intensity, and method of delivering services.
5. A statement of the natural environments in which early intervention services shall appropriately be provided.
6. The projected dates for initiation of services and the anticipated duration of such services.
7. The name of the service coordinator, who is a member of the profession most immediately relevant to the infant's, toddler's, or family's needs, or who is oth-

erwise qualified to carry out all applicable duties, who will be responsible for the implementation of the plan and for coordination with other people and agencies.

8. The steps to be taken to support the transition of the toddler with a disability to services provided by public school districts.

DEVELOPING THE IFSP

In order to develop a meaningful and useful IFSP, the process must be one that encourages and respects families, responds to their priorities and concerns, and builds on their strengths. The development of the IFSP is a cooperative effort. The team members provide their observations and findings from the assessment process. Parents and other family members contribute important information based on their intimate knowledge of the child and their concerns. This sharing of information about the child's strengths and needs leads to a discussion of important and meaningful goals or outcomes. The effects of the services and supports that are provided for the child and family will ultimately be evaluated in relation to the description of the child's level of functioning that appears on the IFSP. Thus, it is important that this description be as careful and accurate as possible.

With the concurrence of the family, the IFSP may also include a statement of the family's resources, priorities, and concerns. The purpose of this component of the IFSP process is to assist the family to identify their hopes and dreams for their child and themselves and to generate ways that they can start to attain these hopes and dreams. Mutual trust and respect are very important in this process. This component of the IFSP is voluntary. A family's participation and openness may change and expand over time as trust and confidence grow among the team members.

The process proceeds to a delineation of target outcomes. Outcomes are positive statements of the changes that the family and other team members want to see for the child and family. They are written in easily understood terms. Outcomes should specify what is to occur and what is expected as a result of these actions. Deal, Dunst, and Trivette (1989) suggested that outcomes be written as "in order to" statements, capturing both the process and the expected outcome. Some examples of outcome statements include the following:

- Midori will develop strength and control of her muscles in order to sit by herself.
- Kim's grandparents, aunts, uncles, and cousins will learn more about supplemental oxygen so that they will not be afraid to play with her.
- Jermaine will use single words to ask for actions or things.
- Someone will be identified to go with the Bower family to medical appointments so that they can get a better understanding of Anthony's health condition.

As outcomes are identified, the discussion expands to include the resources, strategies, and actions that will be useful in meeting the outcomes. Families will contribute their knowledge of their own resources, strengths, and preferences. The professionals will contribute their knowledge of child development, specialized intervention methods, and community resources. The next step is agreement on time lines and criteria. The family will help define what they mean by success or achievement for each of their outcomes.

To illustrate this process, consider the outcome that was identified for Jermaine. Jermaine currently uses gestures (e.g., reaching, bouncing his body) and vocalizing consonant-vowel combinations to make requests. His parents and the rest of the team discussed some of Jermaine's favorite activities and toys and his current turn-taking skills. The speech therapist described some of the usual intermediate steps between Jermaine's current skills and the outcome. The therapist and Jermaine's teacher also contributed some ideas for facilitating Jermaine's development of more sophisticated requesting behaviors. Together the team generates the steps and procedures, and these will appear on his IFSP.

The IFSP also includes a description of the early intervention services that are necessary to meet the needs and concerns of the child and family. This includes the number of days and sessions that a service will be provided, the length of time of each session, and the arrangement and method for delivering the service. For example, a child may receive special instruction through weekly home visits and speech and language therapy in a small play group at a children's center twice a week. The discussion of appropriate settings for services will incorporate the concept of natural environments (i.e., the settings where the child would be if the child did not have a disability). The projected dates for initiation of services and the anticipated duration of early intervention services are also included on the plan.

The name of the service coordinator appears on the IFSP. The roles and responsibilities of the service coordinator are discussed in Chapter 7. A final element of the IFSP document is a plan to support the child's transition to preschool services at age 3 if the child continues to be eligible for special services. This ensures the smooth continuation of services and supports because the lead agency, funding agency, and service delivery system may change at age 3.

A number of safeguards are in place to guarantee that an individualized plan is written and implemented in a timely manner. The plan must be written within 45 days of determination of eligibility. With parental consent, early intervention services may begin immediately upon the determination of eligibility. In this situation, an interim IFSP, with the name of the service coordinator and a description of immediate services, is written and signed. The multidisciplinary assessment and IFSP must still be completed in 45 days.

REVIEW OF THE IFSP

The IFSP must be reviewed every 6 months. Young children grow and change rapidly and their needs may change as well. Furthermore, families of young children are experiencing major changes and their concerns may also change. Thus, IFSP guidelines require 6-month periodic reviews as a minimum. Families have repeatedly told service providers and researchers that they want IFSPs to be dynamic plans that truly reflect their own family's situation and that can be adjusted to meet changing circumstances (Able-Boone, Sandall, Loughry, & Frederick, 1990; Summers et al., 1990).

A review meeting should lend itself to an open discussion of some basic issues. These can be formulated as questions, such as, How are we doing? Is the child/family achieving their outcomes? Do we need to make changes, and if so what should we change? In the past, teams have sometimes been caught in the snare of specific but meaningless criteria for measuring progress toward accomplishment of goals and objectives. Alternatives that are respectful of families and useful to all team members need to be explored. Simeonsson, Huntington, and Short (1982) adapted goal-attainment scaling for early intervention. Dunst, Leet, and Trivette

(1988) provided a rating scale for evaluating the effectiveness of implementation efforts. Such a scale may be particularly useful for family outcomes. Each outcome is evaluated against this scale:

1. Situation changed or worsened; no longer a need, goal, or project
2. Situation unchanged; still a need, goal, or project
3. Implementation begun; still a need, goal, or project
4. Outcome partially attained or accomplished
5. Outcome accomplished or attained, but not to the family's satisfaction
6. Outcome mostly accomplished or attained to the family's satisfaction
7. Outcome completely accomplished or attained to the family's satisfaction

Palisano, Haley, and Brown (1992) described yet another adaptation of goal-attainment scaling. Their version is useful for measuring child behavior change.

To this point, IFSP development may appear to be a highly formalized process. Regulations that are designed to ensure accountability may unfortunately reduce the friendliness and openness of the process. In practice, the steps and activities outlined above should be considered a guiding sequence. The steps and activities are interconnected. The process should be flexible and responsive to an individual family's situation. Families may differ in almost every aspect of the process such as the amount and type of their participation and the time they will spend on the specific topics.

Each IFSP and each meeting will be different. In fact, the regulations do allow for flexibility in conducting these meetings. Participation in the meetings may be by physical presence or by telephone, written reports or records, or presence of a knowledgeable authorized representative. The meetings themselves are held at times and places that are convenient for the family. The meeting might be held at a school or clinic but might also be in the family home or at a community center or even a coffee shop. Families should be involved in planning for these meetings by selecting comfortable and convenient locations. An additional provision is that the meetings must be in the families' native language or mode of communication unless it is not feasible to do so.

The IFSP that was developed for Alicia and her family is shown in the Appendix to this chapter. It is important to repeat that this is just one example of an IFSP, and that the process is more significant than the document. Additional examples of IFSPs and descriptions of the process can be found in McGonigel, Kaufman, and Johnson (1991).

SUMMARY

In their 1995 review article, Gallagher and Desimone noted that the IFSP as a policy has lofty goals: increased accountability and family participation through shared decision making and a more equitable distribution of power between parents and professionals. Achieving these goals takes preparation, organizational support, and commitment.

All of the participants in the IFSP process need ongoing training to ensure their meaningful participation. The professional team members may need assistance in the areas of communication skills and cultural competence, as well as in the details of developing an IFSP. Family members may need information and assistance in the areas of the content and intent of the IFSP, options for their involvement, and specific strategies for involvement. Various formats for providing this preparation can be used including workshops, written materials, and videotapes.

The development of a worthwhile IFSP takes time. All of the organizations and agencies involved in early intervention services need to support their early interventionists by providing time, resources, and the flexibility needed for the development of effective family plans. Development of IFSPs is an early intervention service.

Alicia *(conclusion)*

In planning a time for the IFSP meeting, Mrs. Benson indicated that it needed to be at a time when her husband could attend. The team also discussed inclusion of the clinical nurse specialist who serves as the family's liaison with the various health providers at the HMO and who is familiar with Alicia's medical history. The service coordinator called the Bensons a couple of days later, and they confirmed a date, time, and place. They also discussed the agenda for the meeting. The nurse could not attend, but she prepared a written update on Alicia's health status. The other members of the team were able to attend. As the meeting began, the service coordinator briefly reviewed the purpose. Then the Bensons took their turn. They started by sharing drawings made by James and Mark that showed their family. Then they brought out their crumpled copy of Alicia's "old" IFSP and talked about Alicia's and the family's accomplishments. Then they began the discussion of planning for the next few months.

This chapter has provided information on the content and the process for developing the IFSP as a collaborative effort. The next chapter focuses on implementing services and supports for young children and their families.

SUGGESTED READINGS AND RESOURCES

Bennett, T., Lingerfelt, M.A., & Nelson, M.S. (1990). *Developing individualized family support plans: A training manual.* Cambridge, MA: Brookline Books.

Child Development Resources. (1991). *A family-centered process for IFSP development* [Videotape]. Lightfoot, VA: Author.

Hunt, M., Cornelius, P., Miller, P., Murray, T., & Stoner, G. (1991). *Into our lives.* Tallmadge, OH: Family Child Learning Center.

Interdisciplinary Human Development Institute. (1993). *The family focused individualized family service plan training manual.* Lexington: University of Kentucky, Interdisciplinary Development Institute.

McGonigel, M.J., Kaufmann, R.K., & Johnson, B.H. (Eds.). (1991). *Guidelines and recommended services for the individualized family service plan* (2nd ed.). Bethesda, MD: Association for the Care of Children's Health.

McWilliam, P.J., & McWilliam, R. (1990). *Brass tacks.* Chapel Hill: University of North Carolina, Frank Porter Graham Child Development Center.

Mile High Down Syndrome Association. (1990). *Creating a vision: The IFSP* [Videotape]. Littleton, CO: Author.

REFERENCES

Able-Boone, H., Sandall, S.R., Loughry, A., & Frederick, L.L. (1990). An informed, family-centered approach to Public Law 99-457: Parental views. *Topics in Early Childhood Special Education, 10*(1), 100–111.

Bricker, D. (Ed.). (1993). *Assessment, Evaluation, and Planning System (AEPS) for infants and children: Vol. 1. AEPS measurement for birth to three years.* Baltimore: Paul H. Brookes Publishing Co.

Deal, A.G., Dunst, C.J., & Trivette, C.M. (1989). A flexible and functional approach to developing individualized family support plans. *Infants and Young Children, 1*(4), 32–43.

Dunst, C.J., Leet, H., & Trivette, C.M. (1988). Family resources, personal well-being, and early intervention. *Journal of Special Education, 22*(1), 108–116.

Federal Register. (1989, June 22). Early intervention for infants and toddlers with handicaps: Final regulations. (Vol. 54, 119), pp. 26306–26348. Washington, DC: U.S. Government Printing Office.

Individuals with Disabilities Education Act (IDEA) of 1990, PL 101-476, 20 U.S.C. § 1400 *et seq.*

McGonigel, M.J. (1991). Philosophy and conceptual framework. In M.J. McGonigel, R.K. Kaufmann, & B.H. Johnson (Eds), *Guidelines and recommended practices for the individualized family service plan* (2nd ed., pp. 7–14). Bethesda, MD: Association for the Care of Children's Health.

McGonigel, M.J., Kaufmann, R.K., & Johnson, B.H. (Eds.). (1991). *Guidelines and recommended practices for the individualized family service plan* (2nd ed.). Bethesda, MD: Association for the Care of Children's Health.

Palisano, R.J., Haley, S.M., & Brown, D.A. (1992). Goal attainment scaling as a measure of change in infants with motor delays. *Physical Therapy, 72*(6), 432–437.

Simeonsson, R.J., Huntington, G.S., & Short, R.J. (1982). Individual differences and goals: An approach to the evaluation of child progress. *Topics in Early Childhood Special Education, 1*(4), 71–80.

Summers, J.A., Dell'Oliver, C., Turnbull, A.P., Benson, H.A., Santelli, E., Campbell, M., & Siegel-Causey, E. (1990). Examining the individualized family service plan process: What are family and practitioner preferences? *Topics in Early Childhood Special Education, 10,* 78–99.

10 ACTIVITIES

1. Secure copies of IFSP forms from at least three early intervention programs, school districts, or agencies. Compare these with each other and with the IFSP requirements given in the text. Think about how you would respond to these forms as a parent of an infant or toddler.

2. Use the outcome for Jermaine that was given in the text to develop the steps, procedures, and criteria as they would appear on an IFSP.

3. Obtain permission to observe an IFSP meeting. What did you like about the process? What are some of the difficulties in achieving equitable participation? If you were a member of the team, would you do anything differently?

Appendix

Sample IFSP

The IFSP shown in this Appendix is for Alicia and her family.

IFSP Date: 11-2-95

INDIVIDUALIZED FAMILY SERVICE PLAN

Identifying Information:

Child's Name: Alicia Benson

Date of Birth: 7-30-94

Address: 121 S. Woodland

Phone: 232-5327

County/School District: Locke

Parent(s) or Legal Guardian(s):

Name: Katherine Benson

Phone: 232-5327

Address: 121 S. Woodland

Name: Robert Benson

Phone: 232-5327

Address: 121 S. Woodland

Service Coordination:

Name: Patricia Lee

Phone: 844-6609

Agency: TOTS Program

Family-Professional Team:

Team Members	Relationship/Agency
Katherine Benson	Mother
Robert Benson	Father
Patricia Lee	Physical Therapist, TOTS Program
Sarah Shanklin	Teacher, TOTS
Carol Juarez	Social Worker, TOTS
Lucy Klein	Speech Therapist, TOTS

Child's Name: Alicia Benson

Child's Current Abilities and Needs:

Alicia was assessed on 10-30-95 (see complete assessment report). She is a healthy, happy little girl. She crawls on hands and knees, plays with a variety of toys, uses gestures and vocalizations to communicate. She is beginning to feed herself. Hearing and vision were normal at testing last summer.

Alicia needs to learn to pull-to-stand. When placed in standing her feet point out, hips are abducted. No protective extension to rear. Doesn't use words yet (no mama or dada). Doesn't point at body parts, people, etc.

Family's Resources, Concerns, and Priorities:

We are delighted with Alicia's progress. We both work. Our babysitter has given notice so we need to find child care for Alicia. Also, we would like Alicia to continue to make progress toward walking but we realize that she will probably have to use a walker. We need more information about this. We would also like Alicia to start using words so we need some ideas to help her with talking and understanding more. Her brothers are getting older and beginning to ask more questions about her disability. So we could use some ideas for helping the boys.

(continued)

Early Intervention Services:
(Type, Beginning and Ending Dates, Frequency, Intensity, Method, Location)

1. Physical therapy continues 11-2-95, 1:1, 1x/week, TOTS program, 45 min.
2. Speech therapy continues 11-2-95, integrated sm. group, 1x/week, TOTS, 1 hr.
3. Special Instruction continues 11-2-95, 1:1 & sm. group, 2x/week, TOTS, 1 hr.
4. Home visits continue 11-2-95, 2x/month, Benson's home, 1 hr.
5. Social work 11-2-95, as needed, center or home, problem-solving
6. Sibling Group, 11-2-95, as needed, County ARC
7. __________
8. __________

Summary of Services and Locations:
Alicia is doing well in current program. A second home visit per month will be added. Locations and schedules of services may change when new child care is found.

Is a transition plan needed at this time? No If yes, attach.

Child's Name: Alicia Benson

OUTCOME: Alicia will improve her strength and control so that she can walk with help.

STEPS	PROCEDURE/STRATEGIES	EVALUATION CRITERIA
1. Will pull herself to kneeling at a step or stool.	Individual physical therapy. Practice at home and during play group.	1. maintain position and play.
2. Will pull herself to half-kneeling at a step or chair.	Schedule meeting with parents, PT + physician to discuss walking.	2. Maintain position and play.
3. Will pull herself to standing at a chair or other furniture.		3. Maintain position and play.

Person/Agency Responsible: Patricia Lee, TOTS

(continued)

Child's Name: Alicia Benson

OUTCOME: Alicia will use words to communicate with others.

STEPS	PROCEDURE/STRATEGIES	EVALUATION CRITERIA
1. Alicia will use two or more words to tell what she wants.	Speech Therapist will Consult. Use turn-taking and other interactional methods	1. Use new words at least 5 times. Keep a diary.
2. Alicia will use one or more exclamations such as "uh-oh" in appropriate situations.	Speech therapist and teacher will suggest activities for home.	2. Use her words.
3. Alicia will use Three or more words to name or label people, objects, and toys.		3. Use new words at least 5 times — diary.

Person/Agency Responsible: Lucy Klein, TOTS

Child's Name: Alicia Benson

OUTCOME: Alicia will improve her comprehension skils.

STEPS	PROCEDURE/STRATEGIES	EVALUATION CRITERIA
1. Will point to three or more objects or people when named.	Consultation by Speech Therapist + teacher. Will suggest activities and games for small group + home. Look at books with Alicia.	1. Point consistently – keep notes.
2. Will point to or look at most common objects when they are named.		2. Point or look consistently – keep notes.
3. Will point to three or more body parts when asked.		3. Point consistently – keep notes.

Person/Agency Responsible: Lucy Klein + Sarah Shanklin, TOTS

(continued)

Child's Name: Alicia Benson

OUTCOME: Family will find alternative child care for Alicia.

STEPS	PROCEDURE/STRATEGIES	EVALUATION CRITERIA
1. Identify child care options	Mrs. Benson will talk with friends, neighbors.	Family will make decision by end of February.
2. Contact and visit child care centers or homes.	Sarah will provide list. Carol will contact Child Care referral.	
3. Make decision		

Person/Agency Responsible: Carol Juarez TOTS

Child's Name: Alicia Benson

OUTCOME: Family will get more information on motor and language development to help Alicia.

STEPS	PROCEDURE/STRATEGIES	EVALUATION CRITERIA
1. Gather information and information sources.	Home visits by teacher once a month & by PT or ST once a month.	To family's satisfaction – use goal attainment scaling.
2. Make home visits.	Contact Spina Bifida Association for information, videotapes, etc.	
	Use program's resource files, public library & give suggestions to family.	

Person/Agency Responsible: Sarah Shanklin TOTS

(continued)

Child's Name: Alicia Benson

OUTCOME: Parents would like James and Mark to get more information about spina bifida and to have opportunities to talk about having a sister with a disability.

STEPS	PROCEDURE/STRATEGIES	EVALUATION CRITERIA
1. Get schedule of Sibling Group at The ARC.	Carol will get the schedule and give phone number(s) to Bensons.	To family's satisfaction — use goal attainment scaling.
2. Attend group activities.	Parents will talk to boys about the group. Carol will give/lend books to James and Mark.	

Person/Agency Responsible: Carol Juarez TOTS

Family

We (I) feel that we (I) have had an opportunity to cooperatively develop this plan and that the outcomes reflect our (my) concerns and priorities. We (I) understand that this plan can be changed at any time at our (my) request and that it will be formally reviewed by May, 1996. Based on these understandings, we (I) give permision for the plan to be implemented.

✓ Yes ____ No

Katherine Benson	11-2-95	Robert Benson	11-2-95
Signature	Date	Signature	Date

Other Team Members

The following individuals participated in the development of the IFSP. Each person understands and agrees to carry out the plan as it applies to their role in the provision of services.

Patricia Lee RPT	Sarah Shanklin M.Ed.
Amy Klein MA-CCC-SP	Carl Juang MSW

The IFSP was developed with telephone consultation or a report provided by the following people:

Mary Jo Peterson RN, Lincoln Health, provided written report.

SECTION V

INTERVENTION

CHAPTER 11

Early Intervention Contexts, Content, and Methods

Susan R. Sandall

Objectives

- To be aware of the principles that guide early intervention services and supports for young children and families
- To be able to describe the intervention process and be able to individualize the process
- To understand the influence of contextual variables on early intervention
- To be able to describe the content and methods of early intervention

Early intervention services, supports, and resources are delivered in a variety of settings and in a variety of ways. In this book, infants and toddlers are shown to receive services in homes, centers, clinics, and hospitals. In addition to variation in settings, early intervention programs can differ in intensity, duration, personnel arrangements, and philosophy.

This chapter focuses on the design and delivery of early intervention services, supports, and resources. A primary goal shared by early intervention programs is to support and enhance the development and learning of infants and toddlers who either have disabilities or are at risk for disabilities. This chapter highlights strategies that are aimed at enhancing child development and learning. Much attention is given to center-based and other group forms of care in this chapter. Many of the strategies that are described can be embedded effectively within natural routines at home.

GUIDING PRINCIPLES

In this section, a framework for recognizing and developing quality early intervention services is discussed. This provides the backdrop for planning activities and experiences for young children.

Service Delivery

Regardless of the setting for service delivery, there are some shared indicators of quality. McWilliam and Strain (1993) identified the following five indicators:

- Services should be delivered in the least restrictive and most natural environment.
- Services should be family-centered and responsive to family priorities.
- Service delivery should be transdisciplinary.
- Service delivery should be guided by empirical results and family and professional values.
- Services should be individualized and developmentally appropriate.

Young Children as Learners

In sharing information on service delivery, curriculum design, and implementation, early interventionists are guided by some basic assumptions about young children as learners. First, young children are active learners. Through mental and physical activity, even very young children are working at making sense of their environments. Second, young children can learn as a result of planned interventions. They learn through repeated experiences with people and materials. Thus, early interventionists plan, implement, and repeat activities and experiences. Third, young children learn through social interactions with adults and with other children. They learn best when their teachers, therapists, and other caregivers are responsive to their interests, preferences, abilities, characteristics, and health. Fourth, effective intervention strategies are those that promote learning and development. Thus, early interventionists examine outcomes to evaluate the effectiveness of their intervention efforts.

Theorists and practitioners hold different perspectives as to the relationship between learning and development. Berk and Winsler (1995) summarized these perspectives as follows: A Piagetian perspective views learning and development as separate entities, a behaviorist perspective views learning and development as identical, and a Vygotskian perspective views learning as leading development. Dunst (1993) made these distinctions for early interventionists: "All development involves learning, but not all learning produces development" and "The goal of intervention should be the promotion of development and not simply enhancement of learning" (p. 63). In other words, the activities and experiences designed by interventionists should support valuable, important, and functional learnings that result in significant changes in the ways that the young child acquires, organizes, and uses information.

CURRICULUM THEORY

The *curriculum* is an organized framework that guides intervention. It includes what to teach (content) and how to teach (methods). The curriculum may also include description of the contexts in which teaching and learning occur and the process for identifying the content for individual children. Curricula may differ along several dimensions including theoretical perspective, number and arrangement of content areas, and scope and sequence of objectives or activities. There are a number of reasonable ways to approach curriculum planning. However, early intervention teams need to articulate and use a consistent theoretical perspective to ensure program continuity. This is particularly important in light of the fact that teams often use several published curricula and activity guides as well as their own experiences to design learning activities to meet the individual needs of infants and toddlers.

Several perspectives have influenced curriculum development in early intervention. The *maturational perspective* is closely associated with the work of Arnold Gesell (Gesell, 1925; Gesell & Ilg, 1949). Through careful observations of young children, his developmental schedules were created. These are the bases for many assessment tools and curriculum materials. This perspective emphasizes genetically determined maturation and views development in terms of a linear model. Early experiences are designed to allow the child to act on his or her own innate tendencies toward self-expression. The interventionist's role is to provide the warm, positive atmosphere and age-appropriate enrichment activities.

The *behavioral perspective* influences instructional strategies (the methods of curriculum) rather than content. Associated with the work of Skinner (1976) and others, the behavioral perspective incorporates the importance of planned environmental events and extrinsic motivation of the child. Typically, intervention objectives are specified and systematic instruction is provided through a predetermined series of steps to change or teach new behaviors to attain the targeted objective. The interventionist's role is to identify objectives, plan the environment, sequence activities, and provide reinforcement following demonstration of the targeted objective.

The *cognitive perspective* is typically associated with the work of Piaget (1952, 1970). Important elements of this approach include hierarchical stages, active interaction of the child with the environment, and intrinsic motivation. Varied experiences are provided to ensure that young children initiate interactions and actively experiment. These experiences are carefully sequenced based on observations of the child and knowledge of development. The early interventionist organizes the social and physical environment to engage and challenge the infant or toddler with careful attention to the child's own understanding of the world.

Dialectical theory is another influence on early intervention curricula and intervention strategies. Vygotsky's (1978) work highlights the importance of the social context. He posits that people are products of their social and cultural worlds. Vygotsky's work underlies many of the interactional approaches in early intervention. Adults play an important role in mediating the young child's experiences with the world by establishing joint attention, interacting with the child, and including the child in the culture.

Finally, the *ecological perspective,* developed by Bronfenbrenner (1979), has influenced the design and delivery of early intervention. Infants are viewed as living and developing as members of different ecological settings. The early interventionist must recognize the multiple contexts and interrelationships of infant, family, and community life and must also be aware of the direct and indirect effects of intervention and other systemic changes. Thus, the young child with disabilities is viewed as a dynamic and interactive learner but is not the sole focus of intervention. The various settings must also change to support the child's existing capabilities, to enhance the development of new capabilities, and to buffer stresses. The interventionist mediates systems-level change. This perspective broadens the interventionist's view of early intervention and focuses attention on the goodness-of-fit between the child and environments (Thurman & Widerstrom, 1990).

INTERVENTION GUIDELINES

The following sections focus attention on the design and delivery of activities and experiences to promote learning and development.

Linking Assessment and Intervention

Previous chapters discussed the developmental assessment of young children and presented principles and strategies to guide the process of carefully describing the infant's or toddler's capabilities, interests, and learning strategies. These same principles guide early interventionists' practices when their purpose is to gather information to plan and deliver a child's intervention program and to monitor the effects of the intervention. Effective assessment and intervention are connected and integrated (Bricker, 1989). That is, intervention activities are directly influenced by and depend on assessment information that is gathered before, during, and at the end of intervention.

Curriculum-based measures are listed in the tables in Chapter 9. Curriculum-based procedures are based on the premise that the functional and meaningful behaviors that are assessed and taught are similar. In early intervention, such measures typically encompass a comprehensive set of behaviors that map early development. Thus, in selecting a curriculum-based measure, the team must carefully consider the theory(ies) of child development that it is based upon. The early intervention team, using a curriculum-based measure as the framework for observing, testing, and interviewing, determines the starting points for intervention. These are the outcomes and objectives that appear on the individualized family service plan (IFSP).

Outcomes In selecting child outcomes, team members apply their knowledge of typical child development as well as knowledge of disabling conditions and risk factors and the implications they carry. This knowledge, together with assessment data and the family's concerns, lead to individual child outcomes. Attainment of such outcomes means that the child is becoming progressively more independent, better able to solve problems, and more able to adapt to new situations.

Several steps are necessary to translate child outcomes into effective activities and experiences that promote learning and enhance development. In analyzing assessment information, the team has identified the relative priority given to these outcomes. Furthermore, by looking at the whole child and the environments in which the child interacts, the team gains greater understanding about the variables that may promote or constrain intervention efforts. Outcomes typically represent goals or projects that may take several weeks or months to accomplish.

Intervention Objectives The next step in beginning intervention is to restate the outcome as one or more intervention objectives. Intervention objectives are specific statements about a change in one of a child's repertoire of skills that is expected to occur soon. This change leads the child closer to the identified outcomes. Intervention objectives have three major components: 1) behavior, 2) conditions under which the behavior will occur, and 3) criterion for evaluation. Examples of intervention objectives are shown in Table 11.1.

Table 11.1. Intervention objectives

When an adult places a cup to his lips, Brian will drink from the cup, keeping his lips closed and losing only small amounts of liquid, with jaw support from the side.
After playing social games with an adult, Alberto will initiate playing the game (e.g., pat-a-cake, so big) by vocalizing or making the arm movement and will do so on at least five different occasions.
In a variety of classroom and home situations, Lily will use 10 single words appropriately to refer to objects, people, or actions and will use each word at least three times.

Enabling Steps Objectives can be broken down into smaller components or enabling steps. This can be accomplished by *task analysis*—that is, doing the task for oneself or watching a young child perform the task and writing down the process step-by-step. Another method involves a logical analysis of the behavior drawing on typical developmental sequences. For example, an analysis of the behavior "Says approximation of the word *bottle* upon seeing the bottle" might be broken down to 1) shows excitement upon seeing bottle, 2) vocalizes upon seeing the bottle, and 3) says "ba-ba" upon seeing the bottle. In addition to breaking down objectives into smaller parts or steps, the analysis involves sequencing or arranging the parts or steps for intervention, making adaptations for individual children, and identifying prerequisites.

The use of existing curricula offers a means of translating child outcomes to objectives and learning experiences. Many curricula provide very useful objectives, sequences, and activities. See Table 11.2 for a summary of selected early intervention curricula. Not every young child will fit neatly into a curriculum. Individual children may require smaller steps or alternative responses. Many curricula, for example, do not provide adaptations for children with sensory or physical disabilities (Fewell & Sandall, 1983). Skills in task analysis, logical analysis of behaviors, and adaptations of curricula are valuable for early interventionists.

The process of breaking down the outcomes and objectives is not meant to imply that instruction or therapy is implemented in lock-step fashion. Rather, these smaller steps are incorporated within play and daily routines using the guidelines of active learning, social interaction, and responsivity, as well as careful planning. Interventionists can use their own problem-solving skills to arrive at potentially effective activities. The intervention objective or steps are the "problems." The team (including the family) brainstorms to generate many activities, experiences, toys, materials, and situations. The team uses existing curriculum materials, research findings, child and family preferences, and their own experiences to generate potentially useful "solutions." Then, the team selects those activities that would seem to have the greatest potential in terms of promoting learning and development, and also fit within the child and family's natural environments. During and after implementation, team members assess the effectiveness of the activities in relation to the stated objective(s).

The example in Figure 11.1 shows an example of an activity plan for Lily (see boxed information on p. 268).

The Context for Intervention

This section highlights the importance of setting the stage for effective intervention by describing optimal environments for intervention. Indeed, the environment is a critical component of early intervention and curriculum planning. As Bailey and McWilliam (1990) noted, environmental supports generally represent the least intrusive and most natural interventions.

Table 11.2. Selected curricula for early intervention

Name	Author(s)	Age range	Content	Comments
Assessment, Evaluation, and Programming System (AEPS) for Infants and Children: Curriculum for Birth to Three Years (Vol. 2)	Cripe, Slentz, and Bricker (1993)	Birth–3 years	Fine motor, gross motor, adaptive, cognitive, social-communication, social; supporting information, teaching suggestions, environmental arrangements	Linked to a curriculum-based assessment (Vol. 1), uses activity-based intervention approach, also includes some family materials
The Carolina Curriculum for Infants and Toddlers with Special Needs (2nd ed.)	Johnson-Martin et al. (1991)	Birth–24 months	Traditional domains (fine motor, gross motor, cognition, communication, social, self-help) expanded to 24 areas; supporting information including good chapter on motor development, teaching suggestions	Includes an assessment log, adaptations for children with motor and sensory impairments
Developmental Programming for Infants and Young Children	Schafer and Moersch (1981)	Birth–36 months	Perceptual/fine motor, cognition, language, social/emotional, self-care, gross motor; supporting information, stimulation activities	Linked to assessment tool, includes adaptations for children with motor and sensory impairments
Hawaii Early Learning Profile (HELP)	Furuno et al. (1979)	Birth–36 months	Gross motor, fine motor, cognition, expressive language, social/emotional, self-help; teaching activities	Includes assessment checklists and HELP charts, some adaptations, activities fit into play and caregiving
Partners for Learning	Sparling and Lewis (1984)	Birth–24 months	Covers traditional areas of cognitive/fine motor, social, self-help, motor, language expanded to 23 areas; teaching activities and games, kit	Includes entry assessment, progress charts, naturalistic activities, activity cards, used in the IHDP project
Small Wonder	Karnes (1981)	Birth–36 months	Balance and motion, body awareness, cognition, fine motor, language and listening, self-help, socialization, visual suggested activities	Includes activities for play and routines, progress charts, diary
Teaching the Infant with Down Syndrome: A Guide for Parents and Professionals (2nd ed.)	Hanson (1987)	Birth–3 years	Gross motor, cognitive, fine motor, communication, social, self-help; step-by-step guide to teaching, supporting, information	Designed for parents, background information on Down syndrome
Transdisciplinary Play-Based Intervention: Guidelines for Developing a Meaningful Curriculum for Young Children	Linder (1993)	6 months–6 years	Cognition, social-emotional, communication and language, sensorimotor; rich background information, intervention strategies	Designed to be used with transdisciplinary play-based assessment, activities embedded within play and routines, planning forms

Child: Lily

Outcome: Lily will increase her use of words to communicate with others.

Objective: In a variety of classroom and home situations, Lily will use 10 single words appropriately to refer to objects, people, or actions and will use each word at least three times.

Current Step: Will use three new words for actions.

Activity:

- Implement during Lily's preferred activities (e.g., feeding the fish, painting, eating at snack time).
- Incorporate questions and comments naturally into the play (e.g., "What are you doing?", "What would you like to do next?", "______ is eating his cookie"). Pause following the question/comment.
- If Lily uses an action word, acknowledge it by repeating, expanding, and complying as is appropriate.
- If Lily does not use the action word, model the word.

Potential Words: shake, feed, paint, eat, drink

Alternate Activity: If Lily chooses the book area, use these strategies while looking at books together.

Figure 11.1. Sample activity plan for Lily.

There are several important characteristics that describe optimal environments for early intervention. Optimal learning environments are

- Engaging
- Responsive and predictable
- Filled with opportunities for learning
- Developmentally appropriate
- Safe and hygienic

Engaging Young children, like all people, learn in environments that are engaging. Engaging environments are those that contain people who are available and responsive and toys and materials that are interesting, accessible, and appropriately challenging. These elements are seen in Lily's toddler classroom. Lily is intrigued by the fish and fascinated by the art materials. She has opportunities to make genuine choices, and she has teachers who join her play and help her extend her learning.

Engagement is defined as the amount of time children spend interacting appropriately with their environments (McWilliam, 1991). Engagement is individually determined and varies with context. It is assumed that large proportions of engagement are desirable. McWilliam, Trivette, and Dunst (1986) proposed that a high level of engagement is one indicator of quality programs for young children.

Responsive and Predictable A second characteristic of a positive learning context for early intervention is that it is responsive and predictable. A responsive environment is one that provides feedback for children. Caregivers are sensitive to and responsive to the young child's signals, such as cries, babbles, postural changes, or, for example, Lily's excited bounce. Responses are attuned to the individual child and situation. Social interaction is the basis for learning and development. Early relationships with parents and other caregivers who are responsive and predictable are fundamental.

Lily

Lily kisses her mother good-bye and immediately walks to the fish tank. She watches the goldfish for a few minutes, smiling and pointing at the glass tank while the fish swim in circles. Then Lily looks up in search of Gwen, her teacher. Lily finds her, points, and says "ish, ish." Gwen smiles, walks toward Lily, and asks, "Lily, would you like to feed the fish?" Lily bounces up and down and nods her head. Gwen gets the fish food and helps Lily shake the can two times over the fish tank. Now that the fish are fed, Lily turns for the art table. Gwen follows her, knowing that Lily gets so excited at the prospect of painting that she forgets to put a paint smock on first.

Lily is 2 years old. Every Tuesday and Thursday morning, she attends toddler class at a community preschool. It's a well-established preschool. Lily's sister went to school there and their mother attended the same preschool years ago. Shortly after Lily was born, her parents placed her name on the waiting list. When Lily was diagnosed with Williams syndrome, her parents thought that perhaps she wouldn't be able to attend the preschool. However, their service coordinator helped them work with the school district so that Lily is able to go to the preschool two mornings a week where her teachers make a special point of planning activities and experiences that address Lily's developmental needs. A child development specialist comes to the preschool every other week to help the teachers make adjustments in the curriculum and to help monitor Lily's progress. The teachers have found that most of their usual play centers, toys, and activities require just a few modifications or special instructions for Lily. The child development specialist has provided the most assistance when they've struggled with Lily's challenging behaviors.

Toys and materials also provide feedback contingent on the child's actions. Many infant and toddler toys are designed to do just that. For example, a roly-poly toy jingles when it is batted, and a jack-in-the-box opens when the handle is turned. *Contingency* refers to a perceived relationship between two events. From the literature on infant learning (e.g., Osofsky, 1987), it is known that infants are aware of contingencies and that infants take an active role in perceiving, controlling, and exploring contingencies. Toys and materials should be provided that give feedback contingent on the child's actions. Some children with physical or other disabilities are at a disadvantage because many commercial toys require a motoric response. Toys can be adapted based on the infant's response capabilities. Dunst, Cushing, and Vance (1985) and Sullivan and Lewis (1993) provided examples of successful response-contingent learning by infants with significant disabilities. Simple technology in the form of switch toys and other adapted toys can help children learn this connection (Burkhart, 1980, 1982).

An important consideration in the preparation of a responsive environment is that it is also predictable. Again, this refers to both the social (caregivers) and non-social (toys and materials) aspects of the environment. To learn the relationship between one's behavior and the outcome (contingency), these relationships must be predictable. That is, the roly-poly toy jingles whenever it is batted, the jack-in-the-box opens when the handle is turned, and the caregiver responds predictably to the young child's cues and signals. In this way, the child learns that he or she has some control over the environment. It is also believed that contingent learning experiences enhance the motivation to continue to learn (Sullivan & Lewis, 1993).

Opportunities for Learning An optimal early intervention environment offers many opportunities for learning. These learning opportunities are naturally integrated within typical play activities and caregiving routines whenever possible. Yet the team also understands that interventions must be appropriately matched to the infant's health and alertness. Early interventionists also understand that young children with disabilities or other special needs may require many more learning opportunities than might naturally occur. Thus, the team carefully plans and provides sufficient opportunities so that learning and development take place. This may mean pinpointing definite learning opportunities during play and caregiving routines and also implementing planned activities that the adults specifically organize to provide additional practice (Bricker & Cripe, 1992).

Developmentally Appropriate Optimal environments for infants and toddlers are those that contain materials, toys, and spaces that are developmentally appropriate for young children. In selecting toys and arranging spaces, early interventionists, parents, and other caregivers consider the child's age, interests, and current capabilities and then observe to see if the selections are appropriate. Young children tell us if the toys, materials, or activities are too far below the child's developmental level by expressing boredom or too far above their developmental level by expressing frustration.

There are a number of resources that are helpful in selecting toys for young children (e.g., Bredekamp, 1986; Bronson, 1995; National Association for the Education of Young Children [NAEYC], 1985). The types of toys that should be found in an early intervention environment are described in Table 11.3. Homemade toys and materials can be as appropriate as those that are commercially available.

Table 11.3. Toys for infants and toddlers

Type of toy	Description
Toys to manipulate	Toys or objects that can be mouthed, chewed, touched, dropped, placed, or poked (e.g., busy boxes, texture toys or pieces of fabric, blocks, balls)
Sound makers	Toys or objects that produce a sound if the child does something (e.g., rattles, squeeze toys, chime balls)
Assembly toys	Toys and objects that can be taken apart and put back together (e.g., shape sorters, large pop beads, puzzles, measuring cups, bowls and lids, shoe boxes)
Toys that encourage movement	Toys or objects that help the child see and explore more of the environment (e.g., push- and pull-toys, riding toys, climbers)
Cause-and-effect toys	Toys that help children learn that their actions cause different things to happen (e.g., musical toys, activity centers, push-button or switch toys)
Creative materials	Art-type materials that are provided for the experience of using one's senses and to exercise increasing control (e.g., nontoxic finger paints, play dough, crayons or markers)
Literary materials	Books that encourage language and literacy development. Books may be cloth, cardboard with no words, few words, simple stories, or photograph books and other homemade books.
Dramatic play materials	Toys and materials for beginning dramatic play should be familiar and match the child's own experiences (e.g., dolls, telephones, cooking utensils)

Spaces should also be matched to young children's interests and abilities. Appropriate environments for hospitalized infants were described in Chapters 3 and 7. Regardless of setting, the spatial organization and environmental cues should promote security, learning, and development.

In group settings, the number and type of spaces will depend on the number of children and their developmental ages, and the resources of the program. The environment that is created for very young infants will look different from a center or classroom that serves older toddlers. Centers that serve mixed-age or family groupings will need spaces that can accommodate a range of interests and needs. In general, centers or classrooms for infants and toddlers should have a few, simple inviting interest areas that allow choices and give the young children cues for behavior. Such interest areas promote child initiation, independence, and mastery. These interest areas complement the necessary caregiving spaces.

Family members often remain at the early intervention center with their child. They may observe or participate more actively. The spatial organization should be viewed from both the child's and the family's perspective so that all are welcomed and comfortable.

Because children's interests and abilities will change, early interventionists should monitor how well their spatial arrangements are working. This can be done by periodically checking engagement levels, tracking the children's usage of the spaces in the room, or using an environmental assessment to determine the appropriateness of the physical environment.

Good spaces for infants and toddlers are described in Table 11.4.

Safe and Hygienic Finally, optimal environments for infants and toddlers are safe and hygienic. The toys themselves should be of appropriate size and in good condition. Caregivers should follow the standards outlined by the Consumer Product Safety Commission. The environment should be childproofed (e.g., electrical outlets covered) by following local health and safety guidelines and using other resources (e.g., American Public Health Association [APHA] & American Academy of Pediatrics [AAP], 1992).

Table 11.4. Spaces for infants and toddlers

Space	Description
Spaces for caregiving routines	Spaces devoted to caregiving routines should be comfortable, secure, and pleasant. Areas include a welcoming space for children and families, diapering area, snack or mealtime area, and nap space if needed.
	Keep areas clean, well organized, and equipped with materials to promote social interaction.
Movement areas	Areas should be matched to children's abilities and safety concerns. Areas should promote exploration and motor development and include carpeted or cushioned areas; stable furniture or supports; and climbers, ramps, and stairs.
Sensory centers	Opportunities for exploring sensory stimuli, such as water, sand, and art materials. These spaces also offer children a chance to play near others.
Manipulative areas	Space on the floor for children to play with toys. Toys should be accessible so that children can make choices. Set up another area for tabletop toys. Try to have more than one of each toy for children who are not yet sharing.
Book center	A desirable and inviting area with soft elements such as pillows and stuffed animals. Display the books so that children can make choices and put books away.
House corner	A space dedicated to playing house. Materials should be culturally relevant and similar to the sorts of materials the children see at home.

The use of proper hygiene measures protects both children and staff. Hygienic measures include universal body fluid precautions (UBFP), avoidance of contact with body fluids, and hand washing. Risks may be reduced by wearing gloves whenever contact with body fluids is likely. Surfaces that come in contact with body fluids should be cleaned with a 1- to 10-part solution of bleach and water. The universal use of body fluid protection measures with all children is less stigmatizing for those children who have diagnosed infections.

The single most important component of hygiene is hand washing. The use of gloves is not a substitute. Thorough hand washing is done with soap, lasts at least 10 seconds, includes all hand surfaces and under fingernails, and uses friction as well as running water. Following hand washing, the faucet should be turned off with the paper towel after drying the hands. Caregivers should wash their hands before food preparation, handling, and serving; after toileting or changing diapers; after wiping noses; and after handling animals. Hand washing can be reinforced by the use of posters, convenient and easy-to-use facilities, and staff education conducted at regular intervals. Several excellent resources (e.g., APHA & AAP, 1992; Kendrick, Kaufmann, & Messenger, 1991; University of Colorado Health Sciences Center School of Nursing, 1989a, 1989b) on infection control and safety provide additional information.

Young children with sensory, physical, or special health care needs may need additional modifications to the environment or specialized equipment to ensure their safety and allow their participation. For example, children with sensory or physical needs will benefit from environments in which the furniture is not moved and is arranged to allow children to move and explore as much as they can. It is particularly important that the environment give consistent feedback. Specialized furniture such as wedges, chairs, and standing boards will be necessary for some children to be positioned in such a way as to make better contact with the world and be as independent as possible. Special health care procedures (e.g., tube feeding, suctioning, catheterization) are typically taught to parents by health professionals. Individual programs need to clearly state their policies regarding specialized procedures so that children with special caregiving or health needs can participate, learn, and receive appropriate care.

The larger issue of safety for all children involves access to health care and freedom from danger, violence, disease, overcrowding, and excessive stress (Zero to Three, 1992). It becomes the responsibility of early interventionists in their role as child and family advocates to work for these conditions in their neighborhoods and communities.

Inclusion

The goal of full inclusion for young children has been articulated by the Division for Early Childhood, Council for Exceptional Children (1993). In part, their position reads, "Inclusion, as a value, supports the right of all children, regardless of their diverse abilities, to participate actively in natural settings within their communities" (p. 4). Implicit in the value of inclusion is the concept of belonging. Young children need to truly experience belonging to their families, neighborhoods, and communities (Turnbull, Turnbull, & Blue-Banning, 1994). Thus, early intervention practices must enhance belonging in meaningful ways.

The benefits of carefully planned and implemented inclusive learning opportunities for preschoolers and older children have been reviewed by a number of researchers (e.g., Guralnick, 1990; Odom & McEvoy, 1988). Among the reported benefits are enhanced social and communicative behaviors and improved learning skills. The issues and potential benefits of inclusive practices and inclusive opportunities are somewhat different for infants and toddlers.

One of the primary developmental tasks of infancy is forming an emotional relationship with one or more caregivers. That is, the infant must experience a genuine sense of belonging to the family and eventually to the larger community. The implications for early interventionists are that practices must support these primary relationships, and interventions must support and enhance parent–child interactions. These conditions must be in place in the NICU where policies and practices (e.g., open visiting, physical contact, transportation) should be designed and implemented to help families remain connected with their infant. These conditions must also be in place after the infant moves home, whether to a home-based program or through access to community-based programs. Part of supporting a sense of belonging for the family as well as for the child means that families have true choices, families' preferences are supported, and families have access to the sorts of services and supports that help them maintain their own neighborhood and community networks. A role of early interventionists is to help families in creating the conditions that help them include their child within their own family and community.

As the infant becomes a toddler and becomes increasingly aware of other children, opportunities for learning in social situations can expand. In fact, another critical developmental task of early childhood is to establish oneself as a viable member of a social network of peers. As the infant becomes a toddler, he or she becomes increasingly aware of other children, begins to watch their play, and begins to play in similar ways. Thus, social groupings can be a useful intervention setting. In terms of inclusion, this means that community options must truly be available. Access to community programs and services is supported through the Individuals with Disabilities Education Act (IDEA) of 1990 (PL 101-476) and the Americans with Disabilities Act (ADA) of 1990 (PL 101-336). Community options include group and family child care programs, various social and recreation programs (e.g., baby "gym" classes, mothers'-day-out programs), and infant and toddler "classes" at community centers and places of worship. The team ensures that these are truly learning opportunities by offering its assistance with information materials or consultation as needed.

Emotional Foundations of Early Learning

The value of inclusion is not simply exposure to children without disabilities; rather a child must experience genuine emotional connections with family, neighborhood, and community members. Hyson (1994) and Zero to Three (1992) emphasized the critical importance of the social and emotional foundations of early learning for all young children. Certain characteristics that are formed during the earliest years of life set the stage for positive experiences in school and in life. These characteristics are confidence, curiosity, persistence, self-control, relatedness, the capacity to communicate, and cooperativeness (Zero to Three, 1992). Children will demonstrate these characteristics in individual ways, but it is the role of caregivers (e.g., parents, child care providers, teachers, therapists) to help children establish these characteristics by ensuring that the conditions that support the development of these characteristics are in place. These conditions are health and health care, unhurried time,

responsive caregiving, and safety. Unfortunately, too many children do not have these basic conditions. However, early interventionists, as citizens and child advocates, can work toward providing these conditions. Services can be designed and delivered in ways that promote the emotional foundations of early learning for the children.

INTERVENTION CONTENT AND METHODS

This section begins with the organization and scope of the content of early intervention curricula. This is followed by a discussion of useful strategies and techniques.

Content

Curricula can be organized in a variety of ways. For example, some curricula are organized around themes or units, others around key experiences (e.g., High Scope), others around the environment (e.g., The Creative Curriculum), and others around developmental domains (e.g., The Carolina Curriculum for Infants and Toddlers with Special Needs; Johnson-Martin, Jens, Attermeier, & Hacker, 1991). Traditionally, most curricula in early intervention are organized by developmental domains. When using a curriculum that is organized by domain, it is important for the team to plan in an integrated fashion. That is, experiences and activities should not be designed for a single domain (e.g., cognition) without considering the child's social and communicative competence and movement abilities. An integrated approach also means that, when possible, specialized therapies (e.g, physical therapy, speech therapy) and treatments are integrated within routines and play.

Early interventionists have demonstrated a shift toward building their curriculum around more authentic units (whether routines, or activities, or play centers within the classroom or caregiving and other daily routines at home) while still using developmental domains as the foundation for the curriculum (e.g., Bricker & Cripe, 1992; Linder, 1993). This allows the early interventionist to pinpoint strengths and needs and then integrate this information into meaningful experiences. Early skills are interrelated and interdependent (Berkeley & Ludlow, 1989; Lewis, 1984). The interrelatedness of early development has implications for both assessment and intervention and provides support for a transdisciplinary approach in which all team members are attentive to the whole child.

Thus, the scope of early intervention curricula is grounded in developmental theory and includes the typical developmental accomplishments of infancy and toddlerhood. These accomplishments are the major goals of the curriculum. The curriculum may then break these down into short-term (or intermediate or enabling) objectives that are sequenced. Curricular sequences help interventionists to organize and plan intervention, but rigid adherence to particular sequences may be counterproductive.

When selecting curricula, activity guides, or treatment approaches, the team should ask themselves several questions: Is it based on sound developmental theory? Does it match the philosophy of the program and team? Does it foster collaborative planning and an integrated approach?

Methods

Planning Matrix One way to plan for integrated learning is to use a planning matrix. A matrix allows the team to use the usual routines and to embed instructional or therapeutic opportunities within these routines. Benefits of embedding therapy and instruction include the following:

- Integration of learning experiences, within usual routines and activities, highlights for the child the meaning or use of the learning objectives
- Integration of these planned experiences within routines increases the probability that instruction/therapy will occur
- The use of child-initiated learning experiences capitalizes on the child's attention and motivation
- Learning opportunities that are distributed throughout the day (Bricker & Cripe, 1992; Widerstrom, 1995; Wolery & Wolery, 1992)

An example of a planning matrix for Lily is found in Figure 11.2. Another example using home routines is found in Chapter 13.

Construction of a planning matrix consists of, first, writing down the usual schedule of events and activities on the left side of the matrix. The child's (or children's) current objectives are then written across the top of the matrix. These objectives may be taken directly from the IFSP, but it is likely that they will be smaller, intermediate steps. Next, the team finds the best match between the amount and type of instruction or therapy that the child needs within the usual routine. The team can then mark an "X" in the cell of the matrix corresponding to the best matches. Or, as in the example, the team can write in the names of the people involved, the materials, and the strategies to be used. The team may also want to distinguish between instructional opportunities and practice opportunities.

A matrix helps ensure that planned instruction occurs regularly during the busy day. It also helps the team plan for generalization by planning for instruction

	Objective 1. Use 10 words.	Objective 2. Follow routines in classroom activities.	Objective 3. Initiate positive social interactions with peers.
Arrival/greeting		Verbal or gestural prompts (staff)	
Free choice	Question, comment, and acknowledge (Gwen)	Prompt and let Lily play at the activity (staff)	Model (Maria)
Clean-up		Physically assist with clean-up (staff)	
Snack	Question, comment, and acknowledge (Gwen)		Model (Gwen)
Outside play	Question, comment, and acknowledge (staff)		Model with objects in playhouse (staff)
Closing circle		Let Lily hold a stuffed animal (staff)	Provide affection training in songs (staff)

Figure 11.2. Planning matrix for Lily.

and practice at various times of the day, during various events or activities, and with various people and materials. See Bricker and Cripe (1992), Helmstetter and Guess (1987), and Sandall (1995) for additional versions of planning matrices.

Very Early Intervention Very early intervention may commence in the hospital for preterm infants or at home. Regardless of setting, the team must consider the child's health. The team must also consider and respect the parents in their developmental task of becoming parents whether for the first time or for the first time with this baby. The transition to parenthood, like all family life cycle changes, brings accompanying stress, and the team must appreciate the strategies the parents use to make this transition.

One of the central goals of very early intervention is to help parents and other caregivers learn to read and understand their infant's communicative signals. It is helpful to use an observational tool such as the Infant Behavioral Assessment (IBA) to learn the infant's way of saying, "I'm ready for interaction," or "I'm having fun" as well as those signals that mean "I've had enough and I need to rest." Additional information on parent–infant interaction can be gained from Table 13.1 and the observation tools described in Chapter 9.

Some infants may be experiencing difficulty with state regulation. State, or level of arousal, reflects central nervous system integrity and maturation. One of the goals of learning to read the infant's signals is, in fact, to learn to recognize when the infant is in an alert state and available for social interaction. Methods designed for preterm infants (Als et al., 1986; Hedlund, 1989; Katz, Pokorni, & Long, 1989; Vandenberg, 1985) and infants exposed to alcohol and other drugs (Schneider, Griffith, & Chasnoff, 1989) provide potentially effective intervention strategies. Interventions may involve changing the environment or using particular caregiving techniques. Environmental changes include reducing excess stimulation from noise, light, or activity. Relatively simple changes such as moving or covering the infant's crib may be effective. Other infants may need boundaries within their crib. Positioning with blanket rolls or swaddling are sometimes used. Nonnutritive sucking or finger rolls may increase alertness and self-regulation. By timing and sequencing caregiving according to the infant's sleep–wake cycle and stress responses, the caregiver may also promote state regulation. Intervention also includes the gradual introduction of greater environmental demands.

Temperament refers to behavioral style. Temperament characteristics appear in infancy, are relatively constant, and have a constitutional base but may be influenced by the environment (McDevitt, 1988). Thomas and Chess (1977) described three clusters of temperament characteristics: difficult, slow-to-warm-up, and easy. "Goodness of fit" between the infant and the environment is the critical point rather than assignment of a particular label. Poor fit may lead to behavior problems, especially when temperament patterns do not meet parental expectations. A difficult infant in an accepting environment may be well adjusted; however, in another environment, this infant may do poorly. Intervention is warranted when there is a mismatch. The goal of intervention is to reduce the pattern of mismatch between child and environment by making changes in the environment.

Brazelton (1992) and Cameron and Rice (1986), among others, have described anticipatory guidance as a preventive measure. Guidance involves describing the temperament issue (e.g., mealtime control, sleep problems) to caregivers in positive nonjudgmental terms, outlining why the issue might occur, validating parental feelings that are likely to occur, and suggesting ways to handle or manage the issue.

Another feature of very early intervention is supporting mastery motivation. *Mastery motivation* refers to goal-directed behavior aimed toward mastery of one's social and physical environment. Indicators of mastery motivation include purposeful activity, initiative, and persistence. The team can encourage mastery motivation by careful selection of toys and providing adaptations when needed, allowing choices, and encouraging exploration, effort, and persistence.

Enhancing Movement Skills Movement allows a child to explore the world. Through movement the child interacts with and acts upon the social and physical environment. Many infants with disabilities or other developmental risks demonstrate difficulties in the motor domain. Motor difficulties may limit a child's interaction and exploration and consequently restrict learning opportunities. Moreover, such difficulties may leave children at risk for becoming passively dependent on others.

Children with motor impairments may have limited or poorly controlled movement. They often have difficulty assuming and maintaining postures against gravity (e.g., sitting, standing). In addition, attainment of motor milestones is delayed. While abnormal muscle tone or tension may account for some motor difficulties, other factors include retention of primitive reflexes, delayed development of postural responses, skeletal deformities, abnormal muscle strength, or problems related to speed, accuracy, or timing of movements.

The major goals are to help the child move as normally as possible, to help the child learn to use movement to initiate interactions with and to control aspects of the environment, and to provide opportunities that allow the child to grow and gain independence. Careful identification of individual intervention objectives is particularly important, because the purposes of intervention for infants with neurological impairments is different from intervention for infants with delayed motor development. For the infant with a neurological impairment, intervention may be aimed at preventing abnormal patterns while facilitating independent and functional movement.

The therapist may subscribe to a particular method of treatment such as neurodevelopmental treatment or sensory integration (see Harris & Tada, 1983, for a description). Perhaps the most widely used treatment for individuals with cerebral palsy is the neurodevelopmental treatment (NDT) approach (Bobath & Bobath, 1972). This approach has also been used for children with Down syndrome (Harris, 1981), severe mental retardation (Ellis, 1967), and sensory impairments (Bobath & Bobath, 1964). NDT incorporates handling techniques designed to facilitate normal muscle tone, inhibit abnormal reflex patterns, and facilitate automatic reactions in order to allow the child to move actively and experience normal movement. Four guidelines for positioning and handling the child with motor impairments are useful. These are to use key points of control (head and neck, shoulder girdle, and hips); to work toward symmetry (i.e., equally effective movement of both sides of the body); to work toward midline positioning; and to use only minimal support, thus encouraging maximum independent movement (Hanson & Harris, 1986).

Smith (1989) and Harris (1988) suggested that, in selecting and using this or any other treatment approach, one must consider the child's various environments and ensure that the functional skills that help improve the child's performance in all those environments are included in the child's plan.

Exploring the World During infancy, children extend and integrate sensory and motor actions to produce adaptive responses to the environment. The development of symbolic thought to solve problems marks the end of infancy. Review of early intervention curricula reveals that many base the content of the cognitive domain on Piaget's descriptions of the sensorimotor period. The curriculum-based assessments that accompany such curricula will be helpful for identifying individual objectives. In addition, the Uzgiris and Hunt Scales (Uzgiris & Hunt, 1975) and the Dunst (1980) adaptations are useful. These descriptions detail how the infant constructs reality through such behaviors as looking, listening, and manipulating objects. These early behaviors or schemes are modified, combined, and coordinated to create new schemes. A scheme can be thought of as a basic pattern of action, thought, or knowledge that is used to interact with the environment. Although interaction with objects and the physical environment is critical to early cognitive development, the context for young children to learn cognitive skills is through social interaction with responsive caregivers.

The goal of early intervention in the cognitive domain is to support and enhance the child's own capabilities to remember, gain information, and solve problems. Furthermore, the goal is to support the use of increasingly more conventional forms of those capabilities. That is, functional object use is more conventional than mouthing or poking, and talking is more conventional than vocalizing.

Scaffolding (Vygotsky, 1978) can be an effective intervention method whether used by parents or other members of the intervention team. Bruner (1983) described the parent as providing a "scaffold" for the emerging skills of the child. As the child's skills emerge, the parent (or other team member) supports, encourages, and challenges the child. Another way to think of scaffolding is to set up challenges and assist the child to work "on the edge" of his or her current competence. Vygotsky (1978) used the term *zone of proximal development* to describe the level of development at which the child can function with assistance. The team identifies the child's current competence by carefully observing the child's play using transdisciplinary play-based assessment (TPBA) (Linder, 1993a), the Play Scale, or another measure and combining these observations with their knowledge of child development to then set up appropriate challenges for individual children.

When an adult interacts with an infant or toddler, one must start at the child's level. One way to do this is to mimic the child. Once interaction (several exchanges) has been established, the adult can encourage the child to go a little bit further perhaps by changing the adult's verbal behavior, modifying the way the adult uses the material, or by adding something to the play situation. The adult provides gentle nudges to help the child move ahead (see Widerstrom, 1995, for examples).

In the previous example, imitation (imitating the child) was used to engage the child in an interaction. *Imitation* is a valuable learning strategy for the child to learn as well. By first imitating the child, the adult helps to focus the child's attention. According to Bandura (1985), this is one of the key processes for observational learning. Given these experiences of being imitated, the infant will imitate the adult if the adult is doing a behavior in the child's repertoire. Gradually the infant becomes more able to imitate the sounds, gestures, actions, and sequences of others. Using both immediate and deferred imitation, the young child can learn a variety of new behaviors.

Intervention strategies based on behavioral principles can also be used to facilitate early cognitive and play behaviors (Bricker, 1986; Dunst, 1981). *Reinforcement* is any consequence that immediately follows a behavior and increases the likelihood that the behavior will occur again. Potential reinforcers include smiles, attention, and praise. Contingent reinforcement means that the reinforcer is provided when and only when the behavior occurs.

Assistance provided by the adult before the infant responds is called a *prompt*. There are many types of prompts including gestural prompts (e.g., gesturing with the hand while saying, "Find your shoes"), verbal prompts (e.g., asking "Where's the ball?" to encourage crawling to find a hidden toy), and physical prompts (e.g., guiding at the infant's elbow to assist in reaching for a toy). *Modeling* is a procedure in which a demonstration of the desired behavior is provided by an adult or other child. For example, big brother shows Bella how to hit the xylophone with a hammer, then he gives the hammer to Bella.

Communicating with Others Communication is the transmission of all kinds of messages such as ideas, information, needs, perceptions, and feelings. One may transmit or send messages and one may receive messages. Communication can occur in oral and nonoral modes. Infants communicate in a wide variety of ways such as crying, cooing, wiggling, and kicking.

A substantial number of infants in early intervention programs will have communication needs. Communication and language development can be delayed or different for a variety of reasons. For example, the infant with a hearing loss experiences reduced sensory input, which interferes with output. The infant with Down syndrome may be significantly delayed in acquisition of communication skills. The infant with a motor impairment may be unable to produce gestures or vocalizations that are readily interpreted. Regardless of etiology, communication disorders can have pervasive effects on many features of the child's and family's life.

Goldstein (1993) wrote that a basic guideline for intervention is the presentation of frequent opportunities for children to transmit and receive information in the multitude of ways that communication can be woven into their lives. Intervention efforts should take an interactional approach. This approach emphasizes the social bases of language and assumes that language is based on social interactions and builds from the infant's early nonverbal exchanges with caregivers. Thus, early intervention in the communication domain is aimed at facilitating parent–infant interaction. In using parent–infant strategies, as in other intervention suggestions, the team must consider the family's cultural background and the influence of culture on communication.

A variety of more specific strategies have been described, studied, and refined. The interactional or conversational approach involves establishing a shared topic (often by following the child's lead) and taking turns. Changes in the physical environment may be effective. Other strategies require a more specific response by the conversational partner. Strategies include imitation of sounds, actions, or words to match the child's level (MacDonald & Gillette, 1989; Mahoney & Powell, 1986); use of wait time (Tronick, Als, & Brazelton, 1980) or time delay (Halle, Baer, & Spradlin, 1981) to allow the child the opportunity to take turns; and the use of repetitions and expansions (Scherer & Olswang, 1984) to confirm and extend the child's utterance (Table 11.5). Interventions are then implemented in natural settings to allow multiple, dispersed learning opportunities. Interventions incorporate natural consequences such as attention, continued interaction, and attainment of one's communicative intentions.

Some young children may need augmentative communication methods. Examples include sign language, communication boards, and mechanical or electronic and prosthetic devices. Preparation for and use of augmentative communication are important considerations in program planning.

Developing Self-Help Skills During the early childhood years, children master important skills and develop some measure of independence in the areas of toileting, feeding/eating, dressing, and grooming. For infants, independent feeding is a major accomplishment. Because infants with disabilities often demonstrate delays and difficulties in feeding, this area deserves special attention.

Many children with motor impairments will also have difficulties with feeding. Problems related to abnormal muscle tone, retention of primitive reflexes, structural abnormalities, or abnormal movement. Preterm infants often show feeding problems as well. Infants of less than 32 weeks' gestational age can be expected to have poorly coordinated sucking and swallowing and thus are unable to nipple feed. Alternatives include intravenous feeding and gavage feeding. Careful attention

Table 11.5. Practical strategies to enhance communication

Strategy	Description
Share a topic	Follow the infant's focus of attention. Follow the infant's interests. Use real objects and experiences.
Take turns	Create a conversational atmosphere. Converse about the objects and experiences of interest.
Organize the environment	Have conversational partners available. Provide toys and materials that do interesting things (e.g., roll, make noise, move). To encourage requests, some toys can be in sight but out of reach.
Imitate	Copy or mirror the infant's behavior. This helps keep the infant in the interaction. Children also seem to learn to imitate by having others imitate them.
Use wait time	Take one turn and wait for the infant to take a turn.
Use time delay	Wait 3–5 seconds before reactivating a toy or giving an object. This encourages the intentional infant to request the object or your assistance.
Use repetitions	Repeat or highlight your key words or phrases.
Use expansions	Increase the complexity of the infant's communication slightly, but maintain the intention (e.g., if the child says "key," say "Mommy's keys").

must be given to provide the growing infant with opportunities to suck (finger or pacifier) and to make the transition to bottle or breast. Specialized techniques and lengthy feeding sessions may be required. However, some infants, particularly those who have had multiple intrusive treatments around the mouth, may become resistant to oral feeding. These babies present quite a challenge to their caregivers and may require specialized procedures (Bernbaum, Pereira, Watkins, & Peckham, 1983; Blackman & Nelson, 1985; Harris, 1986; Palmer, Thompson, & Lindsheld, 1975).

Resources that focus on feeding interventions (e.g., Morris & Klein, 1987; University of Colorado Health Sciences Center School of Nursing [UCHSCSN], 1989a, 1989b) are useful in designing interventions that incorporate specialized techniques into normative environments.

Working with Caregivers A fundamental role of the early intervention team is to support and enhance family members as capable and confident caregivers of their child. Whether the setting is the hospital, home, or center, early interventionists must have the skills to interact successfully with family members as well as with the child. Knowledge and use of the family-centered principles described throughout this book establish the foundation. McCollum and Yates (1994) described more specific strategies for working with parents and caregivers. These include acknowledging the parent's competence, providing information, modeling, and suggesting alternatives. The authors also offer guidelines for providing this assistance in sensitive ways. Early interventionists should match their interventions with the individual strengths of the parent, follow the parent's lead, use both direct and indirect instructional strategies, and engage the parent in observing and hypothesizing about his or her child's behavior.

Monitoring Progress

Much time and energy typically go into assessment, identification of outcomes and objectives, design of fun and interesting activities, and the implementation of intervention through those activities. An integral part of the intervention process is monitoring the effects of the intervention. By conducting regular and frequent checks of the child's progress, the team can make accurate decisions about continuing with an activity or strategy; providing additional opportunities; altering the activity, materials, or strategies; or moving on to a new objective. Regular and frequent monitoring tells the early intervention team about the effects of the intervention.

There are a variety of ways by which team members can keep track of progress. Curriculum-based measures are a good choice. The team does not want to limit data collection to a single method. The purpose is to determine whether the child is making adequate progress and to determine whether desired outcomes were achieved. It may be helpful to think of this process as gathering information to tell the "story" of the child's experience in early intervention.

A portfolio is a purposeful collection of a child's work that demonstrates the child's efforts, progress, and achievements over time (Grace & Shores, 1991). A portfolio offers a complex and comprehensive view of a child's performance within natural contexts. An infant or toddler's work samples will be different from those of an older child or adult. Still, by thinking about monitoring progress from a broad perspective, the child's story can be documented.

The actual portfolio items will depend on the child, the outcomes and objectives, and the sorts of activities and experiences that are provided. Suggestions for portfolio entries include work samples, records from observations, and notes from parents or caregivers. Work samples (sometimes called *permanent products*) include audiotapes, videotapes, photographs of a child at play, and drawings or other artwork. Observational methods include anecdotal records, running records, checklists, rating scales, participation charts, and direct observation of target behaviors using time sampling or event sampling techniques. Notes can include phone logs with notes from phone conversations with parents or "back and forth" books that describe the child's day. In Table 11.6, suggestions for methods for monitoring child progress are linked to a sampling of child objectives.

Putting the portfolio together requires some planning, selecting an appropriate container, and organizing the materials by category (e.g., domain, IFSP outcome area) and time sequence. Entry slips should be used on all entries that include the date, the name of the person who entered the sample, and why it was included. Other information that is sometimes in a portfolio includes the child's IFSP, a list of the classroom goals, and special projects or events that the child participated in (e.g., field trip to the petting zoo).

Table 11.6. Suggestions for portfolio items

Brian will drink from the cup.
- Periodic videotapes
- Checklist of steps, record levels of assistance
- Anecdotal record

Alberto will initiate playing social games.
- Parent's diary
- Anecdotal record
- Running record

Lily will use 10 single words.
- Diary at home and school
- Periodic videotapes
- Periodic language sample

The value of the portfolio is in its use. Using the regular, frequent, and repeated information they have collected, the team assesses the child's performance in relation to the child's previous work. The team refers to their previous assessment records that may provide information on the child's own developmental rate and trajectory. The team also uses various sources such as their knowledge of child development and early intervention, developmental assessment tools, and their experiences and expectations to evaluate the child's progress. The team reviews and describes how the child is doing by looking for patterns in the data contained in the portfolio (e.g., increases or improvements, variability, lack of change, declines) and making intervention decisions based on the data.

SUMMARY

This chapter focused on the contexts, content, and methods of early intervention with infants, toddlers, and their families. Interventionists need to be responsive and consistent. They need to intervene through social experiences, caregiving routines, and play. They need to plan, implement, and evaluate their efforts in collaboration with the family and the other members of the team. And they need to enjoy and learn from their experiences with young children and their families.

SUGGESTED READINGS AND RESOURCES

Dunst, C.J. (1981). *Infant learning: A cognitive-linguistic intervention strategy.* Hingham, MA: Teaching Resources.

Fewell, R.R., & Vadasy, P.F. (1983). *Learning through play.* Hingham, MA: Teaching Resources.

Finnie, N.R. (1975). *Handling the young cerebral palsied child at home.* New York: E.P. Dutton.

Furuno, S., O'Reilly, K.A., Inatsuka, T.T., Hosaka, C.M., & Falbey, B.Z. (1993). *Helping babies learn: Developmental profiles and activities for infants and toddlers.* Tucson, AZ: Communication Skill Builders.

Gillette, Y. (1993). *Communicating effectively with young children.* Tucson, AZ: Communication Skill Builders.

Manolson, A. (1985). *It takes two to talk.* Toronto, Ontario, Canada: Hanen Early Language Resource Center.

Mulligan, S.A., Green, K.M., Morris, S.L., Maloney, T.J., McMurray, D., & Kittelson-Aldred, T. (1992). *Integrated child care: Meeting the challenge.* Tucson, AZ: Communication Skill Builders.

Vincent, L.J., Poulsen, M.K., Cole, C.K., Woodruff, G., & Griffith, D.R. (1991). *Born substance exposed, educationally vulnerable.* Reston, VA: Council for Exceptional Children.

REFERENCES

Als, H., Lawhorn, G., Brown, E., Gibes, R., Duffy, F.H., McAnulty, G., & Blickman, J.G. (1986). Individualized behavioral and environmental care for the very low birth weight preterm infant at high risk for bronchopulmonary dysplasia: Neonatal intensive care unit and developmental outcome. *Pediatrics, 78*(6), 1123–1132.

American Public Health Association (APHA) & American Academy of Pediatrics (AAP). (1992). *Caring for our children: National health and safety standards guidelines for out of home child care programs.* Washington, DC: Author.

Americans with Disabilities Act (ADA) of 1990, PL 101-336, 42 U.S.C. § 12101 *et seq.*

Bailey, D.B., & McWilliam, R.A. (1990). Normalizing early intervention. *Topics in Early Childhood Special Education, 10*(2), 33–47.

Bandura, A. (1985). *Social foundations of thought and action: A social cognitive theory.* Englewood Cliffs, NJ: Prentice Hall.

Berk, L.E., & Winsler, A. (1995). *Scaffolding children's learning: Vygotsky and early childhood education.* Washington, DC: National Association for the Education of Young Children.

Berkeley, R.R., & Ludlow, B.L. (1989). Toward a reconceptualization of the developmental model. *Topics in Early Childhood Special Education, 9*(3), 66–77.

Bernbaum, J.C., Pereira, B.R., Watkins, J.B., & Peckham, G.J. (1983). Non-nutritive sucking during gavage feeding enhances growth and maturation in premature infants. *Pediatrics, 71*(1), 41–45.

Blackman, J.A., & Nelson, C.L.A. (1985). Reinstituting oral feeding in children fed by gastrostomy tube. *Clinical Pediatrics, 24*(8), 434–438.

Bobath, K., & Bobath, B. (1964). The facilitation of normal postural reactions and movements in the treatment of cerebral palsy. *Physiotherapy, 50,* 246–252.

Bobath, K., & Bobath, B. (1972). Cerebral palsy. In P.H. Pearson & C. Williams (Eds.), *Physical therapy services in the developmental disabilities* (pp. 31–185). Springfield, IL: Charles C Thomas.

Brazelton, T.B. (1992). *Touchpoints.* Reading, MA: Addison-Wesley.

Bredekamp, S. (1986). *Developmentally appropriate practice in early childhood programs serving children from birth through age 8.* Washington, DC: National Association for the Education of Young Children.

Bricker, D. (1989). *Early intervention for at-risk and handicapped infants, toddlers, and preschool children.* Palo Alto, CA: VORT Corporation.

Bricker, D., & Cripe, J.J.W. (1992). *An activity-based approach to early intervention.* Baltimore: Paul H. Brookes Publishing Co.

Bricker, D.D. (1986). *Early education of at-risk and handicapped infants, toddlers, and preschool children.* Glenview, IL: Scott, Foresman.

Bronfenbrenner, U. (1979). *The ecology of human development: Experiments by nature and design.* Cambridge, MA: Harvard University Press.

Bronson, M.B. (1995). *The right stuff for children birth to 8: Selecting play materials to support development.* Washington, DC: National Association for the Education of Young Children.

Bruner, J.S. (1983). *Child's talk: Learning to use language.* New York: Norton.

Burkhart, L.J. (1980). *Homemade battery powered toys and educational devices for severely handicapped children.* College Park, MD: Author.

Burkhart, L.J. (1982). *More homemade battery devices for severely handicapped children with suggested activities.* College Park, MD: Author.

Cameron, J.R., & Rice, D.C. (1986). Developing anticipatory guidance programs based on early assessment of infant temperament: Two tests of a prevention model. *Journal of Pediatric Psychology, 11*(2), 221–234.

Cripe, J., Slentz, K., & Bricker, D. (1993). *Assessment, Evaluation, and Programming System (AEPS) for infants and children: Vol. 2. Measurement for birth to three years.* Baltimore: Paul H. Brookes Publishing Co.

Division for Early Childhood, Council for Exceptional Children. (1993). DEC position paper on inclusion. *DEC Communicator, 19*(4), 4.

Dunst, C.J. (1980). *A clinical and educational manual for use with the Uzgiris and Hunt Scales of Infant Psychological Development.* Austin, TX: PRO-ED.

Dunst, C.J. (1981). *Infant learning: A cognitive-linguistic intervention strategy.* Hingham, MA: Teaching Resources.

Dunst, C.J. (1993). Interventions to promote cognitive skills. In DEC Task Force on Recommended Practices (Ed.), *DEC recommended practices: Indicators of quality in programs for infants and young children with special needs and their families.* Reston, VA: Council for Exceptional Children.

Dunst, C.J., Cushing, P.J., & Vance, S. (1985). Response-contingent learning in profoundly handicapped infants: A social systems perspective. *Analysis and Intervention in Developmental Disabilities, 5*(1–2), 33–47.

Ellis, E. (1967). Physical management of developmental disorders. *Clinics in Developmental Medicine* (No. 26). London: Heinemann.

Fewell, R.R., & Sandall, S.R. (1983). Curricular adaptations for young children: Visually handicapped, hearing impaired, and physically impaired. *Topics in Early Childhood Special Education, 2*(4), 51–66.

Furuno, S., O'Reilly, K., Hosaka, C., Inatsuka, T., Allman, T., & Zeisloft, B. (1979). *Hawaii Early Learning Profile.* Palo Alto, CA: VORT Corp.

Gesell, A. (1925). *The mental growth of the preschool child.* New York: Macmillan.

Gesell, A., & Ilg, E. (1949). *Child development: An introduction to the study of human growth.* New York: Harper & Row.

Goldstein, H. (1993). Interventions to promote communication skills. In DEC Task Force on Recommended Practices (Ed.), *DEC recommended practices: Indicators of quality in programs for infants and young children with special needs and their families.* Reston, VA: Council for Exceptional Children.

Grace, C., & Shores, E.F. (1991). *The portfolio and its use: Developmentally appropriate assessment of young children.* Little Rock, AR: Southern Association on Children Under Six.

Guralnick, M.J. (1990). Major accomplishments and future directions in early childhood mainstreaming. *Topics in Early Childhood Special Education, 10*(2), 1–17.

Halle, J.W., Baer, D.M., & Spradlin, J.E. (1981). Teachers' generalized use of delay as a stimulus control procedure to increase language in handicapped children. *Journal of Applied Behavior Analysis, 14*(4), 387–400.

Hanson, M.J. (1987). *Teaching the infant with Down syndrome: A guide for parents and professionals* (2nd ed.). Austin, TX: PRO-ED.

Hanson, M.J., & Harris, S.R. (1986). *Teaching the young child with motor delays: A guide for parents and professionals.* Austin, TX: PRO-ED.

Harris, M.B. (1986). Oral-motor management of the high-risk neonate. In J.K. Sweeney (Ed.), *The high-risk neonate* (pp. 231–253). New York: Haworth Press.

Harris, S.R. (1981). Effects of neurodevelopmental therapy on improving motor performance in Down's syndrome infants. *Developmental Medicine and Child Neurology, 23*(4), 477–483.

Harris, S.R. (1988). Neuromotor assessment for infants with Down syndrome. *Down Syndrome: Papers and Abstracts for Professionals, 11*(1), 1–4.

Harris, S.R., & Tada, W.L. (1983). Providing developmental therapy services. In S.G. Garwood & R.R. Fewell (Eds.), *Educating handicapped infants* (pp. 342–368). Rockville, MD: Aspen Publishers.

Hedlund, R. (1989). Fostering positive social interactions between parents and infants. *Teaching Exceptional Children, 21*(4), 45–48.

Helmstetter, E., & Guess, D. (1987). Application of the individualized curriculum sequencing model to learners with severe sensory impairments. In L. Goetz, D. Guess, & K. Stremel-Campbell (Eds.), *Innovative program design for individuals with dual sensory impairments* (pp. 255–282). Baltimore: Paul H. Brookes Publishing Co.

Hyson, M.C. (1994). *The emotional development of young children: Building an emotion-centered curriculum.* New York: Teachers College Press.

Individuals with Disabilities Education Act (IDEA) of 1990, PL 101-476, 20 U.S.C. § 1400 *et seq.*

Johnson-Martin, N.M., Jens, K.G., Attermeier, S.M., & Hacker, B.J. (1991). *The Carolina Curriculum for infants and toddlers with special needs* (2nd ed.). Baltimore: Paul H. Brookes Publishing Co.

Karnes, M.B. (1981). *Small wonder.* Circle Pines, MN: American Guidance Services.

Katz, K.S., Pokorni, J.L., & Long, T.M. (1989). *Chronically ill and at risk infants.* Palo Alto, CA: VORT Corporation.

Kendrick, A., Kaufmann, R., & Messenger, K. (Eds.). (1991). *Healthy young children: A manual for programs* (2nd ed.). Washington, DC: National Association for the Education of Young Children.

Lewis, M. (1984). Developmental principles and their implications for at-risk and handicapped infants. In M.J. Hanson (Ed.), *Atypical infant development* (pp. 3–24). Austin, TX: PRO-ED.

Linder, T.W. (1993a). *Transdisciplinary play-based assessment: A functional approach to working with young children* (Rev. ed.). Baltimore: Paul H. Brookes Publishing Co.

Linder, T.W. (1993b). *Transdisciplinary play-based intervention: Guidelines for developing a meaningful curriculum for young children.* Baltimore: Paul H. Brookes Publishing Co.

MacDonald, J.D., & Gillette, Y. (1989). *Eco: A partnership program (kit).* San Antonio, TX: Special Press, Inc.

Mahoney, G., & Powell, A. (1986). *Transactional intervention program: A child centered approach to developmental intervention with young handicapped children.* [Monograph No. 1]. Farmington: University of Connecticut School of Medicine, Pediatric Research and Training Center.

McCollum, J.A., & Yates, T.J. (1994). Dyad as focus, triad as means: A family-centered approach to supporting parent–child interactions. *Infants and Young Children, 6*(4), 54–63.
McDevitt, S.C. (1988). Assessment of temperament in developmentally disabled infants and preschoolers. In T. Wachs & R. Sheehan (Eds.), *Assessment of young developmentally disabled children* (pp. 255–265). New York: Plenum.
McWilliam, R.A. (1991). Targeting teaching at children's use of time: Perspectives of preschoolers' engagement. *Teaching Exceptional Children, 23*(4), 42–43.
McWilliam, R.A., & Strain, P.S. (1993). Service delivery models. In DEC Task Force on Recommended Practices (Ed.), *DEC recommended practices: Indicators of quality in programs for infants and young children with special needs and their families* (pp. 40–46). Reston, VA: Council for Exceptional Children.
McWilliam, R.A., Trivette, C.M., & Dunst, C.J. (1986). Behavior engagement as a measure of the efficacy of early intervention. *Analysis and Intervention in Developmental Disabilities, 5*(1–2), 33–45.
Morris, S.E., & Klein, M.D. (1987). *Pre-feeding skills.* Tucson, AZ: Therapy Skill Builders.
National Association for the Education of Young Children (NAEYC). (1985). *Toys: Tools for learning.* Washington, DC: Author.
Odom, S.L., & McEvoy, M.A. (1988). Integration of young children with handicaps and normally developing children. In S.L. Odom & M.B. Karnes (Eds.), *Early intervention for infants and children with handicaps* (pp. 241–267). Baltimore: Paul H. Brookes Publishing Co.
Osofsky, J.D. (Ed.). (1987). *Handbook of infant development* (4th ed.). New York: John Wiley & Sons.
Palmer, S., Thompson, R.J., & Linsheld, T.R. (1975). Applied behavior analysis in the treatment of children's feeding problems. *Developmental Medicine and Child Neurology, 17*(3), 333.
Piaget, J. (1952). *The origins of intelligence in children.* (M. Cook, Translator). New York: International Universities Press.
Piaget, J. (1970). Piaget's theory. In P.H. Mussen (Ed.), *Carmichael's manual of child psychology* (3rd ed., pp. 703–732). New York: John Wiley & Sons.
Sandall, S.R. (1995). A planning matrix for play. In A.H. Widerstrom, *Achieving learning goals through play* (pp. 23–38). Tucson, AZ: Communication Skill Builders.
Schafer, D.S., & Moersch, M.M. (Eds.). (1981). *Developmental programming for infants and young children.* Ann Arbor: University of Michigan Press.
Scherer, N., & Olswang, L. (1984). Role of mothers' expansions in stimulating children's language production. *Journal of Speech and Hearing Research, 27*(3), 387–396.
Schneider, J.W., Griffith, D.R., & Chasnoff, I.J. (1989). Infants exposed to cocaine in utero: Implications for developmental assessment and intervention. *Infants and Young Children, (2)*1, 23–36.
Skinner, B.F. (1976). *About behaviorism.* New York: Vintage Books.
Smith, P.D. (1989). Assessing motor skills. In D.B. Bailey & M. Wolery (Eds.), *Assessing infants and preschoolers with handicaps* (pp. 301–338). Columbus, OH: Charles E. Merrill.
Sparling, J., & Lewis, I. (1984). *Partners for learning.* Lewisville, NC: Kaplan School Supply.
Sullivan, M.W., & Lewis, M. (1993). Contingency, means-end skills, and the use of technology in infant intervention. *Infants and Young Children, 5*(4), 58–77.
Thomas, A., & Chess, S. (1977). *Temperament and development.* New York: Bruner-Mazel.
Thurman, S.K., & Widerstrom, A.H. (1990). *Infants and young children with special needs: A developmental and ecological approach* (2nd ed.). Baltimore: Paul H. Brookes Publishing Co.
Tronick, E., Als, H., & Brazelton, T.B. (1980). Monadic phases: A structural descriptive analysis of infant–mother face to face interaction. *Merrill Palmer Quarterly, 26*(1), 3–24.
Turnbull, A., Turnbull, H., & Blue-Banning, M. (1994). Enhancing inclusion of infants and toddlers with disabilities and their families: A theoretical and programmatic analysis. *Infants and Young Children, 7*(2), 1–14.
University of Colorado Health Sciences Center School of Nursing. (1989a). *Feeding infants and young children with special needs* [Videotape]. Lawrence, KS: Learner Managed Designs, Inc.
University of Colorado Health Sciences Center School of Nursing. (1989b). *Infections control in child care settings* [Videotape]. Lawrence, KS: Learner Managed Designs, Inc.

Uzgiris, I., & Hunt, J.M. (1975). *Assessment in infancy: Ordinal scales of psychological development.* Urbana: University of Illinois Press.
Vandenberg, K. (1985). Revising the traditional model: An individualized approach to developmental interventions in the intensive care nursery. *Neonatal Network,* 3(5), 4–9.
Vygotsky, L.S. (1978). *Mind in society: The development of higher psychological functions.* Cambridge, MA: Harvard University Press.
Widerstrom, A.H. (1995). *Achieving learning goals through play.* San Antonio, TX: Communication Skill Builders.
Wolery, M., & Wolery, R. (1992). Promoting functional cognitive skills. In D.B. Bailey & M. Wolery (Eds.), *Teaching infants and preschoolers with disabilities* (2nd ed., pp. 521–572). New York: Macmillan.
Zero to Three. (1992). *Heart Start: The emotional foundations of school readiness.* Washington, DC: National Center for Clinical Infant Programs.

11 ACTIVITIES

1. Locate a program for infants or toddlers and obtain permission to observe. First, ask the teacher to identify the specific intervention objectives for one or more children. Second, observe for use of specific intervention strategies.

2. Interview faculty who teach courses on curriculum or treatment for infants and toddlers in any one of the Part H service areas (e.g., speech therapy, occupational therapy). Ask them about their recommendations for curricula, activity guides, and treatment approaches.

3. Start a resource file. Use a format that will be useful for you both now and in the future. Your entries should include descriptive information and a critique.

4. Design and make a simple toy using easy-to-locate materials for each of the toy categories listed in Table 11.3.

CHAPTER 12

Early Intervention Program Models

Barbara A. Mowder

Objectives

- To define and describe intervention programs
- To evaluate the effectiveness of intervention programs
- To discuss issues in infant intervention programs

Programs for infants and toddlers at risk for or with disabilities are not new, but they have become increasingly important with the passages of PL 99-457, the Education of the Handicapped Act Amendments of 1986 (Lowenthal, 1988; Parson & McIntosh, 1987; Trohanis, 1988), and PL 101-476, the Individuals with Disabilities Education Act (IDEA) of 1990, and the recognition of the importance of developmental intervention in the lives of infants and their families (Lewis & Sullivan, 1994). The implementation of PL 99-457 and IDEA has generated a number of program-related issues (Barnett, 1988; Epps & Jackson, 1991; Garwood, Fewell, & Neisworth, 1988; Harbin, 1988; McLinden & Prasse, 1991; Smith & Strain, 1988), and implementation has taken a variety of forms (Harbin & McNulty, 1990; Walsh, Campbell, & McKenna, 1988). Gallagher (1992) presented the value assumptions that underlie PL 99-457:

- The earlier the intervention occurs, the better.
- It is better that many professional disciplines participate in intervention.
- Families have an important role to play in early intervention.
- It is important that qualified professionals provide early intervention services.
- Children who are at risk are helped with early intervention services.
- Interagency coordinating councils can help in the coordination of intervention services.

In their early stages of development, infant programs tended to focus exclusively on the infant, with a heavy orientation toward infant stimulation and medical interventions. Recently developed programs have moved toward a broader, more comprehensive orientation, incorporating and integrating educational, psychological, and medical perspectives, and including the families in program planning, development, and implementation (see, e.g., Lewis & Sullivan, 1994).

In a review of 12 experimentally designed longitudinal studies of education programs for infants at risk, Ramey and Bryant (1988) found that infant intervention programs vary in their form, duration, and content. The major distinctions they found in the programs are between home- or center-based programs and parent- or child-oriented curricula, but programs also varied along a number of other characteristics:

- The child's age during the intervention
- The intensity of the treatment program
- The number of children involved in the intervention program
- The primary target of the intervention (e.g., the child, one or both parents)
- The program's educational activities
- The site of the intervention (e.g., center, home, a combination of center and home)

Therefore, programs vary according to program factors as well as according to additional variables such as funding; the nature of the population being served; the program's goals, personnel, and theoretical orientation; and prevailing social policy.

Odom, Yoder, and Hill (1988) noted that there are typically three general early intervention program characteristics. The first is an orientation toward prevention of eventual developmental delay; many programs try to prevent or mediate the severity of factors believed to cause or exacerbate a disabling condition. The second characteristic is an orientation toward change in the infant's behavior, development, or relations with caregivers. The third distinguishing aspect is a focus on change within the family system to foster positive changes in the infant.

Infant programs may be discussed and presented in a number of different ways. For the purpose of this chapter, preventive programs, infant-focused intervention programs, and parent–infant programs are discussed first. The chapter continues with infant program evaluation, a discussion of issues in infant intervention programming, and a summary of progress to date in infant program development.

PREVENTIVE INTERVENTION PROGRAMS

Preventive intervention programs are often difficult to describe and justify because they seek to avert a problem that has not yet occurred. Prevention programs, generically described, have three separate levels: primary, secondary, and tertiary (Felner, Jason, Moritsugu, & Farber, 1983; Simeonsson, 1991). The goal of *primary prevention* is the reduction of new disorder cases and the building of skills and competencies as protection against the specified problem. *Secondary prevention* targets early identification and intervention for babies who are displaying initial signs of a disorder, but the difficulty is not yet established. *Tertiary prevention* focuses on the individual with an established disorder, with the goal of reducing the effects of the disorder and rehabilitating the individual to a level at which there is an eventual adjustment to community life.

Women and Infants at Risk

Early preventive intervention programs rarely specifically articulate the level at which they are focused. In general, however, they attempt to identify mothers who are at risk because of environmental or physiological factors for delivering an infant at risk or with disabilities. In that sense, these programs tend to be primary prevention programs. Kopp (1987) identified three group of women at risk: 1) mothers with medical or biological difficulties (e.g., epilepsy, heart disease), 2) mothers from low socioeconomic status groups, and 3) adolescent mothers.

Mothers with Biological Difficulties Programs oriented toward mothers with chronic health problems, a history of reproductive difficulties, or problematic genetic backgrounds try to educate and inform the mother and lessen the effects of these factors on the infant (Odom et al., 1988; Steel, 1985). Program designs include educational instructional programs, nutrition guidance, and pre-pregnancy counseling. Direct medical intervention is also part of these programs, when the mother's or developing infant's physical condition warrants it.

Mothers of Low Socioeconomic Status Mothers from a low socioeconomic background traditionally have many difficulties, including becoming pregnant prematurely, having more children than they can manage, becoming pregnant again at too short an interval, and not having adequate prenatal or obstetrical care or adequate social support systems (Brody, 1988). They are also more likely, as mothers, to be exposed to hazardous experiences and materials during pregnancy and more likely to have infants who are low birth weight or premature than women from higher socioeconomic levels. Liaw and Brooks-Gunn (1994) examined the cumulative familial risks and low birth weight children's behavioral and cognitive development in families that were economically disadvantaged and families that were not. They found that risk factors were more frequent in poor families and that, as the number of risk factors increased, children's measured IQ decreased.

Richey, Lovell, and Reid (1991) reported on a program designed to enhance social support among women at risk for child maltreatment. Mother's at-risk status was defined by a low-income status and a state referral for a therapeutic nursery for their children. The 12-week group training to strengthen interpersonal skills resulted in, among many things, an increase in personal network size, an increase in the quality and duration of daily contacts with others, and an increase in satisfaction with support from friends. There were slight improvements noted in self-esteem, loneliness, and attitudes toward using support resources.

For low socioeconomic status mothers, there are two major federal programs. The Special Supplemental Food Program for Women, Infants, and Children (WIC) (Chelimsky, 1984; Stockbauer, 1987) focuses on nutrition education and the provision of nutritionally strong supplemental foods to low-income women and children. The Maternal and Infant Care (MIC) Programs target medical services for low-income women and children with prenatal and postnatal follow-up examinations.

Pregnant Adolescent Women Adolescent women who become pregnant typically have many birth-related difficulties, including delivery of low birth weight infants, increased levels of infant mortality, and premature delivery (Finkelstein, Finkelstein, Christie, Roden, & Shelton, 1982). In addition, pregnant adolescent women tend to come from low socioeconomic backgrounds and therefore have problems associated with mothers from difficult economic circumstances. Educational and employment opportunities may be limited and repeat pregnancies frequently occur (Chase-Lansdale & Brooks-Gunn, 1994). Stevens-Simon, Kaplan, and McAnarney (1993) identified characteristics of pregnant adolescents associated with preterm deliveries, including vaginal bleeding during the first 8 weeks of gestation, conception within 3 years of menarche, a low body mass index, a socially deviant father of the baby, and a past history of physical or sexual abuse.

Programs for pregnant adolescents tend to provide child development education, health care, instruction on parenting skills, pregnancy and child birth education, and social support (Anastasiow, 1983). In general, they seek to eliminate or minimize the negative consequences of early childbearing and child rearing (McDonough, 1984). Scholl, Hediger, and Belsky (1994) reviewed prenatal care and adolescent maternal health; they found that an increased risk of preterm delivery is associated with young maternal age in both developed and developing countries and that comprehensive prenatal care appears to potentially diminish the risk of many complications.

An important issue in working with adolescent parents is a sensitivity to their developmental level and how their needs change over time as their own skills develop and parenting issues change (Helm, 1988). Trad (1993) noted the developmental obstacles associated with pregnant teenagers, particularly their limited cognitive awareness to predict long-term outcomes. An intervention technique termed *previewing* encourages pregnant adolescents to represent future scenes with their babies as a way of predicting and rehearsing behavioral strategies. Seitz and Apfel (1994) evaluated an alternative public school setting for pregnant teenagers and found that school programs have the potential to provide prenatal intervention to adolescents.

Program Settings

Programs targeting each of these groups of women are usually found in prenatal clinics and in agency, hospital, and school settings (Kopp, 1987). One of the largest issues with preventive approaches and programs is to reach the women and families who cannot or will not use the programs that exist to help them and their infants (Lourie, 1988). The perinatal period, for example, can be an opportunity for enhancing parent–infant communication by teaching parents interaction and communication skills with their infants and thereby preventing parental mistreatment of children (Helfer, 1987). In order to be effective, however, Brody (1988) asserted that prevention programs must view the woman's position within an ecological and social context, including the long-term institutionalized relations between the sexes and between parents and their children. Because there are numerous factors influencing preventive intervention with infants and parents (Greenspan et al., 1987), long-term preventive programming needs to be viewed within a context larger than an agency, community, or governmental action.

INFANT-FOCUSED INTERVENTION PROGRAMS

Infant-focused intervention programs have the longest and most diverse history of all intervention programs in infant programming. Traditionally found in medical settings, many of these programs have come to be identified with the neonatal intensive care unit (NICU), although Gilkerson, Gorski, and Panitz (1990) have discussed approaches linking hospitals with community-based intervention programs.

These infant-focused intervention programs historically tend to be heavily medically oriented, to a great extent overlooking the mother's and infant's many other needs. There is a vast range of infant-focused intervention programs, some found in NICUs, others located in other medical facilities, agency settings, educational facilities, and the home. The focus is as diverse as the locations in which these programs are found. Some are oriented toward a developmental care model, others on remediating perceived deficits, stimulating sensory modalities, teaching skills, or facilitating infant interactions.

Program Settings

Center-based, combination center- and home-based, and home-based programs are examples of some infant-focused intervention programs.

Center-Based Programs Tripp (1988) described a model therapeutic school intervention program to treat emotionally disturbed children. The target population of children was exhibiting anxiety, behavioral difficulties, eating problems, phobias, and sleep disturbances. Interventions addressed their emotional needs and, to a great extent, enabled them to enter and continue in a general education school with an academic program. Furthermore, graduates of the Perry Preschool show a number of benefits of program participation. Berrueta-Clement, Schweinhart, Barnett, Epstein, and Weikart (1984) found that program graduates had better attitudes toward education, had lower rates of special education placement and grade retention, and received better school grades than those children in the control group. Furthermore, Perry Preschool attendance, in the long run, was associated with fewer arrests or criminal charges and, in general, for less serious crimes (Berrueta-Clement et al., 1987). Zigler, Taussig, Cara, and Black (1992) pointed to the Perry Preschool Program and the Syracuse University Family Development Research Program (Lally, Mangione, & Honig, 1988) as examples of programs with the potential to prevent juvenile delinquency.

There are many difficulties in setting up a center-based program and conducting this type of activity, but there are potentially significant rewards for children, parents, and staff. Indeed, Abroms and Bennett (1983) noted that, in addition to helping young children, center-based programs can help parents overcome their sense of aloneness and facilitate their absorption of information related to their child's needs.

Combination Center- and Home-Based Programs The San Francisco Infant Program (Hanson & Krentz, 1986) is a combination program, providing classroom and home education components for infants and toddlers at risk and with disabilities. The focus is on cognitive development, communication skills, gross and fine motor development, self-help issues, and social development. In addition to the infant-focused portion of the program, the San Francisco Infant Program also includes parent training, preservice and in-service training for professionals, and ongoing research on infants. This program is based at San Francisco State University.

Home-Based Programs An example of a home-based infant stimulation program is one carried out by a South Louisiana School District (Aprill & Schifani, 1983). In this program, home teachers helped parents implement an individualized curriculum for their children. In addition, physical therapists and speech therapists were available. The program focused on infant development in cognitive skills, language development, motor areas, self-help skills, and social development; in addition to the services provided children, a parent support group grew out of program efforts.

Other Programs In addition to the center-based, combination, and home-based approaches, a number of specific infant-focused programs have been developed, including programmed instruction, the use of microcomputers, and networking strategies to provide services. A programmed instruction program specifically for infants who were blind or had multiple disabilities focused on infant orientation and mobility. The program concentrated on cognitive development, movement, touch, motor development, and sound localization, and the infants demonstrated significant performance gains in the first three areas.

Behrmann and Lahm (1983) presented an infant program utilizing microcomputers that focused on cognitive, language, and motor development. Infants at risk or with disabilities were taught to interact with microcomputers to foster development in the targeted areas. Brinker (1982, 1984) also found that microcomputers have the potential to teach infants as well as to examine infants' learning and response contingency styles.

Hulme's (1985) Iowa Program provides coordinated services for children needing technical medical care in their home and community. The Iowa Regional Child Health Centers provide services by physicians and pediatric nurse practitioners with a networking approach from a regional community perspective, and the Tennessee Department of Health and Environment established a high-risk registry to enhance infant follow-up program efforts (Riggs, 1985).

Related Issues

Infant-focused intervention programs have been questioned along a number of grounds. For example, Russman (1986) questioned whether children with biologically caused cognitive or motor impairments benefit from infant stimulation programs in the same manner as do children from environmentally deprived situations. Ferry (1986) echoed many of these concerns and found that in some cases (e.g., pediatric brain damage) there is a denial of the permanent, nonfixable nature of the problem. She argued that the program focus should be directed toward helpful aspects of infant intervention, such as fostering ambulation, feeding, posturing, improving communication skills, and strengthening the parent–child relationship. Barnard, Booth, Mitchell, and Telzrow (1988) summed up many of the issues by stating that infant therapy and toddler play groups need to be used in conjunction with interventions directed at mothers if they are to be effective.

PARENT-FOCUSED INTERVENTION PROGRAMS

Programs have been developed to educate, support, and teach parents with babies with special needs. Parents of these babies often face a great amount of stress; sometimes there is the psychological loss of an ideal child who was not born, with the consequent difficulties of handling a new situation (Farran & Sparling, 1988). Trout (1983) cited the many factors that are involved, including the effects of frequent infant hospitalization, father's reactions to a sick youngster, feelings of parental ambivalence, infant–parent interactions, parental grief, sibling issues, and seeking the cause of the illness or disability.

Types of Programs

There are programs, such as counseling programs, parent education programs, and parent interaction skill programs, that are offered for parents to help intervention efforts.

Counseling Programs Many diverse counseling programs for parents have evolved over time. For instance, Walton (1993) reported on a counseling program for parents of children with disabilities that focused on stress management. Procedures for assisting parents in stress awareness and related stress management are emphasized. A parent-focused infant intervention program dealing with infants who have a hearing impairment was developed in which parents were counseled about deaf identity and the deaf community (Clark, 1983). Counseling groups focused on the cultural implications of deafness, implications of a child's hearing impairment on parent issues, and understanding of issues related to hearing impairments. Seligman (1993) offered a group counseling program for parents that centers on ameliorating psychological problems, while Joanning, Demmitt, Brotherson, and Whiddon (1994) saw the individualized family service plan (IFSP) as an excellent avenue for family therapists to provide services to parents.

Parent Education Programs Hedge and Johnson (1986) described an infant intervention program in southeast Kansas that teaches parents to provide daily one-to-one therapy in gross and fine motor development, speech and language development, social adjustment, and behavior management. In general, the evidence on effective parenting is compelling enough to propose mandatory parent education programs (Anastasiow, 1988). Anastasiow found that there is no question that infant cognitive development is facilitated by maternal warmth, responsiveness, low physical punishment, a push to achieve, verbalness, and appropriate toys and exploration. Fine and Gardner (1991) proposed a broadly conceptualized counseling role for those working with parents; this role would include parent education, parent drop-in, and home visitor programs. Finally, Zigler (1994) pointed specifically to parent education as an important component to the effectiveness of early intervention programs.

Parent Interaction Skill Programs Lester (1992) described variations in infants' communication with their parents and, likewise, parents' varying abilities to interpret their children's signals and respond appropriately. He discussed the fit or match between infant and maternal characteristics. Rosenberg and Robinson (1985) described a project to enhance mothers' interactional skills in an infant education program. The focus of the training was on increasing mothers' skills in interacting with their infants or toddlers. Training involved teaching mothers strategies they can use to enhance the quality of interaction with their infants. The results demonstrated that mothers made substantial gains in interaction during the course of the intervention program.

Consistent with this approach is the counseling intervention program described by Pulskamp (1987). She presented a program to train parents in specific positive skills of child rearing, which included four meetings per week in a playroom setting where parents were taught increased interaction time, increased positive interactions, increased positive physical responses, and decreased directiveness.

Program Goals

In general, infant programs that focus on parents seek to improve parent skills in facilitating their infant's growth and development. Programs address different issues in parents' interaction with their children, but the assumption is that improved parent skills and parenting directly affect children's growth and development. Farran and Sparling (1988) found that parent-focused interventions need to anticipate times when parents will need help and to focus on the adaptive, changing capacity of parents. Also, McNaughton (1994) reported on parent views of early childhood intervention programs; in general, the studies he reviewed found high levels of parental satisfaction.

Parent–Infant—Focused Interaction Programs

One of the most striking changes in infant intervention programs since the mid-1970s has been in the role of parents (Guralnick & Bennett, 1987a, 1987b). Initially parents were asked to extend center-based activities into their homes; now, programs are focusing on family systems that emphasize the parent's role and the interaction between the infant and the infant's family. Kysela and Marfo (1983) remarked on the changes in early intervention and focused on a transactional model that emphasizes the child in the context of the parent–child relationship.

Much of the shift to a parent–infant program emphasis is due to the research findings in child development. Early research studies focused either on the parent or on the infant (Barnard et al., 1988), but there is strong increasing evidence that early mutual adaptation between the infant and the parents is important for long-range patterns of development and interaction (Bee et al., 1982; Hammond, Bee, Barnard, & Eyres, 1983). Research findings strongly support the conclusion that desirable cognitive and social-emotional development is related to the quality of the parent–child interaction during infancy (Barnard et al., 1988). McConkey (1994) went further and described five transformations that occur during early intervention services. He cited transformations from a focus on the child to the family, from reliance on specialists to family supporters, from therapy to transactions, from groups of individuals to specific people, and from health systems to community networks.

Parent–Infant Interaction Models and Programs

A number of models of parent–infant interaction and intervention have been developed. The following are some recent examples of parent–infant interaction models and programs.

A Theoretical Model for Parent–Infant Reciprocity Brazelton (1988) described a model for understanding and facilitating parent–infant reciprocity and fostering infant autonomy. According to the model, the parent initially approaches the infant in a specific and direct manner, which includes auditory, tactile, and visual stimulation. After the infant is oriented to the parent, the parent expands the affective and attentional ambiance to maintain the infant's focused state. The infant begins to reciprocate with interaction; the parent maintains the interaction and builds on it, expanding it to include the next infant achievement. When the next achievement occurs, the parent profusely acknowledges it and allows time for the infant to recognize the achievement. This becomes integrated into the infant's sense of competence and leads to the infant's autonomy. By utilizing a model such as this, infant intervention programs can direct their efforts at one or many of the factors influencing the interaction.

Transactional Intervention Program Mahoney and Powell (1988) described the Transactional Intervention Program (TRIP), a program designed to modify patterns of interaction between parents and their infant with disabilities. They found that parents can be very successful at learning turn-taking and interactive match strategies, and parents' efforts at responsiveness, sensitivity, and directiveness increased. Furthermore, they found that their work supports a shift in role for the child educator/therapist from that of a direct provider of services to a parent consultant role. Consistent with this approach is the Social Interaction Assessment/Intervention Model in which caregivers are helped to adjust their interactive styles to their particular infants (McCollum & Stayton, 1985).

Parent and Toddler Training Project Klein, Van Hasselt, Trefelner, and Sandstrom (1988) described the Parent and Toddler Training Project, an intervention program for infants and toddlers with visual impairments and multiple disabilities and their families. The purposes of the program are striking in their focus on family intervention: to increase the social responsiveness of the program's infants with disabilities, to implement a program to develop adequate parenting skills, to initiate treatment approaches with parents to reduce psychological distress and improve the family's quality of life, and to evaluate the progress of all participants in the program.

Medically Oriented Parent–Infant Interaction Programs

The Newborn Nursing Models Project (Barnard et al., 1988) is an empirically designed and tested nursing approach to facilitate parent–child adaptation and synchrony. Three nursing approaches were tested: 1) the Nursing Parent and Child Environments (NPACE), 2) the Nursing Support of Infants' Biobehavior (NSIBB), and 3) the Nursing Standard Approach to Care (NSTAC). These programs had different foci; a comparison of approaches revealed that there were no significant treatment effects. The researchers found that the lack of differences among program groups may have been because all groups were to some extent effective: The NPACE model is best used with families with many needs, the NSIBB model works well for nonmultiproblem families, and the NSTAC model works well with specific family problems.

Related Issues

The physical and occupational therapy literature, as well as the diverse fields of psychiatric and psychological intervention and research on infants with severe mental retardation, is calling for an emphasis on parent–infant interaction. For example, the physical and occupational therapy research finds that infants with disabilities consistently demonstrate difficulties in signaling behaviors and are less engaged and engaging than normal infants in their interactions with their parents. Therefore, O'Sullivan (1985–1986) stressed that early separation should be minimized and positive parent–infant interactions facilitated through intervention strategies.

In an analysis of psychiatric intervention in infancy, Minde and Minde (1982) concluded that treatment of infants must always focus primarily on improving the parent's interaction and child-rearing techniques. Greenspan and Lourie (1981) concurred and maintained that a preventive approach during infancy requires a four-way diagnostic or evaluation process, including assessment of the baby, the mother, the environment, and the cultural milieu of the baby and mother. Even early intervention programs for infants with severe retardation, when issues include life-sustaining technology, susceptibility to disease, and combinations of disabling conditions, stress the importance of social reciprocity and the need to increase interaction between children and their families (Calhoun & Rose, 1988). Stremel-Campbell and Rowland (1987) also asserted that adaptive strategies for infants with severe cognitive, sensory, and motor impairment should focus on and incorporate the process of caregiver–child interactions.

Although the focus on parent–infant intervention is well supported by the research literature and programs are clearly moving in this direction, there is a need to caution parent–infant intervention program developers to capture the uniqueness of each parent–child dyad in order for program strategies to be effective (Guralnick & Bennett, 1987a, 1987b). In addition, Bailey (1987) maintained that interventionists should not attempt to force their values on families but to be sensitive and collaborative in setting goals. Several factors may help interventionists engage in collaborative efforts with families: 1) using effective interviewing and listening techniques, 2) formally assessing family needs (e.g., Turnbull, 1988), 3) using negotiation and case management skills, and 4) viewing families from a systems perspective. The infant research literature and infant program development are moving in the direction of a strong emphasis on parent–infant interaction in infant intervention program models.

EVALUATION OF INTERVENTION PROGRAMS

Wolery (1987) found that the multitude of infant program evaluation studies produced two consistent findings: 1) numerous impact evaluation studies have occurred, and 2) the scientific merit of most of them is questionable. He maintained that evaluation studies of infants with disabilities should be scientifically defensible, and he made specific recommendations on the types of impact studies and specific issues to consider when evaluation studies are conducted.

Wolery (1987) also describes a process for determining if programs meet their stated objectives:

1. Specify the purpose of the evaluation study.
2. Specify objectives of the program to be evaluated and develop goal attainment scales.
3. Generate questions and identify measurement sources related to the program's progress on each objective and suspected areas of need.
4. Develop multiple measurement strategies to answer each question.
5. Collect data from each measurement source.
6. Analyze and summarize data by objective.
7. Present a report of the evaluation study to the decision makers of the program.

Problems with Evaluation Studies

Fewell and Vadasy (1987) reviewed trends in the use of outcome measures in program evaluation efforts, including the use of IQ as a measure, as well as other child-oriented characteristics. They found problems with relying solely on child outcome measures to determine program efficacy and suggest measurement approaches that consider the transactional nature and impact of early interventions on the child and family system. McNaughton (1994) reviewed 14 research articles that reported high levels of parent satisfaction with early intervention services. The analysis of the findings was seriously hampered by incomplete descriptions of the assessment measure as well as of the findings.

Fewell and Sandall (1986) found that program evaluation results vary with each different analysis and therefore lead to varying conclusions regarding program effectiveness. They pointed to problems with measurement, analysis, and methodologies and offered cautions in evaluating infant intervention programs. In particular, they recommended the use of alternative measures of child progress (e.g., multiple measures, expansion of assessed characteristics) in the evaluation of program effectiveness.

Evaluation Models

Meisels, Dichtelmiller, and Liaw (1993) developed a two-dimensional model to describe early intervention service programs. The two dimensions include the importance of parent intervention (from high to low) and the focus on child intervention (from high to low). Based on the two dimensions, four intervention models emerge: 1) low-intensity, 2) child-focused, 3) parent-focused, and 4) dual-focused programs. Interestingly, Upshur (1991) specifically considered parents' ratings of early intervention benefits. She found that services focusing exclusively on parents are less favorably received than those focusing on parents and children together.

Bricker and Gumerlock (1988) described a three-level model evaluation plan for monitoring child progress and program effects. The goals they describe include the following:

- To measure general program impact on participating children
- To monitor child progress toward acquisition of Individualized Education Plan (IEP) long-range goals and short-term objectives
- To gauge child progress toward specific instructional objectives to permit timely program modification (p. 58)

Consistent with the model, there are three different evaluation strategies, depending on the program goals and evaluation content. Despite being a helpful model to evaluate child progress, the plan fails to consider goals, evaluation content, and strategy with regard to families. The latter represents a serious omission in view of the current thrust of embracing families as an integral part of program planning, implementation, and evaluation.

Dickin, McKim, and Kirkland (1983) also discussed suitable designs and evaluation frameworks for evaluating intervention programs for infants at risk. They suggested specific guidelines for the design, implementation, and evaluation of infant intervention programs. The model, which serves as an aid to researchers, service providers, and administrators involved with high-risk infant programs, includes the following components:

- Policy and planning group formation
- Selection of program development model
- Needs assessment
- Literature review and consultation
- Determination of target population
- Selection of theoretical orientation(s)
- Specification of objectives
- Detailing operating components; evaluability assessment; and ethical, institutional, and legal requirements
- Financial viability
- Formal statement
- Community support assessment
- Funding

The implementation portion of the program includes a pilot project, sustaining project, process evaluation, and impact evaluation. They suggested this outline for those interested in considering, implementing, and evaluating infant intervention programs.

Evaluation Study Findings

There have been numerous evaluation studies of infant programs. In general, interventions with more hours of child contact are related to more positive effects on the children, parents, and family circumstances (Bryant & Ramey, 1984).

In one study, Bailey and Bricker (1985) considered the effectiveness of a home- and center-based early intervention program for 36 infants and preschool children with disabilities. The primary outcome variable was child change as measured by the Gesell Developmental Schedules and their own early evaluation and programming system. They found that the program had a positive impact on participating children and their parents. In another evaluation project, Bailey and Bricker (1984) analyzed 13 programs providing early intervention for infants and young children with severe disabilities. Even though the programs varied in terms of population served, interventions delivered, and evaluation methodology, all reported some form of positive outcome data.

Casto and White (1984) examined the efficacy of early intervention programs for infants environmentally at risk using meta-analytic techniques. Their results show some immediate positive effect, but their analysis failed to find long-term benefits and failed to relate the degree of parental involvement to intervention effectiveness. They found that the training of staff and the degree of program structure were positively related to program effectiveness.

In considering the long-term effects of infant stimulation programs for infants with Down syndrome, Sharav and Shlomo (1986) reported that such programs, along with home rearing and training, improved the children's functioning. In a larger project, Gibson and Fields (1984) reviewed the effectiveness of 11 early infant stimulation demonstration programs for children with Down syndrome over a 25-year period. They found there were gains in outcome measures—often at impressive levels—in the short term, but long-term investigations of the outcomes failed to support the gain. (The researchers explained the disparity by asserting that, if treatment was extended in time, intensified, or altered in content, the early gains would serve as building blocks for later cognitive development and academic achievement.) They concluded that future study of early intervention programs must address program definition and differentiation, the characteristics of children with Down syndrome, and the durability of outcome gains.

Marfo and Kysela (1985) analyzed research on the impact of early intervention programs with infants and young children with mental retardation and their families. Their review of 20 studies in five countries from 1975 to 1983 revealed an overemphasis on child developmental progress to the neglect of parental and environmental variables, on which the child's ultimate progress depends.

Bricker (1984) complained that the program evaluation literature addresses issues apart from the effect of the program and provides no objective evaluation outcomes. She found that many variables, including population variability, inability to execute sound designs, and differences in dependent measures and equivalent outcomes, impede firm and generalizable conclusions regarding program effectiveness.

Increasingly, evaluation models will need to be developed that specifically address efficacy concerns related to specific program goals and objectives, infant interaction, and a family orientation. For example, Eayrs and Jones (1992) believed that evaluation of early intervention services should follow the criterion-related evaluation that has become prevalent in adult mental health services. Already, scale development is occurring; for example, Seibert, Hogan, and Mundy (1987) described scales designed to assess social and communication skills acquired in infancy. Increasingly, scale development of this type has become important. Finally, Hauser-Cram (1990) stressed the importance of thoughtful, well-designed evaluations, and Black (1991) was concerned that there remain many unanswered questions regarding early intervention program evaluation.

ISSUES IN INFANT INTERVENTION PROGRAMS

There are many issues that emerge in the discussion of infant intervention programs.

Definition

One of the most fundamental issues is that of definition at all levels of program development, implementation, and evaluation. Dickin et al. (1983) noted that definitions of risk vary from time to time and place to place and are influenced by political and bureaucratic decisions. Definitional issues lead to difficulties in classifying heterogeneous populations of infants and in drawing conclusions on infant interventions studies (Strauss & Brownell, 1984). Definitions, however, guide program development and evaluation and are critical to a discussion of infant programs (Graham & Scott, 1988).

Family Focus

Another obvious issue in infant programs is the increasing family focus. Krauss, Upshur, Shonkoff, and Hauser-Cram (1993), for example, reported on correlates and consequences of professionally organized parent groups for mothers receiving early intervention services for their infants and toddlers with disabilities. To some extent, because program planning has been under the purview of professionals, models for including families in service delivery planning and implementation are in the developmental state. For example, family assessment strategies (e.g., Bailey & Simeonsson, 1988) are just now emerging in the professional literature; the evaluation models incorporating family issues and perspectives have yet to be developed. Because of the increasing strong family focus in infant programs, professionals need to be sensitive to family issues, needs, and priorities. Moreover, a specific program orientation toward integral family involvement is needed in program planning, development, implementation, and evaluation.

Need for Adequate Training

This issue points to a real training need in the preparation of infant specialists and interventionists so the family dynamics and a relationship focus (Affleck, McGrade, McQueeney, & Allen, 1982) become part of professionals' awareness, sensitivity, training, and service delivery. The specific family training needs for infant interventionists beg the question of the actual availability of trained personnel who can provide infant program services. Regardless, the preparation of qualified, well-trained personnel for early intervention is critical to the accomplishment of the goals set forth in PL 99-457 (Gilkerson, Hilliard, Schrag, & Shonkoff, 1987) and IDEA.

Personnel Shortages

The personnel shortages in working with infants and toddlers at risk for or with disabilities and their families lead to many concerns about the implementation of the legislation (Burke, McLaughlin, & Valdivieso, 1988). Historically, in times of personnel shortages, state educators have tended to lower or waive requirements for well-trained professionals. Indeed, the training of well-qualified personnel to serve infants and their families was of high concern in the 1986 report accompanying the U.S. House of Representatives version of PL 99-457; this document specifically identified inadequate training standards for personnel as a major obstacle to implementing quality infant services under PL 99-457 (Campbell, Bellamy, & Bishop, 1988). Klein and Campbell (1990) found that efforts to develop appropriate certification standards are often hampered by the fact that the lead agency is not always the state education department.

Training

The issue of training is related to both preservice and in-service need and is found across educational, medical, and psychological (Mowder, Widerstrom, & Sandall, 1989; Schrag, 1988) disciplines. *Preservice training* applies to the training of all infant specialists needed to carry out various infant and family services (Lourie, 1988). *In-service training* refers to updating the skills of professionals already delivering infant services. Stremel-Campbell and Rowland (1987), for example, found that there is a tremendous research knowledge base in communication intervention with infants, which needs to be part of the updated skills of those already providing infant services. There are also concerns about professionals' abilities and skills regarding professional collaboration (Bailey, Palsha, & Simeonsson, 1991).

As the many infant specialists secure or update their training, there will need to be a sensitivity to multicultural considerations and to working with families from diverse cultural, racial, and socioeconomic backgrounds (Anastasiow & Harel, 1993; Leung, 1987; Smith, 1987; Turner, 1987). A further issue of increasing concern, as professionals from many different specializations work together, will be liaison problems among infant service professionals (Bry, 1985; Early Intervention Project, 1987). Thus, training issues center on content and the process of training (McCollum & Thorp, 1988). For the present, commitment to the education of educators is key to an effective system of care for infants, toddlers, and their families (Iatrides, 1988), and properly preparing trained personnel to work in early intervention programs will be an essential issue for the future (Guralnick & Bennett, 1987a, 1987b).

Policy Issues

There are numerous policy considerations in preparing professional personnel to serve infants and toddlers at risk for or with disabilities and their families (Burke et al., 1988). The issue of trained personnel is not only an educational policy issue but also leads to broader policy issues of who should be served, where, and on what basis (McNulty, Widerstrom, Goodwin, & Campbell, 1988); how societal resources are to be allocated (Garwood et al., 1988); and the role of research and policy formulation (Bricker, 1987). If infant and family needs are to be met in a quality fashion, their needs must be communicated to social planners, economic experts, national

governments, and international decision makers (Lourie, 1988). This is such a concern that Garwood (1987) wondered about the implementation of PL 99-457, given the perceived absence of leadership from the federal level. He would like to see a strategy in place that builds on the existing political culture and ensures that infant needs are met.

Beyond the key policy issues are specific concerns regarding issues such as the right to life and the treatment of infants with disabilities (Ellis & Luckasson, 1986; Shearer, 1985; Smith, 1985; Stark, Menolascino, & McGee, 1984). Legal and ethical issues confront infant caregivers in a number of ways (Stark et al., 1984), including the lengths to which programs are developed and delivered to meet the needs of infants with severe impairments and the perceived cost effectiveness of these programs. Furthermore, Sontag and Schacht (1993) identified significant barriers to early intervention service utilization, specifically among Native American families, low-income families without medical assistance, and infants under 18 months of age.

Integration

There is also the issue of mainstreaming infants at risk or with disabilities with babies without disabilities (Salisbury, 1991). Levine and McColoum (1983) examined this issue and the ways in which babies and toddlers can be included with typically developing children. They make a number of suggestions, including placing infants with disabilities near babies without disabilities; matching younger infants with older children and vice versa, according to their developmental levels and behavioral maturity; and using toys to enhance interactions between infants with and without disabilities. Program guidelines for differing infant needs should be addressed (Dronek & Lundin, 1986). McLean and Hanline (1990) believed that the traditional notion of least restrictive environment should give way to the concept of integration opportunities. They recommended a broad-based view of integration, specifically centered on integration of the child into the family and the integration of the family into the community. Harbin, Danaher, and Derrick (1994) discussed a related but slightly different issue, that of eligibility for infant and toddler programs in contrast to preschool special education programs. They are especially concerned about the eligibility continuity in terms of moving children, who qualify under Part H of IDEA, to programs developed under Part B of IDEA.

Service to Remote Areas

Another issue is serving infants and toddlers and their families when the families reside in rural areas. Creative programs have been developed to serve those in rural areas, but providing services when distance and the availability of trained personnel are issues will continue to be a major concern (Gautt, 1986; Hutinger, 1986). For example, Folio and Richey (1991) described an educational television intervention programs project (ETIPS). This program uses video broadcasts to serve infants, toddlers, their families, and early intervention service providers in rural communities. Furthermore, Flynn and McCollum (1993) found that parents in rural areas want accurate information about and access to their child as well as links to community early intervention services.

Unwarranted Intervention

Gardner, Karmel, and Dowd (1984) discussed the risks involved in prescribing an intervention when it is not necessary; they maintained that interventions should only be attempted when the infant is at risk for poor outcome. Early stimulation of children as a means to enhance development may not always be beneficial for adaptive functioning at later ages.

General Theoretical Issues

General theoretical issues include questions about basic program assumptions (Bryant & Graham, 1993; Ramey & Suarez, 1984), difficulties in classifying heterogeneous populations of infants, questions regarding the conceptual premise of infant stimulation and early intervention (Brownell & Strauss, 1984), the efficacy of stimulation programs (Healy, Keesee, & Smith, 1989), and the future directions for program implementation (Gallagher, 1993). Honig (1984) considered issues regarding infant intervention programs and suggested that a clinical appraisal of model infant intervention projects can influence public policy regarding intervention efforts.

Other theoretical issues about infant intervention programs include the emerging, strong family orientation, multifaceted training issues, political questions regarding the use of resources, the legal and ethical concerns. Professionally, these issues need to be continuously addressed, cooperative professional models developed, and research on infant intervention programs rigorously and comprehensively conducted (Shonkoff, Hauser-Cram, Krauss, & Upshur, 1988).

REFERENCES

Abroms, K.I., & Bennett, J.W. (1983). Current findings in Down syndrome. *Exceptional Children, 49,* 449–450.

Affleck, G., McGrade, B.J., McQueeney, M., & Allen, D.A. (1982). Relationship-focused early intervention in developmental disabilities. *Exceptional Children, 49,* 259–261.

Anastasiow, N.J. (1983). Adolescent pregnancy and special education. *Exceptional Children, 49,* 396–403.

Anastasiow, N.J. (1988). Should parenting education be mandatory? *Topics in Early Childhood Special Education, 8*(1), 60–72.

Anastasiow, N.J., & Harel, S. (Eds.). (1993). *At-risk infants: Interventions, families, and research.* Baltimore: Paul H. Brookes Publishing Co.

Aprill, K.H., & Schifani, J. (1983, April). *Innovative infant stimulation program as being executed by a South Louisiana School District.* Paper presented at the Annual International Conference of the Council for Exceptional Children, Detroit, MI.

Bailey, D.B. (1987). Collaborative goal-setting with families: Resolving differences in values and priorities for services. *Topics in Early Childhood Special Education, 7*(2), 59–71.

Bailey, D.B., Palsha, S.A., & Simeonsson, R.J. (1991). Professional skills, concerns, and perceived importance of work with families in early intervention. *Exceptional Children, 58*(2), 156–165.

Bailey, D.B., & Simeonsson, R.J. (1988). *Family assessment in early interaction.* Columbus, OH: Charles E. Merrill.

Bailey, E.J., & Bricker, D. (1984). The efficacy of early intervention for severely handicapped infants and young children. *Topics in Early Childhood Special Education, 4*(3), 30–51.

Bailey, E.J., & Bricker, D. (1985). Evaluation of a three-year early intervention demonstration project. *Topics in Early Childhood Education, 5*(2), 52–65.

Barnard, K.E., Booth, C.L., Mitchell, S.K., & Telzrow, R.W. (1988). Newborn nursing models: A test of early intervention to high-risk infants and families. In E.D. Hibbs (Ed.), *Children and families: Studies in prevention and intervention.* Madison, WI: International Universities Press.

Barnett, W.S. (1988). The economics of preschool special education under Public Law 99-457. *Topics in Early Childhood Special Education, 8,* 12–23.

Bee, H.L., Barnard, K.E., Eyres, S.J., Gray, C.A., Hammond, M.A., Spietz, A.L., Snyder, C., & Clark, B. (1982). Prediction of IQ and language skill from perinatal status, child performance, family characteristic, and mother–infant interaction. *Child Development, 53,* 1134–1156.

Behrmann, M., & Lahm, L. (1983). *Critical learning: Multiply handicapped babies get on-line.* Paper presented at the Council for Exceptional Children National Conference on the use of Microcomputers in Special Education, Hartford, CT.

Berrueta-Clement, J.R., Schweinhart, L.J., Barnett, W.S., Epstein, A.S., & Weikart, D.P. (1984). *Changed lives: The effects of the Perry Preschool Program on youths through age 19.* Ypsilanti, MI: High/Scope Press.

Berrueta-Clement, J.R., Schweinhart, L.J., Barnett, W.S., & Weikart, D.P. (1987). The effects of early educational intervention on crime and delinquency in adolescence and early adulthood. In J.D. Burchard & S.N. Burchard (Eds.), *Primary prevention of psychopathology: Vol. 10. Prevention of delinquent behavior* (pp. 220–240). Beverly Hills: Sage Publications.

Black, M.M. (1991). Early intervention services for infants and toddlers: A focus on families. *Journal of Clinical Child Psychology, 20*(1), 51–57.

Brazelton, T.B. (1988). Importance of early intervention. In E.D. Hibbs (Ed.), *Children and families: Studies in prevention and intervention.* Madison, WI: International Universities Press.

Bricker, D., & Gumerlock, S. (1988). Application of a three-level evaluation plan for monitoring child progress and program effects. *Journal of Special Education, 22*(1), 55–65.

Bricker, D.D. (1984). The effectiveness of early intervention with handicapped and at-risk infants. *Journal of the Child in Contemporary Society, 17*(1), 51–65.

Bricker, D.D. (1987). Impact of research on social policy for handicapped infants and children. *Journal of the Division for Early Childhood, 11*, 98–105.

Brinker, R.P. (1982). Contingency intervention with the help of microcomputers. *Journal of Special Education Technology, 5*, 37–39.

Brinker, R.P. (1984). The microcomputer as a perceptual tool: Searching for systematic learning strategies with handicapped infants. *Special Services in the Schools, 1*, 21–36.

Brody, E.B. (1988). Advocacy for healthy infancy—Prenatal intervention. In E.D. Hibbs (Eds.), *Children and families: Studies in prevention and intervention*. Madison, WI: International Universities Press.

Brownell, C.A., & Strauss, M.S. (1984). Infant stimulation and development: Conceptual and empirical considerations. *Journal of Children in Contemporary Society, 17*, 109–130.

Bry, T. (1985). *Liaison problems among infant psychiatry, psychology, pediatrics, nursing, and social work in infant mental health care.* Paper presented at the biennial meeting of the National Center for Clinical Infant Programs National Training Institute, Washington, DC.

Bryant, D.M., & Graham, M.A. (1993). *Implementing early intervention: From research to effective practice.* New York: Guilford Press.

Bryant, D.M., & Ramey, C.T. (1984). Prevention-oriented infant education programs. *Journal of Children in Contemporary Society, 17*, 17–35.

Burke, P.J., McLaughlin, M.J., & Valdivieso, C.H. (1988). Preparing professionals to educate handicapped infants and young children: Some policy considerations. *Topics in Early Childhood Special Education, 8*(1), 73–80.

Calhoun, M.L., & Rose, T.L. (1988). Early social reciprocity interventions for infants with severe retardation: Current findings and implications for the future. *Education and Training in Mental Retardation, 23*(4), 340–343.

Campbell, P.H., Bellamy, G.T., & Bishop, K.K. (1988). Statewide intervention systems: An overview of the new federal program for infants and toddlers with handicaps. *Journal of Special Education, 22*(1), 25–40.

Casto, G., & White, K. (1984). The efficacy of early intervention programs with environmentally at-risk infants. *Journal of Children in Contemporary Society, 17*, 37–50.

Chase-Lansdale, P.L., & Brooks-Gunn, J. (1994). Correlates of adolescent pregnancy and parenthood. In C.B. Fisher & R.M. Lerner (Eds.), *Applied developmental psychology* (pp. 207–236). New York: McGraw-Hill.

Chelimsky, E. (1984). Evaluation of the special supplemental program for women, infants, and children (WIC's) effectiveness. *Children and Youth Services Review, 6*, 219–226.

Clark, S. (1983). *Counseling hearing parents of deaf children about deaf identity and the deaf community.* Paper presented at the Annual International Conference of the Council for Exceptional Children, Detroit, MI.

Dickin, K.L., McKim, M.K., & Kirkland, J. (1983). Designing intervention programs for infants at risk: Considerations, implementation, and evaluation. *Early Child Development and Care, 11*, 145–163.

Dronek, M., & Lundin, J. (1986). *Program guidelines for hearing impaired individuals.* Sacremento: California State Department of Education.

Early Intervention Project. (1987). *Summary report, narrative report, and supplemental report.* Augusta: Maine State Department of Mental Health and Mental Retardation.

Eayrs, C.B., & Jones, R.S. (1992). Methodological issues and future directions in the evaluation of early intervention programmes. *Child Care, Health and Development, 18*(1), 15–28.

Education of the Handicapped Act Amendments of 1986, PL 99-457, 20 U.S.C. § 1400 *et seq.*

Ellis, J.W., & Luckasson, R. (1986). Denying treatment to infants with handicaps: A comment on Bowen v. American Hospital Association. *Mental Retardation, 24*(4), 237–240.

Epps, S., & Jackson, B.J. (1991). Professional preparation of psychologists for family-centered service delivery to at-risk infants and toddlers, *School Psychology Review, 20*(4), 489–509.

Farran, D.C., & Sparling, J. (1988). Coping styles in families of handicapped children. In E.D. Hibbs (Ed.), *Children and families: Studies in prevention and intervention.* Madison, WI: International Universities Press.

Felner, R.D., Jason, L.A., Moritsugu, J.N., & Farber, S.S. (1983). Preventive psychology: Evolution and current status. In R.S. Felner, L.A. Jason, J.N. Moritsugu, & S.S. Farber (Eds.), *Preventive psychology: Theory, research and practice.* New York: Pergamon Press.

Ferry, P.C. (1986). Infant stimulation programs: A neurologic shell game? *Archives of Neurology, 43*(3), 281–282.

Fewell, R.R., & Sandall, S.R. (1986). Developmental testing of handicapped infants: A measurement dilemma. *Topics in Early Childhood Special Education, 6*(3), 86–99.

Fewell, R.R., & Vadasy, P.F. (1987). Measurement issues in studies of efficacy. *Topics in Early Childhood Special Education, 7*(2), 85–96.

Fine, M.J., & Gardner, P.A. (1991). Counseling and education services for families: An empowerment perspective. *Elementary School Guidance and Counseling, 26*(1), 33–44.

Finkelstein, J.W., Finkelstein, J.A., Christie, M., Roden, M., & Shelton, C. (1982). Teenage pregnancy and parenthood: Outcomes for mother and child. *Journal of Adolescent Health Care, 3,* 1–7.

Flynn, L.L., & McCollum, J. (1993). Support for rural families of hospitalized infants: The Parents' perspective. *Children's Health Care, 22*(1), 19–37.

Folio, R., & Richey, D. (1991). Public television and video technology for rural families with special needs young children: The ETIPS model. *Topics in Early Childhood Special Education, 10*(4), 45–55.

Gallagher, J.J. (1992). The role of values and facts in policy development for infants and toddlers with disabilities and their families. *Journal of Early Intervention, 16,* 1–10.

Gallagher, J.J. (1993). Policy designed for diversity: New initiatives for children with disabilities. In D.M. Bryant & M.A. Graham (Eds.), *Implementing early intervention.* New York: Guilford Press.

Gardner, J.M., Karmel, B.Z., & Dowd, J.M. (1984). Relationship of psychological development to infant intervention. *Journal of the Child in Contemporary Society, 17*(1), 93–108.

Garwood, S.G. (1987). Political, economic, and practical issues affecting the development of universal early intervention for handicapped infants. *Topics in Early Childhood Special Education, 7*(2), 6–18.

Garwood, S.G., Fewell, R.R., & Neisworth, J.T. (1988). Public Law 99-457: You can get there from here! *Topics in Early Childhood Special Education, 8*(1), 1–11.

Gautt, S.W. (1986). Community linkage development: Expanding services to developmentally delayed infants in rural areas. *Rural Special Education Quarterly, 7,* 17–19.

Gibson, D., & Fields, D.L. (1984). Early infant stimulation programs for children with Down syndrome: A review of effectiveness. In M. Wodrich & D.K. Routh (Eds.), *Advances in developmental and behavioral pediatrics* (Vol. 5, pp. 331–371). Greenwich, CT: JAI Press.

Gilkerson, L., Gorski, P.A., & Panitz, P. (1990). Hospital-based intervention for preterm infants and their families. In S.J. Meisels & J.P. Shonkoff (Eds.), *Handbook of early childhood intervention.* Cambridge, England: Cambridge University Press.

Gilkerson, L., Hilliard, A.G., Schrag, E., & Shonkoff, J.P. (1987). Commenting on PL 99-457. *Zero to Three, 7*(3), 13–17.

Graham, M.A., & Scott, K.G. (1988). The impact of definitions of high risk on services to infants and toddlers. *Topics in Early Childhood Special Education, 8*(1), 23–38.

Greenspan, S.I., & Lourie, R.S. (1981). Developmental structuralistic approach to the classification of adaptive and pathologic personality organization. *American Journal of Psychiatry, 138,* 728–735.

Greenspan, S.I., Weider, S., Lieberman, A., Nover, R., Lourie, R., & Robinson, M. (1987). *Infants in multirisk families: Case studies in preventive intervention.* Madison, WI: International Universities Press.

Guralnick, M.J., & Bennett, F.C. (1987a). Early intervention for at-risk and handicapped children: Current and future perspectives. In M.J. Guralnick & F.C. Bennett (Eds.), *The effectiveness of early intervention for at-risk and handicapped children* (pp. 365–382). New York: Academic Press.

Guralnick, M.J., & Bennett, F.C. (Eds.). (1987b). *The effectiveness of early intervention for at-risk and handicapped children.* New York: Academic Press.

Hammond, M., Bee, H.L., Barnard, K.E., & Eyres, S.J. (1983). *Child health assessment. Part 4: Follow-up at second grade.* Final report of project supported by Grant No. R01-NU-00816, Division of Nursing, Bureau of Health Professions, Health Resources and Services Administration, U.S. Public Health Service.

Hanson, M.J., & Krentz, M.K. (1986). *Supporting parent-child interactions: A guide for early intervention program personnel.* San Francisco: Department of Special Education, San Francisco State University.

Harbin, G.L. (1988). Implementation of P.L. 99-457: State technical assistance needs. *Topics in Early Childhood Special Education, 8,* 24–36.

Harbin, G.L., Danaher, J., & Derrick, T. (1994). Comparison of eligibility policies for infant/toddler programs and preschool special education programs. *Topics in Early Childhood Special Education, 14*(4), 455–471.

Harbin, G.L., & McNulty, B.A. (1990). Policy implementation: Perspectives on service coordination and interagency cooperation. In S. Meisels & J.P. Shonkoff (Eds.), *Handbook of early childhood intervention.* Cambridge, England: Cambridge University Press.

Hauser-Cram, P. (1990). Designing meaningful evaluations of early intervention services. In S. Meisels & J.P. Shonkoff (Eds.), *Handbook of early childhood intervention.* Cambridge, England: Cambridge University Press.

Healy, A., Keesee, P.D., & Smith, B.S. (1989). *Early services for children with special needs: Transactions for family support.* Baltimore: Paul H. Brookes Publishing Co.

Hedge, R., & Johnson, W. (1986, October). *Serving rural families of developmentally disabled in a cost-effective manner.* Paper presented at the annual conference of the National Rural and Small Schools Consortium, Bellingham, WA.

Helfer, R.E. (1987). The perinatal period, a window of opportunity for enhancing parent–infant communication: An approach to prevention. *Child Abuse and Neglect, 11,* 565–579.

Helm, J.M. (1988). Adolescent mothers of handicapped children: A challenge for interventionists. *Journal of the Division for Early Childhood, 12,* 311–319.

Honig, A.S. (1984). Reflections on infant intervention programs: What have we learned? *Journal of Children in Contemporary Society, 17,* 81–92.

Hulme, T.S. (1985). *The Iowa program to provide coordinated services for children who need technical medical care in their home/ community: A network approach.* Paper presented at the Biennial National Training Institute of the National Center for Clinical Infant Programs, Washington, DC.

Hutinger, P.L. (1986). Sharing centers for handicapped infants and toddlers: Settings for parent and child interaction and growth. *Rural Special Education Quarterly, 7,* 6–9.

Iatrides, M. (1988). Educating the educators: Infant caregiving in early childhood education and the training of infant educators. In E.D. Hibbs (Ed.), *Children and families: Studies in prevention and intervention.* Madison, WI: International Universities Press.

Individuals with Disabilities Education Act (IDEA) of 1990, PL 101-476, 20 U.S.C. § 1400 *et seq.*

Joanning, H., Demmitt, A., Brotherson, M.J., & Whiddon, D. (1994). The individualized family service plan: A growth area for family therapy. *Journal of Family Psychotherapy, 5*(3), 69–81.

Klein, B., Van Hasselt, V.B., Trefelner, M., & Sandstrom, D.J. (1988). The parent and toddler training project for visually impaired and blind multihandicapped children. *Journal of Visual Impairment and Blindness, 82*(2), 59–64.

Klein, N.K., & Campbell, P. (1990). Preparing personnel to serve at-risk and disabled infants, toddlers, and preschooler. In S.J. Meisels & J.P. Shonkoff (Eds.), *Handbook of early childhood intervention.* Cambridge, England: Cambridge University Press.

Kopp, C.B. (1987). Developmental risk: Historical reflections. In J.D. Osofsky (Ed.), *Handbook of infant development* (2nd ed., pp. 881–912). New York: John Wiley & Sons

Krauss, M.W., Upshur, C.C., Shonkoff, J.P., & Hauser-Cram, P. (1993). The impact of parent groups on mothers of infants with disabilities. *Journal of Early Intervention, 17*(1), 8–20.

Kysela, G.M., & Marfo, K. (1983). Mother–child interactions and early intervention programs for handicapped infants and young children. *Educational Psychology, 3*(3–4), 201–212.

Lally, R.J., Mangione, P.L., & Honig, A.S. (1988). The Syracuse University Family Development Research Program: Long-range impact on an early intervention with low-income children and their families. In D. Powell (Ed.), *Parent education as early childhood intervention: Emerging directions in theory, research and practice* (pp. 79–104). Norwood, NJ: Ablex.

Lester, B.M. (1992). Infants and their families at risk: Assessment and intervention. *Infant Mental Health Journal, 13*(1), 54–66.

Leung, B. (1987, February). *Cultural considerations in working with Asian parents.* Paper presented at the conference of the National Center for Clinical Infant Programs, Los Angeles.

Levine, M.H., & McColoum, J.A. (1983). Peer play and toys: Key factors in mainstreaming infants.

Lewis, M., & Sullivan, M.W. (1994). Developmental intervention in the lives of infants and parents. In C.B. Fisher & R.M. Lerner, *Applied developmental psychology.* New York: McGraw-Hill.

Liaw, F., & Brooks-Gunn, J. (1994). Cumulative familial risks and low-birthweight children's cognitive and behavioral development. *Journal of Clinical Child Psychology, 23*(4), 360–372.

Lourie, R.S. (1988). Implications for intervention and service delivery: Cross-cultural considerations. In E.D. Hibbs (Ed.), *Children and families: Studies in prevention and intervention.* Madison, WI: International Universities Press.

Lowenthal, B. (1988). United States Public Law 99-457: An ounce of prevention. *Exceptional Child, 35,* 57–60.

Mahoney, G., & Powell, A. (1988). Modifying parent–child interactions: Enhancing the development of handicapped children. *Journal of Special Education, 22*(1), 82–96.

Marfo, K., & Kysela, G.M. (1985). Early intervention with mentally handicapped children. A critical appraisal of applied research. *Journal of Pediatric Psychology, 10*(3), 305–324.

McCollum, J.A., & Stayton, V.D. (1985). Infant/parent interaction: Studies and intervention guidelines based on the S1A1 model. *Journal of the Division for Early Childhood, 9*(2), 125–135.

McCollum, J.A., & Thorp, E.K. (1988). Training of infant specialists: A look to the future. *Infants and Young Children, 1,* 55–65.

McConkey, R. (1994). Early intervention: Planning futures, shaping years. *Mental Handicap Research, 7*(1), 4–15.

McDonough, S.C. (1984). Intervention programs for adolescent mothers and their offspring. *Journal of Children in Contemporary Society, 17,* 67–78.

McLean, M., & Hanline, M.F. (1990). Providing early intervention services in integrated environments: Challenges and opportunities for the future. *Topics in Early Childhood Special Education, 10*(2), 62–77.

McLinden, S.E., & Prasse, D.P. (1991). Providing services to infants and toddlers under PL 99-457: Training needs of school psychologists. *School Psychology Review, 20*(1), 37–48.

McNaughton, D. (1994). Measuring parent satisfaction with early childhood intervention programs: Current practice, problems, and future perspectives. *Topics in Early Childhood Special Education, 14*(1), 26–48.

McNulty, B.A., Widerstrom, A., Goodwin, L., & Campbell, S. (1988). Who should be served, where, and why: Local special education administrators' views. *Topics in Early Childhood Special Education, 8,* 51–60.

Meisels, S.J., Dichtelmiller, M., & Liaw, F. (1993). A multidimensional analysis of early childhood intervention programs. In C.H. Zeanah, Jr. (Ed.), *Handbook of infant mental health.* New York: Guilford Press.

Minde, K.K., & Minde, R. (1982). Psychiatric intervention in infancy: A review. *Annual Progress in Child Psychiatry and Child Development, 2,* 463–483.

Mowder, B.A., Widerstrom, A.H., & Sandall, S.R. (1989). School psychologists serving at-risk and handicapped infants, toddlers and their families. *Professional School Psychology, 4*(3), 159–171.

Odom, S.L., Yoder, P., & Hill, G. (1988). Developmental intervention for infants with handicaps: Purposes and programs. *Journal of Special Education, 22*(1), 11–24.

O'Sullivan, S.B. (1985–1986). Infant–caregiver interaction and the social development of handicapped infants. *Physical and Occupational Therapy in Pediatrics, 5*(4), 1–12.

Parson, A.S., & McIntosh, D.K. (1987). Serving handicapped infants and toddlers in rural areas: Impact of PL 99-457. *Journal of Rural and Small Schools, 2,* 2–7.

Pulskamp, B. (1987). *A model for mother and child counseling intervention.* Paper presented at the National Center for Clinical Infant Programs, Los Angeles, CA.

Ramey, C.T., & Bryant, D.M. (1988). Prevention-oriented infant education programs. In E.D. Hibbs (Ed.), *Children and families: Studies in prevention and intervention.* Madison, WI: International Universities Press.

Ramey, C.T., & Suarez, T.M. (1984). Early intervention and the early experience paradigm: Toward a better framework in social policy. *Journal of Children in Contemporary Society, 17,* 3–13.

Richey, C.A., Lovell, M.L., & Reid, K. (1991). Interpersonal skill training to enhance social support among women at risk for child maltreatment. *Children and Youth Services Review, 13*(1–2), 41–59.

Riggs, K.M. (1985). *HCI-IFU: Infant follow-up services offered by the Tennessee Department of Health and Environment.* Paper presented at the National Center for Clinical Infant Programs, Biennial National Training Institute, Washington, DC.

Rosenberg, S., & Robinson, C. (1985). Enhancement of mothers' interactional skills in an infant education program. *Education and Training of the Mentally Retarded, 20*(2), 163–169.

Russman, B.S. (1986). Are infant stimulation programs useful? *Archives of Neurology, 43*(3), 282–283.

Salisbury, C.L. (1991). Mainstreaming during the early childhood years. *Exceptional Children, 58*(2), 146–155.

Scholl, T.W., Hediger, M.L., & Belsky, D.H. (1994). Prenatal care and maternal health during adolescent pregnancy: A review and meta-analysis. *Journal of Adolescent Health, 15*(6), 444–456.

Schrag, E. (1988). *Sensitivities, skills, and services: Mental health roles in the implementation of Part H of PL 99-457 the Education of the Handicapped Act Amendments of 1986.* Washington, DC: National Center for Clinical Infant Programs.

Seibert, J.M., Hogan, A.E., & Mundy, P.C. (1987). Assessing social and communication skills in infancy. *Topics in Early Childhood Special Education, 7*(2), 38–48.

Seitz, V., & Apfel, N.H. (1994). Effects of a school for pregnant students on the incidence of low-birthweight deliveries. *Child Development, 65*(2), 666–676.

Seligman, M. (1993). Group work with parents of children with disabilities. *Journal for Specialists in Group Work, 18*(3), 115–126.

Sharav, T., & Shlomo, L. (1986). Stimulation of infants with Down syndrome: Long-term effects. *Mental Retardation, 24*(2), 81–86.

Shearer, A. (1985). Everybody's ethics: What future for handicapped babies? *Early Child Development and Care, 18*(3–4), 189–216.

Shonkoff, J.P., Hauser-Cram, P., Krauss, M.W., & Upshur, C.C. (1988). Early intervention efficacy research: What have we learned and where do we go from here? *Topics in Early Childhood Special Education, 8,* 81–93.

Simeonsson, R.J. (1991). Primary, secondary, and tertiary prevention in early intervention. *Journal of Early Intervention, 15*(2), 124–134.

Smith, B.J., & Strain, P.S. (1988). Early childhood special education in the next decade: Implementing and expanding P.L. 99-457. *Topics in Early Childhood Special Education, 8,* 37–47.

Smith, J.D. (1985). Handicapped infants and euthanasia: A challenge to our advocacy. *Exceptional Children, 51*(4), 335–338.

Smith, R.D. (1987). *Multicultural considerations: Working with families of developmentally disabled and high risk children. The Hispanic perspective.* Paper presented at the conference of the National Center for Clinical Infant Programs, Los Angeles, CA.

Sontag, J.C., & Schacht, R. (1993). Family diversity and patterns of service utilization in early intervention. *Journal of Early Intervention, 17*(4), 431–444.

Stark, J.S., Menolascino, F.J., & McGee, J.J. (1984). Major legal-ethical challenges in the care and treatment of the mentally retarded. *Psychiatric Medicine, 2*(3), 295–304.

Steel, K.O. (1985). The satellite clinic: A model for the treatment of handicapped children in towns and rural areas. *Developmental Medicine and Child Neurology, 27,* 355–363.

Stevens-Simon, C., Kaplan, D.W., & McAnarney, E.R. (1993). Factors associated with preterm delivery among pregnant adolescents. *Journal of Adolescent Health, 14*(4), 340–342.

Stockbauer, J.W. (1987). WIC prenatal participation and its relation to pregnancy outcomes in Missouri: A second look. *American Journal of Public Health, 77,* 813–818.

Strauss, M.S., & Brownell, C.A. (1984). A commentary on infant stimulation and intervention. *Journal of Children in Contemporary Society, 17,* 133–139.

Stremel-Campbell, K., & Rowland, C. (1987). Prelinguistic communication intervention: Birth-to-2. *Topics in Early Childhood Special Education, 7*(2), 49–58.

Trad, P.V. (1993). Adolescent pregnancy: An intervention challenge. *Child Psychiatry and Human Development, 24*(2), 99–113.
Tripp, E.D. (1988). Perivolaki: A model therapeutic nursery school. In E.D. Hibbs (Ed.), *Children and families: Studies in prevention and intervention.* Madison, WI: International Universities Press.
Trohanis, P.L. (1988). Public Law 99-457: New programs for infants, toddlers, and preschoolers. *School Law Bulletin, 19,* 7–12.
Trout, M.D. (1983). Birth of a sick or handicapped infant: Impact on the family. *Child Welfare, 62,* 337–348.
Turnbull, A.P. (1988). The challenge of providing comprehensive support to families. *Education and Training in Mental Retardation, 23*(4), 261–272.
Turner, A. (1987). *Multicultural considerations: Working with families of developmentally disabled and high-risk children. The Black perspective.* Paper presented at the conference of the National Center for Clinical Infant Programs, Los Angeles, CA.
Upshur, C.C. (1991). Mothers' and fathers' ratings of the benefits of early intervention services. *Journal of Early Intervention, 15*(4), 345–357.
Walsh, S., Campbell, P.H., & McKenna, P. (1988). First-year implementation of the federal program for infants and toddlers with handicaps: A view from the states. *Topics in Early Childhood Special Education, 8,* 1–22.
Walton, W.T. (1993). Parents of disabled children burn-out too: Counseling parents of disabled children on stress management. *International Journal for the Advancement of Counseling, 16*(2), 107–118.
Wolery, M. (1987). Program evaluation at the local level: Recommendations for improving services. *Topics in Early Childhood Special Education, 7*(2), 111–123.
Zigler, E. (1994). Reshaping early childhood intervention to be a more effective weapon against poverty. *American Journal of Community Psychology, 22*(1), 37–47.
Zigler, E., Taussig, C., Cara, & Black, K. (1992). Early childhood intervention: A promising preventative for juvenile delinquency. *American Psychologist,* 997–1006.

12 ACTIVITIES

1. Design an evaluation of an early intervention program with which you are familiar. Consider a number of variables, such as children's age, duration and intensity of treatment program, and the program's educational activities.

2. Design a preventive intervention program. Specify the prevention goal, target population, and preventive program.

3. Develop a center-based therapeutic school intervention program for young children with emotional disturbances. What are the potential advantages of your program? What difficulties might occur?

4. Develop a parent education program. What is the goal of the program, the curriculum, and the instructional methods you would use?

5. Design a curriculum to sensitize early intervention program professionals to multicultural issues. What experiential exercises might you include?

CHAPTER 13

Home-Based Services and Supports

Susan R. Sandall

Objectives

- To be aware of the history and efficacy of home visiting
- To understand the varied roles and responsibilities of the home visitor
- To become familiar with the process and content of home visits

Home-based intervention is potentially an effective and family-centered form of service delivery in early intervention. Home-based services and regular home visits are used in a variety of situations for children and families with special needs. In part because the family home is thought to be the natural environment for many young children with disabilities, home-based intervention is a popular service delivery option for infants and toddlers.

This chapter explores home-based services in terms of effectiveness for young children and their families. In addition, the process and content of home visits and the roles and responsibilities of the home visitor are examined. The home visitor is critical to the success of any home visiting program. Strategies for managing home visits and providing family support also are included.

Part H of the Individuals with Disabilities Education Act (IDEA) of 1990 (PL 101-476) uses the term *natural environments* to describe the appropriate location of services for infants and toddlers. It is important to note that the term is plural and implies that there is no single best setting for services. Not all services need to be at the same location and the

The Jacksons

Vicki parked her car and glanced at the old gray house on the corner. It was a sunny fall morning, and she had just arrived for her weekly home visit with Frankie and his mother. Vicki hoped they were home. With most of her families she called ahead to confirm a visit, but the Jacksons' telephone was disconnected. Vicki knocked at the back door. She'd been visiting the Jacksons for several months and she'd learned that no one used the front door. From inside the house she heard, "Hi Vicki. Come in." She opened the door and entered the kitchen where 1½-year-old Frankie sat in his high chair. His mother, Carla, was clearing a chair. "We're still having breakfast. Have a seat. Would you like some coffee? she asked. "Sure, thanks," said Vicki. As she moved closer to Frankie, she looked at his oatmeal-covered face and said, "Hi, big guy." Frankie smiled, kicked his legs, and waved his arms. Vicki avoided most of the oatmeal and said, "Hey Frankie, that looks like a yummy breakfast." Frankie waved his arms again. Vicki smiled and nodded at Frankie and sat down. Carla handed her a cup of coffee and sighed. "Well, let me tell you about our night." The Jacksons' home visit had begun.

locations may change over time as child and family needs change. The family plays an important role in determining the natural environments for their child. They can tell providers where their infant or toddler would spend their time if the child were not in need of special services. They can tell providers where the child and the family would be comfortable. For most very young children, the home is a natural environment. Many families select the home as the location (or one of the locations) for early intervention. Home-based services can be a desirable option for families if it is, indeed, a choice.

The principles of family-centered care align nicely with home-based early intervention. Home-based services implicitly recognize that the family is the constant in the child's life. Furthermore, the context for intervention is the home and family. This sets the stage for services and supports that are flexible, culturally competent, and responsive to family-identified needs. The individualized nature of home visits means that the home visitor must allow for and support individual methods of coping, parenting, and participating.

Although home-based early intervention often is viewed as more flexible and personal than other methods of service delivery, it is a formal means of providing help and support to children and families from an outside agency. A number of researchers have described the key assumptions and potential advantages of home-based services (Bailey & Simeonsson, 1988; Gray & Wandersman, 1980; Wasik, Bryant, & Lyons, 1990). These include recognition of the following:

- Parents are usually the most consistent and caring people in the lives of their children.
- Intervention begun early in a child's life can enhance child development.
- An intervention focus on patterns of parent–child interaction can bring about changes that continue beyond intervention.

- Support for the family's concerns may be expedited.
- The nature of services is individualized and personalized.

There are other advantages of home-based services. In general, home-based programs tend to be less expensive on a per-child basis (Barnett & Escobar, 1990), may be suitable for young children with special health care needs, and may fit the conditions of rural areas with sparse populations.

ABOUT HOME VISITS

Home visiting has a long history in health, social services, and early education in Europe and the United States (Wasik et al., 1990). Home visiting is a tool for prevention (e.g., to prevent child abuse and neglect) as well as intervention (e.g., to facilitate learning of young children with disabilities). Home visiting programs have targeted specific populations such as low-income families, adolescent mothers, and families of children with disabilities. Some European countries, however, have a long tradition of universal home health visiting as a means to provide every child with the best possible start. In the United States, the use and proliferation of home-based programs have been influenced by a variety of environmental conditions and societal needs such as disability, developmental risk, and economic disadvantage.

Wasik (1993) reported that home visiting has existed in the United States at least since the 1890s. At the turn of the century, home visiting was one response to the increased numbers of families living in poverty in the cities and the related concerns of contagious diseases, high infant mortality, and school absence and drop out. Given the prevailing belief that child and family outcomes were amenable to change, home visiting was promoted as a direct and formal means of providing help. Volunteers and visiting nurses were soon followed by home teachers and social workers. However, home visiting programs decreased in popularity in the 1920s as beliefs changed about the determinants of personality and cognitive development. The rise of psychoanalytic theory in the field of psychology brought with it an emphasis on the individual in contrast to an emphasis on environmental effects (Roberts, Wasik, Casto, & Ramey, 1991). Then, in the second half of the century, several factors served to reverse this trend and to provide renewed interest in home-based programs. The home was seen as a more appropriate setting for children with disabilities than institutional settings. Parents were seen as key agents in shaping the development of their children. The pernicious effects of poverty and poor health came to the forefront once more. Home visiting was again viewed as one means of changing environmental conditions that were seen as associated with later school and societal problems. The roots of current home-based early intervention programs can be seen in programs of parent education and family support that originated during this period.

The Portage Project was first funded in 1969 to provide a home-based intervention program to young children with disabilities in rural Wisconsin. This project has been very influential in the design and delivery of home-based services in the United States and around the world. In its original form, the Portage Project involved teaching parents to teach their children (Shearer & Shearer, 1976). The family received weekly visits from a home visitor who assessed the child using a developmental checklist, selected weekly teaching goals in concert with the parent, demonstrated teaching procedures to the parent, and taught the parent to collect systematic child data. Parents (most often the mother) implemented the intervention on a daily basis and kept the child's records. At the next weekly visit, the parent and teacher reviewed the child's performance and repeated the cycle. The Portage Project has been replicated in cities, towns, and villages in the United States and around the world. Sturmey et al. (1992) reported that Portage services can and are replicated fairly closely to the original in some locales, but in developing countries services have required substantial modification reflecting available resources, service system infrastructures, and local demography and culture. Examples of modifications include addition of health and nutrition services as critical services, the incorporation of the extended family into service delivery, and substitution of culturally relevant developmental activities. The Portage Project has evolved by building on the results of its home-based model. Its goal has always been to enhance and expand the parent's role in facilitating positive child development outcomes. This entails more than teaching skills to children. It also includes promoting positive child–family interactions, supporting positive family functioning, using multiple strategies, and working with families in a variety of environments (Herwig & Herman, 1993).

Because parent education programs rely on parent participation and respond to parental concerns, the traditional goals revolve around teaching parents to teach their children. Family support or family resource programs emphasize goals such as providing social support, providing encouragement, and helping families become connected with formal and informal means of getting their needs met. The Family, Infant, and Preschool Program in western North Carolina was begun in 1972 to serve young children with disabilities or who are at risk for developmental difficulties and their families. It serves as an example of a family support program that includes home visits; however, the program is highly flexible and individualized. The assessment and intervention approach includes the specification of family needs, mobilization of resources and capabilities within the family, mobilization of resources and supports outside the family, and utilization of a variety of helping and empowering strategies by staff members. Based on research findings that social support and resources have both direct and indirect influences on parent, family, and child functioning (Dunst, Trivette, Hamby, & Pollock, 1990), the model conceptualizes early intervention from a family support perspective (Dunst, Trivette, & Deal, 1988).

Effectiveness of Home-Based Programs

Home-based programs are viewed as particularly appropriate for infants and toddlers in that they meet guidelines for family-centered intervention within natural environments as guided by Part H of IDEA. Given the increased number of home-based programs as well as the continuing calls for expansion of this type of service, it is appropriate to examine the effectiveness of home-based programs.

Research reports on home-based programs most often provide efficacy data using child outcome measures. Less often there are reports that address parent and family outcomes. Studies of home-based programs contend with problems of conceptualization, implementation, and evaluation (Gray & Wandersman, 1980). The program flexibility, which is seen as an advantage of home-based programs, presents methodological problems for researchers.

The Jacksons *(continued)*

Let's take another look at the home-based program for Frankie (who has developmental delays) and his family. This program features both parent education and family support elements. During the visits, the home visitor (Vicki) helps Frankie's mother (Carla) with particular strategies to facilitate Frankie's development and learning of such behaviors as vocalizing to make his intentions known, pulling himself to standing, and turning pages and pointing at pictures in books. Carla (a single mother) also shares some of her other family concerns. Right now she needs to find financial support for child care for Frankie's two preschool-age brothers. Carla is also struggling with making all of Frankie's many appointments because she must rely on public transportation. Finding solutions to these current concerns means that Carla, Vicki, and Carla's social worker from the social services agency must share information and communicate on a regular basis. To address these issues, Vicki has arranged a three-way meeting at the Jackons' house to work on family-level concerns.

In looking at the example of Frankie and his family, Frankie's home visitor is an early intervention teacher who works for a child development center. Like many other children who receive home visits, Frankie also receives a number of other services. He attends a play group at the child development center twice a month, receives physical therapy at a health center once a month, and attends a nutrition and feeding clinic about every 3 months at the hospital. Frankie's family receives social work services from the state social services department. Such a comprehensive and multifaceted set of services is fairly typical for young children in early intervention programs. Yet this diversity of number, type, and intensity of services can be problematic for researchers who are investigating the effectiveness of home-based approaches.

Child and Family Outcomes The complexity of home-based early intervention requires sophisticated research designs. However, many existing studies lack experimental rigor. For example, studies may not have random assignment. Fidelity of the treatment is typically not monitored. Despite these limitations, research reviews (Bailey & Simeonsson, 1988; Casto & Mastropieri, 1986; Halpern, 1984, 1986; White, Bush, & Casto, 1985–1986) have provided modest support for home-based early intervention. Some of the positive child changes that have been reported include enhancement of overall child development, acquisition of functional skills, and improved health status. Measures of cognition are the most frequently reported, although it has been recommended that researchers use multiple measures to assess the effects of programs on children (Roberts et al., 1991).

Reports have described successful home-based programs for children with Down syndrome (Bidder, Bryant, & Gray, 1975; Hanson & Schwarz, 1978), children with moderate and severe developmental delays (Brassell & Dunst, 1978), premature and low birth weight infants (Barrera, Rosenbaum, & Cunningham, 1986; Infant Health and Development Program [IHDP], 1990), and children with hearing

impairments (Strong, 1992). In addition, a variety of programs have addressed the needs of low-income families through home visits. For example, a comprehensive program for low-income children and families in Syracuse looked at both immediate and long-term effects (Lally, Mangione, Honig, & Wittmer, 1988). The follow-up study showed that children in the program were doing better in school (especially the girls) and remaining in school at higher grade levels and that boys were experiencing fewer and less severe problems with the juvenile justice system when compared with children who did not participate in the program.

Home visits may have an impact on parents and other family members as well as the identified child. Potential areas of impact include parenting skills; knowledge of child development, disability, or resources; changes in parent–child interaction; and stress reduction.

Infants with Health Needs Home-based early intervention services are often preferred for very low birth weight infants and other infants at biological risk. The transition from hospital to home for families with infants with special health care needs can be both a welcome and frightening process. Home-based interventions have been designed and studied to assess their effectiveness in promoting the health and development of infants at risk and their families.

Sandall (1991) reviewed experimental studies that were aimed at infants who were premature and who had low birth weight. Intervention approaches varied and included a focus on specific infant behaviors, a focus on parent–infant interaction, a focus on parental support, or some combination of these. The studies suggested that home-based interventions following discharge from the hospital can have positive effects. In general, the effectiveness was best demonstrated by differences in the home environment (as measured by the HOME), increased responsivity and sensitivity by mothers on interaction measures, and, to some degree, by improvements on cognitive measures. Work by Affleck and colleagues (Affleck, Tennen, Rowe, Roscher, & Walker, 1989) demonstrated that interventions need to be individually designed. They found that mothers' perceptions of needs and receptivity to intervention were important variables in trying to understand the effects of support-oriented interventions. VandenBerg and Hanson (1993) provided useful guides for professionals who work with families during this period of transition to life at home and adaptation to parenting an infant who has been hospitalized.

Sufficiency of Service Some researchers have questioned whether home-based programs provide sufficient service and support for young children and their families (LeLaurin, 1992; Roberts et al., 1991; Weiss, 1993). Vulnerable children whose families face multiple risks and challenges or who have minimal resources may need a level of support and services that is not feasible through home visits alone.

Ramey and colleagues studied the effects of either home-based or center-based service or some combination of services for low-income children. From their review of the literature, Ramey, Bryant, and Suarez (1985) concluded that more intense, center-based programs are associated with better outcomes than home-based programs. This contention was studied experimentally through Project CARE (Ramey, Bryant, Sparling, & Wasik, 1985). In this project, 64 children at high risk were randomly assigned at birth to a more intense treatment condition (an educational child care center plus home visits) or a less intense treatment (home visits alone). A no treatment group was also available for comparison. Results at 36 months of age showed that children in the more intense treatment group had gains in IQ scores that were greater than the other two groups, which did not differ significantly from one another. The intense treatment was viewed as having a greater effect on preventing the intellectual decline in children at high risk.

The comprehensive effort studied in Project CARE was extended to low birth weight, preterm infants in the Infant Health and Development Program (IHDP, 1990). IHDP was an eight-site, randomized clinical trial designed to evaluate the effectiveness of the early intervention program in reducing the developmental and health problems seen in these children. Participants were 985 infants who were randomly assigned to either an intervention group or a control group. Both groups received regular, high-quality pediatric services. In addition, the intervention group also received child development and family support services via home visits (weekly for the first year, and every other week thereafter), an enhanced early childhood educational program at a center when the children were 12–36 months of age, and bimonthly parent group meetings. The researchers assessed the effects of the program on the children's cognitive development and behavior, health status and health care utilization, home environment, and parent–child interaction. A number of important findings resulted from this carefully controlled study. Intervention successfully increased children's cognitive development scores (with a greater benefit for the heavier babies). The intervention was differentially effective with children of mothers who had high school educations or less. Children of families that had participated more intensively in home visiting, center attendance, and parent group meetings had higher scores at age 3. At the end of the program, the home environment of families in the intervention group was more conducive to child development. In addition, mothers in this group were more likely to be employed. There were no major differences between groups in medical care utilization or mother's report of children's health or serious illness.

A recurrent theme from research reports and demonstration projects is the admonition that the design and delivery of early intervention services is a complicated matter that involves performing comprehensive child and family needs assessments, matching services with needs, changing service systems to include greater arrays of service options, and ensuring that services and procedures facilitate family choice and optimal child development. As LeLaurin (1992) pointed out, early intervention programs for infants and toddlers often provide only about 1 hour of weekly intervention. Although some parents may be able to provide carryover intervention, the demands on many families preclude regular and systematic intervention with their child, even intervention that is embedded within caregiving routines. The needs of some children necessitate specialized or more intense treatment. Programs that provide limited service (in terms of time) may fail to provide what currently accepted theories of development and research suggest is necessary for improved outcomes for children and families. As Weiss (1993) pointed out, home visiting is a necessary but not sufficient component of programs that seek to address the complicated needs of children and their families.

THE HOME VISITOR

The home visitor is the key to success for any home-based program. The effective home visitor must have knowledge and skills in a variety of areas. Research reports typically describe their home visitors in terms of age, gender, and educational qualifications. In their national survey of home-based programs, Roberts and Wasik (1990) found that the majority of programs reported a bachelor's degree as a minimal requirement for employment. Roberts (1991) reported no comparative information on the relative effectiveness of educational levels in terms of child outcomes. Olds and Kitzman (1993) found that effective home visiting programs are staffed by well-trained professionals. They reported that it is training that is crucial; the educational levels and disciplines may vary among effective home visiting programs.

The home visitor stops by to help and to listen and enters into the home life of the family. It is helpful to use family systems theory (Minuchin, 1974) and ecological theory (Bronfenbrenner, 1979) as frameworks for understanding the influences and effects of home visiting. All parts of the family are interrelated and interdependent. Interventions aimed at one member of the family or one dyad (e.g., mother and child) will have repercussions on other family members and can influence family functioning. Likewise, the home visitor must recognize the larger context of friends and community in addition to family as dynamic influences on family members' lives.

Positive family–home visitor relationships are critical to the effectiveness of home-based services (Roberts et al., 1991; Wayman, Lynch, & Hanson, 1991). While knowledge and skill are important to such a relationship, personal qualities and characteristics of the home visitor are fundamental. Descriptions of home visitors often refer to the importance of interpersonal and communication skills, maturity, and judgment. Wayman et al. (1991) also noted the importance of the home visitor's sensitivity to and appreciation of cultural difference. Interestingly, while the home visitor's skill and relationship with the family are critical to the success of the program, little attention has been given to either the process of home visiting (see, however, Klass, 1996) or to home visitor/family matches in research reports of early intervention (LeLaurin, 1992; Roberts, 1991).

Guiding Principles

Project Copernicus (1991) outlines the principles for delivering family-centered, home-based services:

- Respect the family's values.
- Recognize you are a guest.
- Trust the family.
- Work together.
- Be flexible.
- Relate to the family as people.
- Look at the whole picture.
- Recognize parents as the decision makers.
- Be creative.

The story of Frankie, Carla, and Vicki illustrates some of these guiding principles.

Helping Techniques

As the example of Vicki demonstrates, the home visitor has many roles. Among those roles are direct service provider (e.g., teacher, therapist, nurse) for the child, counselor or teacher for the parent, and consultant to the parent and family. Roberts and Wasik (1990) described some of the many services that the home visitor may provide. Several of these services can be categorized as coordination activities. These include coordination of community services, delivery of information, and coordination of medical services. Other services are in the form of direct assistance to parents. These services might include transportation, respite care, or homemaker training. Another category of services includes psychological support and might include emotional support, family counseling, and stress management. Another set

The Jacksons *(continued)*

Vicki sometimes thinks that the Jacksons test her flexibility. In the past several weeks, she has had other visits in the Jacksons' kitchen. She has spent most of one visit in the bathroom while Frankie took a bath, taken Carla and Frankie to the grocery store when they were out of food, gone for a stroller ride around the neighborhood, and done visits when the house was filled with the neighbor's children while Carla babysat. Carla is always delighted to see her and talk. She talks about her week, about the children, about her former husband, about the neighbors, and about her favorite television shows. Vicki realizes that listening is an important part of the support she provides. After chatting for awhile, she tries to steer her visit toward Frankie's needs. Vicki usually tries to plan three or four goals for her visit and tries to intertwine them with what Carla has shared that day. In this way, Vicki and Carla are usually able to have an "agenda" for the visit that is satisfactory for both of them.

of services is related to enhanced parenting skills. In consideration of these multiple roles and services, two of the important skills of the home visitor are the ability to recognize the home visitor's own strengths and limitations and the willingness to call on others when the needs of the family exceed the visitor's personal expertise. The home visitor's agency or supervisor helps by articulating the boundaries of the home visitor's job.

The effective home visitor uses helping techniques that affirm the parents or primary caregivers as capable decision makers and provide opportunities to use their capabilities and to learn new ones. Sometimes, very skilled clinical practitioners have difficulty with home visits because effective home visits require that the visitor relinquish some of his or her authority and control. The home visitor is a guest in the family's home and must not impose values or changes that conflict with the family. This does not mean that the home visitor ignores his or her talents or skills as a child development specialist. Rather, it means that family and home visitor must form an alliance in which the important question is "How can I help you?" and the important response is to truly listen to and act on the family's answer to that question.

Wasik et al. (1990) detailed four categories of helping techniques that are necessary for the effective home visitor:

1. Competency as a clinician
2. Communication skills (e.g., observing, listening, questioning, probing, prompting)
3. Assessment skills (i.e., assessing family's abilities to problem-solve)
4. Skills in adult teaching and learning

Enhancing Child Development

Some families may request help with specific strategies for helping their young children with disabilities or delays. Many of the instructional and therapeutic strategies that work in the clinic or classroom can be effective at home (e.g., modeling, prompting). There are, however, some important differences. First, the home visitor is at the home for only 1 or 2 hours during a visit. Useful strategies are those that can be incorporated within typical routines such as bathing, feeding, and play time. A planning matrix for embedding child objectives within typical routines is shown in Figure 13.1. Note that, in this example, one of the "routines" that Frankie's mother identified was after one of her favorite television shows. Every family's routines will be just a bit unique and some families will have very few daily routines.

Another difference between homes and clinical settings has to do with the availability of special equipment or materials. Although it may be possible to lend families equipment for short periods of time, it is usually more reasonable for the home visitor to consider using equipment and materials that are available in the home or that can be obtained at minimal cost. For example, most families will not have a therapy ball at home. However, postural reactions can be practiced while the infant is held on a beach ball or on the adult's lap. Similarly, the novelty of the home visitor's special toys may spark a child's curiosity, but the child's own toys should also be used to teach the same behavior. The toys and the activities should be culturally relevant.

Parents are responsible for meeting their family's basic needs, as well as providing emotional and financial support. When helping parents provide additional

Routines	Frankie's objectives				
	Vocalizes wants	Pulls to stand	Turns pages, pats pictures	Plays near others	Gets adequate nutrition
Mealtimes	Encourage asking for "more."				Follow instructions from nutrition clinic.
Bathtime	Encourage asking for more water or more toys.			Take bath with brother.	
Diapering	Encourage asking for "up."				
After nap		Let Frankie pull himself up in crib.			
Watching television		Help Frankie pull to stand at sofa.			
After "Oprah"			Look at picture books together.		
Bedtime routine				Play quiet games with brothers before bed.	

Figure 13.1. An example of a planning matrix for embedding child objectives within the daily routine.

support and attention to their young child with a disability, the home visitor needs to be keenly aware that parents are, first of all, parents and not teachers or therapists. One of the things that parents do with their children is interact and play with them. Home visitors can help parents take advantage of these interactions with their infant. For some parents, these interactions will be reciprocal and fun to watch. For other parents and infants, there may be mismatches. Sometimes, the infant produces behaviors that are infrequent, difficult to interpret, or poorly timed. Sometimes, the adult is unpredictable or has difficulty adjusting to the infant's pace. Drawing from research studies that have examined strategies for strengthening parent–child interaction (e.g., Hanson & Krentz, 1986; MacDonald & Gillette, 1988; Mahoney & Powell, 1988; McCollum & Stayton, 1985), methods that can be incorporated into home visits (as well as center-based programs) have been described. Some of these techniques include getting into position, reading and responding to infant's cues, taking turns, and learning the infant's pace (Table 13.1).

Consultation Skills

It should be apparent that much of the work of the home visitor is similar to that of a consultant. Consultation has been defined as a triadic helping process (Kurpius & Lewis, 1988). The consultant provides services to the child indirectly through a consultee (i.e., parent or caregiver). The aim is to support the child's learning and development by helping the consultee provide more effective help.

Table 13.1. Strategies to enhance interaction

Strategy	Description
Get into position	Interacting with babies usually means getting face-to-face with the baby. With mobile children, this means being available and being willing to follow the child's lead and topic of interest.
Read the infant's cues	Observe and try to understand the infant's cues (e.g., sounds, facial gestures, body movements). Sometimes this requires redefining the "meaning" of a reflex or physiological response.
Respond to the infant's cues	Treat sounds, gestures, and body movements as meaningful. Over time, respond more quickly to more conventional cues.
Follow the infant's lead	Provide a response that is linked to the infant's cue. Respond to infant's current interest or activity.
Imitate the infant	Mimic the infant's action or sound. This is one way of following the infant's lead. It also serves to slow down the adult and allow for turns.
Take turns	Allow the infant the opportunity to behave. Respond to the behavior as meaningful. Use intonation and body language to show that you expect the baby to take another turn.
Learn the infant's pace	Adjust your timing to the infant's. Whether fast or slow, aim for episodes of balanced turns.

Adapted from MacDonald & Gillette (1988) and Mahoney & Powell (1986).

The home visitor often finds him- or herself in the interesting situation of sometimes being the direct service provider and sometimes being an indirect service provider (consultant) all in the same visit. This makes understanding the consultant role even more important.

A model of consultation that is useful for early interventionists is the collaborative consultation model (West & Idol, 1987). In this model, mutual control, mutual goals, and parity among the participants (consultant and consultee) are emphasized.

File and Kontos (1992) reviewed the important variables for effective consultation in early intervention. Many of these are similar to the interpersonal characteristics of effective home visitors that were described in an earlier section. Included are interpersonal skills such as the ability to be caring, respectful, empathic, harmonious, and open. Communication skills are also important. The consultant must be able to communicate clearly in both written and verbal forms, and must be able to listen effectively. Another set of skills has to do with collaborative problem solving. This means that the consultant must be available to the parent, model mutual planning and problem solving, and provide assistance that enables the parent to learn new skills.

Cultural Competence

Home visitors visit a variety of homes and visit a variety of families with a range of values, customs, and beliefs. The home visitor's ability to establish positive relationships with all of those families will depend in part on sensitivity to the cultural background of the families. Lynch and Hanson (1992) have written extensively on developing cultural competence. One of the first steps is for the home visitor to become aware of his or her own cultural heritage, values, and beliefs and to clarify what these mean in relation to providing early intervention services. A second step is for early interventionists to become more knowledgeable about the cultural practices of the families and the communities that they serve. A third step, and one that requires much practice, is to apply this new knowledge. Ideally, the early interventionist can work with a mentor or guide who can assist with this process.

Wayman et al. (1991) provided a set of guidelines for home visitors who work with families whose cultural heritage is different from their own. These guidelines include questions that the home visitor can use informally to gain a greater understanding of the family and their values, beliefs, and practices. These guidelines and questions are grouped around such concerns as family structure, child-rearing practices, caregiving routines and practices, and child guidance issues; perceptions of disability, health and healing, and help seeking; and language and interaction. Home visitors have a unique and sometimes intimate view of family life—a view that is not often provided to nonfamily members. Thus, home visitors must be sensitive, open to new learning, and respectful.

Other Professional Concerns

The variety of ethical questions that is faced by home visitors has been addressed by Bryant, Lyons, and Wasik (1991). Some of these questions are not unique to home visiting, however. Because the context for intervention is the home, the responses to these questions may be more complicated. Possible ethical dilemmas include whether or not to intervene and how best to do so, disclosure of information and issues of confidentiality, and issues related to terminating services. These researchers drew on the work of Reamer (1990) and their experiences to offer a framework for ethical decision making. These guidelines incorporate individual and family's rights, laws and regulations, and clarification of the values and duties of the service provider.

Visiting and helping families can be stressful. As indicated previously, home visitors may find themselves dealing with a variety of ethical dilemmas. They may also find themselves working with families who are in stressful, illegal, or dangerous situations. In addition, because home visitors typically make their visits on their own, they may feel isolated and unsupported. Working and making decisions in such stressful situations is difficult work. As a first step, home visitors need to acknowledge this, and their supervisors and employing agencies need to provide clear guidelines and support. Beyond this, the home visitor will need to acknowledge his or her own values, the limits of his or her current skills, and continually work toward thoughtful and competent actions and appropriate referrals.

A related issue is personal safety. Safety concerns will vary within and across programs. The safety issues in a rural, isolated area may be different from the issues faced by a home visitor in an urban area that is beset with gang activity. Regardless, the home visitor who is distracted by fear is not an effective service provider. The basic guidelines for maintaining personal safety include the following:

1. Using common sense and good judgment
2. Making certain that another staff member knows the visitor's specific schedule
3. Knowing the neighborhood
4. Scheduling visits in the morning or avoiding dangerous areas after dark
5. Learning the safest route to and from a family's home
6. Using reliable transportation
7. Limiting personal possessions
8. Leaving the area if he or she considers him- or herself to be in danger (Wasik et al., 1990)

The Home Visit

Home visitors can be professionals (e.g., teachers, nurses, social workers) or paraprofessionals (e.g., community support workers, "veteran" parents). Visits tend to occur at least once a week. Some programs schedule visits more or less frequently. The potential success of home-based programs seems to be influenced by the frequency of visits (at least once a week), the training and supervision of visitors (intensive and systematic), and program implementation guidelines that are congruent with a well-articulated philosophy (Powell & Grantham-McGregor, 1989; Wasik et al., 1990). The situation of the Jacksons' home visitor is not atypical (see below).

Managing Home Visits

Successful home visiting programs require planning and organization. The first home visit is an important one. This visit should be brief, have a clear focus, and be as friendly and relaxed as possible. In arranging this visit, the home visitor should let the family know the purposes and the estimated length of the visit. The home visitor may want to repeat this information upon arrival at the home. Some of the possible purposes of the first visit are to get acquainted, to describe the sorts of activities that occur during home visits, and to discuss the roles of the home visitor and the family. This visit should also include time for family members to talk about their expectations for home visits and early intervention services.

Subsequent home visits will generally follow four phases: 1) greeting, 2) establishment of a focus or purpose for the visit, 3) implementation of the service(s), and

The Jacksons *(conclusion)*

Frankie's home visitor, Vicki, usually visits Frankie and his mother in their home for about 1½ hours every week. Frankie's comprehensive early intervention program also includes a play group (led by a speech therapist), individual physical therapy, nutrition services, and family social work support. Vicki is the service coordinator for this family. In this role, she must ensure that the services are coordinated, that the schedule is manageable for the family, and that information is shared. She drew from her previous experience, the guidelines of her agency, and suggestions from the other team members, including Carla, to develop an effective communication system. With Carla's agreement, the professional team members (Vicki, the speech therapist, physical therapist, nutritionist, and social worker) have a regularly scheduled monthly conference call. This call lasts anywhere from 10 minutes to 1 hour. The focus is to provide an update on services and progress and to discuss any concerns and possible solutions. Vicki writes a summary of each call, which is shared with Carla and the rest of the team. Team members have their own way of keeping track of services and progress. Vicki completes a reporting form each week for her agency, she also writes extensive notes after her visit, and occasionally uses developmental checklists or rating scales during her visit.

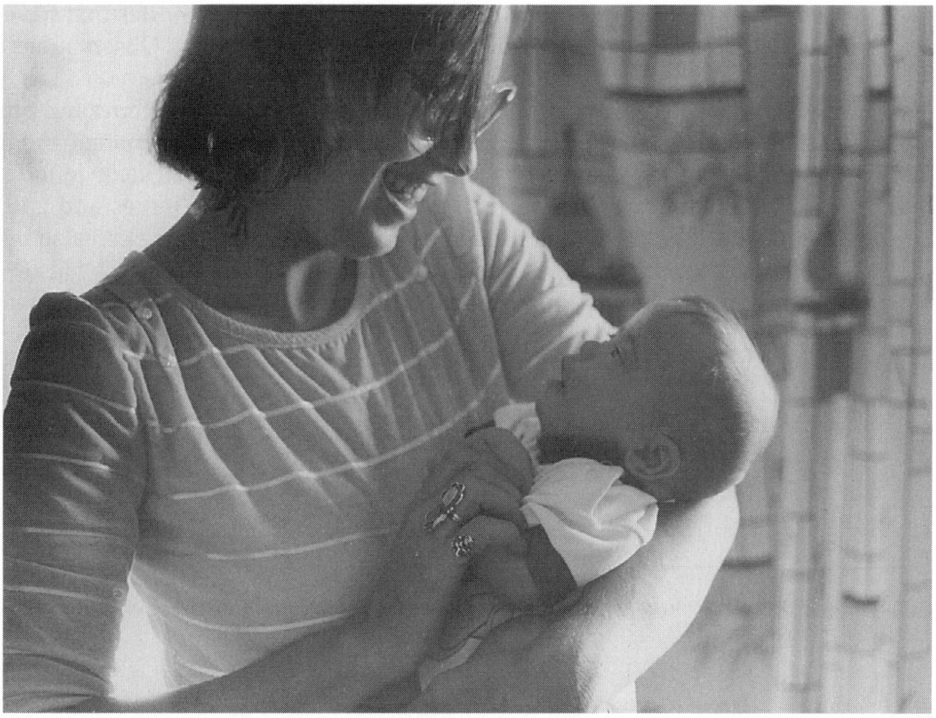

4) closure (Wayman et al., 1991). While this provides a general outline, the amount of time and the content of each phase will vary from family to family and visit to visit. It is possible that, over time, a home visitor and a family become so comfortable with their home visits that they forget to establish the focus for the visit. It is important, however, to do this with every visit so that the visitor and the family have a shared and mutually agreed-upon plan. This will contribute to satisfaction with the services as well as effectiveness.

Scheduling Home visits should be scheduled at times that are mutually convenient. The home visitor has additional considerations of scheduling other visits, travel, and other work. All of these factors will play a part. Many families prefer a regularly scheduled time. However, young children will change their sleeping and eating patterns, so visits may have to change. Families with young children are usually very busy and have many appointments or commitments. Flexibility in scheduling is crucial. Parents who work during the day present a case in point. Ideally, flexible work schedules are an option for home visitors so that visits can be made in the evening or on weekends for some families. As a practical matter, it is helpful, when possible, to confirm appointments by telephone.

Record Keeping Documentation is another component of the home-based program. Home visitors often report that their car has become their office because they keep track of visits and record their notes while in the car. Keeping track of visits usually means completing a form or writing a note that includes the date, length, and participants in the visit; the content or type of visit; and perhaps a brief comment on the nature of the visit. Home visitors also need to keep track of child and family progress toward meeting individualized family service plan (IFSP) outcomes. Many home visitors use notes as their primary method for monitoring progress and for keeping track of the interventions and activities that have been implemented. Notes should include the date, time, and setting. Observations about what occurred should be made distinct from opinions and impressions. The cumulative record of these notes can provide a detailed picture of patterns and progress over time. The home visitor's notes to him- or herself about the content and nature of the visits will add perspective. Examples of notes made by Vicki are found in Figure 13.2. Permanent products such as videotapes or audiotapes and still photographs (with the parent's agreement) or children's drawings can also be used effectively to show changes over time. Checklists and rating scales may also be useful. Family members may use any of these methods, as well, to help document

Home Visit Report

Child's Name: Frankie
Visitor's Name: Vicki

Date: 9-21-95
Time: 9:30 A.M.–10:45 A.M.

Setting(s): Started visit in kitchen and moved to living room after breakfast. Mom and Frankie at visit today.

Observations: Frankie used his whole body to make "requests" for more food. He imitated lip smacks. Said "ba-ba" when Mom asked if he wanted bottle. After Mom cleaned his face, she asked if he wanted up. Frankie lifted his arms.

Played with variety of toys in living room. Smiled and vocalized a lot.

Pulled to stand with a little help (physical assist at his bottom). Did this three or four times. Not yet independent.

Used my new books to get Frankie's interest in the books.

He turned pages with a little help (Mom lifted edge).

Frankie patted pictures with both hands. Very quick. I modeled using intonation and slowing pace.

Frankie showed some interest in playing with shoe box as a container. He looked for toys I hid. I tried to have Frankie put toys in. Not yet.

Comments: Mom very positive with both Frankie and with me. She's glad to have the meeting with the social worker next week. His brothers are not eligible for their preschool after October.

Mom reported that she got several phone calls from her ex-husband last night. She said she would tell her social worker.

Showed Mom how to get more turn-taking when reading books with Frankie.

(Take a look at this next week.)

Mom gave me her latest list of Frankie's sounds.

Frankie was happy and playful for the whole visit.

Figure 13.2. An example of a format for record keeping for home visits.

change. For example, Frankie's mother writes down Frankie's new sounds on a piece of paper that she keeps on the refrigerator. When used systematically, these methods and the information they generate provide a picture of the child's and family's response to the home-based intervention services.

SUMMARY

This chapter provided a review of home-based interventions. Home-based services can be an effective, family-centered method for early intervention. Home visits can offer a friendly, personal, and flexible context for services and supports designed to help the young child and family. Home visits should be an option or component within a larger array of services and service delivery methods. The amount, intensity, and duration of early intervention services should match child and family needs. The importance of the home visitor to the success of home-based services cannot be overemphasized. Suggestions and recommendations for being an effective home visitor were offered.

SUGGESTED READINGS

Hershberger, P. (1991). A naturalistic approach to home-based early intervention. *Infant-Toddler Intervention, 1,* 83–92.

Hussey, B. (1988). *Understanding my signals: Help for parents of premature infants.* Palo Alto, CA: VORT Corp.

Parks, S., Furuno, S., O'Reilly, K., Inastpuka, T., Hosaka, C., & Ziesloft-Falbey, B. (1988). *HELP...at home.* Palo Alto, CA: VORT Corp.

Portage Project. (1993). *Growing: Birth to three Portage Project.* Portage, WI: Author.

Wasik, B.H., Bryant, D.M., & Lyons, C.M. (1990). *Home visiting: Procedures for helping families.* Beverly Hills: Sage Publications.

REFERENCES

Affleck, G., Tennen, H., Rowe, J., Roscher, B., & Walker, L. (1989). Effects of formal support on mothers' adaptation to the hospital-to-home transition of high risk infants: The benefits and costs of helping. *Child Development, 60*(2), 488–601.

Bailey, D.B., & Simeonsson, R.J. (1988). Home-based early intervention. In S.L. Odom & M.B. Karnes (Eds.), *Early intervention for infants and children with handicaps: An empirical base* (pp. 199–216). Baltimore: Paul H. Brookes Publishing Co.

Barnett, W.S., & Escobar, C.M. (1990). Economic costs and benefits of early intervention. In S.J. Meisels & J.P. Shonkoff (Eds.), *Handbook of early intervention: Theory, practice, and analysis* (pp. 560–582). Cambridge, MA: Cambridge University Press.

Barrera, M.E., Rosenbaum, P.L., & Cunningham, C.E. (1986). Early home intervention with low-birth-weight infants and their parents. *Child Development, 57*(1), 20–33.

Bidder, R.T., Bryant, G., & Gray, O.P. (1975). Benefits to Down's syndrome children through training their mothers. *Archives of Disease in Childhood, 50*(5), 383–386.

Brassell, W.R., & Dunst, C.J. (1978). Fostering the object construct: Large-scale intervention with handicapped infants. *American Journal of Mental Deficiency, 82*(5), 507–510.

Bronfenbrenner, U. (1979). *The ecology of human development: Experiments by nature and design.* Cambridge, MA: Harvard University Press.

Bryant, D., Lyons, C., & Wasik, B.H. (1991). Ethical issues involved in home visiting. *Topics in Early Childhood Special Education, 10*(4), 92–107.

Casto, G., & Mastropieri, M.A. (1986). The efficacy of early intervention programs for handicapped children: A meta-analysis. *Exceptional Children, 52*(5), 417–424.

Dunst, C.J., Trivette, C.M., & Deal, A.G. (1988). *Enabling and empowering families: Principles and guidelines for practice.* Cambridge, MA: Brookline Books.

Dunst, C.J., Trivette, C.M., Hamby, D.M., & Pollock, B. (1990). Family systems correlates of the behavior of young children with handicaps. *Journal of Early Intervention, 14*(3), 204–218.

File, N., & Kontos, S. (1992). Indirect service delivery through consultation: Review and implications for early intervention. *Journal of Early Intervention, 16*(3), 221–233.

Gray, S.W., & Wandersman, L.P. (1980). The methodology of home-based intervention studies: Problems and promising strategies. *Child Development, 51*(4), 993–1009.

Halpern, R. (1984). Lack of effects for home-based early intervention? Some possible explanations. *American Journal of Orthopsychiatry, 54*(1), 33–42.

Halpern, R. (1986). Home-based early intervention: Dimensions of current practice. *Child Welfare, 63*(4), 387–398.

Hanson, M.J., & Krentz, M.K. (1986). *Supporting parent–child interactions: A guide for early intervention personnel.* San Francisco: San Francisco State University, Department of Special Education.

Hanson, M.J., & Schwarz, R.H. (1978). Results of a longitudinal intervention program for Down's syndrome infants and their families. *Education and Training of the Mentally Retarded, 13*(4), 403–407.

Herwig, J., & Herman, P. (1993). *Portage multi-state outreach project: Final report.* (Contract No. H023D0031-91). Washington, DC: Early Education Program for Children with Disabilities.

Individuals with Disabilities Education Act (IDEA) of 1990, PL 101-476, 20 U.S.C. § 1400 *et seq.*

Infant Health and Development Program (IHDP). (1990). Enhancing the outcomes of low birth weight premature infants: A multisite randomized trial. *Journal of the American Medical Association, 263*(22), 3035–3042.

Klass, C.S. (1996). *Home visiting: Promoting healthy parent and child development.* Baltimore: Paul H. Brookes Publishing Co.

Kurpius, D.J., & Lewis, J.E. (1988). Assumptions and operating principles for preparing professionals to function as consultants. In J.F. West (Ed.), *School consultation: Interdisciplinary perspectives on theory, research, training, and practice* (pp. 143–154). Austin, TX: The Association of Educational and Psychological Consultants.

Lally, J.R., Mangione, P.L., Honig, A.S., & Wittmer, D.S. (1988). More pride, less delinquency: Findings from the ten-year follow-up study of the Syracuse University Family Development Research Program. *ZERO TO THREE, 12*(3), 1–6.

LeLaurin, K. (1992). Infant and toddler models of service delivery: Are they detrimental for some children and families? *Topics in Early Childhood Special Education, 12*(1), 82–104.

Lynch, E.W., & Hanson, M.J. (Eds.). (1992). *Developing cross-cultural competence: A guide for working with young children and their families.* Baltimore: Paul H. Brookes Publishing Co.

MacDonald, J.D., & Gillette, Y. (1988). Communicating partners: A conversational model for building parent–child relationships with handicapped children. In K. Marfo (Ed.), *Parent–child interaction and developmental disabilities: Theory, research, and intervention* (pp. 220–241). New York: Praeger.

Mahoney, G., & Powell, A. (1986). *Transactional intervention program: A child-centered approach to developmental intervention with young handicapped children.* (Monograph No. 1). Farmington: University of Connecticut School of Medicine, Pediatric Research and Training Center.

Mahoney, G., & Powell, A. (1988). Modifying parent–child interactions: Enhancing the development of handicapped children. *Journal of Special Education, 22*(1), 82–96.

McCollum, J.A., & Stayton, V.D. (1985). Infant/parent interaction: Studies and intervention guidelines based on the SIAI model. *Journal of the Division for Early Childhood, 9*(2), 125–135.

Minuchin, S. (1974). *Families and family therapy.* Cambridge, MA: Harvard University Press.

Olds, D.L., & Kitzman, H. (1993). Review of research on home visiting for pregnant women and parents of young children. *The Future of Children, 3*(3), 53–92.

Powell, C., & Grantham-McGregor, S. (1989). Home visiting of varying frequency and child development. *Pediatrics, 84*(1), 157–164.

Project Copernicus. (1991). *Delivering family-centered, home-based services.* Baltimore: Kennedy Krieger institute.

Ramey, C.T., Bryant, D.M., Sparling, J.J., & Wasik, B.H. (1985). Project CARE: A comparison of two early intervention strategies to prevent retarded development. *Topics in Early Childhood Special Education, 5*(2), 12–25.

Ramey, C.T., Bryant, D.M., & Suarez, T. (1985). Preschool compensatory education and the modifiability of intelligence: A critical review. In D.K. Determan (Ed.), *Current topics in human development* (pp. 247–296). Norwood, NJ: Ablex.

Reamer, F.G. (1990). *Ethical dilemmas in social service.* New York: Columbia University Press.

Roberts, R.N. (1991). The interface of policy, programs, and research. *Infants and Young Children, 4*(2), 33–40.

Roberts, R.N., & Wasik, B.H. (1990). Home visiting programs for families with children birth to three: Results of a national survey. *Journal of Early Intervention, 14*(3), 274–284.

Roberts, R.N., Wasik, B.H., Casto, G., & Ramey, C.T. (1991). Family support in the home: Programs, policy, and social change. *American Psychologist, 46*(2), 131–137.

Sandall, S.R. (1991). Developmental interventions for biologically at-risk infants at home. *Topics in Early Childhood Special Education, 10*(4), 1–13.

Shearer, D.E., & Shearer, M.S. (1976). The Portage Project: A model for early intervention. In T.D. Tjossem (Ed.), *Intervention strategies for high risk infants and young children* (pp. 335–350). Baltimore: University Park Press.

Strong, C.J. (1992). *SKI*HI home-based programming for children with hearing impairments: Demographics, child identification, and program effectiveness (1979–1991).* (Contract No. H023C90117). Washington, DC: Office of Special Education and Rehabilitative Services.

Sturmey, P., Thorburn, M.J., Brown, J.M., Reed, J., Kaur, J., & King, G. (1992). Portage guide to early intervention: Cross-cultural aspects and intra-cultural variability. *Child: Care, Health and Development, 18*(6), 377–394.

VandenBerg, K.A., & Hanson, M.J. (1993). *Homecoming for babies after the neonatal intensive care nursery.* Austin, TX: PRO-ED.

Wasik, B.H. (1993). Staffing issues for home visiting programs. *The Future of Children, 3*(3), 140–157.

Wasik, B.H., Bryant, D.M., & Lyons, C.M. (1990). *Home visiting.* Beverly Hills: Sage Publications.

Wayman, K.I., Lynch, E.W., & Hanson, M.J. (1991). Home-based early childhood services: Cultural sensitivity in a family systems approach. *Topics in Early Childhood Special Education, 10*(4), 56–75.

Weiss, H.B. (1993). Home visits: Necessary but not sufficient. *The Future of Children, 3*(3), 113–128.

West, J.F., & Idol, L. (1987). School consultation (Part I): An interdisciplinary perspective on theory, models, and research. *Journal of Learning Disabilities, 20*(7), 388–408.

White, K.R., Bush, D.W., & Casto, G. (1985–1986). Learning from previous reviews of early intervention research. *Journal of Special Education, 19*(4), 417–428.

13 ACTIVITIES

1. Interview a home visitor and/or parent whose child receives home visits. Ask about their perceptions of home visits, including benefits and drawbacks. Compare these responses with your reading of this chapter.

2. Develop a detailed job description for a home visitor in an early intervention program.

3. In small groups, discuss one or more of the following "problems" that might occur during a home visit:

   a. You arrive and the mother has several of her friends there to visit.

   b. The child you visit has siblings who vie for your attention and want you to play with them.

   c. A female home visitor arrives and is greeted by a man who identifies himself as the baby's uncle. He is caring for the baby. The visitor has never met this man before, and no one else is home.

   d. In the midst of your visit, the parents begin to have a loud argument.

4. Several research projects and demonstration programs were referred to in this chapter. Locate one of these original articles. Describe the services that the families received, and describe how the researchers determined if the program was effective or not. How well does the program meet the guiding principles that were included in this chapter?

CHAPTER 14

Looking Toward the Future

Anne H. Widerstrom

Early interventionists face a paradox. Tremendous advances in technology since the 1980s have made possible the prevention and remediation of disabilities that were previously untreatable. At the same time, funds for human services generally have become less available, particularly for low-income families. The lack of a universal health care system in the United States has contributed to the shortages of medical and other health-related services. In addition, critical educational and social services needs remain unmet.

Although universal health care has not yet become a reality, it remains an important goal for many policy makers. Goals of expanded availability of health care include prenatal care for all pregnant women, family planning, birth control, and genetic counseling for would-be parents.

Prenatal care is particularly scarce for teenage mothers and mothers who are economically disadvantaged. Although the new technologies can be effective in sustaining very young and very small babies, they cannot substitute for preventive measures such as improved access to substance abuse treatment for pregnant women. For preventive care to become available to all pregnant women requires further change in national policy, with the realization that preventive prenatal care is less traumatic and more cost-effective than intensive care.

A study published by the nonprofit Alan Guttmacher Institute (1990) in New York is of interest. In a group of unmarried, young, African American women ages 17 or younger who were pregnant, it was found that teenagers who had abortions fared better economically, suffered less stress, and were more likely to graduate from high school than those who had their babies (Alan Guttmacher Institute, 1990). Researchers found that 82% of the young women who had abortions graduated from high school or remained in school 2 years after the procedure without falling behind, while only 63% of the women who gave birth completed high school or were still in school 2 years later. In addition, women who had abortions were more economically secure 2 years later than young single women who had their babies. Clearly, there is a need for more effective family planning.

It is generally recognized that adequate services for family planning and ready availability of birth control methods for all citizens, particularly for young men and women in their teens, would go a long way toward prevention of unwanted pregnancies, making abortions unnecessary. The lack of access to birth control information is illustrated by a group of interviews with teenagers who were experiencing unwanted pregnancies (Bode, 1980). Most of the young women stated that they did not use any method of birth control because either they or their partners were embarrassed or afraid to go through necessary parental permissions or other required steps. They also stated that they would have used birth control if they had realized what the consequences would be.

In addition, the effectiveness of postnatal assistance programs has been well documented. One of the most successful is the federally funded Women, Infants, and Children (WIC) program that provides food supplements and nutrition information to pregnant women and women with young children as well as to their infants. This program has been credited with reducing risk and preventing disabilities among newborns and infants of low-income parents.

These studies and similar data illustrate the positive impact universally available services can have on preventing developmental problems for infants and their families. The general shortage of such preventive programs in the United States underscores the current and continuing need for addressing this issue.

At the same time, technology will undoubtedly continue to provide treatment for diseases and conditions that were until now fatal or chronic. Daily news releases chronicle the progress that the medical and scientific communities make in extending life expectancy and lowering the neonatal mortality rate. As technology improves to maintain life, early interventionists must grapple with how to improve the quality of life for those infants who are at risk or who have disabilities and for their families. Early interventionists must strive to include families in decisions that affect the life and health of their children.

TECHNOLOGY AND NEONATAL CARE

Every year more than 200,000 premature infants are born in the United States (National Center for Health Statistics, 1993). With advances in neonatal care, infants weighing less than 800 grams and with gestational ages of less than 26 weeks are being kept alive routinely. These very fragile babies require long periods of specialized hospital care in neonatal intensive care units (NICUs), and about one third survive only a few months. More specifically, data from several studies reveal that 39% of preterm, low birth weight babies do not survive (Goldson, 1996). For example, only 2% of infants born at 23 weeks' survived without severe complications that included prolonged ventilator support, retinopathy of prematurity, intraventricular hemorrhage, and severe central nervous system complications, but for those born at 25 weeks' the survival rate was 69%. Many who survive have chronic impairments, physical disabilities, and long-term developmental disorders (Wylie & Allen, 1995). Rates of long-term disability range from 30% to 65% in babies weighing less that 800 grams (Goldson, 1996). In other words, significant neurological and developmental problems affect almost one half of these NICU survivors.

As advances in technology have made it possible to save the lives of very low birth weight and very small babies, questions have been raised about what treatments these tiny babies (those born before 25 weeks' gestational age or weighing less than 750 grams) should receive and who should be making decisions about whether these treatments are implemented (Tyson, 1995). Of particular concern to the babies' parents is what role they will play in the decision-making process during the pregnancy and following birth. Many parents have requested that compassionate limits be set on the use of NICU technology (Harrison, 1994; see Chapter 7), limiting it, for example, to infants weighing more than 750 grams at birth.

In providing family-centered services in early intervention as required by the Individuals with Disabilities Education Act (IDEA) of 1990 (PL 101-476), it is reasonable that parents be given the right to make informed ethical and medical choices about the care of their babies. However, according to a study conducted in the mid-1980s of decision making for infants with birth weights less than 1,000 grams, parents are not routinely invited to participate in ethical decisions affecting their child's resuscitation, treatment planning, or withdrawal from treatment (Rottman, 1986). The study found that medical information is not generally available to parents, and therefore they cannot make truly informed choices. As mentioned in Chapter 7, parents' perceptions of the process are that often information is selectively presented, overly optimistic in prognosis, and reluctantly given.

Nevertheless, some positive changes have begun to be made. The idea of family-centered neonatal care has received nationwide attention in efforts to reform NICU practices (Browne & Smith-Sharp, 1995; Johnson, 1995). For example, an interdisciplinary training model for NICU health professionals in New York stresses the need for family-centered services and emphasizes the parent–professional partnership (Wylie & Allen, 1995). A consortium of intensive care nurseries in Colorado began training staff to deliver individualized, developmentally supportive, family-centered care (Browne & Smith-Sharp, 1995). In Ohio, Arizona, Texas, California, Maryland, and other states, new neonatal care policies are placing parents in responsible roles as decision makers and caregivers in the NICU. These efforts include research projects to test the effectiveness of new developmental care procedures and follow-up and transition programs. They depend on training to effect changes in staff attitudes toward families (Johnson, 1995).

Avoiding the routine use of invasive procedures may improve outcomes for infants. For example, a survey of neonatal units revealed a high survival rate coupled with an unusually low incidence of bronchopulmonary dysplasia at a unit where very low birth weight babies *were not* routinely intubated (Avery et al., 1987). As with the related issue of pain, the impact of the NICU environment and the effects of routine procedures require more thorough investigation. Until more is known, the prudent and humane course would appear to be to protect babies as fully as possible from unnecessary light, noise, handling, uncomfortable positioning, and sleep disruptions.

To provide babies with individualized protective care, primary care nurses need extensive training in the developmental needs of premature infants. Such training is currently available in the form of the Newborn Individualized Developmental Care and Assessment Program (NIDCAP) developed by Als and her colleagues (Als et al., 1994; Als & Gilkerson, 1995). The NIDCAP model, developed as a framework for the delivery of developmental care in the NICU, has received widespread support from parents and professionals. It includes a systematic method for the detailed observation of infant behavior and for the use of each infant's unique repertoire of strategies as a guide for caregiving. The resulting detailed reports include suggestions to support the infant's physiological stability, behavioral organization, and developmental progression, and this information is shared freely with family members and caregivers (Als & Gilkerson, 1995). Although long-term outcome data are not yet available on the effectiveness of the NIDCAP model, it appears to represent a positive step in the direction of more sensitive neonatal care and more involvement of the family in care-related decisions.

Despite these efforts, full provision of family-centered care has not yet been achieved in most intensive care nurseries, particularly in the area of making decisions about what treatments will or will not be given to premature infants. Concerns remain that, without informed and empowered parents to set some limits, babies in the NICU may be exposed to overtreatment. Parents worry that their babies may be subjected to unnecessary pain and emotional isolation during treatments that may result in little more than keeping the child alive. At the same time they worry about the moral and ethical implications of removing life supports and allowing infants to die. Many parents maintain, however, that, whatever the implications, the final decision should be made by the parents.

Medical Information

Parents primarily request sufficient information to make informed decisions about their infants and the opportunity to participate in the decision. Parents have said that they do not wish to be pressured into agreeing to medical procedures that may cause unnecessary pain or suffering for their children or to subject children to procedures that may not result in better outcomes. They worry that there is a serious lack of follow-up care for their children with a disability and that they will be forced to shoulder the financial and emotional burdens of such care alone (Harrison, 1992; Tyson, 1995). They are concerned that advanced NICU technologies may save their children's lives but leave them with disabilities requiring long-term treatment and care (Hack, Klein, & Taylor, 1995).

By bringing family-centered care to the NICU, an attempt is being made to address some of these concerns. In this model, emphasis is placed on collaboration between family and professionals. With a family-centered approach, staff no longer see families as visitors to the NICU but as the infants' primary caregivers and essential partners of the staff. Families then can be included in policy development and program planning through participation in advisory councils, in peer support groups, in staff in-service training activities, and other collaborative activities (Johnson, 1995). Moreover, information about their infant can be openly shared with parents in a family-centered NICU. Nevertheless, despite sincere efforts on the part of NICU staff to be more inclusive with parents in NICU practices and to provide more developmentally based care to infants in the NICU, parents' questions about long-term outcomes for their baby largely remain unanswered (Hack et al., 1995; Paneth, 1995). Hack et al. (1995) reported that long-term follow-up studies conducted on children born in the 1960s indicated that the adverse consequences of being born with low birth weight were still apparent in adolescence.

Follow-Up Neonatal Care

For parents who take home from the hospital a small, sick baby, the issue of follow-up care is important. Because low birth weight and premature infants are part of a population that has never before survived, and because they have been exposed to

innovative and experimental treatments, it is important that outcome data be collected and published. School systems and social services agencies need to know the scope of the resources they will be asked to provide as these babies grow to school age and into adulthood. For these purposes, both long-term follow-up studies and randomized clinical trials are needed (Brown & Valluzzi, 1995; Gross, Slagle, D'Eugenio, & Mettleman, 1992; Guillemin, 1992; Hack et al., 1992).

SERVICE DELIVERY SYSTEMS

Because of declining revenues, it is safe to guess that service delivery will be quite different in the future from what it is today. At present, it is an expensive, labor-intensive system dominated by professionals from various disciplines, with little input from consumers. Much of it, particularly in areas employing new technology, is hospital based. NICUs, although very effective in saving the lives of preterm and low birth weight infants, are very expensive to maintain. The technological advances that have increased the survival rate of the tiniest infants have led to increased concern about the demands these survivors place on their families and the rest of society.

Almost all infants weighing less than 2,500 grams require special attention. Although many function normally during childhood and beyond, they are more likely than children of typical birth weight to experience health and developmental problems (Lewit, Baker, Corman, & Shiono, 1995). Several studies have reported that low birth weight children use more special education services. One such study found that children ages 6–15 who weighed less than 2,500 grams at birth were almost 50% more likely than children with typical birth weight to be enrolled in some type of special education program. Costs of special education programs have been estimated to be twice as high as costs of general education programs (Chaikind & Corman, 1991). Almost one third of low birth weight children will repeat a grade by Grade 10, compared with about one quarter of children with typical birth weight (Corman & Chaikind, 1993).

High Costs of Low Birth Weight

In an attempt to determine the direct cost of low birth weight in the United States, Lewit et al. (1995) used figures released for 1988, the most recently available at the time of publication. They estimate that, of $11.4 billion spent on health care for infants that year, $4 billion, or 35%, was for the additional costs incurred by low birth weight infants. This total averaged about $15,000 extra cost per infant born under 2,500 grams. If those weighing less than 1,000 grams at birth or experiencing respiratory distress syndrome are separated, their extra cost per infant is $33,900. This group of infants accounted for 45% of the additional or incremental cost associated with low birth weight. In 1988, that total cost exceeded $5.4 billion (Lewit et al., 1995). It is interesting to note that only smoking and alcohol abuse carry higher direct health care costs. The annual direct cost of low birth weight among children birth to age 15 is several times that of the cost of AIDS among people of all ages (Lewit et al., 1995).

In addition to the economic costs of low birth weight children who require additional health and educational services, there are emotional and psychological costs borne by the families. These are eloquently described in Chapter 7. The best solution to the problem of high costs of low birth weight is ultimately prevention. There will always be a need, however, for neonatal intensive care and early intervention programs for children with disabilities. Whether such programs can withstand serious budget cutting and the move to managed health care is questionable. Rather, it seems likely that future service delivery systems will have the following characteristics:

Service Delivery Systems Will Be Less Labor Intensive Several trends combine to predict that future service delivery must be less dependent on the ample availability of highly trained professionals from numerous disciplines. First, the number of families with special concerns is increasing, for reasons previously discussed. Second, training programs in health and human services fields are not significantly increasing the number of graduates they prepare (Widerstrom & Abelman, 1996) and in some cases are facing serious funding cutbacks. Third, salaries in these fields, except for medicine, are generally not competitive with salaries available in the private sector. This implies a shortage of recruits for training, and the end result is more clients and fewer professionals to serve them.

The Consumer Will Have Larger, More Responsible Role In the case of early intervention, parents will have more responsibility, both in decision making and in carrying out those decisions. In fact, there is accumulating evidence that increasing family involvement in early intervention is not only cost-effective but more efficacious than other models. In a research review illustrating some emerging trends in the field, Guralnick (1989) noted that there is strong potential for parent-mediated early intervention to yield clinically significant benefits. "By enhancing natural parenting skills and providing the conditions for families to become more competent and more confident in their unique relationships with their children, conditions for optimal child development may well be created" (p. 12). Guralnick (1989) further stated that models that encourage optimal parent–child relationships and emphasize parent empowerment may prove to be more effective than the more traditional models with a didactic focus that require parents to carry out instructional activities.

In health-related fields, the more active and assertive role of families is illustrated by the acknowledgment of infants' needs for social interactions, especially interactions with their parents, when they are confined to neonatal special care and follow-up programs in hospitals (Als & Gilkerson, 1995). Allowing parents into the NICU on a regular basis, based on a realization of the positive effect they have on their infant's development in that environment, represents a step forward in the field of neonatal care.

Early Intervention Services Will Be Provided Through Health Care System Based on Managed Care Managed care has as its primary objective the containment of the cost of services. For those individuals participating in the system, costs are reduced by offering to a limited number of providers (e.g., pediatricians) the opportunity to increase their "market share" of service provision (e.g., pediatric care) by reducing the cost of their services and therefore the amount of their reimbursements from insurance companies. Thus, economies of scale are effected (Frederick, 1996). A second objective of managed care is to reduce the utilization of health care services by requiring a "gatekeeper" or primary care physician to carefully monitor (and restrict) consumers' access to specialist care.

The prospect of a managed care system of health services has important implications for families with a young child with disabilities, especially low-income families. As Frederick (1996) stated,

> As managed care scenarios are implemented, families may be forced to change providers. The new providers may or may not have pediatric experience or knowledge of and commitment to Part H goals and objectives. Families might be forced to travel far distances for services. Even worse, they may find that appropriate services are only available through nonmanaged-care–approved sources and they may be forced to bear all or part of the cost of services themselves. (p. vii)

Frederick (1996) also raised some important questions. Will managed care providers be willing to adhere to Part H guidelines (PL 101-476) that call for services in natural settings, family-centered approaches, and specific procedures for monitoring service delivery and for conflict resolution? What will become of current service providers? Will they perhaps be excluded from the managed care system because they cannot afford to provide the services at the reimbursement levels allowed? Frederick (1996) raised the unfortunate prospect of an economic subculture of Part H–eligible families unable to afford private provider services and therefore relegated to a limited number of possibly unqualified managed care providers. Although much of this discussion is speculative, early interventionists must remain alert in order to preserve the effective and nearly universal service delivery system put in place by the hard work and cooperation of many parents and professionals.

Public Schools Will Become Centers for Comprehensive Services in Each Community Ideally, public services should include education for all children from infancy, comprehensive child care from infancy, community health clinics including family planning clinics, well-baby clinics, teen pregnancy programs, early intervention/prevention programs, and social services programs for low-income families (Zigler, 1990). It is natural for the community public school to become the hub for community services because it has taken on an increasingly broader and more comprehensive role in serving children and families in recent years, particularly in urban environments. Teen health clinics, parent–infant programs for teenage parents, and after-school child care are examples of programs that are currently offered in many high schools. Because of the Education of the Handicapped Act Amendments of 1986 (PL 99-457), and the requirement for infant intervention services, public schools have begun to take a larger role in serving infants and toddlers and their families.

Such a comprehensive community-based service delivery system has several obvious advantages. First, it ensures a wide distribution of service centers geographically within the community, making services readily available to those families without transportation. In many cases, the comprehensive busing system in place in most public schools could be adapted to include these children and families. Second, it avoids duplication and promotes coordination of services by health, education, and social service providers when all available services are under one roof. Third, such a comprehensive setting allows for a truly multidisciplinary team concept in the delivery of services. Such a neighborhood-based network could result in a more personal and more humane service delivery system in which professionals and the families they serve would have the opportunity to develop mutually beneficial long-term relationships. Fourth, such services could be responsive to the special needs of varying cultural groups found in a community, while at the same time be tailored to the individual needs of a particular family.

Of course, there are potential disadvantages to such a system, too. Critics of public schools assert, with some justification, that in the past schools have not shown themselves to be very responsive to community needs. Some public schools, actively or by default, have discouraged parent participation, and many parents undoubtedly view their child's school as a place with which they have contact only in times of trouble. Although public schools and churches in this country have traditionally occupied the center of community life, that tradition is no longer as strong as it once was, particularly in urban communities. Some, therefore, question whether public schools in the present environment can introduce a service delivery system that is truly family-centered in the spirit of PL 99-457.

With the disappearance of the neighborhood school concept in many communities and the accompanying reliance on busing, most public schools no longer serve a geographically restricted community. This makes it more difficult to implement a neighborhood-based service system. These reservations are shared by many early intervention professionals and must be adequately addressed before a comprehensive, community-based system of human services can become a reality.

Long-Term Intervention and Care Will Be Based in Home and Community In realizing the goal of providing more comprehensive services with reduced revenues, intervention services will gradually move from expensive settings like hospitals and clinics to community-based and home-based settings. This will mean less reliance on hospitals for long-term care of infants and children and a greater emphasis on parents carrying out intervention with the assistance of home visitors (service providers).

This trend is compatible with the renewed movement toward normalization that is currently influencing public schools to follow a policy of *full inclusion.* This

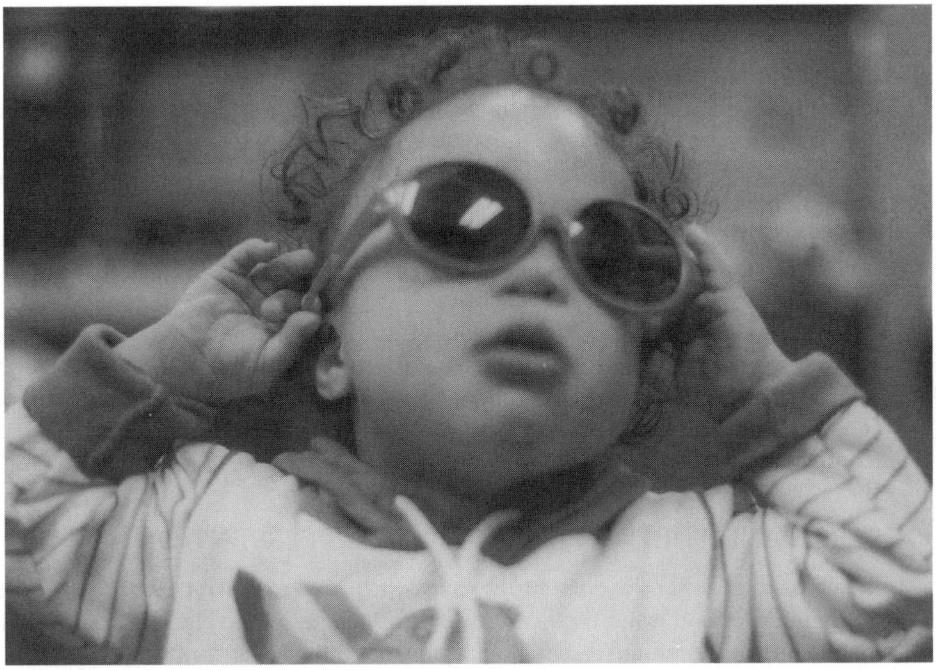

means integrating all children, whatever their needs or abilities, into programs with typically developing children. This point of view emphasizes the community as the proper setting for all but the most technical service delivery.

THE TRANSDISCIPLINARY TEAM

A continuing thread running through this book has been the role of the multidisciplinary team in providing early intervention to infants and toddlers, and it seems that this emphasis will continue and probably intensify. Certainly the transdisciplinary approach to teams as described in Chapter 11, with its emphasis on role release and role sharing, appears to be the most favored at present and is likely to continue, given the current economic climate. The number of professionals working with any given infant or toddler may be fewer, but through transdisciplinary practice the needed intervention can be provided.

In short, regardless of funding availability, it is likely that teams will expand their scope and the number of disciplines represented will increase. As early intervention services become better coordinated and more community based, a combination of services from health, education, and social services individualized to each family's special needs will gradually become available in a single setting. This will undoubtedly mean a more important role for service coordinators to act as liaison between professionals and families.

It is hoped that training for professionals to provide early intervention will be expanded in future years through both in-service and preservice activities. A major concern in the implementation of PL 99-457 and IDEA has been the preparation of professional personnel to ensure an adequate supply of service providers of quality for infant and toddler programs. Universities must increase their efforts to prepare a new cadre of professionals for work on infant teams, and those already-existing team members must continually update their skills and knowledge (Widerstrom & Abelman, 1996).

Following a transdisciplinary model, training should be coordinated between disciplines, so that professionals in health, psychology, education, and speech-language, for example, share course work and internship experiences. In addition, training should also be coordinated within each discipline, so that professionals serving infants and toddlers have contact with those serving preschool and older children with disabilities. In this way, preparation for interagency coordination and interdisciplinary cooperation can begin at the initial level of training (Bricker & Widerstrom, 1996).

A related issue is the development of training materials for both in-service and preservice programs. The need is great for curriculum guides and instructional materials in both print and videotape formats for training of early interventionists. The need for training programs and instructional materials underlines the need for continuing research in early intervention.

RESEARCH AND PUBLIC POLICY IN EARLY INTERVENTION

It seems likely that the current trend toward more extensive research addressing early intervention issues will continue through the 2000s. The emphasis should be to develop more refined research methods that offer better control of validity threats and improved designs for conducting longitudinal, multivariate research. Subjects of research studies in the future should include technological advances; the development of assessment models and techniques that have better predictive validity; the examination and refinement of intervention models and techniques; and further examination of the role of the family in infant growth and development, including family-focused early intervention. It is important to include both quantitative and qualitative designs and methods in carrying out this research agenda. For this to happen, far more resources need to be channeled into these areas of research.

With the emerging consensus on the validity of early intervention, future research should take a longitudinal approach (e.g., questions concerning the long-term implications of varying intervention practices, the predictive validity of assessment measures, the long-term outcomes of parenting variables). If the gap between research and practice can be more efficiently bridged than at present, the ultimate result should be more effectively trained professionals, more effective instructional materials, and more appropriate and cost-effective programs.

If early intervention efficacy data continue to impress policy makers, it could mean the further adoption of laws to ensure universal availability of services. At the same time, there should emerge an emphasis on developing preventive educational programs to address the enormous problems of substance abuse, violent crime, and other social ills. It is hoped that policy makers will begin to recognize the cost benefits of prevention as opposed to treatment, whether it be in a drug rehabilitation clinic, hospital, or prison.

REFERENCES

Alan Guttmacher Institute. (1990). The urban adolescents choose abortion. *Perspectives, 21*(6), 18–23.

Als, H., & Gilkerson, L. (1995). Developmentally supportive care in the neonatal intensive care unit. *Zero to Three, 15*(6), 1–10.

Als, H., Lawhon, G., Duffy, F.H., McAnulty, G.B., Gibes-Grossman, R., & Blickman, J.G. (1994). Individualized developmental care for the very low birthweight preterm infant: Medical and neurofunctional effects. *Journal of the American Medical Association, 272*(11), 853–858.

Avery, M.E., Tooley, W.H., Keller, J.B., Hurd, S.S., Bryan, M.H., Cotton, R.B., Epstein, M.F., Fitzhardinge, P.M., Hansen, C.B., Hansen, T.N., Hodson, W.A., James, L.S., Kitterman, J.A., Nielson, H.C., Poirier, T.A., Truog, W.E., & Wang, J.-T. (1987). Is chronic lung disease preventable? A survey of eight centers. *Pediatrics, 79*(1), 26–30.

Becker, P.T., Grunwald, P.C., Moorman, J., & Stuhr, S. (1993). Effects of developmental care on behavioral organization in very low birthweight infants. *Nursing Research, 42*(4), 214–220.

Bode, J. (1980). *Kids having kids: The unwed teenage parent.* New York: Franklin Watts.

Bricker, D., & Widerstrom, A. (Eds.). (1996). *Preparing personnel to work with infants and young children and their families: A team approach.* Baltimore: Paul H. Brookes Publishing Co.

Brown, S.E., & Valluzzi, J.L. (1995). Do not resuscitate orders in early intervention settings: Who should make the decision? *Infants and Young Children, 7*(3), 13–27.

Browne, J.V., & Smith-Sharp, S. (1995). The Colorado consortium of intensive care nurseries: Spinning a web of support for Colorado infants and families. *Zero to Three, 15*(6), 18–23.

Chaikind, S., & Corman, H. (1991). The impact of low birth weight on special education costs. *Journal of Health Economics, 10*(3), 291–311.

Corman, H., & Chaikind, S. (1993, July). *The effect of low birth weight on the health, behavior and school performance of school-aged children.* Working Paper No. 4409. Cambridge, MA: National Bureau of Economic Research.

Education of the Handicapped Act Amendment of 1986, PL 99-457, 20 U.S.C. §1400 *et seq.*

Frederick, J. (1996). Implications of managed care on early intervention services for infants and toddlers. *Infants and Young Children, 8*(3), vi–viii.

Goldson, E. (1996). The micropremie: Infants with birth weight less than 800 grams. *Infants and Young Children, 8*(3), 1–10.

Gross, S.J., Slagle, T.A., D'Eugenio, D.B., & Mettleman, B.B. (1992). Impact of a matched term control group on interpretation of developmental performance in preterm infants. *Pediatrics, 90*(5), 681–687.

Guillemin, J.H. (1992). The problem of probable outcome. *Birth, 19*(3), 155–156.

Guralnick, M. (1989). Recent developments in early intervention efficacy research: Implications for family involvement in PL 99-457. *Topics in Early Childhood Special Education, 9*(3), 1–17.

Hack, M., Horbar, J.D., Malloy, M.H., Tyson, J.E., Wright, E., & Wright, L. (1992). Very low birth weight outcomes of the National Institute of Child Health and Human Development Neonatal Network. *Pediatrics, 87*, 587–597.

Hack, M., Klein, N.K., & Taylor, H.G. (1995). Long-term developmental outcomes of low birth weight infants. *The Future of Children, 5*(1), 176–196.

Harrison, H. (1992). Very low birth weight outcomes. *Pediatrics, 89*, 357–361.

Harrison, H. (1994, October 14). *Parents' perspectives on neonatal ethics: Setting compassionate limits to the use of technology.* Paper presented at Grand Rounds, Community Hospital, Santa Rosa, CA.

Individuals with Disabilities Education Act (IDEA) of 1990, PL 101-476, 20 U.S.C. §1400 *et seq.*

Johnson, B.H. (1995). Newborn intensive care units pioneer family-centered change in hospitals across the country. *Zero to Three, 15*(6), 11–17.

Lewit, E.M., Baker, L.S., Corman, H., & Shiono, P.H. (1995). The direct cost of low birth weight. *The Future of Children, 5*(1), 35–56.

National Center for Health Statistics. (1993). Advance report of final natality statistics for 1991: Final data from the National Center for Health Statistics. *Monthly Vital Statistics Report, 42*(3).

Paneth, N S. (1995). The problem of low birth weight. *The Future of Children, 5*(1), 19–34.

Rottman, C.J. (1986, September 12). *How neonatologists influence parents' decision making concerning their low birth weight infants.* Paper presented at the Parent Care Third Annual Conference, Indianapolis, IN.

Tyson, J. (1995). Evidence-based ethics and the care of premature infants. *The Future of Children, 5*(1), 197–213.

Widerstrom, A.H., & Abelman, D. (1996). Issues in team training. In D. Bricker & A. Widerstrom (Eds.), *Preparing personnel to work with infants and young children and their families: A team approach* (pp. 23–42). Baltimore: Paul H. Brookes Publishing Co.

Wylie, V., & Allen, J. (1995). Early intervention and the NICU health professional: An interdisciplinary training model. *Zero to Three, 15*(6), 30–35.

Zigler, E. (1990, January). *Child care and children at risk.* Keynote address at the annual Queens College School Psychology Conference, Queens, NY.

Index

Page numbers followed by "f" and "t" indicate figures and tables, respectively.